THE FATHERS
OF THE CHURCH

A NEW TRANSLATION

VOLUME 80

THE FATHERS OF THE CHURCH

A NEW TRANSLATION

EDITORIAL BOARD

Thomas P. Halton
The Catholic University of America
Editorial Director

M. Josephine Brennan, I.H.M.
Marywood College

Kathleen McVey
Princeton Theological Seminary

Elizabeth Clark
Duke University

Daniel J. Sheerin
University of Notre Dame

Hermigild Dressler, O.F.M.
Quincy College

Robert D. Sider
Dickinson College

Robert B. Eno, S.S.
The Catholic University of America

Michael Slusser
Duquesne University

David J. McGonagle
Director
The Catholic University of America Press

FORMER EDITORIAL DIRECTORS

Ludwig Schopp, Roy J. Deferrari, Bernard M. Peebles,
Hermigild Dressler, O.F.M.

Cindy Kahn
Warren J. A. Soule
Staff Editors

ORIGEN
COMMENTARY ON THE GOSPEL ACCORDING TO JOHN
BOOKS 1–10

Translated by
RONALD E. HEINE
Emmanuel School of Religion
Johnson City, Tennessee

THE CATHOLIC UNIVERSITY OF AMERICA PRESS
Washington, D.C.

Copyright © 1989
THE CATHOLIC UNIVERSITY OF AMERICA PRESS, INC.
All rights reserved

LIBRARY OF CONGRESS CATALOGING-IN-PUBLICATION DATA
Origen.
 [Origenous tōn eis to kata Iōannēn Euangelion exēgētikōn. English. Selections]
 Commentary on the Gospel according to John : books I, II, IV V, VI, X / Origen : translated by Ronald E. Heine.
  p. cm.—(The Fathers of the church ; v. 80)
 Translation of: Origenous tōn eis to kata Iōannēn Euangelion exēgētikōn.
 Bibliography: p.
 Includes index.
 1. Bible. N.T. John—Commentaries—Early works to 1800.
 I. Heine, Ronald E. II. Title. III. Series.
 BR60.F3060 [B2615] 270 s—dc19 [226'.507] 88-20406

ISBN 0-8132-1029-1 (pbk.)
ISBN-13: 978-0-8132-1029-2 (pbk.)

CONTENTS

Abbreviations	vii
Select Bibliography	ix
Introduction	3
Book 1	31
Book 2	95
Book 4	158
Book 5	160
Book 6	168
Book 10	253
Indices	
Index of Proper Names	331
Index of Holy Scripture	336

ABBREVIATIONS

ACW   Ancient Christian Writers. New York, New York/Mahwah, New Jersey: Newman Press, 1946–.
ANF   Ante-Nicene Fathers. Grand Rapids: Erdmans, 1969 (reprint).
EP   *The Encyclopedia of Philosophy.* 8 vols. New York: Macmillan, 1967.
FOTC   The Fathers of the Church. New York and Washington, D.C., 1947–.
GCS   Die griechischen christlichen Schriftsteller der ersten drei Jahrhunderte. Leipzig, 1897–.
JThS   *Journal of Theological Studies*
LCL   Loeb Classical Library
LSJ   *A Greek-English Lexicon.* ed. H. G. Liddell, R. Scott and H. S. Jones. Oxford: at the Clarendon Press, 1940.
LXX   *Septuagint.* Ed. A. Rahlfs. 2 vols. Stuttgart. 1935.
NAB   *The New American Bible.* Patterson, New Jersey, 1970.
OCD   *Oxford Classical Dictionary.* 2d ed. ed. N. G. L. Hammond and H. H. Scullard. Oxford, 1970.
ODCC²   *The Oxford Dictionary of the Christian Church.* 2d ed., ed. F. L. Cross and E. A. Livingstone. Oxford, 1984.
PGL   G. W. H. Lampe, *A Patristic Greek Lexicon.* Oxford: at the Clarendon Press, 1961.
RSV   The Holy Bible, Revised Standard Version.
SC   Sources chrétiennes. Paris, 1942–.
SP   Studia Patristica. ed. E. A. Livingstone.
SPCK   Society for Promoting Christian Knowledge.
TU   Texte und Untersuchungen zur Geschichte der Altchristlichen Literatur. Berlin, 1882–.
VC   *Vigiliae Christianae.*

Abbreviations of Classical and Patristic texts follow OCD and ODCC².

SELECT BIBLIOGRAPHY

Texts and Translations

Balthasar, H. Urs von, ed. *Origen: Spirit and Fire.* Tr. R. J. Daly. Washington, D.C.: The Catholic University of America Press, 1984.
Blanc, C., ed. and tr. *Origène: commentaire sur saint Jean.* SC 120 (1966) and 157 (1970).
Brooke, A. E., ed. *The Commentary of Origen on S. John's Gospel.* 2 vols. Cambridge: University Press, 1896.
Butterworth, G. W., tr. *Origen: On First Principles.* New York: Harper & Row, 1966.
Cadiou, R. *Commentaires inédits des Psaumes: études sur les textes d'Origène contenus dans le manuscrit Vindobonensis 8.* Paris: société d'édition *les belles lettres*, 1936.
Corsini, E., tr. *Commento al Vangelo di Giovanni di Origene.* Torinese: Unione Tipografico-Editrice, 1968.
Gögler, R., tr. *Origenes: Das Evangelium nach Johannes.* Zürich-Köln: Benziger Verlag Einsiedeln, 1959.
Harl, M. et Lange, N. De, eds. and trs. *Origène: Philocalie, 1–20 sur les écritures.* SC 302 (1983).
Heine, R. E., tr. *Origen: Homilies on Genesis and Exodus.* FOTC 71 (1982).
Lawson, R. P., tr. *Origen: The Song of Songs Commentary and Homilies.* ACW 26 (1956).
Menzies, A., tr. *Origen's Commentary on the Gospel of John.* ANF 10 (1969).
Preuschen, E., ed. *Origenes Werke: Der Johanneskommentar.* GCS 4 (1903).
Rauer, M., ed. *Origenes Werke: Die Homilien zu Lukas in der Übersetzung des Hieronymus und die griechischen Reste der Homilien und des Lukas-Kommentars.* GCS 9 (1959).
Tollinton, R. B., ed. and tr. *Selections from the Commentaries and Homilies of Origen.* Translations of Christian Literature. Series 1: Greek Texts. London: SPCK, 1929.

Other Works

Brooke, A. E. *The Fragments of Heracleon.* Texts and Studies 1. Cambridge: University Press, 1896.
Campenhausen, H. von. *The Formation of the Christian Bible.* Tr. J. A. Baker. Philadelphia: Fortress Press, 1972.
Colson, F. H., tr. *Philo.* Vol. 7. LCL (1950).
Courcelle, P. *Late Latin Writers and Their Greek Sources.* Tr. H. Wedech. Cambridge: Harvard University Press, 1969.
Crouzel, H. *Origène.* Paris: Éditions Lethielleux, 1985.
Daniélou, J. *Gospel Message and Hellenistic Culture.* Tr. J. A. Baker. Philadelphia: The Westminster Press, 1973.

———. *Origène*. Paris: La Table Ronde, 1948.
Faye, E. de. "De l'influence du Gnosticisme sur Origène." *Revue de l'histoire des religions* (1923), 181–235.
Foerster, W. *Gnosis: A Selection of Gnostic Texts*. Tr. R. McL. Wilson. Oxford: Clarendon Press, 1972.
Ginzberg, L. *The Legends of the Jews*. 7 vols. Philadelphia: The Jewish Publication Society of America, 1909–1938.
Gögler, R. *Zur Theologie des biblischen Wortes bei Origines*. Düsseldorf: Patmos-Verlag, 1963.
Gorday, P. *Principles of Patristic Exegesis: Romans 9–11 in Origen, John Chrysostom, and Augustine*. Studies in the Bible and Early Christianity 4. New York: The Edwin Mellen Press, 1983.
Grant, R. M. *The Letter and the Spirit*. London: SPCK, 1957.
Grobel, K. *The Gospel of Truth*. London: Adam & Charles Black, 1960.
Hanson, R. P. C. *Allegory and Event*. Richmond, Virginia: John Knox Press, 1959.
———. Review of *Origène: Philocalie 1–20* by M. Harl and N. De Lange. *Patristics* (July, 1985), 3.
Harl, M. *Origène et la fonction révélatrice du verbe incarné*. Paris: Éditions du Seuil, 1958.
Harnack, A. von. *Der kirchengeschichtliche Ertrag der exegetischen Arbeiten des Origenes* II. TU 42.4.
Heine, R. E. "Can the Catena Fragments of Origen's Commentary on John be Trusted?" *VC* 40 (1986), 118–134.
———. "Gregory of Nyssa's Apology for Allegory." *VC* 38 (1984), 360–370.
Hennecke, E. *New Testament Apocrypha* 1. Ed. W. Schneemelcher, tr. R. McL. Wilson. Philadelphia: Westminster Press, 1963.
Janssens, Y. "L'épisode de la Samaritaine chez Héracléon." *Sacra Pagina* 2. Bibliotheca Ephemeridum Theologicarum Lovaniensium XII–XIII. Paris: Librairie Lecoffre, 1959.
Kasser, R., Malinine, M., Puech, H., Quispel, G., and Zandee, J., eds. *Tractatus Tripartitus* 1, *De Supernis*. Bern: Francke Verlag, 1973.
Koch, H. *Pronoia und Paideusis*. Berlin: Walter de Gruyter, 1932.
Lagarde, P. de. *Onomastica Sacra*. Hildesheim: Georg Olms Verlagsbuchhandlung, 1966.
Lejewski, C. "Logic, History of." *EP* 4.513–520.
Lubac, H. de. *Histoire et esprit: l'intelligence de l'écriture d'après Origène*. Paris: Aubier, 1950.
Macleod, C. W. "Allegory and Mysticism in Origen and Gregory of Nyssa." *JThS* n.s. 22 (1971), 362–379.
Mates, B. *Stoic Logic*. Berkeley: University of California Press, 1961.
Nardoni, E. "Origen's Concept of Biblical Inspiration." *The Second Century* (1984), 9–23.
Nautin, P. *Origène: sa vie et son oeuvre*. Paris: Beauchesne, 1977.
Pagels, E. *The Johannine Gospel in Gnostic Exegesis: Heracleon's Commentary on John*. New York: Abingdon, 1973.
Pazzini, D. *In Principio era il Logos. Origene et il prologo del vangelo di Giovanni*. Studi Biblici 64. Brescia, 1983.
Puech, H. and Quispel, G. "Le quatrième écrit Gnostique du codex Jung." *VC* (1955), 65–102.
Quispel, G. "From Mythos to Logos." *Gnostic Studies* 1. Istanbul, 1974.

SELECT BIBLIOGRAPHY   xi

Quispel, G. "Origen and the Valentinian Gnosis." *VC* (1974), 29–42.
Rist, J. M. "The Importance of Stoic Logic in the *Contra Celsum*." *Neoplatonism and Early Christian Thought: Essays in Honour of A. H. Armstrong*. Ed. H. J. Blumenthal and R. A. Markus. London: Variorum Publications, Ltd., 1981.
Robinson, J. W., ed. *The Nag Hammadi Library*. New York: Harper & Row, 1977.
Rudolph, K. *Gnosis*. Tr. R. McL. Wilson. San Francisco: Harper & Row, 1983.
Schürer, E. *The Literature of the Jewish People in the Time of Jesus*. Tr. P. Christie and S. Taylor. New York: Schocken Books, 1972.
Tanner, T. M. "A History of Early Christian Libraries from Jesus to Jerome." *The Journal of Library History* (1979), 407–435.
Torjesen, K. J. *Hermeneutical Procedure and Theological Structure in Origen's Exegesis*. Patristische Texte und Studien 28. Berlin: de Gruyter, 1986.
———. "Origen's Interpretation of the Psalms." *SP* 17, 2.944–958.
Trigg, J. W. "The Charismatic Intellectual: Origen's Understanding of Religious Leadership." *Church History* (1981), 5–19.
———. *Origen: The Bible and Philosophy in the Third-century Church*. Atlanta: John Knox Press, 1983.
Ullmann, W. "Hermeneutik und Semantik in der Bibeltheologie des Origenes dargestellt anhand von Buch 10 seines Johanneskommentares," *SP* 17, 2.966–977.
Wiles, M. F. "Origen as Biblical Scholar." *The Cambridge History of the Bible* 1. Ed. P. R. Ackroyd and C. F. Evans. Cambridge: University Press, 1970.
———. *The Spiritual Gospel: The Interpretation of the Fourth Gospel in the Early Church*. Cambridge: University Press, 1960.
Wutz, F. *Onomastica Sacra*. Leipzig: J. C. Hinrichs'sche Buchhandlung, 1914.

INTRODUCTION

INTRODUCTION

THE STUDY OF THE BIBLE stood at the center of Origen's life and work. The majority of his writings are either commentaries on books of the Bible or homilies preached on biblical texts. His exegesis is interlaced with texts from the Bible. His mind wandered at ease through its pages, plucking appropriate phrases and arranging them artfully in his pursuit of the spiritual meaning he perceived to be latent in each word and phrase. "There has never been a theologian in the church," Harnack observed, "who was (and wished to be) so exclusively a biblical exegete as Origen."[1]

(2) Perhaps no book of the Bible, certainly none of the New Testament, was so suited to Origen's exegetical approach as the Gospel of John. In his *Commentary on the Gospel of John* we have the greatest exegetical work of the early church. He himself praises it in the *Commentary* as the high point of all Scripture.[2] The nature of the Gospel of John, which early earned it the title, "the spiritual Gospel,"[3] makes this particular commentary from the early Church of continued interest. M. F. Wiles has noted that while modern critical approaches to the Bible have so completely revolutionized our interpretation of some books that we find little in patristic exegesis that is of value in understanding them, "there is probably no book of which this is less true than the Fourth Gospel. It is of such a nature," he says, "that it seems to reveal

---

1. A. von Harnack, *Der kirchengeschichtliche Ertrag der exegetischen Arbeiten des Origenes* (1919) 2.4, as quoted in H. von Campenhausen, *The Formation of the Christian Bible*, tr. J. A. Baker (Philadelphia: Fortress Press, 1972), 307.

2. *Comm. Jn.* 1.23.

3. See Eusebius *H.E.* 6.14.7, quoting the *Hypotyposeis* of Clement of Alexandria.

its secrets not so much to the skillful probings of the analyst as to a certain intuitive sympathy of understanding."[4]

Date and Place of Writing

(3) This magisterial treatise was begun rather early in Origen's career while he was still at Alexandria, but was finished much later, after he had taken up residence in Caesarea.[5] Origen indicates in Book 1 that he began to work on it shortly after returning to Alexandria following an absence of some duration.[6] He gives no indication of where he had been. Nautin thinks this absence was his visit to Palestine which was precipitated by tension between Origen and Demetrius, bishop of Alexandria, over the publication of his *Commentary on Genesis* and his treatise *On First Principles*.[7] The fragment preserved in the *Philocalia*, from the preface to Book 5, indicates that he was again away from Alexandria.[8] Nautin surmises that this absence coincided with Origen's trip to Antioch at the invitation of the mother of Alexander Severus in A.D. 231–232.[9] This would place the composition of the first four books in Alexandria in A.D. 230–231,[10] and part, at least, of Book 5 in Antioch in A.D. 231–232. Origen says he dictated the words of the commentary as far as the fifth book at Alexandria, and began the sixth book there.[11] The trouble between him and Demetrius heated up and became so disruptive of his scholarly tranquillity, however, that he ceased work on the commentary until after he had abandoned Alexandria and settled in Caesarea.[12]

---

4. M. F. Wiles, *The Spiritual Gospel: The Interpretation of the Fourth Gospel in the Early Church* (Cambridge: University Press, 1960), 1.
5. For a brief sketch of Origen's life see *Origen: Homilies on Genesis and Exodus*, tr. R. E. Heine, FOTC 71, 7–25. For a fuller account see H. Crouzel, *Origène* (Paris: Éditions Lethielleux, 1985); and J. W. Trigg, *Origen: The Bible and Philosophy in the Third Century Church* (Atlanta: John Knox Press, 1983).
6. *Comm. Jn.* 1.12–13.
7. P. Nautin, *Origène: sa vie et son oeuvre* (Paris: Beauchesne, 1977), 366–70; 423–27.
8. *Comm. Jn.* 5.1.
9. Nautin, *Origène*, 427, based on Eusebius *H.E.* 6.21.3–4.
10. Cf. Nautin, *Origène*, 425–27.   11. *Comm. Jn.* 6.8.
12. Ibid., 6.9.

INTRODUCTION 5

(4) He seems to have returned to his work on the commentary soon after his move to Caesarea, but says he had to begin the sixth book over since what he had dictated at Alexandria had not been brought.[13] The move to Caesarea probably occurred in A.D. 234.[14] This provides a date for when he began working on Book 6, but no clue as to when he completed the commentary. Book 6 is still discussing chapter 1 of the gospel. The introductory section to Book 32, the last preserved book of the *Commentary* and probably the last written by Origen on this gospel,[15] indicates a weariness with the work and an uncertainty that it will be completed.[16] Book 32 was written after he had delivered his *Homilies on Luke*, for he refers to one of them in the book.[17] All of Origen's homilies, if we accept Nautin's dating,[18] were delivered sometime between A.D. 238 and 244. Nautin puts the composition of Book 32 of the *Commentary* in A.D. 248;[19] there is, however, no clear evidence for assigning a specific date to its composition. The best we can do with assurance is to say that it appears to have been written late in Origen's life. The composition of the *Commentary on the Gospel of John*, therefore, spans a large portion of Origen's scholarly career.

Occasion for the Composition of the Commentary

(5) The *Commentary on the Gospel of John*, as several other of Origen's writings,[20] was addressed to Ambrose, and was probably written at his instigation. He is directly addressed in the opening section of each book that is complete at the beginning.[21] The comments in the fragments of Book 5 sound as

13. Ibid., 6.10–12.   14. See Nautin, *Origène*, 431–32.
15. See the Introduction below on the size and preservation of the *Commentary*.
16. *Comm. Jn.* 32.1–3.
17. Ibid., 32.5. The homily referred to, however, is not extant. See my note on the passage.
18. Nautin, *Origène*, 401–9.   19. Ibid., 412.
20. See, for example, *Against Celsus*, Preface 1; and *On Prayer* 2.1.
21. *Comm. Jn.* 1.9; 2.1; 6.6; 13.1; 20.1; 28.6; 32.2. Book 19 clearly lacks the opening section; Book 10 appears also to lack the opening. The second person singular pronoun in 10.2 presumably refers to Ambrose, as do the comments in sections 1, 2, 4, and 8 of the fragments of Book 5.

though Origen had entered an agreement with Ambrose to produce a commentary on John's Gospel, and that Ambrose was prodding him to keep working at it even when he was away.[22] It was Origen's love for Ambrose which caused him to persevere in producing the books of the commentary.[23]

(6) Ambrose, Eusebius says, had been a Valentinian before Origen converted him.[24] This may provide the reason Ambrose was interested in a commentary on John's Gospel. E. Pagels has pointed out that it was the Gospel most used by Gnostics, and that the Valentinians especially used it.[25] Irenaeus refers to the extensive use of John by the Valentinians;[26] and Heracleon, the disciple of Valentinus whom Origen quotes in the *Commentary,* wrote the earliest commentary on the gospel known to us. Ambrose must have known this Gnostic exegesis of John, and particularly that of Heracleon, and wanted a counterpart from the Church.

(7) While Origen obviously intended to refute Heracleon's understanding of John, he seems to have had a broader goal in mind. Heracleon's comments are not the focus of Origen's arguments in the *Commentary on the Gospel of John* in the way that Celsus' comments are the focus of his arguments in the *Against Celsus.* The latter work is structured by Celsus' attacks on Christians and Origen's responses to those attacks. There are, however, large sections in the *Commentary on the Gospel of John* where there is no reference to Heracleon. Heracleon's

---

22. See *Comm. Jn.* 5.1 and 2. Cf. Jerome, *Lives of Illustrious Men* 61, where he says Ambrose urged Origen to write commentaries on Scripture, provided him with secretaries and copyists, and exacted work from him on a daily basis. For this reason, he says, Origen called Ambrose his taskmaster in one of his letters.
23. *Comm. Jn.* 5.4.
24. Eusebius *H.E.* 6.18.1. Jerome, *Lives of Illustrious Men* 56 and 61, says Ambrose had been a Marcionite before Origen converted him. Since Ambrose appears to have been from Alexandria where Valentinus had taught, it is more likely that Eusebius is correct. Origen says in *Comm. Jn.* 5.8 that Ambrose had followed the heterodox before he abandoned them by using his own understanding.
25. E. Pagels, *The Johannine Gospel in Gnostic Exegesis: Heracleon's Commentary on John* (New York: Abingdon, 1973), 16. See also K. Rudolph, *Gnosis,* tr. R. McL. Wilson (San Francisco: Harper & Row, 1983), 17.
26. *Adv. Haer.* 3.11.7.

work may have been the stimulus that moved Origen to action, but he seems to have intended to write a commentary that would be independent of Heracleon's work, and that would provide an interpretation of John's Gospel that would appeal to Christian intellectuals.[27]

(8) He says as much in a fragment of Book 5 where he notes that the heterodox were composing numerous books interpreting both the Gospels and the Epistles, and that these books had an appeal to inquisitive minds. "For this reason," he says, "it seems necessary to me that one who is able intercede in a genuine manner on behalf of the teaching of the Church and reprove those who pursue the knowledge falsely so-called."[28] Origen's method for achieving this, however, was not simply to take up the various interpretations of Heracleon and the Gnostics and argue against them, but to set forth his own interpretation in line with the teaching of the Church. He grappled with the kinds of questions raised by an intelligent reading of the Gospel, such as points of difference between John and the Synoptics, as well as with specific differences of interpretation between Heracleon and himself.

The Size and Preservation of the Commentary

(9) The *Commentary on John* became a massive production. At the end of six books Origen had reached only John 1.29. The three of the first six books which are preserved total 159 pages in Preuschen's Greek text. If the other three were of approximately the same size, Origen devoted over 300 pages to verses 1–29 of John's Gospel. In successive books he went into less detail than he had in the earlier ones, but by the end of Book 32, the last book of the *Commentary* known to us, he had reached only John 13.33.

(10) There is no evidence to suggest that Origen wrote more than thirty-two books on John. Jerome knew only thirty-two. He says in the preface to his translation of Origen's *Homilies on Luke* that Blesilla's request that he translate

---

27. Cf. C. Blanc, *Origène: commentaire sur saint Jean* I, SC 120.10 (1966); and Trigg, *Origen*, 149.
28. *Comm. Jn.* 5.8.

into Latin Origen's twenty-six books on Matthew, five on Luke, and thirty-two on John was beyond his strength, his leisure, and his energy.[29] In his list of Origen's works in Epistle 33 he again refers to thirty-two books on John.[30] There is only one fragment on a passage beyond John 13, the chapter covered in Book 32.[31] We have already noted that Origen expresses some doubt at the beginning of Book 32 that he will complete the commentary. It is also significant that Book 32 closes with no indication that anything will follow. Books 13, 20, and 28 all close with statements which anticipate what will be taken up in the next book.[32] All the evidence available points to Book 32 being the last book of the *Commentary* Origen composed.

(11) Nine of these thirty-two books have been preserved in more or less complete form in Greek—1, 2, 6, 10, 13, 19, 20, 28, and 32. Book 19 lacks several pages at both the beginning and end of the book. Book 2, in my view, lacks a few pages at the end; it closes by introducing the second half of John 1.7 for discussion. The entire verse had been presented for discussion earlier,[33] and the first half discussed. We have no example elsewhere in the *Commentary* of Origen referring a part of a verse he has already quoted for discussion in one book to the next. Book 6 also lacks something at the end, and Book 10 at the beginning. The latter begins with a quotation of John 2.12–25, the passage of Scripture which is discussed in the book. Preuschen suggested that this quotation was added by someone after the opening page had been lost, because Origen nowhere else quotes the entire scriptural text for a book of the *Commentary* in one place.[34]

---

29. *Origenes Werke: Die Homilien zu Lukas in der Übersetzung des Hieronymus und die griechischen Reste der Homilien und des Lukas-Kommentars*, ed. M. Rauer, GCS 1 (1959).
30. Nautin, *Origène*, 228–29.
31. Frag. 105 does not come from Origen, but from Theodore of Mopsuestia. Frag. 106 is on Jn 20.25. See note 41 below on the questionable authenticity of the fragments.
32. See *Comm. Jn.* 13.455; 20.422; 28.249.
33. *Comm. Jn.* 2.199.
34. See my note 2 in Book 10 below.

(12) We do not know when or how the other books of the *Commentary* were lost.³⁵ It seems doubtful that they were intentionally destroyed because someone found their contents unacceptable. It is more likely that they perished because the work was too large to be copied in its entirety, the fate which the *Hexapla* also seems to have suffered. The *Commentary* would have been kept in the library at Caesarea which Pamphilus established.³⁶ By the mid–fourth century that collection was in danger of extinction because of the fragility of the papyrus on which it was written. Bishops Acasius (340–366) and Euzoius (369–376) each commissioned the library's scriptorium to transcribe the papyrus documents onto parchment.³⁷ We do not know, however, how much had already been lost before it could be copied onto parchment, nor do we know what kind of decisions may have had to be made about abbreviating documents because of the exigencies of cost and time.³⁸

(13) In addition to the nine books of the commentary that have been preserved, a large number of fragments containing comments on John's Gospel ascribed to Origen are extant.³⁹ The authenticity of five of these fragments, which are drawn from the *Philocalia* by Basil and Gregory of Nazianzus, the *Church History* of Eusebius, and the *Apology for Origen* by Pamphilus, is not questioned.⁴⁰ The remainder of the fragments,

---

35. For the preservation of Origen's works in general, see my discussion in FOTC 71, 25–27.

36. See Jerome, *Lives of Illustrious Men* 75.

37. See T. M. Tanner, "A History of Early Christian Libraries from Jesus to Jerome," *The Journal of Library History* (1979), 419; and P. Courcelle, *Late Latin Writers and Their Greek Sources*, tr. H. Wedech (Cambridge: Harvard University Press, 1969), 103–4.

38. Rufinus, for example, who translated many of Origen's works into Latin in the fourth century, notes in the preface to his translation of the *Commentary on Romans* that he had been asked to abbreviate the *Commentary* as well as translate it into Latin. He also notes that some of the books of the *Commentary* were missing.

39. A. E. Brooke, *The Commentary of Origen on S. John's Gospel* 2 (Cambridge, 1896), appends 110 fragments to his edition; E. Preuschen, *Origenes Werke: Der Johanneskommentar* GCS 4 (1903), appends 140 to his.

40. The fragments from the Philocalia (M. Harl and N. De Lange, SC 302.269–305) and from Eusebius (*H.E.* 6.25.7) constitute the fragmentary text of Books 4 and 5 which are translated in this volume.

however, which are found in catenae are of questionable authenticity. Several have been discovered to belong to the works of other Fathers. Of the remaining fragments, twenty-five cover passages in John's Gospel which are treated in the extant books of the *Commentary*, but only ten of them can be found in Origen's comments on these passages, and they have sometimes been severely abbreviated, and even altered. This raises serious questions about trusting those fragments that cover sections of the gospel not treated in the extant books. It means that where we have no corroborating evidence from other texts of Origen that we can never be certain that we have his thoughts, much less his words, in a fragment from the catenae.[41] It is for this reason that the fragments from the catenae contained in Preuschen's text are not included in this translation.

Origen's Hermeneutics in the Commentary on John

(14) This is not the place to attempt a comprehensive presentation of Origen's hermeneutic. To borrow a statement he sometimes makes of various subjects that come up in his exegetical discussions, such a study would demand a volume of its own. A number of fine studies on this subject and narrower aspects of it have already been written.[42] We have the

---

41. For a more complete presentation of the evidence against the trustworthiness of most of the fragments attributed to Origen among the catenae, see R. E. Heine, "Can the Catena Fragments of Origen's Commentary on John be Trusted?" *VC* 40 (1986) 118–134.

42. See, for example, J. Daniélou, *Gospel Message and Hellenistic Culture*, tr. J. A. Baker (Philadelphia: The Westminster Press, 1973), 273–288; Peter Gorday, *Principles of Patristic Exegesis: Romans 9–11 in Origen, John Chrysostom, and Augustine*, Studies in the Bible and Early Christianity 4 (New York: The Edwin Mellen Press, 1983); R. M. Grant, *The Letter and the Spirit* (London: SPCK, 1957); R. P. C. Hanson, *Allegory and Event* (Richmond, Virginia: John Knox Press, 1959); M. Harl and N. De Lange, *Origène: Philocalie, 1–20 sur les écritures*, SC 302.42–157 (1983); H. de Lubac, *Histoire et Esprit: l'intelligence de l'écriture d'après Origène* (Paris: Aubier, 1950); K. J. Torjesen, *Hermeneutical Procedure and Theological Structure in Origen's Exegesis*. Patristische Texte und Studien 28 (Berlin: de Gruyter, 1986); idem, "Origen's Interpretation of the Psalms," *SP* 17, 2.944–958; W. Ullmann, "Hermeneutik und Semantik in der Bibeltheologie des Origenes dargestellt anhand von Buch 10 seines Johanneskommentares," *SP* 17, 2.966–977.

INTRODUCTION 11

more modest goal of observing how Origen works at the text of John's Gospel and presenting these observations in a somewhat systematic fashion. In the *Commentary on John* there are approaches to Scripture which we would expect to find in Origen, along with a few surprises.

(15) Origen lays out a theoretical hermeneutic in *On First Principles* which corresponds to the tripartite division of man: "Just as man consists of body, soul and spirit, so in the same way does the Scripture."[43] He attempts to base this threefold level of meaning in Scripture on Proverbs 22.20–21.[44] The "flesh" of Scripture is to edify the simple, its "soul" is for the man who has made some progress, and the spiritual level is for the perfect.[45] Origen then notes that some passages lack a bodily or literal meaning and possess only those higher levels of meaning corresponding to the soul and the spirit of man. This, he suggests, may be the reason the waterpots at the wedding in Cana are said to contain two or three measures apiece.[46] Two measures means that sometimes there is only the soul meaning and the spiritual meaning in a passage of Scripture, at other times, as those containing three measures suggest, all three levels of meaning are present in a text.

(16) In practice, Origen rarely speaks of three levels of meaning in his exegesis. And, when he deals with two, it is usually the literal and the spiritual which he discusses. The intermediate level of meaning receives almost no attention in Origen's exegesis.[47] K. J. Torjesen has correctly said, "The contemporary consensus about the allegorical method holds that it proceeds in two distinct stages. The first stage is an exposition of the historical sense. And the second stage is an exposition of the allegorical or spiritual sense."[48] This must be taken one step further, however, in regard to Origen's ex-

---

43. Origen, *Princ.* 4.2.4. Quotations from this work are from *Origen: On First Principles*, tr. G. W. Butterworth (New York: Harper & Row, 1966).
44. See W. Ullmann, "Hermeneutik und Semantik," 968.
45. Origen, *Princ.* 4.2.4.   46. Jn 2.6; Origen, *Princ.* 4.2.5.
47. Cf. M. F. Wiles, "Origen as Biblical Scholar," *The Cambridge History of the Bible*, ed. P. R. Ackroyd and C. F. Evans (Cambridge: Cambridge University Press, 1970), 1.467–470.
48. Torjesen, "Origen's Interpretation of the Psalms," 944.

egesis of John. Quite frequently he deals with only one sense of Scripture. One of the surprising features of Origen's exegesis in the *Commentary on John* is that there are so many extended discussions which begin and end with the literal level, and make no suggestions concerning a higher level of meaning. Furthermore, his usual approach when he discusses both the literal and the spiritual level is to demonstrate that the problems involved in the text at the literal or historical level cannot be solved at that level of meaning. Consequently, the sole purpose of his discussion of the literal meaning in those cases is to show that there must be some meaning in the text at a higher level of interpretation. The literal level, therefore, is discussed only to be dismissed, not to provide edification at its own level. This, too, must be considered an interpretation of only one sense of Scripture, i.e., the spiritual sense. Origen's exegesis of John may be summarized, then, by saying that sometimes he offers an interpretation at only the literal level, sometimes at only the spiritual, and occasionally an interpretation at both levels. We shall attempt to offer some illustrations of each of these in the following discussion.

Spiritual Exegesis

(17) Origen's spiritual exegesis is rooted in his view of Scripture. While he does not deny the human agency in the writing of the Scriptures, the ultimate author of all Scripture for Origen, as for the early church in general, is the Holy Spirit. The meaning that one finds in Scripture, then, must be worthy of the Spirit from whom it comes. When the text of Genesis relates that Abraham was standing under a tree, "we ought not," Origen says, "believe that it was of greatest concern to the Holy Spirit to write in the books of the Law where Abraham was standing. For what does it help me," he continues, "who have come to hear what the Holy Spirit teaches the human race, if I hear that 'Abraham was standing under a tree'?"[49] And when Rebecca is said to come daily to the wells, Origen remarks, "Do you think these are tales and

---

49. *Gn. Hom.* 4.3; and FOTC 71.106.

that the Holy Spirit tells stories in Scriptures? This is instruction for souls and spiritual teaching which instructs . . . you to come daily to the wells of the Scriptures, to the waters of the Holy Spirit. . . ."[50]

(18) On the other hand, the human agents who put the teachings of the Spirit in written form were not ignorant of the spiritual meanings in the material they wrote. Moses knew the allegorical meanings in the Law and in the stories he recorded; Joshua understood "the true distribution of the land"; and the Prophets perceived the meanings of their visions.[51]

(19) Such a view of Scripture demands that the exegete search for spiritual meaning in each detail of the text. It demands also that the exegete be filled with the same Spirit that filled the authors of Scripture.[52] Origen says as much in an analogy he draws at the beginning of Book 6 of the *Commentary on John*. He compares himself as the composer of the *Commentary* to the builder in Jesus' parable who counted the cost to see if he had sufficient resources to complete the building of a tower. Origen finds his own resources inadequate for the project. "We have, however," he says, "trusted in God who enriches us in all speech and knowledge, trusting that he will enrich us as we struggle to keep the spiritual laws. On the basis of what he supplies, we anticipate advancing in the construction even to the parapet of the house."[53]

(20) This view of Scripture and of the exegete must be kept in mind as the background to the introduction to the *Commentary* which Origen provides in Book 1. There he offers an elaborate discussion of the Gospels as the firstfruits of all the Scriptures, and John's Gospel as the firstfruits of the Gospels.[54] The meaning of such a Gospel standing at the pinnacle

---

50. Ibid., 10.2; and FOTC 71.160.   51. *Comm. Jn.* 6.22–23.
52. See R. E. Heine, "Gregory of Nyssa's Apology for Allegory," *VC* 38 (1984), 362; E. Nardoni, "Origen's Concept of Biblical Inspiration," *The Second Century* 4 (1984), 20; and J. W. Trigg, "The Charismatic Intellectual: Origen's Understanding of Religious Leadership," *Church History* 50 (1981) 10–11.
53. *Comm. Jn.* 6.7. Cf. *Comm. Jn.* 1.89; 20.1; 28.6; 32.1–3.
54. Ibid., 1.12–23.

of all Scripture is not open to just anyone. The one who would understand it must have leaned on Jesus' breast, and have received Mary to be his mother. The latter means that he must have, in some sense, become Jesus, for Mary had only one son. Therefore, when Jesus said to Mary, "Behold your son," it was as though he had said, "Behold, this is Jesus whom you bore." This, Origen finds to be in harmony with Paul's statement that the one who has been perfected "no longer lives, but Christ lives in him."[55] The words of John's Gospel, then, which in their physical sense as language can be read or heard by anyone, can be accurately understood only by one who can say, "'But we have the mind of Christ, that we may know the things that are given us by God.'"[56]

(21) Origen calls this higher level of insight attained by the Spirit-led exegete the spiritual gospel. John, he thinks, alludes to it in his reference to the eternal gospel in Revelation 14.6.[57] This spiritual gospel is the reality of which Christ's acts were symbols; it is the secrets hidden in the mysteries of Christ's words.[58] There are, then, two gospels. The one is perceptible to the senses, the gospel consisting of the language which tells of the teachings and activities of Jesus which all can read. The other is the spiritual gospel, the bare truth behind the types in the gospel perceptible to the senses. The task of the exegete is "to translate the gospel perceptible to the senses into the spiritual gospel."[59]

(22) We must note here that this spiritual translation includes more than allegorical interpretation. It includes, for one thing, what modern scholars call typological interpretation. J. Daniélou has called attention to the following Old Testament types found in the commentary: various crossings of the Jordan serve as types of baptism in Book 6; the paschal

55. Ibid., 1.23.   56. Ibid., 1.24.
57. Cf. R. Gögler, *Origines: Das Evangelium nach Johannes* (Zürich, Köln: Benziger Verlag Einsiedeln, 1959), 74. In *Lev. Hom.* 4.10 Origen links the "eternal law" of Lv 6.15 (LXX) with the "eternal gospel" of Rv 14.6, and in the same paragraph equates the "eternal law" with the "spiritual law" of Rom 7.14. Cf. R. Gögler, *Zur Theologie des biblischen Wortes bei Origenes* (Düsseldorf: Patmos-Verlag, 1963), 384–5.
58. *Comm. Jn.* 1.40.   59. Ibid., 1.44–46.

lamb is a type of the crucified Christ in Book 10; the tabernacle and the temple are viewed as types of Christ and the Church in Book 10.[60] Origen is "an innovator," Daniélou says, "in the extent to which he brings the New Testament into the typological process."[61] This means that Origen sees certain things in the New Testament to be types of spiritual realities just as certain things in the Old Testament were types of corresponding things in the New Testament. For example, his discussion of the pasch in John 2.13 proceeds from the pasch in Exodus to Christ via 1 Corinthians 5.7, and from there to the Christian eucharist via John 6.53–56. The process does not stop here, however, but he goes on to suggest that there will be "a third pasch which will be celebrated with 10,000 angels in a most perfect assembly and a most blessed exodus."[62]

(23) Origen does not, however, see typological exegesis to consist primarily, if at all, in finding correspondences between various historical realities, as earlier exegetes such as Justin had done. "We must not suppose," he says, "that historical things are types of historical things, and corporeal of corporeal. Quite the contrary: corporeal things are types of spiritual things, and historical of intellectual."[63] Origen makes little discernible distinction between typological and allegorical interpretation. What modern scholars would distinguish as typological and allegorical exegesis are woven together indiscriminately by Origen in this discussion as he pursues the spiritual meaning of the simple statement, "And the pasch of the Jews was near."

(24) Fulfillment of prophecy is closely related to typology in the Christian tradition. Origen also uses this in the *Commentary on John*.[64] He attacks the heterodox who deny the va-

---

60. J. Daniélou, *Gospel Message*, 276–8. See also J. Daniélou, *Origène* (Paris: la table ronde, 1948), 145–147. Daniélou's sharp distinction between typology as belonging to the tradition of the Church, and allegory as a part of the Hellenistic tradition, has been rightly criticized by Hansen, *Allegory and Event*, 97–129.
61. Daniélou, *Gospel Message*, 278.
62. *Comm. Jn.* 10.67–111. 63. Ibid., 10.110.
64. See, e.g., *Comm. Jn.* 1.142–150; 2.166.

lidity of the prophecies about Christ.⁶⁵ Prophetic testimony, he argues, is one of the proofs of the Incarnation.⁶⁶ This is similar to the type of arguments advanced in the New Testament and by later Christians such as Justin in his *Dialogue with Trypho*. As in the case of typology, however, Origen does not stop by seeing historical connections between the word of the prophet in the Old Testament and its fulfillment in the historical life of Christ depicted in the New Testament. The prophetic testimonies may, in addition, teach theology concerning such things as the relationship between the Father and the Son.⁶⁷ Prophetic testimonies that have historical fulfillment in Christ in the Gospels also have higher, spiritual meanings. Zacharias' prophecy, for example, which the evangelists quote in connection with the triumphal entry foretells more than "the bodily event which is revealed in the Gospels."⁶⁸ Prophecies, therefore, as well as types contain spiritual meanings which transcend whatever literal fulfillment they may have had.

(25) Origen's spiritual exegesis also, of course, contains classical examples of allegorical interpretation. In his treatment of John 1.1, he cites Revelation 19.11ff. as an ancillary passage, in which a rider appears in heaven on a white horse. He then proceeds through the passage object by object giving special meanings to each in typical allegorical fashion.⁶⁹ The mention of the shoes of Jesus which John the Baptist was not worthy to unloose leads Origen to suggest that one of the shoes is the Incarnation, and the other the descent into Hades.⁷⁰ Sometimes he offers more than one possible meaning in his allegories. The ass and colt, for example, which Jesus rode into Jerusalem at one point are the Old and New Testaments,⁷¹ but a little later he suggests that they are "those of the circumcision and those from the gentiles who believed later."⁷²

(26) Although there are exceptions, in general Origen al-

---

65. Ibid., 2.199–205.
66. Ibid., 2.202.
67. Ibid., 2.205.
68. Ibid., 10.161.
69. Ibid., 2.45–63.
70. Ibid., 6.174.
71. Ibid., 10.174–5.
72. Ibid., 10.185–6.

legorizes narratives and metaphors.⁷³ His allegorization of narratives arises from his assumption that all the biblical texts must offer spiritual lessons. Historical statements, as we pointed out above, lack religious value in his judgment. They are, therefore, given religious value by allegorization. Some have suggested that he allegorized metaphors because he lacked poetic sensitivity.⁷⁴ It seems more likely to me that he saw poetic statements, like historical statements, to be devoid of religious value in themselves. While a metaphor is not an historical statement, it shares with historical statement the fact that it involves the physical world. There is a sense, indeed, in which it is correct to say that Origen saw the whole physical world as a metaphor for spiritual realities. As H. Koch has noted, in Origen's view the invisible, eternal world is now hidden from souls because of the fall. Consequently, God created the visible world in such a way that each thing in it is an image of something eternal so that human reason can lift itself to the heavenly world by contemplating the objects in the physical world.⁷⁵ Origen appeals to this cosmological basis for his hermeneutic in his discussion of the simile in Song of Songs 2.9: "My lover is like a roe or a young hart upon the mountains of Bethel." "Paul teaches us," he says,

that the invisible things of God are understood by means of things that are visible, and that the things that are not seen are beheld through their relationship and likeness to things seen. He thus shows that this visible world teaches us about that which is invisible, and that this earthly scene contains certain patterns of things heavenly. Thus it is possible for us to mount up from things below to things above, and to perceive and understand from the things we see on earth the things that belong to heaven.... And perhaps, even as God made man in his own image and likeness, so also did he create the other creatures after the likeness of some other heavenly patterns. And perhaps the correspondence between all things on earth and their celestial prototypes goes so far, that even *the grain of mus-*

---

73. For an example of the latter, see *Comm. Jn.* 2.193–5.
74. Wiles, "Origen as Biblical Scholar," 470; so also R. P. C. Hanson in his review of *Origène: Philocalie 1–20* in *Patristics* 14 (July, 1985), 3.
75. H. Koch, *Pronoia und Paideusis* (Berlin: Walter de Gruyter, 1932), 45–6.

tard seed, . . . which is the least of all seeds, has something in heaven whose image and likeness it bears. . . .[76]

(27) All of this comprises what Origen calls the translation of "the gospel perceptible to the senses into the spiritual gospel."[77] While Origen thinks the gospel perceptible to the senses is not of much value without this translation, he does not completely despise it. Just as Paul made certain concessions to those of the circumcision in order to gain them, so the one who would benefit the multitudes cannot do so by "inward Christianity alone." "This is why," he says, "we must live as a Christian in a spiritual and in a physical manner." And when necessary, we must preach the literal gospel, declaring "nothing except Jesus Christ, and him crucified."[78]

Literal Exegesis

(28) As we have already noted, Origen sometimes interprets a passage at both the literal and spiritual levels. Such is the case when he discusses John 1.6: "There was a man sent from God." At the literal level, he says, this means he was sent to Israel and to those who heard him preach in the wilderness. At the deeper level, it means he was sent into the world. The implications of the latter meaning are then pursued in relation to the question of whence he was sent. This leads finally to the conclusion that John was an angel who assumed a body to bear testimony to the light.[79] The fragment of Book 5 preserves another clear example of both a literal and spiritual meaning being given to a statement. There Origen is reflecting on the length of his *Commentary* in light of Ecclesiastes 12.12: "My son, beware of making many books." At the literal level this may mean either that one ought not own many books, or that one ought not compose many books. While there is much to commend the historical meaning of this text, Origen notes that if this is all it means, Solomon himself

---

76. *Comm. Cant.* 3.12; translation from *Origen: The Song of Songs Commentary and Homilies,* ACW 26.218–19.
77. *Comm. Jn.* 1.45.
78. Ibid., 1.42–43. Cf. W. Ullmann, "Hermeneutik und Semantik," 970.
79. *Comm. Jn.* 2.175–192.

sinned in relation to it, for he spoke 3000 parables and 5000 odes. This leads him to search for a deeper meaning, which is that all truth is one word, regardless of how many words or books express it, while error consists of a multitude of words.[80]

(29) In the two examples cited in the preceding paragraph the literal meaning is preserved, although its significance is subordinated to the deeper meaning. There are other instances in the *Commentary*, however, where the literal meaning is investigated only to show that it is impossible, and that one must look for a spiritual meaning. This is especially the case where there are differences in parallel passages in the Gospels. The problem of fitting John 2.12–25 into the chronology of the Synoptics leads Origen to say that "the truth of these accounts lies in the spiritual meanings."[81] If this solution is not accepted he fears that many will dismiss "credence in the Gospels as not true, or not written by a divine spirit, or not successfully recorded."[82] The problem in this passage, Origen notes, is not an isolated case. There are so many disagreements between the Gospels at the historical level that one would become dizzy examining them.[83] Origen proposes a kind of parable to explain how the truth can be communicated through so many discrepancies. Suppose, he says, that God reveals things to four different men in different places who all see in the spirit. Each one would report what he had seen and heard. Let them agree with one another in some things, he says, and disagree in others. Let one man report that God appeared to someone in a particular form in one place, and another report that he appeared to someone else in another place at the same time. Anyone, he asserts, who thinks that what these men write is history, and that God shares in the limitations of space and time, will have to conclude that they cannot be telling the truth. The only way their accounts could be harmonized would be to see that they were trying to communicate the things they had seen in their mind

---

80. *Comm. Jn.* 5.2–8.
81. Ibid., 10.10.
82. Ibid.
83. Ibid., 10.14.

by means of a type. So it is with the four evangelists. "In some places they have interwoven in Scripture something made clear to them in a purely intellectual manner, with language as though it were something perceptible to the senses."[84] Sometimes they have even altered what happened historically for the sake of the spiritual meaning.

> Their intention was to speak the truth spiritually and bodily at the same time where that was possible, but where it was not possible in both ways, to prefer the spiritual to the bodily. The spiritual truth is often preserved in the bodily falsehood, so to speak.[85]

(30) It remains to set forth examples where Origen discusses the literal meaning of a passage and does not move beyond this to a spiritual meaning. There are several places where Origen deals only with the literal sense in his debate with Heracleon. For example, Heracleon, Origen asserts, attributed certain words in the prologue of John's Gospel to the Baptist which should be attributed to the disciple, and vice versa.[86] There follows a lengthy and circuitous argument which, nevertheless, moves at the literal level of interpretation. The argument closes with a statement stressing the importance of paying close attention to the details of Scripture at the historical level. "The one who will read Scripture accurately must," Origen says, "pay attention everywhere, to observe, when necessary, who is speaking, and when it is spoken, that we may discover that words are appropriately matched with characters throughout the Holy Books."[87]

(31) In another place he reconciles a discrepancy in the way a saying of the Baptist is reported in the different Gospels at the literal level by saying that he made both statements, but

---

84. Ibid., 10.15–18.
85. Ibid., 10.20. Origen sets forth a similar hermeneutic for the entire Bible in *Princ.* 4.3.1–5. Cf. Harl's comments in Harl and De Lange, *Philocalia, 1–20,* 97–101; 190–191. Wiles, "Origen as Biblical Scholar," 470–71, notes that once Origen accepted the principle that some things stated as historical facts in the Bible are not true historically, he was surprisingly reluctant to use it. He does, however, use it several times in Book 10 of the *Commentary on John.* See, for example, in addition to the passage discussed here, 10.119–130; 10.199–200.
86. *Comm. Jn.* 6.13–14. 87. Ibid., 6.13–53.

at different times. This reconciliation is offered to preserve the credibility of the evangelists,[88] something which he attempts in other places by denying the historicity of the differing accounts in favor of the spiritual meaning.[89] The fact that he chose to reconcile the differences at the historical level here shows that he did not take the historical sense lightly, but dismissed it as impossible only in those places where he could see no way of harmonizing the accounts at the historical level.

(32) Large portions of Books 1 and 2 consist of literal exegesis directed at theological problems posed by various groups, some Gnostic, some the simple pious, and others unidentified.[90] No spiritual meaning is offered for anything contained in the first five verses of John's Gospel. Allegorical interpretations are sometimes offered for ancillary passages that are discussed in conjunction with these verses,[91] but these verses themselves are not allegorized.

(33) We noted earlier that Origen usually allegorized narratives and metaphors. He considered the opening verses of John, however, to be theological propositions. The first two verses of the gospel, he asserts, consist of four propositions:[92] (1) "In the beginning was the Word"; (2) "The Word was with God"; (3) "And the Word was God"; (4) "The same was in the beginning with God." The first three propositions teach us "in what the Word was, namely 'in the beginning,' and with whom he was, namely 'with God,' and who the Word was, namely 'God.'"[93] The fourth teaches "that 'he was in the beginning' and 'in the beginning' he was 'with God,' neither being only 'with God' since 'he was' also 'in the beginning,' nor being only 'in the beginning,' and not being 'with God,' since 'the same was in the beginning with God.'"[94] While Origen rambles over numerous subjects, and quotes and interprets several texts from both the Old and New Testaments in

---

88. Ibid., 6.170–172.
89. See note 85 above.
90. See, for example, *Comm. Jn.* 2.155; 2.171; 2.16; 2.73–4.
91. As, for example, the treatment of Rv 19.11–16 in *Comm. Jn.* 2.45–63.
92. *Comm. Jn.* 2.11–12; 2.34–5; 2.64–68.
93. Ibid., 2.35.
94. Ibid., 2.69.

the course of discussing these first two verses of the Gospel, the exegesis he offers of the verses themselves is literal.

(34) The treatment of John 1.3 is structured by two problems posed by Heracleon's exegesis of the verse, (1) What does the expression "all things" include? and (2) What is the significance of "through him"? He concludes that "all things" must include everything (even the Holy Spirit) except the aspects which are in Christ (i.e. the life, the light of men, etc.), and that "through him" means that all things have been made *through* the Word *by* the creator.[95] This, again, is interpretation at the literal level.

(35) While Origen does not call John 1.4 a paradox, it reminds him of the Stoic paradoxes, and his interpretation is modeled on those paradoxes:

Now if life is equivalent to the light of men, no one who is in darkness is alive, and no one who is alive is in darkness, but everyone who is alive is also in light, and everyone who is in light is alive. Consequently only the one who is alive, and everyone who is alive, is a son of light.[96]

(36) John 1.5 is treated as an extension of verse four. After pursuing the concepts of light and darkness through various biblical passages, Origen offers this interpretation of the verse:

This light, indeed, which was made in the Word, which also is life, 'shines in the darkness' of our souls. It has come to stay where the world rulers of this darkness live (who by wrestling with the human race struggle to subject those who do not stand firm in every manner to darkness), that, when they have been enlightened, they may be called sons of light. And this light shines in the darkness and is pursued by it, but it is not overcome.[97]

(37) The nomenclature of literal and spiritual interpretation does not appear in relation to these first five verses of John. Origen offers one interpretation and gives no indication that he thinks another to be possible at another level of understanding the text. When he comes to verse six, however,

95. Ibid., 2.70–104. 96. Ibid., 2.132.
97. Ibid., 2.167.

he offers an interpretation "according to the literal account," followed by an interpretation "according to the deeper meaning."[98] John 1.6 marks the beginning of the narrative about John the Baptist: "There was a man sent from God, whose name was John," and consequently, the beginning of Origen's allegorization of the words of the Gospel.

Heracleon and the Tripartite Tractate

(38) Our knowledge of Heracleon, the second century Gnostic whose exegesis of John Origen occasionally quotes and attacks in the *Commentary*, is very limited. Origen tells us that he was said to have been a pupil of Valentinus,[99] and Clement of Alexandria calls him the most famous of the Valentinian school.[100] Irenaeus,[101] Tertullian,[102] and Hippolytus[103] connect him with Ptolemaeus and the Italian branch of the school of Valentinianism. Ps.–Tertullian refers to him as sharing some views with Valentinus, but differing in others.[104]

(39) None of Heracleon's writings have been preserved except for forty-eight fragments quoted in Origen's *Commentary on John*, two fragments quoted by Clement of Alexandria, and an allusion to a viewpoint of Heracleon in Photius.[105] The Nag Hammadi documents have shed some uncertain light on Heracleon.[106] Y. Janssens thinks the *Gospel of Truth*, which some have attributed to Valentinus,[107] has a number of ap-

---

98. Ibid., 2.175.
99. *Comm. Jn.* 2.100.
100. *Strom.* 4.9.71.1.
101. *Adv. Haer.* 2.4.1.
102. *Adv. Val.* 4.
103. *Ref.* 6.35.
104. *Haer.* 4.
105. The fragments in the *Commentary on John* are found in Books 2, 6, 10, 13, 19, and 20. They are printed in block quotations in this translation. Those in Clement are in *Eclogae Propheticae* 25.1 and *Strom.* 4.9.71.1–73.1; that in Photius is in *Ep.* 134. These fragments are conveniently collected and translated in W. Foerster, *Gnosis: A Selection of Gnostic Texts*, tr. R. McL. Wilson (Oxford: Clarendon Press, 1972), 162–183.
106. For a convenient English translation of the documents see *The Nag Hammadi Library*, ed. J. M. Robinson (New York: Harper & Row, 1977). All translations from the Nag Hammadi documents in this introduction are from this volume.
107. See G. W. MacRae's comments in the introduction to his translation of the treatise in *The Nag Hammadi Library*, 37, and K. Grobel, *The Gospel of Truth* (London: Adam & Charles Black, 1960), 26–27.

parent contacts with the fragments of Heracleon.[108] More direct light on Heracleon's thought may come from another treatise from Nag Hammadi which has been named the *Tripartite Tractate* by modern scholars. H. Puech and G. Quispel have argued that Heracleon may have been the author of this treatise.[109] Quispel is certain that the *Tripartite Tractate* "reflects the views of the Western school of Valentinianism and more specifically those of the school of Heracleon."[110] Whether Heracleon was the actual author of this treatise will probably never be known. There are, nevertheless, some striking similarities between the viewpoint expressed in a few of the fragments of Heracleon preserved by Origen in the *Commentary on John* and viewpoints set forth in the *Tripartite Tractate*.[111]

(40) The most striking contact between a fragment of Heracleon and the *Tripartite Tractate* is found in the fragment Origen quotes in Book 2 of the *Commentary*.[112] The discussion in the *Commentary* concerns the meaning of John 1.3: "All

108. Y. Janssens, "L'épisode de la Samaritaine chez Héracléon," in *Sacra Pagina* 2, *Bibliotheca Ephemeridum Theologicarum Lovaniensium* XII–XIII (Paris: Librairie Lecoffre, 1959), 82.
109. H. Puech and G. Quispel, "Le quatrième écrit Gnostique du codex Jung," *VC* (1955), 65–102. See also G. Quispel, "From Mythos to Logos," *Gnostic Studies* 1 (Istanbul, 1974), 165–6; idem, "Origen and the Valentinian Gnosis," *VC* (1974), 29–42; and the notes of G. Quispel and J. Zandee in *Tractatus Tripartitus*, Part 1 *De Supernis*, ed. by R. Kasser, M. Malinine, H. Puech, G. Quispel, and J. Zandee (Bern: Francke Verlag, 1973), 311ff.
110. Quispel, "Origen and the Valentinian Gnosis," 35. The followers of Valentinus were divided into an Oriental branch represented in the writings of Theodotus, and a Western or Italian branch headed by Ptolemaeus and Heracleon. The Western branch introduced a number of new elements into the teachings of Valentinus which brought them nearer to certain views of the Catholic Church (Ibid., 33–4).
111. There are more numerous contacts between viewpoints Origen expresses as his own and certain views in the *Tripartite Tractate* if one looks beyond the *Commentary on John* to other works of his as the *On First Principles*. These similarities led Quispel, "Origen and the Valentinian Gnosis," 33, 36–42, to suggest an evolution of certain concepts from Valentinus via Heracleon to Origen. Daniélou, *Origène*, 190–198, had already shown the influence of Heracleon's exegetical approach on Origen, and E. de Faye, long before the discoveries at Nag Hammadi argued for Gnostic influence on Origen's view and treatment of the Bible, and on all the major points of his theology in "De l'influence du Gnosticisme sur Origène," *Revue de l'histoire des religions* (1923) 181–235.
112. *Comm. Jn.* 2.100–104. See note 135 on this passage.

INTRODUCTION 25

things were made through him." There are two problems, Origen notes, with Heracleon's interpretation of this statement. First, he limits the expression "all things" to this world and its contents, excluding all the beings of the higher realms. Second, he identifies the *logos* not with the agent of creation, but with the cause, making the creator lower than the *logos*. These same views can be found in the *Tripartite Tractacte*, though they are not connected with John 1.3. Here the higher realm, called the *aeon*, and the beings of the higher realm, called *totalities* or *aeons*, come forth from the Father independent of the logos, who is also one of the *aeons*, prior to the creation of the world and the things in it.[113] The *logos*, on the other hand, is the cause of the creation of the world and the lower beings, including mankind, but is not the agent. The *archon* is the agent of creation, being used by the *logos* as a "hand."[114] Consequently, the *logos* is higher than the creator of the world in the *Tripartite Tractacte*. This is precisely what Origen accuses Heracleon of saying.

(41) A somewhat lesser point of contact is found in Heracleon's identification of the *logos* as the Savior,[115] and the appearance of the same identification in the *Tripartite Tractacte*.[116] The significance is to be seen in connection with our discussion in the preceding paragraph, i.e. both Heracleon and the *Tripartite Tractate* identify the *logos* as the cause of creation and as the Savior.

(42) Another similarity between Heracleon and the *Tripartite Tractate* lies in the way they each describe the response of pneumatics to redemption once it is revealed to them. In the *Tripartite Tractate* the spiritual race responds immediately to the light once it is revealed.[117] Heracleon "praises the Samaritan woman because she demonstrated a faith that was unhesitating and appropriate to her nature, when she had no doubt about what he said to her."[118] E. Pagels takes the frag-

---

113. *Tripartite Tractate*, 59.5–64.35.
114. Ibid., 100.30–34; 114.7–8.   115. *Comm. Jn.* 6.108.
116. *Tripartite Tractate* 113.38–39; 114.7–8; 115.26–29.
117. Ibid., 118.29–37; 123.4–11.
118. *Comm. Jn.* 13.63. Cf. 13.92.

ments of Heracleon on the Samaritan woman to be dealing with the subject of pneumatic conversion.[119] "Hearing the Savior's offer of 'living water,'" she says, "the Samaritan responds with spontaneous recognition, as if hearing what she already has known intuitively. Her answer is 'immediate, uncritical, undiscriminating'—a response 'appropriate to her nature' . . . since she is already one of those 'chosen by the Father.' "[120]

(43) The metaphor of marriage in relation to the final state of the elect appears to be another point of contact between the *Tripartite Tractate* and Heracleon. In the *Tripartite Tractate* it is said that "the election shares body and essence with the Savior, since it is like a bridal chamber because of its unity and its agreement with him."[121] Heracleon thinks that "the husband of the Samaritan woman mentioned by Jesus is her pleroma, so that, on coming to the Savior, she may obtain from him power, unity, and union with her pleroma."[122]

(44) These similarities are not all of equal significance, nor are they sufficient in their totality to prove Heracleon to have been the author of the *Tripartite Tractate*. They do suggest, however, a similarity of viewpoint between Heracleon and the *Tripartite Tractate* and consequently, if used with prudence, may help us better understand the theological position of Heracleon, and even of Origen himself.

Manuscripts, Editions, and Translations of the Commentary on John

(45) While there are eight, and possibly nine or ten,[123] Greek manuscripts containing the *Commentary on John*, they are all dependent on one thirteenth century manuscript Codex Monacensis 191 (M) which is located in Munich. This

---

119. E. Pagels, *The Johannine Gospel*, 86–92.
120. Ibid., 87.
121. *Tripartite Tractate* 122.14–16. Cf. Quispel, "Mythos," 169.
122. *Comm. Jn.* 13.67. Cf. Pagels, *The Johannine Gospel*, 88.
123. For the uncertainty of whether there is a ninth, and even a tenth manuscript of the commentary, see A. E. Brooke, *The Fragments of Heracleon*, Texts and Studies 1, ed. J. A. Robinson (Cambridge: University Press, 1891), 6; idem, *The Commentary of Origen on S. John's Gospel* 1, 12.

INTRODUCTION 27

dependence on Codex Monacensis has been established by A. E. Brooke[124] and E. Preuschen,[125] and is accepted by C. Blanc in the only critical edition of the commentary to appear after the editions of Brooke and Preuschen.[126] This means that our knowledge of the text of the commentary is completely dependent on this one manuscript. Consequently, wherever there are lacunae in this manuscript, and there are several, we must either resort to conjecture or leave gaps in the text. And wherever the reading of the manuscript appears incorrect, we must either offer emendations or mark the text as corrupt at that point.

(46) The first edition of the *Commentary* was produced by Huet in 1668, based on the sixteenth century manuscript Codex Regius of Paris. The Delarue edition of all of Origen's works, based on the sixteenth century manuscript Barberinus and the seventeenth century manuscript Bodleianus was produced in 1733–1759. Lommatzsch's edition of Origen's works appeared in 1831–1848 and was based on the work of his predecessors. Migne reproduced the edition of Delarue in 1857.[127] A. E. Brooke produced his new edition based on his study of Codex Monacensis in 1896. This was followed in 1903 by the edition of E. Preuschen based on the same manuscript. The edition of C. Blanc, which is based on that of Preuschen,[128] is still in process of appearing.[129]

(47) In the sixteenth century Ambrosius Ferrarius translated the commentary into Latin from the fourteenth century Codex Venis. There are four translations of the commentary into modern languages in various degrees of completeness. A. Menzies translated Books 1 through 10 into English. His

---

124. See the works by Brooke cited in the preceding note.
125. Preuschen, GCS 4.9–61.   126. Blanc, SC 120.41.
127. See the discussion of these editions by E. Corsini, *Commento al Vangelo di Giovanni di Origene* (Torinese: Unione Tipografico-Editrice, 1968), 93–4; and by A. Menzies, ANF 10.294.
128. Blanc, SC 120.41.
129. The first volume, containing Books 1–5, appeared as SC 120 (1966); the second, containing Books 6 and 10, appeared as SC 157 (1970); the third, containing Book 13, appeared as SC 222 (1975); and the fourth, containing Books 19 and 20, appeared as SC 290 (1982).

translation now appears in The Ante-Nicene Fathers 10. No date accompanies the translation, but Menzies says in a note that the edition of A. E. Brooke appeared too late to be used in his translation.[130] The translation is based on the text of Lommatzsch. There is an Italian translation by E. Corsini (1968), based on the text of Preuschen.[131] R. Gögler produced a partial translation of the commentary in German in 1959, also based on the text of Preuschen.[132] This translation contains sections from each of the nine extant books of the commentary, with some of the books translated in their entirety. C. Blanc is producing a French translation based on her edition of the text. This is now complete through Book 20 of the *Commentary*.[133] There are, in addition, two anthologies of texts of Origen which contain some selections from the *Commentary on John*. One was done by R. B. Tollinton in 1929,[134] and the other by H. Urs von Balthasar in 1938. The latter was translated into English by R. J. Daly in 1984.[135]

(48) Our translation is based on the text of Preuschen. The editions of Brooke and Blanc, however, have been constantly at hand and have been consulted on all passages where there are difficulties in the text. All places where we have deviated from Preuschen's text have been noted in footnotes. As in my translation of Origen's *Homilies on Genesis and Exodus* (FOTC 71), I have followed the Douay version of the Bible for the spelling of all names of biblical persons and places.[136]

130. ANF 10.294.
131. Corsini, *Commento al Vangelo di Giovanni*, 110.
132. Gögler, *Origenes: Das Evangelium nach Johannes*, 89.
133. See note 129 above.
134. R. B. Tollinton, *Selections from the Commentaries and Homilies of Origen*, Translations of Christian Literature, Series 1: Greek Texts (London: SPCK, 1929). See also, C. M. Moss, *Origen's Commentary on John, Book 13*: a translation with annotations [Ph.D. Diss] Louisville, Ky.: The Southern Baptist Theological Seminary, 1982.
135. H. Urs von Balthasar, tr. R. J. Daly, *Origen: Spirit and Fire* (Washington, D.C.: The Catholic University of America Press, 1984).
136. The reason for following the spelling in this version is given in FOTC 71.42–3.

COMMENTARY ON THE GOSPEL OF JOHN BOOKS 1–10

BOOK 1

UST AS THE PEOPLE of old, who were called the people of God,[1] were divided into twelve tribes plus the Levitical order, and this order itself, which engaged in service of the Divine, was divided into additional priestly and Levitical orders, so, I think, all the people of Christ according to "the hidden man of the heart,"[2] who bear the name "Jew inwardly" and who have been circumcised "in spirit,"[3] possess the characteristics of the tribes in a more mystical manner. This can be learned most clearly from John in the Apocalypse, although the other prophets are not silent for those who know how to understand such matters.

(2) John speaks as follows: "And I saw another angel ascending from the rising of the sun, having the seal of the living God, and he cried out with a loud voice to the four angels to whom it was given to hurt the earth and the sea, saying, 'Hurt not the earth, nor the sea, nor the trees, until we seal the servants of our God on their foreheads.' And I heard the number of those who were sealed, 144,000 were sealed of every tribe of the children of Israel; 12,000 were sealed from the tribe of Juda; and 12,000 from the tribe of Ruben."[4]

(3) And after enumerating the remaining tribes consecutively, except for Dan, he adds further on, "And I saw, and behold the lamb stood upon Mount Sion and with him 144,000, having his name and the name of his Father written on their foreheads. And I heard a voice from heaven, as the noise of many waters, and as the sound of loud thunder; and the voice which I heard was as the voice of harpists playing

---

1. Cf. Nm 27.17.
2. 1 Pt 3.4.
3. Rom 2.29.
4. Rv 7.2–5.

on their harps. And they sing a new song before the throne and before the four living creatures and the elders; and no one could learn the song except the 144,000 who were purchased from the earth. These are those who were not defiled with women, for they are virgins. These are those who follow the Lamb wherever he goes. These were purchased from men, the firstfruits for God and for the Lamb, and no lie was found in their mouth, for they are blameless."[5]

(4) Now the following words point to the conclusion that John says these things of those who have believed in Christ and who themselves are from the tribes, even though their physical race does not appear to go back to the seed of the patriarchs. "Hurt not," the angel says, "the earth, nor the sea, nor the trees, until we seal the servants of our God on their foreheads. And I heard the number of those who were sealed, 144,000 sealed of every tribe of the children of Israel."[6]

(5) Those, therefore, from every tribe of the children of Israel who are sealed on their foreheads are 144,000 in number. These 144,000 are later said by John to have the name of the Lamb and of his Father written on their foreheads, being virgins and not defiled with women.

(6) What else, then, would the seal on the foreheads be than the name of the Lamb and of his Father? In both passages the foreheads are said to have, in one place, the seal, and in the other, the letters containing the name of the Lamb and the name of his Father.

(7) But also, if those "from the tribes" are the same as the virgins, as we showed previously, and a believer from Israel according to the flesh is rare, so that one might perhaps dare to say that the number of the 144,000 is not filled up with believers from Israel according to the flesh,[7] it is clear that the 144,000 is composed of those gentiles who come to the divine Word, who are not defiled with women. Consequently, he who declares that the virgins of each tribe are its firstfruits would not be wrong.

5. Cf. Rv 14.1–5. 6. Rv 7.3–4.
7. Cf. 1 Cor 10.18.

COMMENTARY ON JOHN, BOOK 1   33

(8) For he also adds, "These were purchased from men, the firstfruits for God and for the Lamb, and no lie was found in their mouth, for they were blameless."[8] Now we must not be unaware that the saying about the 144,000 virgins admits an anagogical sense.[9] But at this time it would be superfluous and not in accord with our purpose to compare the prophetic texts which teach us the same thing about those from the gentiles.

(9) What, indeed, do all these things mean for us? You will raise this question when you read these words, Ambrose, since you are truly a man of God,[10] and a man in Christ,[11] and are eager to be spiritual, no longer being man.[12] Those from the tribes, on the one hand, offer tithes and firstfruits to God through the Levites and priests, not having all things as firstfruits or tithes. But the Levites and priests, although all their possessions consist of tithes and firstfruits, offer tithes to God through the high priest and, I think, firstfruits too.

(10) Most of us who approach the teachings of Christ, since we have much time for the activities of life and offer a few acts to God, would perhaps be those from the tribes who have a little fellowship with the priests and support the service of God in a few things. But those who devote themselves to the divine Word and truly exist by the service of God alone will properly be said to be Levites and priests in accordance with the excellence of their activities in this work.

(11) And, perhaps, those who excel all others and who hold, as it were, the first places of their generation will be high priests according to the order of Aaron, but not according to the order of Melchisedech.[13] If someone should object to this, thinking that we are impious when we prescribe the title of high priest for men, since Jesus is proclaimed as great priest in many places—for we have "a great high priest who

---

8. Rv 14.4–5.   9. *Anagōgē*. PGL, 100.
10. Cf. 1 Tm 6.11.   11. 2 Cor 12.2.
12. Blanc (SC 120.62), calls attention to *Comm. Jn.* 2.138, where Origen discusses the distinction between being "spiritual" and being "man."
13. Cf. Heb 7.11.

has passed through the heavens, Jesus the Son of God"[14]—, we would have to say to him that the apostle indicated this when he said that the prophet said of Christ, "You are a priest forever according to the order of Melchisedech,"[15] and not according to the order of Aaron. On this basis we too say that men can be high priests according to the order of Aaron but only the Christ of God according to the order of Melchisedech.

(12) Since we are eager for those things which are better, all our activity and our entire life being dedicated to God, and we wish to have all our activity as the firstfruits of many firstfruits—unless, indeed, we are mistaken when we think this—what more excellent activity ought there be, after our physical separation from one another, than the careful examination of the gospel? For, indeed, one might dare say that the gospel is the firstfruits of all the Scriptures.

(13) What other firstfruits of our activities ought there to have been, then, since we have come home to Alexandria, than that devoted to the firstfruits of the Scriptures?[16] But we ought to know that firstfruits and firstling are not the same.[17]

14. Heb 4.14. 15. Heb 7.17; 5.6.
16. On the historical significance of this statement, see FOTC 71.15; and Nautin, *Origène*, 366–67.
17. *Aparchē* and *prōtogennēma*, Origen seems to have exaggerated the distinction between the two terms. *Prōtogennēma*, according to E. Hatch and H. A. Redpath, *A Concordance to the Septuagint*, 2 vols. (Graz, Austria: Akademische Druck-U Verlagsanstalt, 1954) is used in the LXX for the Hebrew *bikkûrîm*, "firstfruits," being "the first of grain and fruit that ripened and was gathered and offered to God according to the ritual" (this and the following definitions of Hebrew words are from F. Brown, S. R. Driver, and C. A. Briggs, *A Hebrew English Lexicon of the Old Testament* [Oxford: At the Clarendon Press, 1959]). It also translates the Hebrew *rē'šit* which can also mean "firstfruits" in the sense of first of fruits. *Aparchē* too, however, is used by the LXX to translate *rē'šit*. In addition, *aparchē* translates the following Hebrew words in the LXX: (1) *hēleb*, in the sense of "choicest" or "best part" of the products of the land; (2) *Ma'ăśēr* meaning "tithes"; (3) *t'nûpâh*, "offering," and (4) *t'rûmâh*, "contribution" or "offering." Philo uses the two terms nearly synonymously. He defines *prōtogennēma* in this way: "One explanation of the name, 'Feast of the First-products' (*prōtogennēmatōn*) is that the first produce of the young wheat and the earliest fruit to appear is brought as a sample offering (*aparchē*) before the year's harvest comes to be used by men" (*De Specialibus Legibus* 2.179; tr. F. H. Colson, *Philo*, LCL, 7 (1950). Cf. *De Specialibus Legibus* 1.183 and *De Decalogo* 160). The Mishnaic treatise *Bikkurim* refers to no such distinctions in "offerings."

For firstfruits are offered after all the fruits, but the firstling is offered before.

(14) One would not go wrong, then, in saying that of the Scriptures which are in circulation in all the churches of God and which are believed to be divine, the law of Moses is the firstling, but the gospel is the firstfruits. For the perfect Word has blossomed forth after all the fruits of the prophets up to the time of the Lord Jesus.

(15) But if someone should object, because of the idea inherent in the explanation of firstfruits, and say that the Acts and the Epistles of the apostles were brought forth after the Gospels, and that the statement that the gospel is the firstfruits of all Scripture would not still prevail in accordance with our previous explanation of firstfruits, we would surely have to say that you have in the Epistles which are in circulation the understanding of wise men who have been aided by Christ, who need the testimonies contained in the words of the law and Prophets in order to be believed. Consequently we must say that the apostolic writings are wise and trustworthy and most beneficial; they are not, to be sure, on a par with, "Thus says the Lord almighty."[18]

(16) And in relation to this, consider if Paul also includes his own writings when he says, "All Scripture is inspired of God and profitable."[19] Do not his statements, "I speak, and not the Lord,"[20] and "I ordain in all churches,"[21] and "Such things as I suffered at Antioch, at Iconium and at Lystra,"[22] and words similar to these which he wrote from time to time, present[23] the apostolic ... authority ... , but not the absolute character of divinely inspired words?

(17) We must note in addition that the Old Testament is not gospel since it does not make known "him who is to come,"[24] but proclaims him in advance. On the other hand,

---

18. 2 Cor 6.18.
19. 2 Tm 3.16.
20. 1 Cor 7.12.
21. 1 Cor 7.17.
22. 2 Tm 3.11.
23. The MS. is damaged here. Brooke prints *parechonta*; Preuschen, and Blanc following him, leaves a lacuna.
24. Cf. Mt 11.3.

all the New Testament is gospel, not only because it declares alike with the beginning of the Gospel, "Behold the Lamb of God who takes away the sin of the world,"[25] but also because it contains various ascriptions of praise and teachings of him on account of whom the gospel is gospel.

(18) Furthermore, if God placed apostles, prophets, and evangelists,[26] and pastors and teachers, in the Church,[27] when we examine what the task of the evangelist is, we see that it is not exclusively to narrate in what way the Savior healed a man blind from birth,[28] how he raised a dead man beginning to stink,[29] or how he performed any of his incredible deeds. Since the gospel is characterized also by hortatory discourse to confirm the things concerning Jesus, we shall not hesitate to say that the things written by the apostles are, in a certain way, gospel.

(19) But as regards the second explanation, we must say to the one who objects that we are not correct in naming all the New Testament gospel because the Epistles are not entitled gospel, that in many passages of the Scriptures, when two or more things are given the same name, the name applies more appropriately in the case of one of the things mentioned. For example, although the Savior says, "Call no one teacher on the earth,"[30] the apostle says that teachers also have been appointed in the Church.

(20) These, then, will not be teachers as far as the precise sense of the expression in the gospel. In the same way, everything written in the Epistles will not be gospel when it is compared with the narrative of the deeds, sufferings and words of Jesus. The gospel, however, is the firstfruits of all Scripture, and we offer the firstfruits of all our future activities to the firstfruits of the Scriptures, as we have vowed.

(21) Now, in my opinion, there are four Gospels, as though

---

25. Jn 1.29.
26. *Evangelistēs*. The word "gospel" is *evangelion*. Origen is taking the work of the *evangelistēs*, i.e. the author of a gospel, to be the same as that of the *evangelistēs* which Paul discusses. Cf. Eph 4.11.
27. Cf. 1 Cor 12.28; Eph 4.11.   28. Cf. Jn 9.1.
29. Cf. Jn 11.39.   30. Cf. Mt 23.8.

they were the elements[31] of the faith of the Church. (The whole world which has been reconciled to God consists[32] of these elements, as Paul says: "God was in Christ, reconciling the world to himself."[33] Jesus took away the sin of this world, for the word which is written, "Behold the Lamb of God who takes away the sin of the world,"[34] is about the world of the Church.) But I think that John's Gospel, which you have enjoined us to examine to the best of our ability, is the firstfruits of the Gospels. It speaks of him whose descent is traced, and begins from him who is without a genealogy.

(22) For since Matthew, on the one hand, writing for the Hebrews awaiting the son of Abraham and David, says, "The book of the generation of Jesus Christ, son of David, son of Abraham,"[35] and Mark, knowing what he is writing, relates the "beginning of the gospel,"[36] perhaps we find its goal in John [when he tells of][37] the Word "in the beginning,"[38] the Word being God. But Luke also, . . . ;[39] but indeed he reserves for the one who leaned on Jesus' breast[40] the greater and more perfect expressions concerning Jesus, for none of those manifested his divinity as fully as John when he presented him saying, "I am the light of the world";[41] "I am the way, and the truth, and the life";[42] "I am the resurrection";[43] "I am the door";[44] "I am the good shepherd";[45] and in the

---

31. *Stoicheia.* This term was commonly used in philosophy after the time of Plato (cf. *Tht.* 201e) of the four basic components of the world: earth, air, fire, and water. Origen is alluding to this philosophical view in the analogy he presents here.

32. Cf. Col 1.17. 33. 2 Cor 5.19.
34. Cf. Jn 1.29. 35. Mt 1.1.
36. Mk 1.1.

37. *Diēgoumenō* is supplied by Brooke. The codex is damaged. He supplies the dative in agreement with John. It is possible that a passive participle in agreement with goal might be correct. "In John," *para tō Jōannē*, would then become "by John."

38. Cf. Jn 1.1.

39. Lacuna in the text. Brooke's emended text reads, "But Luke also having said in the beginning of Acts, 'The former treatise I made of all things which Jesus began to do and teach.'"

40. Cf. Jn 13.25. 41. Jn 8.12.
42. Jn 14.6. 43. Jn 11.25.
44. Jn 10.9. 45. Jn 10.11.

Apocalypse, "I am the alpha and the omega, the beginning and the end, the first and the last."[46]

(23) We might dare say, then, that the Gospels are the firstfruits of all Scriptures, but that the firstfruits of the Gospels is that according to John, whose meaning no one can understand who has not leaned on Jesus' breast nor received Mary from Jesus to be his mother also. But he who would be another John must also become such as John, to be shown to be Jesus, so to speak. For if Mary had no son except Jesus, in accordance with those who hold a sound opinion of her, and Jesus says to his mother, "Behold your son,"[47] and not, "Behold, this man also is your son," he has said equally, "Behold, this is Jesus whom you bore." For indeed everyone who has been perfected "no longer lives, but Christ lives in him,"[48] and since "Christ lives" in him, it is said of him to Mary, "Behold your son," the Christ.

(24) How great, then, must be our understanding, that we may be able to understand in a worthy manner the word which is stored up in the earthen treasures[49] of paltry language, whose written character is read by all who happen upon it, and whose sound is heard by all who present their physical ears? What also must we say? For he who will understand these matters accurately must say truthfully, "But we have the mind of Christ, that we may know the graces that have been given us by God."[50]

(25) Now it is possible to introduce evidence from Paul's words on our point that the whole New Testament is the gospel when he writes somewhere, "according to my gospel."[51] For among Paul's writings we do not have a book called a "gospel" in the usual sense, but everything which he preached and said was the gospel. And the things which he preached and said he also wrote. What he wrote, therefore, was "gospel."

46. Rv 22.13.
47. Jn 19.26.   48. Cf. Gal 2.20.
49. Cf. 2 Cor 4.7.
50. 1 Cor 2.16.12. See R. E. Heine, "Gregory of Nyssa's Apology for Allegory," *VC* (1984):361.
51. Rom 2.16.

(26) But if the writings of Paul were gospel, it is consistent with that to say that Peter's writings also were gospel and, in general, those which present the sojourn of Christ and prepare for his coming and produce it in the souls of those who are willing to receive the Word of God who stands at the door and knocks[52] and wishes to enter their souls.

What is a "gospel"?

(27) It is now time, however, to examine what the term "gospel" means, and why these books have this title. The gospel, therefore, is a discourse containing a report of things which, with good reason, make the hearer glad whenever he accepts what is reported, because they are beneficial. Such a discourse is no less gospel should it also be examined with reference to the hearer's attitude. The gospel is either a discourse which contains the presence of a good for the believer, or a discourse which announces that an awaited good is present.

(28) All the definitions which we have already mentioned fit those books entitled the gospels. For each gospel brings cheer with good reason. Each is a composition of declarations which are beneficial to the one who believes them and does not misconstrue them since it produces a benefit in him. Each gospel teaches about the saving sojourn with men of Christ Jesus, "the firstborn of every creature,"[53] a sojourn which occurred on account of men. But it is also clear to everyone who believes, that each gospel is a discourse which teaches about the sojourn of the good Father in his Son with those who are willing to receive him.

(29) And it is also obvious that these books announce something good which has been awaited. For John the Baptist summed up more or less the voice of all the people when he sent to Jesus and said, "Are you he who is to come, or do we look for another?"[54] For the Christ was the good awaited by the people. The prophets preached about him until even all

---

52. Cf. Rv 3.20.   53. Col 1.15.
54. Mt 11.3.

the common people who were under the Law and prophets had their hopes in him, as the Samaritan woman testifies when she says, "I know that the Messias is coming, who is called Christ. When he comes, he will tell us all things."[55]

(30) But Simon and Cleophas too, talking "together of all the things which had happened"[56] to Jesus, say to the risen Christ himself, though they did not yet know that he had risen from the dead, "Are you alone a stranger in Jerusalem, and do not know the things that have been done there in these days?" And he said, "What things?" and they answered, "The things concerning Jesus of Nazareth, who was a prophet, mighty in work and word before God and all the people; and how our chief priests and princes delivered him to be condemned to death, and crucified him. But we hoped that it was he who would redeem Israel."[57]

(31) Besides these, when Andrew, the brother of Simon Peter, found his own brother Simon, he said, "We have found the Messias, which is being interpreted, the Christ."[58] And a little later, when Philip found Nathanael, he said to him, "We have found him of whom Moses in the law, and the prophets, wrote, Jesus the son of Joseph of Nazareth."[59]

(32) But someone may think he must object to the first definition since those writings not entitled gospels also fall under it. For the Law and the prophets are believed to be discourses containing a report of things which, with good reason, make the hearers glad whenever they accept the things which are reported, because they are beneficial.

(33) One might reply to this, however, that before the coming of Christ, the Law and the prophets did not contain the proclamation which belongs to the definition of the gospel since he who explained the mysteries in them had not yet come. But since the Savior has come, and has caused[60] the gospel to be embodied in the gospel, he has made all things gospel, as it were.

---

55. Jn 4.25.
57. Lk 24.18–20.
59. Jn 1.45.
56. Lk 24.14.
58. Jn 1.41.
60. Accepting *poiēsas*, the reading of M, with Brooke and Blanc. Preuschen has *thelēsas*.

(34) And I would not be off target to use the example, "A little leaven leavens the whole lump."[61] Because . . .[62] sons of men in his divinity, when he had removed the veil on the Law and prophets,[63] he showed the divine nature of them all when he presented clearly to those wanting to become disciples of his wisdom what things were true in the law of Moses, which the ancients cultivated in a copy and shadow,[64] and what the truth was in the events in the stories, which "happened to them in a figure, and were written" on account of us "on whom the ends of the world have come."[65]

(35) Everyone, then, in whom Christ has dwelt, worships God neither in Jerusalem nor on the mountain of the Samaritans, but because he has learned that "God is spirit," serves him spiritually "in spirit and truth,"[66] and no longer worships the Father and creator of all things figuratively.

(36) Nothing of the ancients was gospel, then, before that gospel which came into existence because of the coming of Christ. But the gospel, which is a New Testament, made the newness of the Spirit which never grows old shine forth in the light of knowledge. This newness of the Spirit removed us from "the antiquity of the letter."[67] It is proper to the New Testament, although it is stored up in all the Scriptures. But that gospel which produced the gospel thought to exist in the Old Testament too, had to be called "gospel" in a special sense.

(37) We must not fail to remark, however, that Christ came spiritually even before he came in a body. He came to the more perfect and to those who were not still infants or under pedagogues and tutors,[68] in whom the spiritual "fullness of the time"[69] was present, as, for example, the patriarchs, and Moses the servant,[70] and the prophets who contemplated the glory of Christ.

(38) But just as Christ visited the perfect before his sojourn

---

61. Gal 5.9.
62. Lacuna in the text.
63. Cf. 2 Cor 3.15.
64. Cf. Heb 8.5.
65. 1 Cor 10.11.
66. Jn 4.24.
67. Rom 7.6.
68. Gal 3.25; 4.2.
69. Gal 4.4.
70. Cf. Heb 3.5.

which was visible and bodily, so also he has not yet visited those who are still infants after his coming which has been proclaimed, since they are "under tutors and governors"[71] and have not yet arrived at "the fullness of the time."[72] The forerunners of Christ have visited them—words with good reason called "pedagogues" because they are suited to souls which are children—but the Son himself, who glorified himself as the Word who is God,[73] has not yet visited them, because he awaits the preparation which must take place in men of God who are about to receive his divinity.

(39) And we must also know that just as there is a "law" which contains a "shadow of the good things to come,"[74] which have been revealed by the law proclaimed in accordance with truth, so also the gospel, which is thought to be understood by all who read it, teaches a shadow of the mysteries of Christ.

(40) And that which John calls an eternal gospel,[75] which would properly be called a spiritual gospel, clearly presents both the mysteries presented by Christ's words and the things of which his acts were symbols, to those who consider "all things face to face"[76] concerning the Son of God himself. Consistent with these matters, we understand that just as one is a Jew outwardly and cir[cumcised], there being both an outward and inward cir[cumcision],[77] so it is with a Christian and baptism.

(41) Both Paul and Peter, formerly being Jews outwardly and circumcised, later received from Jesus to be such also inwardly, not only confessing in words, but demonstrating in deeds[78] that they were Jews outwardly for the salvation of the many in accordance with the dispensation. And one must say the same thing also of their Christianity.

(42) Just as Paul cannot help those Jews in the flesh unless,

---

71. Cf. Gal 4.2.
72. Ibid.
73. Cf. Jn 1.1.
74. Heb 10.1.
75. Cf. Rv 14.6.
76. Cf. Prv 8.9.
77. Cf. Rom 2.28–29. There are some textual uncertainties in this passage.
78. Cf. Jas 2.18.

when reason persuades, he circumcise Timothy,[79] and, when it is reasonable, be shaved[80] and offer an offering and, in general, become a Jew to the Jews, that he might gain the Jews,[81] so he who is set out for the benefit of many cannot, through inward Christianity alone, improve those who are instructed in the basic principles of outward Christianity and lead them forth to better and higher things.

(43) This is why we must live as a Christian in a spiritual and in a physical manner. And wherever it is necessary to preach the literal[82] gospel declaring among the carnal[83] that we "know nothing except Jesus Christ, and him crucified,"[84] we must do this. But whenever we find those who are established in the Spirit and are bearing fruit in him[85] and desiring the heavenly wisdom, we ought to share with them the Word who was restored from being made flesh to what "he was in the beginning with God."[86]

(44) We do not think our discussion was in vain when we examined these matters about the gospel, distinguishing in concept, as it were, the gospel which is perceptible by the senses from the intelligible and spiritual gospel.

(45) And, indeed, the task before us now is to translate the gospel perceptible to the senses into the spiritual gospel. For what is the interpretation of the gospel perceptible to the senses unless it is translated into the spiritual gospel? It is little or nothing, even though the common people believe they receive the things which are revealed from the literal sense.

(46) But all kinds of difficulties stand in our way as we attempt to reach into the depths of the meaning of the gospel and examine the bare truth of the types in it.

The contents of the gospel

(47) If the good things in the proclamation of those who preach the good news are investigated, the apostles preach

---

79. Cf. Acts 16.3.
80. Cf. Acts 21.24.
81. Cf. 1 Cor 9.20.
82. Or, bodily (*sōmatikon*).
83. Cf. 1 Cor 3.1.
84. 1 Cor 2.2.
85. Cf. Col 1.10.
86. Jn 1.2.

Jesus. They are said, however, to preach him as good, and the resurrection. The resurrection is Jesus in some way, for Jesus says, "I am the resurrection."[87] Jesus, however, preaches the things stored up for the saints as good news to the poor,[88] inviting them to accept the divine promises.

(48) And the divine Scriptures bear witness both to the preaching of the gospel by the apostles and to that by our Savior. David, on the one hand, says of the apostles, and perhaps also of the evangelists, "The Lord shall give the word to them that preach good tidings with great power; the king of powers is of the beloved."[89] At the same time he also teaches that it is not the composition of a speech and the utterance of sounds and the practised beauty of speech that produce persuasion, but the provision of divine power.

(49) Wherefore Paul also says somewhere, "I will know not the speech of them that are puffed up, but the power. For the Kingdom of God is not in speech, but in power."[90] And elsewhere, "And my speech and my preaching were not in the persuasive words of wisdom, but in a demonstration of the Spirit and power."[91]

(50) Simon and Cleophas testify to this power and say, "Was not our heart burning on the road as he opened the Scripture to us?"[92] And since the quantity of power God supplies to those who speak also differs, the apostles had great power in accordance with David's statement: "The Lord shall give the word to them that preach good tidings with great power."[93]

(51) Isaias, on the other hand, declares, "How beautiful are the feet of those who announce good things!"[94] Since Isaias perceived the beautiful and opportune preaching of the apostles who follow him who said, "I am the way,"[95] he praises the "feet" which proceed over the intelligible way, which is Christ Jesus, and go in to God through the door.[96] But these, whose feet are beautiful, announce Jesus as "good things."

---

87. Jn 11.25.
88. Cf. Mt 11.5.
89. Ps 67.12 (LXX).
90. 1 Cor 4.19–20.
91. 1 Cor 2.4.
92. Lk 24.32.
93. Ps 67.12 (LXX).
94. Cf. Is 52.7. Origen quotes it, however, as it appears in Rom 10.15.
95. Jn 14.6.
96. Cf. Jn 10.9.

(52) And let no one be surprised if we have understood Jesus to be announced by the plural "good things." For when we have understood the things of which the names which the Son of God is called are predicated, we will understand how Jesus, whom these whose feet are beautiful preach, is many good things.

(53) For life is one good thing, and Jesus is life. And "the light of the world"[97] is another good thing, which is "the true light"[98] and "the light of men."[99] The Son of God is said to be all these. The truth is another good thing in concept over and above the life and the light; the way which leads to it is a fourth in addition to these. Our Savior teaches that he himself is all these when he says, "I am the way, and the truth, and the life."[100]

(54) And is it not a good thing to shed the grave and death, and to rise obtaining this from the Lord insofar as he is resurrection, since he says, "I am the resurrection"?[101] But the door too, through which one enters into the highest blessedness, is a good thing, and Christ says, "I am the door."[102]

(55) And what must we say of wisdom which "God created as the beginning of his ways for his works"?[103] Her Father rejoiced at her, rejoicing in her manifold spiritual beauty which only spiritual eyes see. Wisdom's divine heavenly beauty invites the one who contemplates it to love. For the wisdom of God which is proclaimed along with the good things mentioned previously by those whose "feet are beautiful" is a good thing.

(56) But the power of God too, which Christ is,[104] is now the eighth good thing in our list.

(57) And we must not pass over in silence the Word who is God after the Father of all things. For this too is a good thing, no less than any other. Blessed, therefore, are those who comprehend these good things and receive them from those whose feet are beautiful, and who proclaim them.

97. Jn 8.12.
98. Jn 1.9.
99. Jn 1.4.
100. Jn 14.6.
101. Jn 11.25.
102. Jn 10.9.
103. Cf. Prv 8.22.
104. Rom 1.16.

(58) But even if one who is a Corinthian, since Paul judges to know nothing with him except "Jesus Christ, and him crucified,"[105] should, when he learns this, receive him who became man because of us, he is "at the beginning" of good things when he becomes a "man of God" by the man Jesus and dies to sin by his death, for he too, "in that he died to sin, died once for all."[106]

(59) Everyone, however, who has become conformed to his resurrection receives the power to live unto God from his life since Jesus, "in that he lives, lives unto God."[107] And who will doubt that absolute righteousness is a good thing, and absolute holiness, and absolute redemption? Those who proclaim Jesus proclaim these very things too, saying that he has become righteousness for us from God, and holiness, and redemption.[108]

(60) But one who presents how Jesus is a multitude of good things can infer from these innumerable things written about him that the things which are in him in whom all the fullness of divinity "was pleased" to dwell "bodily"[109] are by no means contained in writings.

(61) And why do I say "in writings," when John says even of the whole world, "The world itself, I think, would not be able to contain the books that would be written."[110]

(62) It is the same thing, therefore, to say that the apostles preach the Savior and that they preach good things. For he is the one who received from the good Father that he be good things, in order that each one who received through Jesus the thing or things he is capable of, might engage in good things.

(63) But the apostles too, whose "feet are beautiful," and their emulators, could not have announced the good things had Jesus not previously announced good things to them, as Isaias says, "I myself who speak am here; as the springtime upon the mountains, as the feet of him who announces a message of peace, as one announcing good things, because I

---

105. 1 Cor 2.2.
107. Ibid.
109. Cf. Col 2.9; 1.19.
106. Rom 6.10.
108. Cf. 1 Cor 1.30.
110. Jn 21.25.

shall make your salvation heard, saying to Sion, Your God shall reign."[111]

(64) For what are the mountains on which the speaker acknowledges that he is present except those who are inferior to none of the highest and greatest on earth? Those who are fit ministers of the New Testament[112] must seek these out that they may keep the commandment which says, "Go up onto a high mountain, you who bring good tidings to Sion; lift up your voice with strength, you who bring good tidings to Jerusalem."[113]

(65) But do not be surprised if Jesus announces the good things which happen to be nothing other than himself to those who are about to announce the good things. For the son of God announces the good things of himself to those who are able to learn of him without the aid of others. But he who treads upon the mountains and announces the good things to them does not despise the poor in soul since he was instructed by the good Father who makes "the sun" rise "on the bad and good" and rains "on the just and unjust."[114]

(66) For he brings good news to these too, as he himself testifies when he took Isaias and read, "The Spirit of the Lord is upon me, therefore he has anointed me to bring good news to the poor; he has sent me to preach deliverance to the captives and recovery of sight to the blind." For "when he closed" the book and "gave it back to the attendant, he sat down," and when all fix their eyes on him he says, "Today this Scripture is fulfilled in your ears."[115]

(67) We ought to know that every good deed done to Jesus is also included in so great a gospel. For example, there was the woman who had performed wicked deeds and repented. She was able to anoint Jesus with a fragrant substance because of her genuine repentance of evil deeds, and she produced the scent of ointment in the whole house, perceptible to everyone there.[116]

(68) For this reason it is also written, "Wherever this gospel

111. Is 52.6–7.
113. Is 40.9.
115. Lk 4.18–21; cf. Is 61.1.
112. 2 Cor 3.6.
114. Cf. Mt 5.45.
116. Cf. Lk 7.37; Jn 12.3.

is preached among all the nations, that also which she has done shall be told for a memory of her."[117] Now it is clear that the things done to Jesus' disciples [also] happen to him. Therefore, when he points out those who have received benefits, he says to those who have done the beneficial deeds, "What you did to these, you did to me."[118] Consequently, every good deed which we perform for our neighbor is taken up into the gospel which is written in the tablets of heaven and read by all those worthy of knowledge of all things.

(69) But also, on the contrary, the sins committed against Jesus are a part of the gospel for the accusation of those who have committed them.

(70) Judas' betrayal, therefore, and the outcry of the impious people who said, "Away with such an one from the earth,"[119] and, "Crucify him, crucify him,"[120] and the mockery of those who crowned him with thorns, and the things like these have been included in the Gospels.

(71) Consequently, we should understand that everyone who betrays Jesus' disciples has been reckoned a betrayer of Jesus. Therefore, [he said] to Saul while he was still a persecutor, "Saul, Saul, why do you persecute me?" And, "I am Jesus whom you are persecuting."[121]

(72) But who are those who have the thorns with which they crown Jesus to dishonor him? Those who have received the Word of God and "yield no fruit," because they are choked "by the cares and riches and pleasures of life."[122]

(73) For this reason we must beware lest perhaps we too, as though crowning Jesus with our own thorns, be recorded to be like these and be read about by those who learn the Jesus who is in and with all spiritual or holy persons. They learn how he is anointed with ointment, entertained, and glorified, or, on the contrary, how he is dishonored, mocked, and beaten.

(74) We have made these comments out of necessity, then,

---

117. Mt 26.13.
118. Mt 25.40.
119. Acts 22.22.
120. Lk 23.21.
121. Acts 9.4–5.
122. Lk 8.14.

Angels, the Old Testament and the gospel

(75) But if there are among men those who are honored with the ministry of evangelists, and Jesus himself preaches the good news and preaches the gospel to the poor, there was no need that the "angels" who had been made "spirits" by God and who were "flames of fire," "ministers" of the Father of all things, should themselves be deprived of being evangelists too.[124]

(76) It was for this reason also that an angel stood by the shepherds and, when he had made glory shine around them, said, "Fear not, for behold I bring you good tidings of great joy, which shall be to all people, for today a Savior is born to you in the city of David, who is Christ the Lord."[125] And when people do not yet understand the mystery of the gospel, their superiors, being a heavenly army of God, praise God and say, "Glory to God in the highest and on earth peace, good will among men."[126]

(77) After the angels said these things, they withdrew from the shepherds into heaven and left us to consider how the "joy" announced to us through the birth of Christ Jesus is "glory to God in the highest," since those who were humbled to the dust return "to" their "rest"[127] and are about to glorify God "in the highest" through Christ.

(78) But the angels marvel too at the peace Jesus shall bring to earth, the battlefield to which "Lucifer, who rises early," fell "from heaven,"[128] and where he is crushed by Jesus.

(79) In addition to what has been said, we must know this too about the gospel. First of all, it is the gospel of Christ Jesus, the head of the whole body of the saved, as Mark says:

---

123. Dn 12.2.
124. Heb 1.7; Ps 103.4. I have followed Brooke's punctuation. Preuschen has a question mark, followed by Blanc.
125. Lk 2.9–11.
126. Lk 2.14.
127. Cf. Ps 114.6–7; 43.25.
128. Is 14.12.

"The beginning of the gospel of Christ Jesus."[129] But further, it is also the gospel of the apostles, on account of which Paul says, "According to my gospel."[130]

(80) But the beginning of the gospel (for its greatness consists of a beginning, a sequence, a middle, and end) is either all the Old Testament, John being its type, or, because of the connection of the New with the Old, the final events of the Old Testament which were presented through John.

(81) For the same Mark says, "The beginning of the gospel of Jesus Christ. As it is written in Isaias the prophet, Behold I send my angel before your face, who shall prepare your way. A voice of one crying in the desert, Prepare the way of the Lord, make his paths straight."[131]

(82) This passage causes me to wonder how the heterodox attribute the two testaments to two gods, when they are refuted no less even by this word. For how could John, the man of the demiurge, and ignorant of the new deity, as they suppose, be the beginning of the gospel, as they themselves think, when he belongs to a different God?

(83) The angels, however, are not merely entrusted with one brief service pertaining to the gospel, nor merely with visiting the shepherds. At the end of time an angel flying in mid-air with the gospel will proclaim good news to every nation, since the good Father has not completely forsaken those who have fallen away from him.

(84) Wherefore, John, the son of Zebedee, says in the Apocalypse, "And I saw an angel flying in the midst of heaven having the eternal gospel to preach to those who sit upon the earth, and to every nation, and tribe, and tongue, and people, saying with a loud voice, 'Fear God and give him glory because the hour of his judgment has come; and adore him who made heaven, and earth, and the sea, and the fountains of waters.'"[132]

(85) Since, then, according to one interpretation, we presented all the Old Testament, which is indicated by John's

---

129. Mk 1.1.
131. Mk 1.1–3.
130. Rom 2.16.
132. Rv 14.6–7.

name, to be "the beginning of the gospel," we shall juxtapose from Acts what is said of the royal Ethiopian eunuch and Philip, so that this interpretation will not be without a witness. For "Philip," Scripture says, "preached the Lord Jesus to him, beginning from the Scripture of Isaias which reads, 'He was led as a sheep to the slaughter; and like a lamb without voice before his shearer.' "[133] Now how does he preach Jesus, beginning from the prophet, unless Isaias was some part of the beginning of the gospel?

(86) But at the same time this can also be shown from our remarks in the beginning about all divine Scripture being capable of being gospel. For indeed if the one who preaches "preaches good things," and all those before Christ's bodily sojourn preach Christ as being "the good things" as we demonstrated, the words of all of these are in some way part of the gospel.

(87) Since whatever is called gospel is spoken in the whole world, we understand that it is proclaimed in the whole world, not only in the surrounding earth, but also in the whole system of heaven and earth, or of the heavens and earth.

Conclusion

(88) And why must we prolong further our discourse on what the gospel is? The remarks we have made are quite sufficient. On the basis of these words, which are not inappropriate, it is possible to gather comparable things from the Scriptures and see what the glory of the good things in Jesus Christ is from the gospel. The gospel is served by men and angels and, I think, also by principalities and powers and thrones and dominions "and every name that is named, not only in this world, but also in that which is to come,"[134] since indeed it is also served by Christ himself. Here, perhaps, we shall stop the preliminaries to our reading together the things which have been written.

(89) Let us now ask God to work with us through Christ in the Holy Spirit to explain the mystical meaning stored up like a treasure in the words.

133. Acts 8.35.32 (Is 53.7).   134. Eph 1.21.

In the beginning was the Word.

Sense of the term "beginning"

(90) It is not only the Greeks who say that the designation "beginning" means many things. For, indeed, if anyone should observe this title, collecting its occurrences from every source, and should wish, by careful examination, to understand its application in each passage of the Scriptures, he will discover many meanings of the expression even in the word of God.

(91) One meaning involves change, and this belongs, as it were, to a way and length which is revealed by the Scripture: "The beginning of a good way is to do justice."[135] For since a "good way" is very great, we must understand that the practical, which is presented by the phrase "to do justice," relates to the initial matters, and the contemplative to those that follow. I think its stopping point and goal is in the so-called restoration because no one is left as an enemy then, if indeed the statement is true, "For he must reign until he has put all his enemies under his feet. And the last enemy to be destroyed is death."[136]

(92) For at that time those who have come to God because of the Word which is with him[137] will have the contemplation of God as their only activity, that, having been accurately formed[138] in the knowledge of the Father, they may all thus become a son, since now the Son alone has known the Father.

(93) For if someone should carefully examine when it is that those shall know the Father to whom the Son who has known the Father reveals him,[139] and should see that the one who sees now sees "through a mirror and indistinctly"[140] not yet having known "as he ought to know,"[141] he would be correct to say that no one has known the Father even if he be an apostle or prophet,[142] but that it will occur whenever they become one as [the] Son and the Father are one.[143]

---

135. Prv 16.7 (LXX).
136. 1 Cor 15.25–26. On *apokatastasis* see *PGL*, s.v. 195.
137. Cf. Jn 1.1.
138. Cf. Gal 4.19.
139. Cf. Mt 11.27; Lk 10.22.
140. 1 Cor 13.12.
141. 1 Cor 8.2.
142. Cf. Eph 3.5.
143. Jn 10.30.

(94) But if anyone should think that we have digressed by explaining one meaning of "beginning" and making these remarks, we must show that the digression was necessary and useful for that which lies ahead. For if "beginning" has to do with change and a way and length, "and the beginning of a good way is to do justice,"[144] it is possible to know that every good way has "doing justice" as a "beginning" in some manner, and after the beginning, contemplation, and in what manner it has contemplation.

(95) There is also a "beginning" of creation, however, which would seem to be its use in the statement, "In the beginning God made heaven and earth."[145] But I think what is meant is stated more clearly in Job in the statement, "This is the beginning of the Lord's creation,[146] made to be mocked by his angels."[147]

(96) For someone might suppose that "heaven and earth" were made "in the beginning" of those things which happened to exist in the genesis of the world. But it is better to say, as with the second quotation, that of those many beings which have come into existence with bodies, the first of those with bodies was that called a dragon, and named also perhaps "the great sea-monster"[148] which the Lord subdued.

(97) And we must raise the question if, while the saints continued to live a completely immaterial and bodiless life in blessedness, he who is called a dragon deserved to be bound to matter and a body before all others because he fell from the pure life, so that this is why the Lord should say through storm and clouds as a warning, "This is the beginning of the work of the Lord, made to be mocked by his angels."[149]

(98) Nevertheless, it is possible that the dragon is not the beginning of the work of the Lord in general, but is the be-

---

144. Prv 16.7 (LXX; 16.5 Douay-Rheims).
145. Gn 1.1.
146. *Plasma*, something molded or formed, as by a potter.
147. Jb 40.14 (19). 148. Jb 3.8.
149. Jb 40.14 (19). In *Princ.* 1.5.5 Origen quotes Jb 40.20 and identifies the dragon with the devil in a discussion of the fall of Satan from heaven. He makes the same identification in *Princ.* 2.8.3. Origen is thinking here of the original fall of souls from God, in which the devil fell furthest.

ginning of the many made with a body "to be mocked by his angels," since some can exist with a body in another manner. For the soul of the sun is in a body too, as is true also of all creation, of which the apostle says, "All creation groans and travails until now."[150]

(99) Perhaps the following statement is also about that: "Creation was subjected to vanity, not willingly, but because of him who subjected it in hope,"[151] that bodies and doing bodily things, which is ... necessary ... for one in a body, might be vanity.[152] He who is in a body does bodily things unwillingly. For this reason creation was subjected to vanity unwillingly.

(100) And he who does bodily things unwillingly does what he does because of hope. It is as if we should say that Paul wishes "to remain in the flesh,"[153] not willingly, but because of hope. For though he preferred "to depart and be with Christ,"[154] considered by itself, it was not irrational for him to wish "to remain in the flesh" because of the benefit to others and progress in the things hoped for, not only his own progress, but also that of those benefited by him.

(101) And in relation to this, we will be able to understand what is meant by the beginning of creation, and what Wisdom says in Proverbs: "For God," she says, "created me the beginning of his ways for his works."[155] It is possible, of course, for this also to be referred to our first meaning, i.e. that pertaining to a way,[156] because it is said, "God created me the beginning of his ways."

(102) But someone will say with good reason that the God of all things is clearly a beginning too, proposing[157] that the Father is the beginning of the son, and the creator[158] is the beginning of the things created and, in general, God is the beginning of the things which exist. And by understanding

---

150. Rom 8.22.   151. Rom 8.20.
152. There are two lacunae in the text.
153. Cf. Phil 1.24.   154. Cf. Phil 1.23.
155. Prv 8.22.
156. See above, paragraphs 91ff.
157. Accepting Preuschen's suggested emendation of *proballōn* for *propiptōn*.
158. *Dēmiourgos*.

the Son to be the Word, he will justify his view by the statement, "In the beginning was the Word,"¹⁵⁹ because what is said to be in the Father is in the beginning.

(103) And third, that from which something comes, as the underlying matter, is thought to be a beginning by those who understand matter to be uncreated, but not by us who believe that God made the things which are from that which does not exist, as the mother of the seven martyrs in Machabees taught, and the angel of repentance in the *Shepherd of Hermas*.¹⁶⁰

(104) In addition to these definitions, that "according to which" something is made, as according to its form, is also a beginning in the following manner. Since the firstborn of all creation is the image of the invisible God,¹⁶¹ the Father is his beginning. And likewise also Christ is the beginning of those made according to the image of God.¹⁶²

(105) For if men are "according to the image," and the image according to the Father, the "according to which" of Christ, on the one hand, is the Father, his beginning but, on the other hand, Christ is the "according to which" of men, who are made, not according to that of which Christ is the image, but according to the image.¹⁶³ The statement, "In the beginning was the Word," will fit the same paradigm.

(106) There is also a beginning that pertains to learning, according to which we say that the letters of the alphabet are the beginning of writing.¹⁶⁴ In accordance with this the apostle says, "Although, because of the time, you should be teachers, you have need that someone teach you again the rudiments of the beginning of the oracles of God."¹⁶⁵

(107) Now the beginning pertaining to learning is twofold. One involves its nature and the other its relation to us. It is as if we should say in the case of Christ that, on the one hand,

---

159. Jn 1.1.
160. Cf. 2 Mc 7.28; Hermas *Mand.* 1.1; *Vis.* 1.1.6.
161. Col 1.15.   162. Cf. Gn 1.27.
163. See Blanc, *Origène* (SC 120.115), n. 4.
164. Grammar was the beginning level of the ancient Greek and Roman school curriculum; cf. Plato, *Sophist* 253.
165. Heb 5.12.

in his nature, divinity is the beginning. But, on the other hand, in his relation to us who are not able to begin from the greatness of the truth about him, it is his humanity, according to which Jesus Christ, and he crucified, is proclaimed to infants.[166] So in accordance with this we say that in nature Christ is the beginning of learning insofar as he is "the wisdom" and "power of God."[167] But in his relation to us the beginning of learning is "the Word became flesh,"[168] that he might dwell among us who are able to receive him only in this manner at first.

(108) And perhaps, for this reason, he is not only the firstborn of all creation, but also Adam, [which] means "man." And because he is Adam, Paul says, "The last Adam has become a life-giving spirit."[169] There is also a beginning which pertains to action, in which action there is some goal after the beginning. And consider if wisdom, since it is the beginning of God's actions,[170] can thus be understood as a beginning.

Application to the Son of God

(109) Although so many meanings of "beginning" have occurred to us at the present time, we are investigating how we ought to take the statement, "In the beginning was the Word."[171] It is clear that we are not to understand it in its meaning related to change, or a way and length. And we should certainly not take it in its meaning related to creation.

(110) But it is possible that he is the "by which," which is effective, since "God commanded and they were created."[172] For Christ is perhaps the creator to whom the Father says, "Let there be light," and "Let there be a firmament."[173]

(111) But it is as the beginning that Christ is creator, according to which he is wisdom. Therefore as wisdom he is called the beginning. For wisdom says in Solomon, "God

---

166. 1 Cor 2.2; 1.24. 167. Cf. 1 Cor 1.24.
168. Jn 1.14. 169. 1 Cor 15.45.
170. Cf. Prv 8.22. 171. Jn 1.1.
172. Ps 148.5. Blanc (SC 120.118–19), notes that Origen alludes to the four causes of Aristotle in the following sections: Material cause (103), formal cause (104–5), final cause (108), and efficient cause (110–111).
173. Gn 1.3.6.

created me the beginning of his ways for his works,"[174] that "the Word might be in the beginning,"[175] in wisdom. It is wisdom which is understood, on the one hand, taken in relation to the structure of the contemplation and thoughts of all things, but it is the Word which is received, taken in relation to the communication of the things which have been contemplated to spiritual beings.

(112) And it is not extraordinary if, as we have said before, the Savior being many good things has conceived in himself things which are first and second and third. John, therefore, added, declaring of the Word, "What came to be in him was life."[176] Life, therefore, came to be in the Word. And neither is the Word other than the Christ, God the Word, the one with the Father, through whom all things came to be, nor is the life other than the Son of God who says, "I am the way and the truth and the life."[177] Just as life, then, came to be in the Word, so the Word was in the beginning.

(113) But consider if it is possible also for us to take the statement, "In the beginning was the Word,"[178] in accordance with this meaning, so that all things came to be in accordance with the wisdom and plans of the system of thoughts in the Word.

(114) For I think that just as a house and a ship are built or devised according to the plans of the architect, the house and the ship having as their beginning the plans and thoughts in the craftsman, so all things have come to be according to the thoughts of what will be, which were prefigured by God in wisdom, "For he made all things in wisdom."[179]

(115) And we must say that after God had created living wisdom, if I may put it this way, from the models in her he entrusted to her [to present] to the things which exist and to matter [both] their conformation and forms, but I stop short of saying their essences.

174. Prv 8.22.
175. Jn 1.1.
176. Jn 1.3–4.
177. Jn 14.6.
178. Jn 1.1.
179. Ps 103.24. On *protranoomai* (not in LSJ) "prefigure," see *PGL*, s.v., 1190.

(116) On the one hand, it is not difficult to say, roughly speaking, that the son of God is the beginning of the things which exist, since he says, "I am the beginning and the end, the alpha and the omega, the first and the last."[180] But, on the other hand, we must know that he himself is not the beginning according to everything which he is named.

(117) For insofar as he is life, how can he be the beginning? This life came to be in the Word, which clearly is its beginning. And it is even clearer that he cannot be the beginning insofar as he is the "firstborn of the dead."[181]

(118) And if we should carefully consider all the concepts applied to him, he is the beginning only insofar as he is wisdom. He is not even the beginning insofar as he is the Word, since "the Word" was "in the beginning,"[182] so that someone might say boldly that wisdom is older than all the concepts in the names of the firstborn of all creation.

(119) God, therefore, is altogether one and simple. Our Savior, however, because of the many things, since God "set" him "forth as a propitiation"[183] and firstfruits of all creation,[184] becomes many things, or perhaps even all these things, as the whole creation which can be made free needs him.[185]

(120) And for this reason he becomes the light of men when men, darkened by evil, need the light which shines in the darkness and is not grasped by darkness.[186] He would not have become the light of men if men had not been in darkness.

(121) And it is possible to perceive a similar thing also in the case of him being the firstborn [from] the dead.[187] For if, by way of supposition, the woman had not been deceived and Adam had not fallen into sin,[188] but the man created for incorruption had grasped incorruption, he would have neither descended "into the dust of death"[189] nor died since there

---

180. Rv 22.13.
181. Col 1.18.
182. Jn 1.1.
183. Cf. Rom 3.25.
184. Cf. Jas 1.18.
185. Cf. Rom 8.21.
186. Cf. Jn 1.5.
187. Cf. Col 1.18.
188. Cf. Gn 3.
189. Cf. Ps 21.16.

would have been no sin for which he had to die because of his love for men. And if he had not done these things, he would not have become the "firstborn from the dead."[190]

(122) We must also consider whether he would not have become a shepherd if man had not been compared "to senseless beasts nor become like them." For if "God saves men and beasts,"[191] he saves what beasts he saves by granting a shepherd to those who lack the capacity for a king.

(123) Once we have collected the titles of the Son, therefore, we must test which of them came into existence later, and whether they would have become so numerous if the saints had begun and continued in blessedness. For perhaps wisdom alone would remain, or word, or life, and by all means truth, but surely not also the other titles which he took in addition because of us.

(124) And blessed indeed are all who, although they need the son of God, have become such that they no longer need him as physician who heals the sick,[192] or as shepherd,[193] or redemption,[194] but as wisdom, and word, and righteousness,[195] or if there is any other title for those who, because of their perfection, can receive his noblest titles. Enough said on the phrase, "In the beginning."

Explication of "the Word," the title of the Son of God

(125) But let us consider more carefully what the Word is which is in the beginning. I frequently marvel when I consider the things said about the Christ by some who wish to believe in him. Why in the world, when countless names are applied to our Savior, do they pass by most of them in silence? Even if they should perhaps remember them, they do not interpret them in their proper sense, but say that these name him figuratively. On the other hand, they stop in the case of the title "Word" alone, as if they say that the Christ of God is "Word" alone; and they do not investigate, consistent with the

---

190. Cf. Col 1.18.
192. Cf. Mt 9.12.
194. Cf. Rom 3.24.
191. Ps 48.13, Ps 35.7.
193. Cf. Jn 10.2.
195. Cf. 1 Cor 1.30.

rest of the names, the meaning of what is indicated by the term "Word."

(126) Now what I mean when I say I marvel at many people—for I shall speak more clearly—is this. The son of God says somewhere, "I am the light of the world."[196] In other places he says, "I am the resurrection,"[197] and again, "I am the way, and the truth, and the life."[198] It is also written, "I am the door."[199] And it is said, "I am the good shepherd."[200] And to the Samaritan woman who says, "We know that the Messias is coming who is called Christ; whenever he comes, he will tell us all things," he answers, "I who speak to you am he."[201]

(127) In addition to these, when he washed the disciples' feet, he confessed that he was their Lord and teacher by these words: "You call me Teacher and Lord, and you speak correctly, for I am."[202]

(128) But he also announces clearly that he is the Son of God when he says, "Do you say of him whom the Father sanctified and sent into the world, you blaspheme, because I said, I am the Son of God?"[203] And, "Father, the hour has come; glorify your Son, that the son may glorify you."[204]

(129) We find him announcing also that he is king, as when in response to Pilate's question, "Are you the king of the Jews?"[205] he says, "My kingdom is not of this world; if my kingdom were of this world, my servants would strive that I should not be delivered to the Jews, but now my kingdom is not thence."[206]

(130) And we have read, "I am the true vine and my Father is the husbandman."[207] And again, "I am the vine, you are the branches."[208]

(131) Let the saying also be taken into account with these:

196. Jn 8.12.
197. Jn 11.25.
198. Jn 14.6.
199. Jn 10.9.
200. Jn 10.11.
201. Jn 4.25–26.
202. Jn 13.13.
203. Jn 10.36.
204. Jn 17.1.
205. Jn 18.33.
206. Jn 18.36.
207. Jn 15.1.
208. Cf. Jn 15.5.

"I am the bread of life,"[209] and again, "I am the living bread which came down out of heaven" and "gave life to the world."[210] We have presented these titles which suggested themselves at present from those which occur in the Gospels. The Son of God says that he is all these things.

(132) But he also says in the Apocalypse of John, "I am the first and the last and the living one, and I was dead, and behold I am living forever and ever."[211] And again, "I am the alpha and the omega, and the first and the last, the beginning and the end."[212]

(133) The discerning reader of the Holy Books can take several similar things also from the prophets. For example, he calls himself a "chosen arrow" and a "servant of God" and a "light of the gentiles."[213]

(134) Isaias speaks as follows to be sure: "From my mother's womb he called me by my name and he made my mouth like a sharp sword and he hid me under the shadow of his hand. He made me as a chosen arrow and hid me in his quiver. And he said to me, You are my servant Israel, and in you I will be glorified."[214]

(135) And a little further he said: "And my God shall be my strength. And he said to me, This is a great thing for you to be called my servant, to establish the tribes of Jacob and to turn back the diaspora of Israel. Behold I have set you for a light of the gentiles that you might be for salvation to the end of the earth."[215] But also in Jeremias he likens himself to a lamb as follows, "I was as an innocent lamb led to be slaughtered."[216]

(136) Therefore, he applies these and similar titles to himself. But it is possible to collect 10,000 times as many titles which are applied to the Son of God in the Gospels by the apostles and the prophets. These represent either those who wrote the Gospels setting out their own idea of what he is, or the apostles praising him on the basis of what they have

209. Jn 6.35.
210. Jn 6.51.33.
211. Rv 1.17–18.
212. Rv 22.13; 21.6.
213. Is 49.2.3.6.
214. Is 49.1–3.
215. Is 49.5–6.
216. Jer 11.19.

learned, or the prophets proclaiming in advance his coming sojourn and declaring the things about him with different names.

(137) John the Baptist, for example, calls him "Lamb of God," when he says, "Behold the Lamb of God who takes away the sin of the world."[217] And he calls him "man" in these words: "This is he of whom I said, After me comes a man who ranks before me because he was before me, and I did not know him."[218]

(138) In the catholic epistle John declares that he is an "advocate" with the Father concerning our souls when he says, "And if anyone sin, we have an advocate with the Father, Jesus Christ the just."[219]

(139) And he adds, "And he is the propitiatory for our sins."[220] In a similar manner Paul says that he is a "propitiation," when he declares, "Whom God proposed to be a propitiation through faith in his blood, for the remission of former sins, in the forbearance of God."[221]

(140) And he has been proclaimed according to Paul to be the wisdom and power of God, as he says in the Epistle to the Corinthians that Christ is the power and wisdom of God.[222] In addition to these titles, he states that he is both "sanctification" and "redemption," for he says, "God made him our wisdom, and justice, and sanctification, and redemption."[223]

(141) But he also teaches us that he is a great high priest, when he writes to the Hebrews, "Having, therefore, a great high priest who has passed into the heavens, Jesus the son of God, let us hold fast our confession."[224]

(142) But in addition to these, the prophets also apply other names to him. Jacob calls him Juda in the blessing to his sons: "Juda, may your brothers praise you; may your hands be on the back of your enemies; [the sons of your father shall bow down to you];[225] Juda is a lion's whelp; you

---

217. Jn 1.29.
218. Jn 1.30–31.
219. 1 Jn 2.1.
220. 1 Jn 2.2.
221. Cf. Rom 3.25–26.
222. Cf. 1 Cor 1.24.
223. 1 Cor 1.30.
224. Heb 4.14.
225. Preuschen thinks this clause was omitted in the MSS. by homoiote-

COMMENTARY ON JOHN, BOOK 1   63

sprung up, my son, from a shoot; you lay down and slept as a lion and as a whelp; who shall awaken him?"[226] ... But this is not the time to present in plain language how the things said to Juda pertain to Christ.

(143) But even the objection which can reasonably be adduced, "A ruler shall not fail from Juda, and a leader from his thighs,"[227] will be solved more appropriately in other places.

(144) And Isaias knows that the Christ is named Jacob and Israel, when he says, "Jacob is my servant, I will help him; Israel is my elect, my soul has accepted him. He shall proclaim judgment to the gentiles. He shall not contend or cry out, nor shall anyone hear his voice in the streets. A bruised reed he shall not break, and smoking flax he shall not quench until he send forth judgment to victory,[228] and the gentiles shall hope in his name."[229]

(145) For Matthew shows clearly in his gospel that it is the Christ concerning whom these things have been prophesied when he recalls a portion of the passage and says, "That that which was said might be fulfilled, he shall not contend or cry out," and the rest.[230]

(146) But David also is called the Christ, as when Ezechiel prophesied to the shepherds and added, in the person of God, "I will raise up David my servant, who will shepherd them."[231] For the patriarch David will not be raised up to shepherd the saints, but Christ.

(147) And in addition, Isaias calls the Christ "rod" and "flower," in the statement: "And a rod shall come forth out of the root of Jesse, and a flower shall rise up out of his root. And the spirit of God shall rest upon him, a spirit of wisdom and understanding, a spirit of counsel and strength, a spirit

---

leuton and that its inclusion is necessary to bring out the Messianic significance of the citation. Blanc omits it.

226. Gn 49.8–9.   227. Gn 49.10.

228. Accepting Preuschen's suggestion to read *eis nikos* with the text of Mt 12.20. He prints *ek nikous* and marks it as a textual corruption.

229. Is 42.1–4. After the first sentence, Origen follows the text as it appears in Mt 12.18–21.

230. Mt 12.17.19.   231. Cf. Ez 34.23.

of knowledge and godliness, and a spirit of the fear of God shall fill him."[232]

(148) And also in the Psalms our Lord is said to be a "stone" as follows: "The stone which the builders rejected, the same became the head of the corner. This was done by the Lord, and it is wonderful in our eyes."[233]

(149) Now the gospel, and Luke in Acts, reveal that the stone is no other than the Christ. The gospel has it this way: "Have you never read: the stone which the builders rejected, the same has become the head of the corner? Everyone who has fallen on this stone shall be broken; and it shall crush him on whom it falls."[234]

(150) And Luke writes in Acts: "This is the stone which was rejected by you the builders, which has become the head of the corner."[235] One of the names, of course, attributed to the Savior, but not used by him, and which has been recorded by John is also, "The Word in the beginning with God, God the Word."[236]

Sense of these titles

(151) It is worthwhile to consider those who disregard so many names and treat this one as special. And again, they look for an explanation in the case of the other names, if someone brings them to their attention, but in the case of this one they believe they have a clear answer to what the Son of God is, when he is named Word. This is especially obvious since they continually use the verse, "My heart uttered a good word,"[237] as though they think the Son of God is an expression of the Father occurring in syllables. And in accordance with this view, if we inquire of them carefully, they do not give him substance nor do they elucidate his essence. I do not yet mean that it is this or that, but in what manner he has essence.

(152) For it is impossible for anyone to understand a proclaimed word to be a son. Let them declare to us that God the Word is such a word, having life in himself, and either is

---

232. Is 11.1–3.
234. Mt 21.42.44; Lk 20.18.
236. Cf. Jn 1.1.
233. Ps 117.22–23.
235. Cf. Acts 4.11.
237. Ps 44.2.

not separated from the Father and, in accordance with this position, does not subsist nor is he a son, or is both separated and invested with substance.

(153) We must say, therefore, that just as in the case of each of the previously mentioned names we must disclose the meaning of what is named from the title, and produce appropriate proof to show how the Son of God is said to be this name, so must we also do in the case of him being named "Word."

(154) For what absurdity not to hold to the letter in the case of each title, but to investigate, for example, how we must understand him to be a "door," and in what manner he is a "vine," and for what reason he is a "way,"[238] but not to do this only when it is recorded that he is the "Word"!

(155) That we may, therefore, with more conviction recognize what will be said on the questions concerning how the Son of God is Word as correct, we must begin from those names of him previously set forth.

(156) We know that such a procedure will seem excessively digressive to some. But the attentive person will find it useful for what is proposed to test the concepts in relation to which the titles are used, and an understanding of the concrete realities will serve as preparation for what is to come.

(157) And once we have taken up the theology of the Savior, and discover the things about him which can be learned by inquiry, we shall of necessity understand him more fully not only insofar as he is the Word, but also insofar as he is the other things as well.

(158) He said, therefore, that he was the "light of the world."[239] We must also examine the expressions that are closely related to this, since some think they are not only closely related, but the same.

(159) Now these titles are, "the light of men,"[240] "the true light,"[241] and the "light of the gentiles."[242] The title, "the light of men," occurs in the beginning of the gospel lying before

---

238. Cf. Jn 15.1.5; 14.6.
240. Jn 1.4.
242. Is 49.6.
239. Jn 8.12.
241. Jn 1.9.

us, for John says, "What was made in him was life, and the life was the light of men; and the light shines in the darkness, and the darkness did not grasp it."[243] He is called the true light in the words which follow the same Scripture: "The true light which enlightens every man was coming into the world."[244] But it is in Isaias that he is called the "light of the gentiles," as we said before when we quoted the statement, "Behold I have given you for a light of the gentiles that you might be for salvation to the ends of the earth."[245]

(160) The sun is the light of the world perceived by the senses, and after it the moon and stars will appropriately be given the same title.

(161) But since these are light perceived by the senses, which are said in Moses to have come into existence on the fourth day, they are not the true light because they enlighten the things on the earth. The Savior, on the other hand, is the light of the spiritual world because he shines on those who are rational and intellectual, that their mind may see its proper visions. Now I mean he is the light of those rational souls which are in the sensible world, of which the Savior teaches us that he is the maker, being, perhaps, its directing and principal part, and, so to speak, the sun of the great day of the Lord.[246]

(162) Because of this day he says to those who partake of his light, "Work while it is day; the night is coming when one can no longer work. As long as I am in the world, I am the light of the world."[247] But in addition he says also to his disciples, "You are the light of the world," and, "Let your light shine before men."[248]

(163) Now we understand the moon and stars to be analogous to the bride, the Church, and the disciples, who have their own light or a light acquired from the true sun to illuminate those who have not been able to provide a source of light in themselves. For example, we will say that Paul and

---

243. Jn 1.3–5.
244. Jn 1.9.
245. Is 49.6. See above, section 135.
246. Cf. Rv 16.14; 6.17; Jl 2.11; Zep 1.14.
247. Cf. Jn 9.4–5.
248. Mt 5.14.16.

Peter were a "light of the world," but the world of which the apostles were a light was the general run of those instructed by them, who, while they were illuminated, on the one hand, could certainly not illuminate others.[249]

(164) The Savior, however, being the "light of the world," does not illuminate corporeal natures. He illuminates the incorporeal spirit with an incorporeal power in order that each of us, being illuminated as though by the sun, may also be able to see the other spiritual beings.

(165) And just as the ability of the moon and stars to give light becomes faint when the sun is shining, so those who are illuminated by Christ and have received his rays have no need of any ministering apostles and prophets—for we must dare to speak the truth—or angels. And I will add that they do not need the more excellent powers either, since they are instructed by the firstborn light himself.

(166) The ministering saints, however, provide a light which is much weaker than the previously mentioned one, for those who do not receive the rays of the sun which come from Christ. These people are scarcely able to receive even this light, and are filled by it.

(167) But Christ, who is the light of the world, is the true light in contradistinction to that which is perceptible by the senses, since nothing perceptible by the senses is true. It does not follow, however, that because that which is perceptible by the senses is not true, it is false. For what is perceptible by the senses can have a resemblance to that which is apprehended by the intellect. Everything which is not true certainly cannot correctly be designated false.

(168) But I am investigating whether the title "light of the world" is identical with "light of men." I think that a greater power of light is expressed when Christ is designated "light of the world" than when he is designated "light of men," for, according to one interpretation, "the world" is not only "men."

(169) Paul, in the first letter to the Corinthians, will demonstrate that the world is more, or other than, men when he

---

249. Cf. Origen, *Gn. Hom.* 1.5–7.

says, "We were made a spectacle to the world, both to angels and to men."[250]

(170) But consider if, according to another interpretation, the "world" is the creation which is freed "from the slavery of corruption into the freedom of the glory of the children of God," "the expectation" of which "awaits the revelation of the sons of God."[251]

(171) Now we added "consider," because the corresponding statement made by Jesus to the disciples, "You are the light of the world,"[252] can be compared to the statement, "I am the light of the world."[253]

(172) For there are those who understand those men who have been truly instructed by Jesus to be greater than the other creatures, some being such, some think, by nature, others, according to others, also by the principle[254] related to the more difficult struggle.

(173) For those who are in flesh and blood have more troubles and a more precarious life than those in an ethereal body. Should the lights in heaven assume earthly bodies, they would not pass through life here free from danger and without any sin at all. And the defenders of this position will use the texts of the Scriptures which set forth the greatest things about men, which declare the incomparability of the promise that extends to men, texts which do not at all relate this same thing also concerning the creation, or the world, as we understood it.[255]

(174) For the statements, "As you and I are one, that they too may be one in us,"[256] and, "Where I am, there also shall my servant be,"[257] have clearly been written of men, but of the creation it is said that it is freed "from the slavery of corruption into the freedom of the glory of the children of God."[258] And they will add that if it is freed it does not already also share in "the glory of the children of God."

---

250. 1 Cor 4.9.
251. Rom 8.21.19.
252. Mt 5.14.
253. Jn 8.12.
254. *Logos*.
255. See above, sections 168–9.
256. Cf. Jn 17.21.
257. Jn 12.26.
258. Cf. Rom 8.21.

(175) These people will also voice the fact that the firstborn of all creation became man because man is more honored than all creatures; he did not, indeed, become some being in heaven. In addition, the star which appeared in the East was created second, as both a minister and servant of the knowledge of Jesus, being either like the other stars, or perhaps even greater, since it was a sign of him who surpasses all.

(176) And if the boasts of the saints are in their tribulation, since they know "that tribulation produces patience, and patience trial, and trial hope, and hope is not disappointed,"[259] the creation which has not been afflicted will have neither the same patience, nor trial, nor hope, but a different one, since "the creation was subjected to vanity, not willingly, but because of him who subjected it, in hope."[260]

(177) But he who does not dare attribute such great things to man, at the same time when he has confronted this problem will say that the creation, which is subjected to vanity, is afflicted, groaning more than those who are in the temporary habitation,[261] since creation, too, is enslaved to vanity for a very long time, much longer than the trial that humans experience.

(178) For why does it do this "not willingly"? Doubtless because it has been subjected to vanity contrary to its nature and lacks its previous condition of life which it will take up again when it is set free and released from the vanity of bodies in the destruction of the world.

(179) But since we seem to have spoken about a larger problem and one not related to that set before us, we shall return to our starting point, suggesting why the Savior is said to be "light of the world," "true light," and "light of men." For, on the one hand, we have explained that he is said to be "true light" because of the light of the world which is perceptible to the senses, and that the expression "light of the world" is either equivalent to "the light of men" or is capable on examination of not being equivalent.

259. Rom 5.3–5.
260. Rom 8.20.
261. Cf. 2 Cor 5.4.

(180) Now we have had to investigate these matters because of those who have no understanding of the fact that the Savior is the Word, on the one hand, that we might be persuaded not to stop absurdly with the concept and title[262] "Word" without interpreting the change of meaning and, on the other hand, that we might interpret anagogically and allegorically the expression "light of the world" and the many others which we have cited.

(181) Now just as he is "light of men" and "true light" and "light of the world"[263] because he enlightens and illuminates the intellects of men or, in general, of spiritual beings, so he is called "the resurrection"[264] from the fact that[265] he effects the putting away of all that is dead and implants the life which is properly called life, since those who have genuinely received him are risen from the dead.

(182) Now he effects this not only for those who can say at the present, "We have been buried together with Christ by baptism"[266] and we have risen with him, but much more when someone has completely put away all that is dead, even that related to the Son himself, and walks in newness of life; that is, when we have been aided in so remarkable a manner, "we always carry about here the dying of Jesus in our body that the life of Jesus may be made manifest in our bodies."[267]

(183) But also the journey in wisdom, that is the active journey of the saved which takes place in him by means of discussions concerning truth in the divine Word and activities in conformity with the true righteousness, enables us to perceive how he is the way[268] on which one needs to take nothing, neither travelling bag nor garment. The traveller does not even have to have a rod or put sandals on his feet.[269]

(184) For the way itself is sufficient in place of any provisions; no traveller on this way has any need, since he has been

---

262. Accepting Lommatzsch's emendation: *prosēgonas*.
263. Jn 1.9; 8.12; 9.5.   264. Jn 11.25.
265. Omitting *dia tou* with Brooke and Blanc. Preuschen brackets the words.
266. Cf. Rom 6.4.   267. 2 Cor 4.10.
268. Jn 14.6.
269. Cf. Lk 9.3; Mk 6.8; Mt 10.10.

adorned with a garment befitting one invited to a wedding,[270] and no difficulty can encounter him on this road. For, according to Solomon, it is impossible to discover the paths of a serpent on a rock,[271] and I say that the same is also impossible of any beast at all.

(185) Therefore, there is no need for a rod on a way which lacks the tracks of adversaries and, because of its firmness, for which it is called a rock, does not admit wicked men.

(186) And the only begotten is truth since, according to the will of the Father, he has embraced the whole principle of the universe with all clarity, and, insofar as he is truth, he has shared it with each one as he deserves.

(187) But someone may inquire if our Savior understands everything known by the Father in the depth of his wealth and wisdom and knowledge,[272] and in the delusion of glorifying the Father, he may declare that something known by the Father is not known by the Son who refuses[273] to be made equal to the perceptions of the unbegotten God. If this inquiry should be made, we must consider that he is the Savior on the basis that he is truth, and we must apply the consideration that if the truth is complete, he is ignorant of nothing true, lest the truth stumble because it lacks those things which it does not know, which, according to those, are in the Father alone. Or let someone show that there are things which are known which do not belong to the appellation truth, but are beyond it.

(188) Now it is clear that the principle of the life which is pure and unmixed with anything else is properly in the firstborn of all creation.[274] The participants in Christ truly live because they receive their life from this life, while just as those who are thought to live without him do not have the true light, so neither do they live the true life.

---

270. Cf. Mt 22.10–11.
271. Cf. Prv 24.54 (30.19).   272. Cf. Rom 11.33.
273. Blanc takes the participle *diarkountos* to have this meaning here. The phrase is obscure. For the way others have interpreted it, see Blanc (SC 120.152–3).
274. Cf. Col 1.15.

(189) The Savior has also been recorded to be a door since it is not possible to be in the Father or beside the Father if one has not first taken the initiative to ascend from below to the divinity of the Son through which one can be led also to the blessedness of the Father.

(190) And since he is benevolent and is in favor of helping souls improve in any way possible, he becomes a shepherd for those who do not hasten to reason, but are like sheep which, in an unexamined and non-rational way, are gentle and meek. "For the Lord saves men and beasts,"[275] and both Israel and Juda are sowed with the seed not only of men but also of beasts.

(191) In addition to these titles, we must consider first of all the title Christ, and we must add that of king, to perceive the difference by the juxtaposition. In Psalm 44 he who has loved justice and hated iniquity more than his fellows[276] is said to be anointed because he has thus approached justice and hated iniquity. Consequently, he did not receive the anointing at the same time with his being, as something coexistent and created at the same time with himself. Anointing is a symbol of sovereignty among mortals, and sometimes also of priesthood. Is, then, the sovereignty of the Son of God added later and not congenital with him?

(192) And how could the firstborn of all creation, when he was not a king, later have become a king because he had loved justice, and that when he happened to be justice? His human nature, however, never escapes our notice when he is Christ, especially when he is considered in relation to the soul which became both troubled and sorrowful[277] because of his humanity. On the other hand, his kingly nature is obvious when he is considered according to the divine.

(193) And I support this from Psalm 71 which says, "Give to the king your judgment, O God; and your justice to the king's son, to judge your people with justice, and your poor with judgment."[278] For clearly the Psalm, which has been ascribed to Solomon, prophesies of Christ.

---

275. Cf. Ps 35.7.
277. Cf. Jn 12.27; Mt 26.38.
276. Cf. Ps 44.8.
278. Ps 71.1–2.

(194) And it is worthwhile to see to what king the prophesy prays that God give judgment, and to what son of a king, and of what kind of a king justice.

(195) I think, then, that "king" is used of that preeminent nature of the firstborn of all creation.[279] Judgment is given to this nature because it transcends. And "the king's son" is used of the human nature which is assumed, which is formed and shaped in accordance with justice by that nature.

(196) And I am led to accept that this is so from the fact that both have been brought together into one Word, and the fact that the things which are added are no longer related as of two individuals, but as of one.

(197) For the Savior had made "both one,"[280] having made them according to the firstfruits of both which came to be in himself before all things. And I say "of both" also in the case of men in whose case each man's soul has been mixed with the Holy Spirit and each of those who are saved has become spiritual.

(198) Just as there are some, then, of whom Christ is shepherd because, as we said previously, they are meek and tranquil, and more irrational, so also there are some over whom he is king insofar as they approach piety in a more rational manner.

(199) There are also differences between those who are governed by a king. They are governed either in a manner that is more mystical, esoteric and worthy of God, or in a manner that is inferior.

(200) I would also say that those who have contemplated the bodiless realities called "invisible" and "not seen" [281] by Paul, who exist by reason[282] apart from everything perceptible by sense, are ruled by that preeminent nature of the only begotten.[283] But those are ruled by the Christ who have arrived at the rational principle[284] of those things perceptible by the senses, and through them glorify the one who made them,

---

279. Cf. Col 1.15.
280. Cf. Eph 2.14.
281. Cf. Col 1.16; Rom 1.20; 2 Cor 4.18.
282. *Logō.*
283. Cf. section 195.
284. *Logon.*

and are themselves ruled by reason. But let no one take offense when we distinguish the aspects in the Savior, thinking that we also do the same with his essence.

(201) Now it is very clear even to the common crowd how our Lord is teacher and interpreter for those striving for piety, and lord of servants who have "the spirit of bondage in fear."[285] But when they progress and hasten to wisdom and are judged worthy of it—since "the servant does not know what his lord wishes"[286]—he does not remain their lord; he becomes their "friend."

(202) He himself teaches this, declaring somewhere when his hearers were still servants, "You call me teacher and lord, and you speak correctly, for I am."[287] And elsewhere, "No longer do I call you servants, for the servant does not know what the will of his lord is, but I call you friends," because you have continued "with me in all my temptations."[288]

(203) Those, therefore, who live in the fear which God demands of those who are not good servants (as we have read in Malachi, "If I am a lord, where is my fear?")[289] are servants of a lord who is called their Savior.

(204) But the noble origin of the Son is not presented clearly by all these titles. It is, however, when God, with whom it is always "today," says to him, "You are my Son, today have I begotten you."[290] There is no evening of God possible and, I think, no morning, but the time, if I may put it this way, which is coextensive with his unoriginated and eternal life, is today for him, the day in which the son has been begotten. Consequently neither the beginning nor the day of his generation is to be found.

(205) We must add to what has been said a discussion of how the Son is the "true vine."[291] Now this will be obvious to those who understand the following statement in a manner worthy of the grace the prophets received: "Wine cheers the heart of man."[292]

285. Rom 8.15.
286. Cf. Jn 15.15.
287. Jn 13.13.
288. Cf. Jn 15.15; Lk 22.28.
289. Mal 1.6.
290. Ps 2.7; Heb 1.5; cf. Lk 3.22.
291. Cf. Jn 15.1.
292. Ps 103.15.

(206) For if the heart is the intellectual part, and what cheers it is the most delectable reason, which completely rids it of human concerns and causes it to experience ecstasy and to be intoxicated with an intoxication which is not irrational, but divine—I think it is this intoxication with which Joseph also intoxicates his brothers,[293]—it is reasonable that he who brings the wine which cheers the heart of man is the "true vine." He is "true" because he has the truth as grapes, and as branches he has the disciples, his imitators, who themselves also bear the truth as fruit.

(207) It is difficult, however, to present the difference between the bread and the vine, since he says he is not only the "vine," but also the "bread of life."[294]

(208) But see if, perhaps, it is like this. As bread nourishes and strengthens and is said to sustain the heart of man, but wine pleases and cheers and confounds, so the ethical teachings, since they preserve life for the one who learns and carries them out, are the bread of life (these would not be said to be the fruit of the vine), but the esoteric and mystical doctrines[295] come from the "true vine" and are called "wine" because they cheer and produce ecstasy, being present in those who delight in the Lord and desire not only to be nourished, but also to revel in him.

(209) In addition to these names [we must consider][296] how he is described in the Apocalypse as the "first and last."[297] As first, he is different from the alpha and the beginning, and as last, he is not the same as the omega and the end.

(210) I think, therefore, since rational creatures are represented in many forms, that one of them is first, and another second, and third, and so on to the last.

(211) And to say precisely what is first, and of what sort the second is, and upon what basis the third is true, and so on to the last, is not possible for man at all, but is beyond our nature.

---

293. Cf. Gn 43.34.   294. Cf. Jn 6.48.
295. *Theōrēmata*. Origen contrasts this with the earlier *mathēmata* ("teachings").
296. *Epistateon*. Conjecture of Preuschen adopted by Blanc.
297. Rv 22.13.

We shall attempt to stop, however, and treat the subjects in the passage as we are able.

(212) There are certain gods of whom God is god, as the prophecies say, "Give thanks to the God of gods," and, "The God of gods, the Lord has spoken, and has called the earth."[298] And according to the gospel, "he is not God of the dead, but of the living."[299] Those gods, therefore, of whom God is god, are also living.

(213) The Apostle also acknowledges this when he writes in his letter to the Corinthians, "Just as there are many gods and many lords."[300] He understood the term gods to mean existing beings, in accordance with the prophetic writings.

(214) There are other beings besides the gods of whom God is god. Some of these are called "thrones," others are said to be "principalities," and others besides these are called "dominations and powers."[301]

(215) And because of the saying, "Above every name that is named, not only in this world, but also in that which is to come,"[302] we must believe that there are other spiritual beings besides these, to whom we do not usually give a name. The Hebrew used to call one species of these beings Sabai (who was their ruler and none other than God), and from which the name Sabaoth was derived. In addition to all these, man is a mortal spiritual being.

(216) The God of the universe, therefore, has created a spiritual race, first in honor, composed, I think, of those beings called gods. Let us say for the moment that "thrones" are second, and "principalities," without doubt, third. In this way we must descend in thought to the last spiritual being which, perhaps, is none other than man.

(217) The Savior, therefore, in a way much more divine than Paul, has become "all things to all," that he might either "gain" or perfect "all things."[303] He has clearly become a man to men, and an angel to angels.

---

298. Ps 135.2; cf. 49.1.
299. Mt 22.32.
300. 1 Cor 8.5.
301. Cf. Col 1.16.
302. Cf. Eph 1.21.
303. Cf. 1 Cor 9.22.

(218) No believer will have any doubt that he became a man; and we may be convinced that he became an angel if we observe the appearances and words of the angels when [some angel appears with authority][304] in certain passages of Scripture when the angels speak. For example, "An angel of the Lord appeared in the fire of a burning bush. And he said, I am the God of Abraham, and of Isaac, and of Jacob."[305] But also Isaias says, "His name shall be called angel of great counsel."[306]

(219) The Savior, therefore, is first and last,[307] not that he is not what lies between, but it is stated in terms of the extremities to show that he himself has become "all things."[308] But consider whether the "last" is man, or those called the underworld beings, of which the demons also are a part, either in their entirety or some of them.

(220) We must inquire about those beings to whom the Savior says through the Prophet David when he also became one of them, "And I have become as a man without help, free among the dead."[309] Just as he was more than man insofar as his birth from a virgin was concerned, and the rest of his astounding life, so was he among the dead insofar as he was the only free man there; his soul was not left in Hades.[310] So, then, he is "first and last."[311]

(221) But if there are letters of God, as there are, which the saints read and say they have read what is written in the tablets of heaven, those letters are the thoughts about the Son of God which are broken up into alpha and the letters that follow to omega, that heavenly matters might be read through them.

(222) And again the same one is beginning and end, but he is not the same insofar as the aspects are concerned. For he is the beginning insofar as he is wisdom, as we have learned in Proverbs. Therefore it has been written, "God created me the beginning of his ways for his works."[312] But insofar as he

304. This is Preuschen's conjecture for the text at this point.
305. Ex 3.2.6.
306. Is 9.5 (LXX).
307. Cf. Rv 22.13.
308. Cf. Col 3.11.
309. Ps 87.5–6.
310. Cf. Ps 15.10; Acts 2.27.
311. Rv 22.13.
312. Cf. Prv 8.22.

is Word he is not the beginning, for "in the beginning was the Word."³¹³

(223) His aspects, therefore, have a beginning, and something that is second beyond the beginning, and third, and so on to the end. It is as if he had said, "I am the beginning insofar as I am wisdom," and second, if there should be such, "insofar as I am invisible," and third, "insofar as I am life," since "what came to be in him was life."³¹⁴

(224) And if someone is able, by close examination, to perceive the meaning of the Scriptures, perhaps he will discover many things about the order and the end. For I do not think that he will discover everything. But beginning and end seem rather clearly to be applied usually to what is united, as the foundation is the beginning of a house, and the parapet its end.

(225) And because the Christ is the "chief cornerstone,"³¹⁵ we must indeed adapt the illustration to the whole united body of the saved, for Christ the only begotten is also "all in all";³¹⁶ for example, he is the beginning in the man which he assumed, but the end in the last of the saints—being, of course, also in those in between—, or, he is the beginning in Adam, but the end in his sojourn among us, according to the saying, "The last Adam became a life-giving spirit."³¹⁷ But this saying will apply also to the interpretation of "first and last."³¹⁸

(226) By observing, however, the things said about "first and last" and about "beginning and end,"—in some places we referred the argument to the forms of spiritual beings, and in others to the differences in the aspect of the Son of God—we have gained also a distinction between "first" and "beginning," between "last" and "end," and further also between the "Alpha" and the "Omega."³¹⁹

(227) Nor is it obscure why he is called the "living" and the "dead," and the one who lives forever and ever after death.³²⁰ For since we were not benefitted from his superior life while

---

313. Jn 1.1.
314. Jn 1.4.
315. Eph 2.20; Is 28.16.
316. Cf. 1 Cor 15.28.
317. 1 Cor 15.45.
318. Cf. Rv 22.13.
319. Ibid.
320. Cf. Rv 1.18.

we were in sin, he came down to our mortality, that when he died to sin,[321] we, by bearing about in the body the mortification of Jesus,[322] might be able to receive in due order his life forever and ever after our mortality. For those who always bear Jesus' death about in their bodies will also have the life of Jesus manifested in their bodies.

(228) He made these statements, which are found in the books of the New Testament, about himself. But in Isaias he declared that his "mouth" was made by the Father "as a sharp sword," and that he was hidden "under the shadow of his hand," being likened to a chosen arrow hidden "in the quiver" of the Father. The Father calls him "servant" of the God of the universe, "Israel," and "the light of the gentiles."[323]

(229) The mouth of the Son of God, therefore, is a sharp sword, since "the word of God" is "living and effectual, and more piercing than any two-edged sword, and reaching to the division of the soul and the spirit, of the joints and also the marrow, and is a discerner of the thoughts and intentions of the heart."[324] Above all, since he came not to cast peace on the earth, that is on the things which are corporeal and perceived by the senses, but a sword,[325] and since he cuts through, if I may speak in this way, the harmful friendship of soul and body, that the soul, by devoting herself to the spirit which fights against the flesh,[326] might be made a friend of God, he had his mouth as a sword, or as a sharp sword as the word of the prophet has it.[327] But also when one sees so many wounded by the divine love, like the bride who confesses that she has so suffered in the Song of Songs by the words, "I have been wounded by love,"[328] he will find the arrow which has wounded the souls of so many in regard to the love of God to be none other than him who said, "He made me as a chosen arrow."[329]

(230) And further, everyone who has understood how Jesus

---

321. Cf. Rom 6.10.
323. Is 49.2, 3 and 6.
325. Cf. Mt 10.34.
327. Cf. Is 49.2.
329. Is 49.2.

322. Cf. 2 Cor 4.10.
324. Heb 4.12.
326. Cf. Gal 5.17.
328. Song 2.5.

was to his disciples, not as the one who is at table, but as the one who serves,[330] since the Son of God took the form of a servant[331] for the freedom of those enslaved to sin, will not fail to recognize how the Father says to him, "You are my servant," and a little further on, "This is a great thing for you, that you are called my servant."[332]

(231) For we must dare say that the goodness of Christ appeared greater and more divine and truly in accordance with the image of the Father when "he humbled himself and became obedient unto death, even death on a cross," than when "he had considered being equal to God robbery,"[333] and had not been willing to become a servant for the salvation of the world.

(232) For this reason, wishing to teach us that to have served in this way was a great gift which he had received from the Father, he says, "And my God shall be my strength. And he said to me, This is a great thing for you, that you are called my servant."[334] For if he had not become a servant he would not have established "the tribes of Jacob" nor converted "the diaspora of Israel"; neither would he have become the "light of the gentiles" to "be for salvation to the end of the earth."[335]

(233) And although the Father says it was great, the fact that he became a servant was moderate indeed compared to the fact that he became an innocent little lamb and a lamb. For the Lamb of God became as an innocent little lamb led to be slaughtered that he might take away "the sin of the world."[336] He who bestowed speech[337] on all is compared to a lamb dumb "before his shearer,"[338] that we might all be cleansed by his death which is distributed like a drug against the adverse influences and against the sin of those who wish to receive the truth. For the death of Christ has made the powers which war against the human race ineffectual, and, by

---

330. Cf. Lk 22.27.
331. Cf. Phil 2.7.
332. Cf. Is 49.3.6.
333. Phil 2.8.6.
334. Is 49.5.6.
335. Is 49.6.
336. Cf. Is 53.7; Jn 1.29.
337. *Logos.*
338. Is 53.7.

an ineffable power, has brought the life in sin in each believer to an end.³³⁹

(234) And because he takes away sin until all his enemies are abolished, and death is the last indeed,³⁴⁰ that the whole world might be without sin, John points to him and says, "Behold the Lamb of God who takes away the sin of the world."³⁴¹ He does not say he who will take it away but is not already also taking it away; and he does not say he who took it away but is not also still taking it away.

(235) For the "taking away" affects each one in the world until sin be removed from all the world and the Savior deliver to the Father a prepared kingdom³⁴² in which there is no sin at all, a kingdom which permits the Father's rule and again admits all things of God in its whole and total self, when the saying is fulfilled: "That God may be all in all."³⁴³

(236) But also in addition to these things a "man" is mentioned who comes after John, who existed before him and who was before him, that we might learn also that the human nature of the Son of God which was united with his divinity antedates his birth from Mary.

(237) The Baptist says "he did not know" this man.³⁴⁴ But how did he not know, he who leaped for joy while he was still an infant in the womb of Elizabeth when "the sound" of Mary's "greeting" reached "the ears" of Zachary's wife?³⁴⁵

(238) Consider, then, if the phrase "he did not know" can refer to what preceded his physical existence. And also, if he did not know him before he came in the body, but did know him while he was still in his mother's womb, perhaps he learns something about him other than what he knew, namely that he on whom the spirit descended and remained "is the one who baptizes with the Holy Spirit and fire."³⁴⁶

(239) For even if he knew him still from his mother's womb,

---

339. *Exeleusesthai.* The text is corrupt here.
340. Cf. 1 Cor 15.26.
341. Jn 1.29.
342. Cf. 1 Cor 15.24.
343. Cf. 1 Cor 15.28.
344. Cf. Jn 1.30.31.
345. Cf. Lk 1.41.44.
346. Cf. Jn 1.33.

he certainly did not know everything about him, and perhaps he also did not know that "this is the one who baptizes with the Holy Spirit and fire," when he had seen "the Spirit descending and remaining on him."[347] John did not know, however, that he was a "man," and the first man.

(240) But none of the previously mentioned names reveals his patronage for us with the Father, when he intercedes and is merciful on behalf of human nature, as "the advocate,"[348] and "[the] propitiation,"[349] and "the propitiatory."[350] The "advocate" is mentioned in the Epistle of John: "For if anyone sin we have an advocate with the Father, Jesus Christ the just, and he is the propitiation for our sins."[351] And in the same Epistle "the propitiation" is said to be the "propitiation for our sins."[352] And, likewise, also in the Epistle to the Romans he is called the "propitiatory": "Whom God has proposed to be a propitiatory through faith."[353] The golden propitiatory lying on the two cherubim in the innermost places and the holy of holies was a kind of shadow of the propitiatory.[354]

(241) But how could he have become advocate and propitiation and propitiatory without the power of God which completely destroys our weakness, a power furnished by Jesus which flows in the souls of believers? He is before this power, the very power of God itself, on account of whom one might say, "I can do all things in Christ Jesus who strengthens me."[355]

(242) For this reason we know that Simon the magician, who called himself "the power of God which is called great," has departed with his money into ruin and destruction.[356] We, however, confessing that Christ is truly the "power of God,"[357] have believed that all things which have received power anywhere at all participate in him insofar as he is "power."

347. Ibid.
348. 1 Jn 2.1.
349. 1 Jn 2.2.
350. Rom 3.25. This word and the preceding one are sometimes used synonymously meaning "propitiation." It was used of the mercy-seat in the OT (see, for example, Ex 25.17–20).
351. Cf. 1 Jn 2.1–2.
352. 1 Jn 2.2.
353. Rom 3.25.
354. Cf. Ex 25.17–19.
355. Cf. Phil 4.13.
356. Cf. Acts 8.10.20.
357. Cf. 1 Cor 1.24.

COMMENTARY ON JOHN, BOOK 1   83

(243) And we must not pass over in silence the fact that he is, with just cause, the "wisdom of God,"³⁵⁸ and for this reason is called this. For his wisdom does not exist merely in the mental images of the God and Father of the universe in a way analogous to the images in human thoughts.

(244) But if someone is able to comprehend an incorporeal existence comprised of the various ideas which embrace the principles of the universe, an existence which is living and animate, as it were, he will understand the wisdom of God which precedes all creation, which appropriately says of herself, "God created me the beginning of his ways for his works."³⁵⁹ It is because of this creation that the whole creation has also been able to subsist, since it has a share in the divine wisdom according to which it has been created, for according to the Prophet David, God made "all things in wisdom."³⁶⁰

(245) Many creatures, on the one hand, have come into existence by participation in wisdom, while they do not apprehend her by whom they have been created. Very few, however, comprehend not only the wisdom concerning themselves, but also that concerning many beings, for Christ is all wisdom.

(246) But each of the wise participates in Christ to the extent that he has the capacity for wisdom, insofar as Christ is wisdom, just as each one who possesses power has obtained greater power to the extent that he has shared in Christ, insofar as Christ is power.

(247) We must also consider sanctification and redemption in the same way. For Jesus has become sanctification itself for us,³⁶¹ whence the saints are sanctified, and has become redemption. And each of us is sanctified by that sanctification and redeemed in relation to that redemption.

(248) But consider if the Apostle uses the expression "for us" in vain when he says, "Who became for us³⁶² wisdom from

---

358. Cf. 1 Cor 1.25.   359. Cf. Prv 8.22.
360. Cf. Ps 103.24.
361. Reading *autos* with Brooke and Blanc. Preuschen has *auto*. This may be a printing error as neither his text nor Brooke's notes anything in the apparatus.
362. The NAB and RSV translate the dative *hēmin* as possessive. Origen, however, seems to have understood it as a dative of advantage. This under-

God, and justice, and sanctification, and redemption."[363] And consider if, in other statements about the Christ, insofar as he is "wisdom" and "power," the statement is not made absolutely that "Christ is the power of God and the wisdom of God,"[364] even if we have assumed that he was not absolutely the "wisdom" and "power of God," but was such "for us." Now, however, in the case of "wisdom" and "power," we have the unqualified expression recorded in addition to the qualification "for us." The same expression, however, has not been used in the case of "sanctification" and "redemption."

(249) For this reason, since "he who sanctifies and they who are sanctified are all of one,"[365] consider if the Father is the "sanctification" of our sanctification himself, in the same way as the Father is the head of Christ, while Christ is our head.[366]

(250) And Christ is our redemption, because we have been taken captive and need redemption. I do not ask, however, about the redemption of him who has been tempted "in all things as we are, without sin,"[367] and has never been taken into captivity by his enemies.

(251) But once the distinction has been made between "for us" and the unqualified state, "sanctification" and "redemption," on the one hand, being "for us" and qualified, and "wisdom" and "power" being both "for us" and unqualified, we must not leave unexamined the statements concerning "justice." It is clear, on the one hand, that Christ is justice "for us," from the text, "Who became wisdom for us from God, and justice, and sanctification, and redemption."[368]

(252) But if we should not find that he is "justice" absolutely, just as he is "wisdom" and the "power of God" absolutely, we must examine if the Father is "justice" for Christ himself also,

---

standing created a problem for his theology, for he divided the titles given to Christ into those which designated things he became on account of man's salvation and those which he was by his nature. Wisdom belonged to the latter group and, therefore, was not one of the things Christ became for us. See M. Harl, *Origène et la fonction révélatrice du verbe incarné* (Paris: éditions du Seuil, 1958), 121–22.

363. 1 Cor 1.30.
365. Heb 2.11.
367. Heb 4.15.
364. 1 Cor 1.24.
366. Cf. 1 Cor 11.3.
368. 1 Cor 1.30.

just as he is his "sanctification." For there is, indeed, no injustice with God; he is both a just and holy Lord; his judgments are in justice, and being just, he manages all things justly.³⁶⁹

(253) I think the distinction made by some heretics between the just one and the good one is deceptive.³⁷⁰ They have not made clear in what way they think the creator is just, but the Father of Christ good. If the matter is investigated carefully, I think the distinction can be made in the case of the Father and the Son. The Son, on the one hand, is justice, who received the "right to perform judgment"³⁷¹ because he is the Son of man and "will judge the world in justice."³⁷² After the kingdom of Christ, however, the Father, by doing good to those disciplined by the justice of the Son, will demonstrate the title "good" by his works, when God becomes "all in all."³⁷³

(254) And perhaps the Savior, by his own justice, is preparing all things in their appropriate times by reason, and discipline, and punishments and, if I may put it this way, by his resources for spiritual healing, that they may receive the Father's goodness at the end. Because he understood the Father's goodness, he says to the only man who addresses him as "good teacher": "Why do you call me 'good'? No one is good except one, God the Father."³⁷⁴

(255) We have shown the same thing in other matters, even in the case of someone being greater than the creator. We understood the Christ to be the creator, but the Father is greater. He, indeed, who is such great things as "the advocate," "the propitiation," "the propitiatory,"³⁷⁵ because he showed compassion "on our weaknesses" in experiencing temptation "in all things" human "in our likeness, without sin," is a "great high priest"³⁷⁶ who offered himself as the sacrifice offered once for all,³⁷⁷ not for men alone, but also for

---

369. Cf. Rom 9.14; Rv 16.5 and 7.
370. This distinction was made by Marcion.
371. Jn 5.27. 372. Cf. Acts 17.31.
373. 1 Cor 15.28. 374. Cf. Mk 10.18.
375. 1 Jn 2.1.2; Rom 3.25. 376. Heb 4.15.14.
377. Cf. Heb 9.28.

every spiritual being. For "apart from God he tasted death for all."³⁷⁸ This appears in some copies of the Epistle to the Hebrews as "by the grace of God."³⁷⁹

(256) But whether "apart from God he tasted death for all," he died not only for men but also for the rest of the spiritual beings, or "by the grace of God he tasted death for all," he died for all apart from God, for "by the grace of God he tasted death for all."

(257) And, indeed, it would be strange to declare that he tasted death for human sins, but not further also for any other creature, in addition to man, which happened to be in sins, for instance for the stars, since not even the stars are absolutely pure before God, as we have read in Job: "And the stars are not pure in his sight,"³⁸⁰ unless this was said hyperbolically.

(258) For this reason he is a "great high priest,"³⁸¹ since he restores all things to the kingdom of the Father, causing the things which are wanting in each of the creatures to be supplied that they may be able to receive the Father's glory.

Title given by the Prophets

(259) This high priest is named "Juda" according to a somewhat different aspect from those which have been mentioned.³⁸² This is so that those who are Jews in secret³⁸³ might be called Jews, not from Juda, the son of Jacob, but from this man, being his brothers and praising him because they share in the freedom with which he made them free when he delivered them from their enemies, having placed his hands on their back and subjected them.

(260) In addition, because he supplanted³⁸⁴ the activity of the adversary, and because he alone sees the Father he is "Jacob" and "Israel"³⁸⁵ when he has become man; as we become light because he is the light of the world, so we become Jacob

---

378. Cf. Heb 2.9.
379. This textual variation in Heb 2.9 is still noted in modern critical editions of the NT. "Grace" (*chariti*), however, has much stronger manuscript support than "apart from" (*chōris*).

380. Cf. Jb 25.5.	381. Heb 4.14.
382. Cf. Gn 49.8.	383. Cf. Rom 2.29.
384. Cf. Gn 25.25.	385. Cf. Is 49.5–6.

because he is called "Jacob," and Israel, because he is named "Israel."

(261) And further, the Christ receives the kingdom from the king whom the children of Israel appointed for themselves because they began with him[386] apart from the will of God, and they did not consult God. He fights the battles of the Lord and prepares peace for his son, his people.[387] Perhaps it is for this reason that he is called "David," and later "rod"[388] for those who need direction that is painful and harsh and who have not offered themselves to the love and meekness of the Father.

(262) For this reason, if he is called rod, "he shall come forth,"[389] for he does not remain in himself, but appears to leave his preceding condition behind.

(263) After he has come forth and become a "rod," he does not remain a "rod," but after the "rod" he becomes a "flower" springing up.[390] This "flower" has been revealed to be the goal for which he is a "rod" to those who have experienced his visitation as a "rod," for God will visit "with a rod," that is, the Christ, "the iniquities of those" whom he will visit.[391] But he will not take his mercy from him,[392] for he shows mercy to him when the Father has mercy on those whom the son wishes to receive mercy. But it is also possible to take the fact that he becomes a "rod" and a "flower" not to be related to the same people, but to understand that he became a "rod" to those in need of punishment, and a "flower" to those being saved. I think, however, that the former interpretation is better.

(264) We must add at this point, however, that perhaps, if he becomes a "rod" to someone, he will, by all means, be a "flower" because of the goal. If he becomes a "flower" to someone, however, it does not necessarily follow that he will also have to be a "rod" to that person, unless, perhaps, because one flower is more perfect than another, and those which are

---

386. Preuschen thinks that there is a difficulty in the text here.
387. Cf. 1 Sm 25.28; 1 Kgs 2.33.
388. Cf. Is 11.1.
389. Ibid.
390. Ibid.
391. Ps 88.33.
392. Cf. Ps 88.34.

not as yet bearing fruit perfectly are said to flower, the perfect receive that which is beyond the flower of Christ. Those, however, who have experienced him as a rod will not participate in his perfection at the same time with the rod, but only in the flower which precedes his fruits.

(265) Finally, before we discuss the "Word," Christ was a "stone" rejected by the builders and appointed head of the corner.[393] For since living stones[394] are built upon the foundation with other stones which are "the apostles and prophets, Christ Jesus," our Lord, "himself being the chief cornerstone,"[395] he is called "stone" because he is a part of the building made of living stones "in the land of the living."[396]

The "Word"

(266) We have said all these things wishing to show the random and unexamined procedure followed by many interpreters. Although so many names are applied to Christ, they stop with the term "Word" alone, and do not investigate why "the Son of God" has been recorded to be the Word, God, who was in the beginning with the Father, through whom all things came into being.

(267) As, therefore, he is entitled "light of the world"[397] because of his activity of enlightening the world of which he is the light, and he is called "resurrection"[398] because he causes those who genuinely draw near to him to put off that which is dead and, rising, to assume newness of life, and because of other actions he is called "shepherd,"[399] "teacher,"[400] "king,"[401] "chosen arrow,"[402] "servant,"[403] and, in addition, "advocate," "propitiation,"[404] and "propitiatory,"[405] so also he is called "Word," because he removes everything irrational from us and makes us truly rational beings who do all things for the

---

393. Cf. Ps 117.22.
394. Cf. 1 Pt 2.5.
395. Eph 2.20.
396. Cf. Ps 141.6.
397. Cf. Jn 9.5.
398. Cf. Jn 11.25.
399. Cf. Jn 10.11.12.
400. Cf. Jn 13.13.
401. Cf. Zec 9.9; Jn 12.15; Mt 21.5.
402. Cf. Ps 44.6; Is 49.2.
403. Cf. Is 49.3.
404. 1 Jn 2.1.2.
405. Cf. Rom 3.25.

glory of God, even to eating and drinking,[406] so that we perform both the more common and the more perfect works of life to the glory of God because of reason.[407]

(268) For if, by participating in him, we arise and are enlightened, and perhaps also are shepherded or ruled, it is clear that we also become rational in a divine manner when he destroys in us all that is irrational and dead insofar as he is "Word" and "resurrection."[408]

(269) But consider if, perhaps, all men participate in him insofar as he is Word. This is why the Apostle teaches us that he is sought within the seekers[409] by those who choose to find him when he says, "Do not say in your heart, 'Who shall ascend into heaven?' that is, to bring Christ down; or, 'Who shall descend into the deep?' that is, to bring up Christ again from the dead. But what does Scripture say? The Word[410] is near you, even in your mouth, and in your heart,"[411] as though Christ and the Word which is sought are the same.

(270) But also when the Lord himself says, "If I had not come and spoken to them, they would not have sin; but now they have no excuse for their sin,"[412] we must understand that the Word is saying nothing other than that there is no sin in those in whom he has not yet been completed, but that these are guilty of sin who, when they have already partaken of him, act contrary to the concepts by which he has been completed in us. Only as it is understood in this way is the saying true, "If I had not come and spoken to them, they would not have sin."[413]

(271) Come, then, consider this in the case of the visible Jesus, as the many will imagine him. How is it true that these

406. Cf. 1 Cor 10.31.
407. *Logos.* The same term (rendered "word") occurs earlier in this sentence where it is applied to Christ. The two adjectives, *alogon* ("irrational") and *logikous* ("rational"), chosen by Origen to describe the work of Christ as the *Logos*, show that he understands the term, here at least, to mean reason.
408. Cf. Jn 1.1, 11.25.
409. Literally, "not outside of the seekers."
410. *Hrēma.*
411. Rom 10.6–8; cf. Dt 30.12–14.
412. Jn 15.22.   413. Ibid.

to whom he has not come have no sin? For all who lived before the sojourn of the Savior will be freed from all sin since the Jesus seen in the flesh had not come.

(272) But all those, too, will have no sin to whom the message about him has never been proclaimed, and obviously those who have no sin are not liable to judgment.

(273) Now "reason"[414] which is in men, in which we have said our species participates, is spoken of in two ways: according to the perfecting of concepts which occurs in everyone who has gone beyond childhood, the exceptional being excluded, or according to the excellence which is found in the perfect alone.

(274) Therefore, the words, "If I had not come and spoken to them, they would not have sin; but now they have no excuse for their sin,"[415] must be interpreted according to the first view, but, "All who have come before me are thieves and robbers, and the sheep did not hear them,"[416] must be interpreted according to the second.

(275) For before the perfection of reason, all men's thoughts are blameworthy inasmuch as they are deficient and inadequate. The irrational elements in us, which are figuratively said to be "sheep," do not obey these perfectly. And, perhaps, it is according to the first view that "the Word became flesh,"[417] but according to the second that "the Word was God."[418]

(276) But subsequent to this it is possible to ask [if] it is possible to perceive [anything] in human terms between the statement, "The Word became flesh," and, "The Word was God,"[419] as if the Word was resolved into its original elements after it had become flesh and, little by little, was reduced until it should become what it was in the beginning, namely God, the Word with the Father.[420] It was the glory of this Word which John saw to be truly the only begotten as from the Father.[421]

(277) But the Word can also be "the Son" because he an-

---

414. *Logos.*
415. Jn 15.22.
416. Jn 10.8.
417. Jn 1.14.
418. Jn 1.1.
419. Ibid.
420. Cf. Jn 1.1.
421. Jn 1.14.

nounces the secrets of his Father, who is "mind" analogous to the Son who is called "Word." For as the word in us is the messenger of what the mind perceives, so the Word of God, since he has known the Father, reveals the Father whom he has known, because no creature can come into contact with him without a guide.

(278) "For no one has known the Father but the Son and he to whom the Son will reveal him."[422] And to the extent that he is the Word, he is the "messenger of great counsel" "upon whose shoulder the authority"[423] has come to rest, for he has become king because he suffered the cross. And in the Apocalypse the Word which is faithful and true is said to be seated on a white horse,[424] to demonstrate, in my opinion, the clarity of the voice on which the Word of truth rides which comes to reside in us.

(279) But this is not the time to show that the term "horse" is applied to the voice in many passages of Scripture, in which are found the prescribed teachings by which we are benefitted if we obey the divine teachings. But we must mention only one or two passages: "A horse is deceptive for safety,"[425] and, "Some trust in chariots and some in horses, but we will be exalted in the name of the Lord our God."[426]

(280) We must not, however, leave unexamined what is recorded in Psalm 44, which many cite very frequently as if they understood it: "My heart has uttered a good word; I speak my works to the king."[427] Grant that the Father speaks these words.

(281) What, then, is his "heart," that "the good word" should appear subsequent to his heart? For if the term "word" does not need interpretation, as they suppose, obviously neither does the term "heart." It is very strange to suppose that the heart is a part of God, similar to the heart in our body.

(282) But we must remind them that as God's hand, and arm, and finger are mentioned, we do not attach our understanding to the literal sense, but examine how we should

422. Cf. Mt 11.27.
424. Cf. Rv 19.11.
426. Ps 19.8.
423. Is 9.5 (LXX).
425. Ps 32.17.
427. Ps 44.2.

understand these expressions correctly and in a manner worthy of God, so also must we take God's heart to be his intellectual and purposeful power concerning the universe, and the term "word" to be the expression of those matters in that heart.

(283) But who, other than the Savior, announces the will of the Father to the creatures who are worthy, and who has come into existence in accordance with them? Perhaps also the term "uttered"[428] was used intentionally, for a number of other expressions could have been used in place of "uttered." For example, "My heart cast forth a good word"; "My heart spoke a good word." But perhaps as a belch is the emergence of hidden wind into the open, as though the one belching exhales in this way, so the Father belches forth visions of the truth in a disconnected manner and produces their form in the Word, and for this reason the Word is called the image of the invisible God.[429] We have said these things that we may accept that the Father said, "My heart has uttered a good word,"[430] in agreement with the view of the many interpreters mentioned previously.

(284) But we must not yield to them completely, as if it were the common consent that God pronounced these words. For why would it not be the prophet, filled with the Spirit and bringing forth a good word concerning a prophecy about Christ, who, when he is not able to restrain it, says, "My heart has uttered a good word; I speak my works to the king. My tongue is the pen of a scribe who writes swiftly. You are fairer in your beauty than the sons of men." Then he says to the Christ himself, "Grace has been poured forth on your lips."[431]

(285) For if the Father said these things, how, after he had said, "Grace has been poured forth on your lips," were the

---

428. *Exereugesthai* means to "belch forth," and then, metaphorically, to "utter speech."

429. Cf. Col 1.15.

430. Ps 44.2. Cf. R. Cadiou, *Commentaires inédits des Psaumes: étude sur les textes d'Origène contenus dans le manuscrit Vindobonensis 8* (Paris, 1936), 77, where these words are not taken to be spoken by God, but by one "fed on spiritual bread."

431. Ps 44.2–3.

words added, "Therefore God has blessed you forever," and a little later, "Therefore God, your God, has anointed you with the oil of gladness above your fellows"?[432]

(286) But someone who wishes these words in the Psalm to be pronounced by the Father may offer as an objection the saying, "Hear, O daughter, and see; incline your ear, and forget your people and your father's house."[433] For it is not the prophet who will say to the Church, "Hear, O daughter."

(287) It is not difficult, however, to show from other Psalms that changes of persons occur frequently, so that here too it is possible that the Father is speaking, beginning with the words, "Hear, O daughter."

(288) We must also add to our investigation concerning the Word the verse, "By the Word of the Lord the heavens were established; and all their power by his spirit."[434] Some think that these words apply to the Savior and the Holy Spirit,[435] although they can show that the heavens were established by the Word of God. As we might say that a house has come into existence by the word of an architect, and a ship by the word of a shipbuilder, so, then, the heavens have been established by the Word of God. Because they have the distinction of being of a more divine body, which is also called firm because it is not subject, for the most part, to the flux and dissolution of other inferior bodies, the heavens have been special to the divine Word.

Conclusion

(289) Since, then, our purpose is to perceive clearly the statement, "In the beginning was the Word,"[436] and wisdom, with the aid of testimonies from the Proverbs, has been ex-

---

432. Ps 44. 3 and 8.
433. Ps 44.11. In *Ex. Hom.* 2.4 Origen takes this verse to refer to the gentile church.
434. Cf. Ps 32.6. The verb translated "established" in this verse is a form of *stereoō*, which means "to make something firm or solid." It is related to the noun *stereōma*, "firmament," in Gn 1.6–8. It is this connection which underlies the exegesis Origen is discussing here, and also underlies his use of the adjective *stereos*, "firm," of the heavens.
435. Cf. Ireneaus, *Adv. Haer.* 3.8.3.   436. Jn 1.1.

plained to be called "beginning,"[437] and wisdom has been conceived as preceding the Word which announces her, we must understand that the Word is always in the beginning, that is, in wisdom. Being in wisdom, however, which is called "beginning," does not prevent the Word from being "with God," and himself being God, and not merely being "with God," but since he is "in the beginning," that is in wisdom, the Word is "with God."[438]

(290) The Scripture, indeed, says in addition, "The same was in the beginning with God."[439] It could have said, "The same was with God." But just as "he was in the beginning," so also "he was in the beginning with God." Furthermore, "all things were made by him"[440] who was "in the beginning," for according to David, God made "all things in wisdom."[441]

(291) In addition, to signify that the Word has his own individuality, that is to say, lives according to himself, we must speak also of powers, not only of power. "For thus says the Lord of the powers" is a phrase which occurs in many places,[442] certain divine spiritual beings being named powers. The highest and best of these powers was Christ who is called not only the "wisdom of God," but also the "power."[443]

(292) As, therefore, there are many powers of God, each of which has its own individuality, which the Savior excels, so also the Christ, on the basis of our previous investigation, will be understood to be the "Word"—although the reason which is in us has no individuality apart from us—possessing substance "in the beginning," that is in wisdom. This will be sufficient for us at the present on the statement, "In the beginning was the Word."[444]

---

437. Cf. Prv 8.22.
438. Cf. Jn 1.1. 439. Jn 1.2.
440. Jn 1.3. 441. Cf. Ps 103.24.
442. Blanc (SC 120.206), lists Ps 23.10; 58.6; 79.5 and 8. In all of these passages God is addressed as Lord or God of the powers. The sentence Origen cites appears in the LXX only in 2 Kgs 19.20. Preuschen lists no reference though he puts the sentence in quotations in his text.
443. Cf. 1 Cor 1.24. 444. Jn 1.1.

BOOK 2

And the Word was with God, and the Word was God.[1]
Presence of the Word with God and with men

SINCE WE HAVE, in the preceding pages, discussed as sufficiently as we can at present, holy brother Ambrose, who have formed yourself according to the gospel, what the beginning is in which the Word was, and what Word was in the beginning, we now consider subsequently how "the Word was with God."[2]

(2) It is useful, moreover, to reconcile with this statement the "word" which is recorded to have come[3] to certain men. For example, "The word of the Lord which came to Osee the son of Beeri,"[4] and, "The word which came to Isaias the son of Amos concerning Judea and Jerusalem,"[5] and, "The word which came to Jeremias concerning the drought."[6]

(3) We must consider, then, how "the word of the Lord" came to Osee, and how it is the word which came to Isaias the son of Amos, and again how "the word" came to Jeremias concerning "the drought," that we can discover how "the Word was with God,"[7] since it is closely related.

(4) Most people will understand what is said of the prophets in a simple manner, as though the word of the Lord or the word came to them. But perhaps, as we say someone

---

1. Jn 1.1. 2. Ibid.
3. The verb is *ginesthai* in each of the examples from the LXX, and means literally "to come to be." Origen draws a contrast between this verb and *einai*, "to be," in Jn 1.1. These three examples from the Old Testament seem to have been chosen because the construction is exactly parallel with Jn 1.1 (i.e., *logos* is the subject, and the verb is followed by the preposition *pros* and a personal object). See Harl, SC 302.122, on the distinction between *einai* and *ginesthai* in Origen's Christology.
4. Hos 1.1. 5. Cf. Is 2.1.
6. Cf. Jer 14.1. 7. Jn 1.1.

comes to someone, so the "son," who is now acknowledged as divine, came to Osee as the "Word," sent to him by the Father. According to the literal sense, he was sent to the son of Beeri, the prophet Osee, but according to the mystical meaning, he was sent to the one who is saved—for Osee means "saved." The son of Beeri means "wells,"[8] for each of the saved becomes a son of the spring which gushes forth from the depth of the wisdom of God.

(5) It is not strange for the saint thus to be a son of wells, for a son frequently receives his name from virtuous deeds. One may be called a son "of light" because "his works" shine "before men,"[9] another a son "of peace" because he has the "peace of God which surpasses all understanding,"[10] and further, one may be called a "child of wisdom" because of the benefit that comes from wisdom, for Scripture says, "Wisdom is justified by her children."[11]

(6) So, therefore, he who searches all things by the divine Spirit, even the depths of God,[12] in order to speak plainly about him—"O the depth of the riches and wisdom and knowledge of God!"[13]—can be a "son of wells" to whom the Word of the Lord comes.

(7) Likewise the word also comes[14] to Isaias teaching him the things that will come upon Judea and Jerusalem in the last days. And in a similar manner the word comes also to Jeremias, lifted up with a divine exaltation, for his name means "the lifting up of Iao."[15]

(8) The word *comes to be*, however, with men who could not previously receive the sojourn of the Son of God who is the Word. On the other hand, he does not *come to be* "with God"[16]

---

8. For the interpretation of Osee, see Paul de Lagarde, *Onomastica Sacra* (Hildesheim: Georg Olms Verlagsbuchhandlung, 1966), 82.15; and Franz Wutz, *Onomastica Sacra* (Leipzig: J. C. Hinrichs'sche Buchhandlung, 1914), 128. For Beeri see Lagarde *Onomastica* 29.21, and Wutz *Onomastica* 530.

9. Cf. Mt 5.16; Jn 12.36; 1 Thes 5.5.
10. Cf. Phil 4.7; Lk 10.6.   11. Cf. Lk 7.35; Mt 11.19.
12. Cf. 1 Cor 2.10.   13. Rom 11.33.
14. Here Origen uses *erchetai*. Cf. note 3 above.
15. On the interpretation of Jeremias, see Lagarde *Onomastica* 94.6, 199.59, 203.69, and Wutz *Onomastica* 132, 1023.
16. Jn 1.1.

as though previously he were not with him, but because he is always with the Father, it is said, "And the Word *was* with God,"[17] for he did not "*come to be* with God."

(9) And the same verb, "was," is predicated of the Word when he "was in the beginning" and when he "was with God." He is neither separated from the beginning nor does he depart from the Father. And again, he does not *come to be* "in the beginning" from not being "in the beginning," nor does he pass from not being "with God" to coming to be "with God," for before all time and eternity "the Word was in the beginning," and "the Word was with God."[18]

(10) Since, then, to discover the meaning of the statement, "and the Word was with God,"[19] we compared prophetic texts relating how the word came to Osee and Isaias and Jeremias, and we observed the significant difference between the expressions "he has come to be" or "he came to be," compared with "he was"; we shall add that by coming to the prophets he enlightens them with the light of knowledge, causing them to see things which they had not perceived before his coming as if they saw them before their eyes. In being with God, however, the Word[20] is God because he is with him.

(11) Perhaps John, seeing some such order in the argument,[21] did not place "the Word was God" before "the Word was with God," so that we might not be hindered in seeing the individual meaning of each of the propositions in the affirmations of the series. For the first proposition is this: "In the beginning was the Word"; and the second: "The Word was with God"; and the next: "And the Word was God."[22]

17. Ibid.   18. Ibid.
19. Ibid.
20. Accepting Preuschen's emendation.
21. *Logō.* "Argument" was one of the technical meanings of *logos* in Stoic logic. See Benson Mates, *Stoic Logic* (Berkeley: University of California Press, 1961), 134. For Origen's thorough knowledge of Stoic logic see J. M. Rist, "The Importance of Stoic Logic in the *Contra Celsum*" in *Neoplatonism and Early Christian Thought: Essays in honour of A. H. Armstrong*, ed. H. J. Blumenthal and R. A. Markus (London: Variorum Publications Ltd., 1981), 64–78. The term *axiōma*, "proposition," which occurs twice in this section, is also a term from Stoic logic.
22. Jn 1.1.

The difference between "the God" and "a God"

(12) But since the proposition, "In the beginning was the Word," has been placed first, perhaps it indicates some order; in the same manner, next, "And the Word was with God," and third, "And the Word was God." Perhaps he says, "And the Word was with God," then, "And the Word was God," that we might understand that the Word has become God because he is "with God."

(13) John has used the articles in one place and omitted them in another very precisely, and not as though he did not understand the precision of the Greek language. In the case of the Word, he adds the article "the," but in the case of the noun "God," he inserts it in one place and omits it in another.

(14) For he adds the article when the noun "God" stands for the uncreated cause of the universe, but he omits it when the Word is referred to as "God." And as "*the* God" and "God" differ in these places, so, perhaps, "*the* Word" and "Word" differ.

(15) For as the God who is over all is "*the* God" and not simply "God," so the source of reason[23] in each rational being is "*the* Word." That reason which is in each rational being would not properly have the same designation as the first reason, and be said to be "*the* Word."

(16) Many people who wish to be pious are troubled because they are afraid that they may proclaim two Gods and, for this reason, they fall into false and impious beliefs. They either deny that the individual nature of the Son is other than that of the Father by confessing him to be God whom they refer to as "Son" in name at least, or they deny the divinity of the Son and make his individual nature and essence as an individual to be different from the Father.

(17) Their problem can be resolved in this way. We must say to them that at one time God, with the article, is very God, wherefore also the Savior says in his prayer to the Father, "That they may know you the only true God."[24] On the

---

23. *Logos.* 24. Jn 17.3.

other hand, everything besides the very God, which is made God by participation in his divinity, would more properly not be said to be "*the* God," but "God." To be sure, his "firstborn of every creature,"[25] inasmuch as he was the first to be with God and has drawn divinity into himself, is more honored than the other gods beside him (of whom God is God as it is said, "The God of gods, the Lord has spoken, and he has called the earth"[26]). It was by his ministry that they became gods, for he drew from God that they might be deified, sharing ungrudgingly also with them according to his goodness.

(18) *The* God, therefore, is the true God. The others are gods formed according to him as images of the prototype. But again, the archetypal image of the many images is *the* Word with *the* God, who was "in the beginning." By being "with *the* God" he always continues to be "God." But he would not have this if he were not with God, and he would not remain God if he did not continue in unceasing contemplation of the depth of the Father.

Use of the words "God" and "Word"

(19) Some, however, have probably taken offense at what we said when we described the Father as the true God but, in addition to the true God, said many gods have come into existence by participation in *the* God. These people might fear that the glory of the one who transcends all creation is put on a level with the others who happen to have the title "god." Because of this we must set forth this explanation in addition to the difference which has already been explained in relation to which we declared that God the Word is the minister of deity to all the other Gods.[27]

(20) The reason which is in each rational being has the same position[28] in relation to the Word which is in the beginning with God, which is God the Word, which God the Word has with God.[29] For as the Father is very God and true God

---

25. Col 1.15. 26. Ps 49.1.
27. See above, *Comm. Jn* 2.17.
28. Accepting Preuschen's suggestion to read *topos* instead of *logos*.
29. *Logos* has been translated by both "reason" and "Word" in this and the following sentence.

100   ORIGEN

in relation to the image and images of the image (wherefore also men are said to be "according to the image,"[30] not "images"), so is the very Word in relation to the reason in each one. For both hold the place of a source; the Father, that of divinity, the Son, that of reason.

Classing men with "the God" or "the Word" according to which they belong

(21) As, therefore, there are many gods, but for us there is "one God, the Father," and there are many lords, but for us there is "one Lord, Jesus Christ,"[31] so there are many words, but we pray that the Word who is in the beginning, who is with God, God the Word, may be with us.

(22) For he who does not receive this Word which was in the beginning with God will either devote himself to him who became flesh, or will share with those who have partaken of something of this Word, or, after he has fallen away from sharing with him who has partaken, will remain in that so-called [word] which is totally foreign to *the* Word.

(23) Now what has been said will be clear from the examples we have given about God and the Word of God, and about gods who either participate in God or are said to be gods, but are not gods at all; and again about the Word of God and the Word which became flesh, and words which either participate in some way in the Word, words of the second or third rank next to the Word who is before all things, words thought, on the one hand, to be words, but which are not truly words, if I may speak in this way, words which are wholly irrational in this respect, even as in the case of those said to be gods which are not gods, one might substitute "gods which are not gods" for words which are irrational.[32]

(24) The God of the universe, therefore, is God of the elect[33] and, much more, of the Savior of the elect; then he is God of those who are truly gods, and, in general, he is God of the living and not of the dead.[34] And perhaps God the

---

30. Cf. Gn 1.26.
31. Cf. 1 Cor 8.5–6.
32. *Alogōn logōn.*
33. Cf. Rom 11.7.
34. Cf. Mt 22.32.

Word is God of those who place everything in him and think of him as Father.

(25) But the sun, moon, and stars, as some of our predecessors have related, were assigned to those who were not worthy that the God of gods be claimed to be their God.[35] They understood it in this way, moved by the words in Deuteronomy which go like this: "Lest when you have lifted your eyes to heaven and have seen the sun and the moon and all the host of heaven, you be deceived and adore them and serve them, which the Lord your God assigned to all the nations. But the Lord your God did not give them thus to you."[36]

(26) For how did God assign the sun, moon, and all the host of heaven to all the nations when he had not given them to Israel in this way? He did it so that those who are not able to rise to the spiritual nature, being moved concerning deity by gods perceived by the senses, might stand contentedly in these and not fall to idols and demons.

(27) Some, therefore, have the God of the universe as God. Others, second after these, take their stand still on the Son of God, his annointed. And others, in third rank, have the sun, moon, and all the host of heaven. These have wandered from God, but their wandering differs greatly from, and is better than, those who give the name of gods to the works of men's hands, gold and silver, and the inventions of art.[37] And those are last who devote themselves to things said to be gods, but which are in no way gods.

(28) So, then, some participate in the Word "in the beginning" himself, even the Word "with God" and "God" the Word,[38] as Osee and Isaias and Jeremias and any other who has proven himself to be such that "the Word of the Lord"[39] or "the Word"[40] has come to him.

(29) But second are those who have known nothing "except

---

35. Cf. Clement, *Strom.* 6.14.110.
36. Cf. Dt 4.19 and 20. Preuschen includes the last statement in the quotation. It is, however, quite different from the LXX text of Dt 4.20.
37. Cf. Ps 113.12 (LXX).   38. Cf. Jn 1.1.
39. Cf. Hos 1.1.   40. Cf. Is 2.1; Jer 14.1.

Jesus Christ and him crucified,"[41] having supposed that the Word which became flesh was the totality of the Word, who know Christ only according to the flesh.[42] Such is the multitude of those who are considered to have believed.

(30) And third are those who have devoted themselves to words[43] which participate in some way in *the* Word,[44] supposing that they transcend every word. And these, perhaps, are those who follow the popular and prevailing schools in philosophy among the Greeks.

(31) And fourth, besides these, are those who have believed in words[45] which are altogether corrupt and godless, which do away with providence which is self-evident and more or less perceptible to the senses, and which approve some other goal than the good.[46]

(32) Although we seem to have digressed, I think that it is relevant that we have made this point so we can see clearly that there are four orders in relation to the noun "God," and four in relation to "Word." There was "*the* God" and "God," then "gods" in two senses. "God the Word" transcends the higher order of these gods, himself being transcended by "*the* God" of the universe. And again there was "*the* Word," and perhaps also "Word," comparable to "*the* God" and "God," and "the words" in two senses. And as for men,[47] some belong to the Father, being his portions, and similar to these are those whom our discourse just now presented more clearly, who have previously come to the Savior and have placed everything in him. And those previously mentioned are third, who suppose the sun, moon, and stars to be gods and who take their stand on them. But in addition to all these also in the region below are those who are addicted to idols which are soulless and dead.

41. 1 Cor 2.2.
42. Cf. 2 Cor 5.16.
43. *Logois*.
44. *Tou logou*.
45. *Logois*.
46. These were the common charges leveled at the Epicureans. Blanc, SC 120.226, notes that they were sometimes also applied to the followers of Aristotle.
47. Accepting *anthrōpoi* with Lommatzsch, Brooke, and Blanc. Preuschen has *anthrōpinoi*.

(33) But we find an analogy also in these concerning the Word. For some have been ruled by the Word himself, others by something similar to him and appearing to be with the first Word himself. These are those who have known nothing "except Jesus Christ and him crucified,"[48] who see the Word as flesh. And third, there are those whom we mentioned a little earlier. But why should I speak of those who are considered to be in the Word, but who have fallen away, not only from the good itself, but also from the traces of those who share in it?

The same was in the beginning with God.

Recapitulation of that which precedes

(34) After the evangelist has taught us the three orders through the three propositions which were previously mentioned, he sums up the three under one head, saying, "The same was in the beginning with God."[49]

(35) Now we have learned from the three propositions first, in what the Word was, namely "in the beginning," and with whom he was, namely "with God," and who the Word was, namely "God."[50] It is as if, therefore, he indicates the previously mentioned God the Word by the expression "the same," and gathers the three, "In the beginning was the Word," and, "The Word was with God, and the Word was God,"[51] into a fourth proposition and says: "The same was in the beginning with God."[52]

The beginning is also the creation

(36) The expression "beginning," however, can be taken also with reference to the beginning of the cosmos. We learn through what is said that the Word was older than the things which were created from the beginning. For if "in the beginning God made heaven and earth,"[53] but the expression, "was

---

48. 1 Cor 2.2.
50. Cf. Jn 1.1.
52. Jn 1.2.
49. Jn 1.2.
51. Jn 1.1.
53. Gn 1.1.

in the beginning,"⁵⁴ is clearly older than what was made in the beginning, the Word is not only older than the firmament and dry land,⁵⁵ but also than heaven and earth.⁵⁶

There is only one "Word" in its proper sense

(37) Someone perhaps may ask with good reason why it was not said, "In the beginning was the Word" of God, "and the Word" of God "was with God and the Word" of God "was God."⁵⁷ But it follows that one who asks why it has not been written, "In the beginning was the Word of God," etc., is proposing that there are many words, and perhaps different kinds of words of which one is the Word of God, and another, let us say, is the word of angels, and another the word of men, and so for the remaining words.

(38) Now if the Word is like this, perhaps "wisdom" and "justice" are too. It is absurd, however, to think that several beings properly possess the title "Word," and "Wisdom," and "Justice."⁵⁸ And we will be compelled by a consideration of the concept of truth to admit that we must not seek more Words and Wisdoms and Justices in the proper sense.

(39) For every person imaginable would admit that the truth is one. For no one would dare say, in the case of it too, that the truth of God is one thing, and that of the angels is another, and that of men still another. For it belongs to the nature of beings⁵⁹ that the truth concerning each is one.

(40) Now if truth is one, it is clear that its elaboration and demonstration, which is wisdom, would reasonably be thought of as one, since everything considered wisdom would not properly be called wisdom if it did not possess the truth. And if truth is one and wisdom is one, the Word also, who an-

---

54. Jn 1.1.
55. Cf. Gn 1.6 and 9.
56. Cf. Gn 1.1.
57. Jn 1.1.
58. Origen appears to be using the principles of Stoic logic in this section. See *EP* 4:519, and note 21 above. The second inference schema of Chrysippus was, "If the first then the second; but not the second; therefore, not the first" (*EP* 4:519). Origen's reasoning is, (1) If there are several "Words," then (2) there may be several "wisdoms" and "justices." The second proposition is absurd, therefore, the first is false.
59. *Tōn ontōn*.

nounces the truth and wisdom simply and openly to those capable of apprehending it, would be one.[60]

(41) And we say these things, not to deny that the truth and wisdom and the Word are of God, but to show the advantage of the omission of the phrase "of God," and of not having written, "In the beginning was the Word of God."

The Word in the Apocalypse

(42) The same John, however, in the Apocalypse, also mentions him with the addition of the term *God* when he says, "And I saw heaven opened, and behold, a white horse; and he that sat upon him was called faithful and true, and he judges and fights with justice. And his eyes were as a flame of fire, and on his head were many diadems, and he had a name written, which no one knows but himself. And he was clothed with a garment sprinkled with blood; and his name was called 'The Word of God.' And his armies in heaven followed him on white horses clothed in pure fine linen. And a sharp sword proceeds from his mouth, that he may strike the nations with it, and he will rule them with an iron rod; and he treads the winepress of the fierceness of the wrath of God the Almighty. And he has a name written on his garment and on his thigh: 'The king of kings and Lord of lords.'"[61]

(43) Now of necessity he has been said to be the Word both without qualification and with the addition, "Word of God." If one of these were omitted we would have grounds to misunderstand and fall away from the truth concerning the

60. The principles of Stoic logic appear again (see note 58 above) to be the basis of Origen's reasoning in section 40. Chrysippus' first inference schema was, "If the first then the second; but the first; therefore, the second" (*EP* 4:519). Origen's reasoning is, (1) If the truth is one, then (2) the Word must be one. The truth is obviously one, therefore the Word is one. He has shown, therefore, in sections 38–40 that one must not think that there is more than one Word, by using the first two inference schemata of Chrysippus. It should also be noted that Origen developed this whole section on the basis of what the Bible did *not* say. C. W. MacLeod, "Allegory and Mysticism in Origen and Gregory of Nyssa," *JThS*, n.s. 22 (1971), 374, notes that this is a technique of Gregory of Nyssa in developing "his theology of divine infinity." Perhaps Gregory learned it from Origen.
61. Cf. Rv 19.11–16.

Word. For if "Word" had been recorded, but "Word of God" had not been mentioned, we would not learn clearly that this Word is the "Word of God."

(44) And again, in turn, if he were called "Word of God" but not said to be "Word" without qualification, we might imagine that there are many words so far as the category pertains to each of the rational beings, and we might falsely accept that many are properly so named.

(45) Nevertheless the Apostle and Evangelist—but also now a prophet in addition through the Apocalypse—says correctly, as he describes the things concerning the Word of God in the Apocalypse, that he saw the Word of God riding on a white horse in the opened heaven.[62]

(46) But to advance even more in understanding the matters pertaining to the "Word of God," we must contemplate what is suggested in the heaven being opened, the white horse, and the fact that the one called the Word of God, who, in addition to being the Word of God, is also said to be faithful and true, and one who judges and fights with justice, is seated on the white horse.

(47) Now I think that heaven has been closed to those who are impious and who bear "the image of the earthly," but opened to those who are just and who have been adorned with "the image of the heavenly."[63] For the higher things have been closed to the first group, inasmuch as they are below and are still in the flesh, because they cannot understand them nor their beauty, for they do not wish to perceive them, in that they are stooped over and do not devote themselves to lifting up their heads. But he opened the heavenly places with the key of David[64] to be contemplated by the superior group, inasmuch as they have citizenship in heaven.[65] The divine Word opens them and explains them by riding a horse. The horse is the words which proclaim the meanings.[66] He is white

---

62. Cf. Rv 19.11.
63. Cf. 1 Cor 15.49.
64. Cf. Rv 3.7.
65. Cf. Phil 3.20.
66. Cf. Origen, *Comm. Jn.* 1.278–279. The word rendered "words" here and in section 48 is *phōnais*. The same word appears in the singular in 1.278–279, where I have translated it "speech."

because the nature of the knowledge is remarkable and white and luminous.

(48) And he who is called "faithful" sits on the white horse,[67] seated more firmly and, if I may so speak, royally, on words which cannot be overturned, words which run faster and swifter than any horse, and which surpass every opponent in their rush, that is, every supposed word which is a dissembler of the Word, and every dissembler of truth which seems to be truth.

(49) But he who is on the white horse is called "faithful," not so much because he trusts, as because he is trustworthy, that is, he is worthy of being trusted, for according to Moses, the Lord is faithful and true.[68] For he is also true in contradistinction to a shadow and a type, and an image, since the Word in the opened heaven is such. For the Word on earth is not like the Word in heaven, inasmuch as he has become flesh and is expressed by means of a shadow and types and images.[69]

(50) And the multitudes of those who are considered to have believed are instructed by the shadow of the Word and not by the true Word of God who is in the opened heaven. For this reason Jeremias says, "The breath of our person, Christ the Lord, of whom we said, 'In his shadow we shall live among the Gentiles.'"[70]

(51) This Word of God, indeed, who is called faithful is also called true, and he judges and fights with justice. He has received the ability from God to impart what each creature deserves and to judge with absolute justice and judgment.

(52) For no one who participates in justice and the power to judge people will be able to receive the impressions of justice and of judging so completely in his own soul that he falls short of absolute justice and judgment in no way, just as a painter will not be able to give a share of all the unique features of what is being painted to his painting.

(53) For this reason, indeed, I think David says, "No one

67. Cf. Rv 19.11.   68. Cf. Dt 32.4.
69. The influence of Plato is obvious in this statement.
70. Cf. Lam 4.20.

living shall be justified before you."[71] For he did not say in general, "no man," or "no angel," but "no one living," because even if someone should partake of the life and completely repel mortality, not even in this way will he be able to be justified with you in a manner equal to the life. It is not possible that one who shares in the life, and for this reason is called living, has himself become life; and that one who shares in justice, and for this reason is called just, has been made equal to justice in every way.

(54) Now just as it is said that the task of the Word is to judge with justice, so also his task is said to be to fight with justice, that by thus fighting the soul's enemies with reason and justice, he may dwell in it and justify it when the irrational elements and injustice are destroyed. He casts out the hostile elements from that soul which, if I may speak in this way, has been taken captive by Christ for salvation.

(55) Now it is possible to see the war which the Word wages even better, when he, on the one hand, advocates the cause of truth but, on the other hand, he who is not the Word pretends to be the Word, and one who proclaims himself the truth when he is not the truth but a lie, declares that he is the truth.[72] For then the Word, having fully armed himself against the lie, "destroys it with the breath of his mouth, and annihilates it by the appearance of his presence."[73]

(56) And see if it is possible that these matters are presented in a spiritual sense by the apostle in the epistle to the Thessalonians. For what is it which is destroyed by the breath of Christ's mouth except the lie, since Christ is the Word, and Truth, and Wisdom? And what is it which is annihilated by the appearance of Christ's presence, when he is understood as Wisdom and Word, except everything which is announced to be wisdom, but is one of these things which God seizes "in their craftiness"?[74]

Further, John says most admirably in his statements about

71. Ps 142.2.
73. Cf. 2 Thes 2.8.
72. See above, section 48.
74. 1 Cor 3.19.

the Word mounted on the white horse also, "His eyes were as a flame of fire."[75]

(57) For as the flame is bright and at the same time illuminating, and further also has a nature that is fiery and consumes the more material elements, so the eyes of the Word, if I may speak in this way, with which he sees, and everyone who participates in him, destroy and obliterate the more material and gross elements of thoughts by grasping them by means of the spiritual powers inherent in him. Everything false, in any way whatsoever, has fled the subtlety and precision of the truth.

(58) And in a very orderly manner after [mentioning] the one who judges with justice and who fights in accordance with his just judgments, and next in order to the fighting, the one who enlightens, he adds that there are many diadems on his head. For if the lie were one and simple against which the Word who is "faithful and true"[76] prevailed, who received the crown when the lie was overcome, the Word who became master of God's opponents would also reasonably have been recorded to wear one diadem.

(59) But now, since the lies which profess the truth are many against which the Word has fought and is crowned, there are many diadems surrounding the head of him who has conquered them all. And also because he prevailed over each rebellious power, he put on many diadems for conquering.

(60) Next, after the diadems, he is recorded to have "a name written which no one knows except himself,"[77] for this living Word alone understands some things because of the natural inferiority in those who came into existence after him. None of them can contemplate all the things which he grasps. And perhaps also only those who share in the Word, in contradistinction to those who do not, know what the latter are missing.[78]

---

75. Rv 19.12.
76. Cf. Rv 19.11.
77. Rv 19.12.
78. Literally, "the things which do not come to the latter."

110   ORIGEN

(61) Now John does not see the Word of God mounted on a horse naked. He is clothed with a garment sprinkled with blood, since the Word who became flesh, and died because he became flesh, is invested with traces of that passion, since his blood also was poured forth upon the earth when the soldier pierced his side.[79] For, perhaps, even if in some way we attain the most sublime and highest contemplation of the Word and of the truth, we shall not forget completely that we were introduced to him by his coming in our body.

(62) All the hosts in heaven follow this Word of God.[80] They follow the Word who leads them, and imitate him in all things, especially in having mounted white horses like him, for all things are open to those who understand.[81] And just as "pain and grief and groaning fled"[82] at the end of things so, I think, obscurity and dismay fled when all the mysteries of God's wisdom burst forth with precision and clarity.

(63) And consider the white horses of those who follow the Word, clothed in "pure white linen."[83] [What does this mean] unless the linen garments, since linen comes from the earth, are types of the languages on earth in which the sounds have been clothed which indicate the realities in a pure manner? These matters indeed have been discussed rather fully from the Apocalypse which teaches about the Word of God, that we might understand the things about him more accurately.

The same was in the beginning with God.

The refrain "The same was in the beginning with God"

(64) The evangelist will seem to repeat himself to those who do not thoroughly understand the different propositions in what is proclaimed, saying nothing more in the statement,

79. Cf. Jn 19.34.   80. Cf. Rv 19.14.
81. Cf. Prv 8.9.   82. Is 35.10.
83. Cf. Rv 19.14. The participle, "clothed," is in agreement with "horses" rather than with "those who follow." The same is true in the longer quotation above in section 42. This peculiarity appears also in the text of codex Sinaiticus, a Greek text of the Bible from Egypt dated in the fourth century, which is one of the major witnesses to the text of the New Testament accepted today, and in a few other MSS.

"The same was in the beginning with God," than in, "And the Word was with God."[84]

(65) It must be observed, however, that in the one, "The Word was with God," we do not learn when or in what he "was with God."[85] This information is added in the fourth axiom, for there are four axioms here, which some call propositions,[86] the fourth of which is, "The same was in the beginning with God."[87]

(66) Now the statement, "The Word was with God," and the statement, "The same was" not simply with God, but when or in what he was with God, are not the same, for he says, "The same was in the beginning with God."[88] But also the reader who does not investigate very carefully will assume that the expression "the same," adduced in its demonstrative force, is applied to the Word or to God. His purpose will be to discover a common predicate[89] of the earlier propositions, both of the conception "Word," and "God," which occurs in the expression, "the same," that the demonstrative might gather the differences in conception into one.

(67) For the conception "Word" does not contain the conception "God," nor does the conception "God" contain that of "Word." But perhaps it sums up the three propositions in one, namely, "The same was in the beginning with God."[90] For insofar as "the Word was in the beginning,"[91] we had not learned that he was "with God," and insofar as the Word was "with God," we could not have known clearly that he was in the beginning with God, and insofar as "the Word was God," it could not be revealed that he was "in the beginning" nor that he was "with God."

(68) But in the statement, "The same was in the beginning

---

84. Jn 1.1 and 2.   85. Jn 1.1.
86. Origen may be referring to the Stoics in this parenthetical remark. See note 21 above, and Mates, *Stoic Logic* 132–133.
87. Jn 1.2.   88. Jn 1.1 and 2.
89. *Syllēpsin*. This term was used in rhetoric of "a figure by which a predicate belonging to one subject is attributed to several" (LSJ, s.v. Syllēpsin). This appears to be the way Origen is using the term here as he discusses the fourth proposition as a summing up of the preceding ones.
90. Jn 1.2.   91. Jn 1.1.

with God," the expression "the same" being considered with reference to the Word and God, and the phrase "in the beginning" being thus attached, and the phrase "with God" being added, nothing is lacking of the things in the three propositions which is not summed up when they are gathered into one.

(69) But consider if it is possible for us to learn two things in that "in the beginning" is mentioned twice. One is that "in the beginning was the Word," as if he were by himself, and not with anyone at all; the other being that "in the beginning" he "was with God." I think that it is not false to say of him that "he was in the beginning" and "in the beginning" he was "with God," neither being only "with God" since "he was" also "in the beginning," nor being only "in the beginning," and not being "with God," since "the same was in the beginning with God."[92]

All things were made through Him.
The Word, the instrumental cause

(70) The expression "through whom" never has the first position, but always the second, as in the Epistle to the Romans: "Paul," he says, "a servant of Christ Jesus, called to be an apostle, set apart for the gospel of God, which he announced before through his prophets in the holy Scriptures concerning his Son, who was born of the seed of David according to the flesh, who was predestined Son of God in power according to the spirit of holiness by the resurrection from the dead, Jesus Christ our Lord, through whom we have received grace and apostleship for the obedience of faith in all the nations for his name."[93]

(71) For God announced his gospel before through the prophets. The prophets were his servants, and had an understanding[94] of the "through whom." And again God gave Paul and the others "grace and apostleship for the obedience of

---

92. Jn 1.2.
94. *Logon.*
93. Rom 1.1–5.

faith in all the nations,"[95] and he gave it through Christ Jesus, the Savior, who had the "through whom."

(72) And in the Epistle to the Hebrews the same Paul says: "At the end of days he has spoken to us in a Son whom he has appointed heir of all things, through whom also he made the worlds,"[96] teaching us that God has made the worlds through the son since the only begotten had the "through whom" when the worlds were made. So here too, therefore, if all things were made through the Word, they were not made by [97] the Word, but by one better and greater than the Word. And who would this other one be except the Father?

The Holy Spirit

(73) But if it is true that "all things were made through him,"[98] we must investigate if the Holy Spirit, too, was made through him. I think that one who declares that he was made and who advances the statement, "All things were made through him,"[99] must accept that the Holy Spirit too was made through the Word, since the Word is older than he. But it follows that one who does not wish the Holy Spirit to have been made through the Christ, if he judges the things in this Gospel to be true, says he is "unbegotten."

(74) But there will be a third person also besides these two, I mean besides the one who accepts that the Holy Spirit was made through the Word, and the one who supposes him to be unbegotten. This third person teaches that the Holy Spirit has no distinctive essence different from the Father and the Son. But he may perhaps propose rather, if he thinks the Son is different from the Father, that the Spirit is the same with the Father, since a commonly acknowledged distinction between the Holy Spirit and the Son is revealed in the statement, "Whoever speaks a word against the Son of man shall

---

95. Rom 1.5.
96. Cf. Heb 1.2.
97. Here Origen switches from the preposition *dia* (through) which usually expresses instrumentality, to the preposition *hypo* (by), which expresses the personal agent. The significance of this distinction lies in his debate with Heracleon, which is set out explicitly below in sections 102–104. See, in particular, footnote 135 below.
98. Jn 1.3.
99. Ibid.

be forgiven, but whoever blasphemes the Holy Spirit will not have forgiveness in this world or in the world to come."[100]

(75) We, however, are persuaded that there are three hypostases, the Father, the Son, and the Holy Spirit, and we believe that only the Father is unbegotten. We admit, as more pious and as true, that the Holy Spirit is the most honored of all things made through the Word, and that he is [first] in rank of all the things which have been made by the Father through Christ.

(76) Perhaps this is the reason the Spirit too is not called son of God, since the only begotten alone is by nature a son from the beginning. The Holy Spirit seems to have need of the Son ministering to his hypostasis, not only for it to exist, but also for it to be wise, and rational, and just, and whatever other thing we ought to understand it to be by participation in the aspects of Christ which we mentioned previously.

(77) I think, if I may put it this way, that the Holy Spirit supplies the material of the gifts from God to those who are called saints thanks to him and because of participation in him. This material of the gifts which I mentioned is made effective from God; it is administered by Christ; but it subsists in accordance with the Holy Spirit.

(78) Paul moves me to assume that these things are this way when he writes somewhere of gifts as follows: "Now there are diversities of gifts, but the same Spirit; and there are diversities of ministries, and the same Lord; and there are diversities of operations, and it is the same God who works all in all."[101]

(79) There is an additional problem, however, both because of the statement, "All things were made through him,"[102] and the consequence that the Spirit, having an origin, has been made through the Word. How is the Spirit honored, as it were, above the Christ in some Scriptures? In Isaias, Christ admits that he has not been sent by the Father alone, but also by the Holy Spirit (for he says, "And now the Lord has sent

---

100. Cf. Mt 12.32; Mk 3.29.   101. Cf. 1 Cor 12.4–6.
102. Jn 1.3.

me, and his Spirit"¹⁰³). And in the gospel he proclaims forgiveness in the case of sin against himself, but declares of blasphemy against the Holy Spirit, that there will be no forgiveness for the one who speaks ill of him, not only "in this world," but not even "in the world to come."¹⁰⁴

(80) Perhaps it is not at all because the Holy Spirit is more honored than the Christ that there is no forgiveness for the one who has sinned against him,¹⁰⁵ but because all spiritual beings have a share in Christ, to whom pardon is given when they turn from their sins. But it is reasonable that there is no pardon for those who have been considered worthy of the Holy Spirit when, with such a great help toward the good, they still fall away and turn from the counsels of the Spirit which is in them.

(81) And if our Lord says, according to Isaias, that he has been sent by the Father and his Spirit,¹⁰⁶ it is possible even there to allege of the Spirit which sent the Christ, that he does not excel him in nature, but that the Savior was made less than him because of the plan of the incarnation of the Son of God which was taking place.

(82) But if [someone] takes offense when we say that the Savior was made less than the Holy Spirit when he became man, we must approach him from what is said in the Epistle to the Hebrews, when Paul also declared that Jesus was made less than angels because he suffered death. For he says, "But we see Jesus, who was made a little less than the angels because he suffered death, crowned with glory and honor."¹⁰⁷

(83) Or perhaps it is also possible to say that the creation (but also the human race), in order to be set free from the slavery of corruption,¹⁰⁸ was in need of an incarnate, blessed, and divine power which would also restore the things on earth to order. This activity fell, as it were, in some way to the

---

103. Cf. Is 48.16.   104. Cf. Mt 12.32.
105. Accepting Delarue's neuter *auto* with Blanc. Preuschen and Brooke both have the masculine *auton*. Origen has consistently used the neuter pronoun of the Spirit in this entire discussion of the Holy Spirit.
106. Cf. Is 48.16.   107. Heb 2.9.
108. Cf. Rom 8.21.

Holy Spirit. Since the Spirit cannot bear it, he sends forth the Savior because he alone is able to bear such a great conflict. And although it is the Father, as leader, who sends the Son, the Holy Spirit joins in sending him in advance,[109] promising to descend to the Son of God at the right time and to cooperate in the salvation of men.

(84) And this he has done when he lights upon the Savior in bodily form as a dove after his baptism, and remains and does not pass on.[110] Perhaps he would have passed on among men who cannot constantly bear his glory. Wherefore, in regard to his knowledge of who is the Christ, John indicates that it is not only the descent of the Spirit on Jesus, but in addition to the descent, it is the fact that he abides in him.

(85) For it is written that John said, "He who sent me to baptize said, 'He on whom you see the Spirit descending and remaining on him, he it is who baptizes with the Holy Spirit and with fire.'"[111] For he does not say, "He on whom you see the Spirit descending" only—perhaps he has also descended on others—but "descending and remaining on him."

(86) Now these things have been examined extensively because we have wished to see more clearly how, if all things were made through him, and the Spirit was made through the Word, the Spirit is one of the "all things" considered to be inferior to him through whom he was made, although some texts seem to draw us to the opposite views.

(87) But if someone accepts the Gospel according to the Hebrews, where the Savior himself says, "My mother, the Holy Spirit, took me just now by one of my hairs and carried me off to the great mountain Thabor,"[112] he will question how the "mother" of Christ can be "the Holy Spirit" which was made through the Word.

---

109. The text has two verbs here: "the Holy Spirit joins in sending him and joins in sending him in advance."

110. Cf. Lk 3.22; Jn 1.33.   111. Cf. Jn 1.33.

112. Origen quotes the same words in *Hom. Jer.* 15.4, but he does not identify the source there. On the *Gospel of the Hebrews* see E. Hennecke, *New Testament Apocrypha*, ed. W. Schneemelcher, R. McL. Wilson (Philadelphia: Westminster Press, 1963) 1. 158–165.

(88) But it is not difficult to interpret these words also as follows. If he who does "the will of the Father in heaven is" his "brother and sister and mother,"[113] and the expression "brother of Christ" is applicable, not only to the human race, but also to beings which are more divine than the human race, it will not be strange at all for the Holy Spirit to be his "mother," since every woman is called the "mother of Christ" because she does the will of the Father in heaven.

The attributes of Christ

(89) We must investigate these things further also in relation to the statement, "All things were made through him."[114] The Word is different from the life in aspect, and what was made in the Word "was life, and the life was the light of men."[115] Therefore, as all things were made through him, was the life too, which is "the light of men," and the other aspects of the Savior made through him, or must we understand the statement, "All things were made through him,"[116] to exclude the aspects which were in him? The latter seems better to me.

(90) For supposing that this may be allowed because the life was made the light of men, what must we say of wisdom which is conceived as preceding the Word? For that which is before[117] the Word has not been made through the Word, I presume. Consequently, apart from the things which are observed in Christ, all things have been made through the Word of God, since the Father made them in wisdom. For Scripture says, "You made all things in wisdom."[118] It does not say, "You made them through wisdom."

---

113. Cf. Mt 12.50.
114. Jn 1.3.
115. Jn 1.4.
116. Jn 1.3.
117. Preuschen prints *para ton logon* ("what is beyond the Word"), the emendation suggested by Wendland. Blanc and Brooke have *peri ton logon* ("what concerns the Word"). It seems to me that the problem raised by Origen in the preceding question demands the meaning "before the Word," which would be *pro tou logou*.
118. Ps 103.24.

118 ORIGEN

*Seeming superfluity of the phrase
"without him nothing was made"*

(91) Now let us see why the statement, "And without him nothing was made," is added.[119] Some may think it superfluous to subjoin "without him nothing was made" to "all things were made through him."[120] For if every conceivable thing has been made "through the Word," nothing has been made "without the Word." That all things have been made *through* the Word, however, does not now follow from the assertion that nothing has been made without the Word. For if nothing has been made without the Word, it is possible that not only have all things been made *through* the Word, but also that some things have been made *by* the Word.

Evil is "nothing" and was not created by God

(92) We must know, therefore, how the expression "all things" is to be understood, and how "nothing." For it is possible, if both expressions have not been made clear, to take it to mean that if all things were made through the Word, and evil and all the profusion of sin and wickedness belong to the "all things," that these too, were made through the Word. But this is a false conclusion. For, on the one hand, it is not surprising that all creatures have been made through the Word (we must also understand that of necessity the acts of bravery and all virtuous actions have been performed by the blessed through the Word), but this does not now follow also for acts of sin and falling away.

(93) Some, therefore, because evil is unsubstantial (for it neither was from the beginning nor will it be forever),[121] have understood these things to be the "nothing." And as certain Greeks say that the genus and species,[122] such as living being and man, belong to the category of "no things,"[123] so they have supposed "nothing" to be everything which has received

---

119. Jn 1.3.
120. Ibid.
121. Cf. Origen, *Princ.* 3.6.2.
122. *Genē* and *eidē*.
123. Cf. Plato, *Parmenides* 130 c.

its apparent constitution neither from God nor through the Word.

(94) Let us see if we can prove these things in a striking way from the Scriptures. So far as the meaning of "nothing" and "not being" are concerned, they will appear to be synonyms. "Not being" would be meant by "nothing," and "nothing" by "not being." The Apostle indeed appears to use the expression, "those things that are not," not for things which exist nowhere, but for things which are wicked, considering "those things that are not" to be things which are bad. For he says, "God called those things that are not as those that are."[124]

(95) And in Esther, according to the *Septuagint*, Mordochai calls Israel's enemies "those who are not," when he says, "Lord, do not hand your scepter over to those who are not."[125] We can also introduce how the wicked are called "those who are not" because of evil, from the name of God recorded in Exodus. "For the Lord said to Moses, 'He who is, this is my name.'"[126]

(96) Now according to us who boast that we belong to the Church, it is the good God who speaks these words. This is the same God the Savior honors when he says, "No one is good except the one God, the Father."[127] "The one who is good," therefore, is the same as "the one who is." But evil or wickedness is opposite to the good, and "not being" is opposite to "being." It follows that wickedness and evil are "not being."

(97) Perhaps it is this that deceived those who said the devil is not a creation of God. For insofar as he is the devil, he is not a creation of God, but to the extent that it falls to the devil "to be," being made, since there is no creator except our God, he is a creation of God. It is as if we should say also that a murderer is not a creation of God, while we do not annul the fact that *qua* man, he has been made by God.

(98) For when we assume that *qua* man he has received his

---

124. Cf. Rom 4.17.
125. Cf. Est 4, Chap. C. 22. (NAB).   126. Cf. Ex 3.14.
127. Cf. Mk 10.18; Lk 18.19.

being from God, we do not also assume that *qua* murderer he has received this from God. All, therefore, who share in "being"—and the saints share in it—would properly be called "those who are." But those who have turned away from sharing in "being" have, by having deprived themselves of "being," become "those who are not."

(99) Now we said before that "not being" and "nothing" are synonyms, and for this reason those "who are not" are "nothing," and all evil is "nothing," since it too is "not being." And evil, which is called "nothing" has been made without the Word, not being included in the "all things."[128] We have presented, therefore, to the best of our ability, what the "all things" are which have been made through the Word, and what that is which was made without him, and, because it never was, is also for this reason called "nothing."

Refutation of a theory of Heracleon

(100) Heracleon, who is said to be a disciple of Valentinus, in explaining the statement, "All things were made through him,"[129] has, in my opinion, violently and without proof understood "all things" to mean the cosmos and what is in it. At the same time, to suit his own purpose, he excludes from "all things," those things which exceed the world and the things in it. For he says: "Neither the aeon nor the things in the aeon have been made through the Word." He thinks these things were made before the Word. And he adopts a rather shameless attitude to the statement, "And without him nothing was made,"[130] because he does not respect the saying, "Add not to his words, lest he reprove you and you be a liar."[131] He adds to "nothing" the words, "of the things in the cosmos and in the creation."

(101) And since it is clear that his statements are exceedingly distorted and made contrary to manifest facts, if what is divine according to his way of thinking is excluded from the "all things," but those things which are utterly destroyed, as he thinks, are properly called "all things," we must not spend more time refuting statements which are obviously absurd. For example, when Scripture says, "Without him nothing was made," he adds, without warrant from Scripture, the words, "of the things in the cosmos and in the creation." Nor does he prove this with plausible argument, since he considers him-

128. Cf. Jn 1.3.
130. Ibid.
129. Jn 1.3.
131. Prv 30.6.

self worthy to be believed like the prophets or apostles who, in an authoritative manner and beyond criticism, left writings of salvation for their contemporaries and those who would come after themselves.

(102) Furthermore, he also understands "all things were made through him" in a peculiar way when he says, "The one who provided the creator with the cause for making the world, that is the Word, is not the one 'from whom,' or 'by whom,' but the one 'through whom', taking what has been written contrary to the customary usage of the phrase. For if the truth of things were as he understands it, it would have had to be written that all things have been made by the Word through the creator, and not contrariwise through the Word by the creator.

(103) We, on the one hand, by using the phrase "through whom" properly in its customary usage have not left our interpretation unattested. He, however, by not having supported his private understanding from the divine Scriptures, appears both to have suspected the truth and to have opposed it shamelessly. For he says, "The Word himself did not create as though under the impulse of another, that the phrase, 'through him,' should be understood in this way,[132] but another created under his impulse."

(104) But this is not the time to prove that the Creator did not become the servant of the Word and make the world, and to show that the Word became the servant of the creator and prepared the world. For according to the prophet David, "God spoke and they were made; he commanded and they were created."[133] For the uncreated God "commanded" the firstborn of all creation[134] and "they were created." This includes not only the cosmos and the things in it, but also all that remains, "whether thrones, or dominations, or principalities, or powers; for all things have been created through him and for him, and he is before all things."[135]

---

132. This clause appears to be an insertion by Origen into the statement by Heracleon.
133. Cf. Ps 148.5. 134. Cf. Col 1.15.
135. Cf. Col 1.16 and 17. There is a general agreement between what is said in this fragment from Heracleon and the teaching in the *Tripartite Tractate* (100.19ff.) from Nag Hammadi concerning the relationship between the Logos and the creator. Heracleon, Origen says, excludes from the "all things" of Jn 1.3 those things which are above the world which include the aeon and the things in the aeon. In the *Tripartite Tractate* it is said that the aeon (= the pleroma) and the things in the aeon (= the totalities or aeons) were not made through the Logos, but were produced prior to the Logos by the Father. The role of the Logos in creation in both this fragment of Heracleon and the *Tripartite Tractate* is limited to the material world. Origen also notes that Heracleon has the Logos higher than the creator, considering the Logos to be "the

Sin: the presence of the "Word" renders spiritual creatures accountable

(105) One thing more on the statement, "Without him nothing was made."[136] We must also not leave the explanation concerning evil unexamined, for even if it appear exceedingly incongruous, it does not seem to me to be entirely negligible. For we must inquire if evil too has been made through the Word, the Word[137] which is in each one now appropriately being understood since it too has originated in each one from the Word who was "in the beginning."[138]

(106) The Apostle, therefore, says, "Without the law sin was dead,"[139] and adds, "But when the commandment came, sin revived."[140] He is teaching in general that sin has no actuality before the law and the commandment. But how can[141] the Word be the law and commandment, and there be no sin if there is no law ("For sin is not imputed when there is no law"[142])? Again, there would be no sin if there were no Word ("For if I had not come," he says, "and spoken to them, they would not have sin"[143]).

(107) Every excuse is removed from the one who wishes to defend his own sin, when he does not obey the word which is in him and shows him what he must do. Perhaps, then, all things, including even the very bad, have been made through

---

one who provided the creator with the cause for making the world." If this were the case, Origen argues, Jn 1.3 should have said that "all things have been made by the Logos through the creator, and not contrariwise." This, in fact, is what the *Tripartite Tractate* teaches. There, the archon (i.e. the creator) is the agent or "hand" of the Logos in creation. The Logos is also referred to as "the cause of the things which have come into being" (114.7–8), as Heracleon presents him. See also the comments of G. Quispel and J. Zandee in *Tractatus Tripartitus* 1. 384–5.

136. Jn 1.3.
137. Origen continues to use *logos*, but probably in its sense of "reason."
138. Cf. Jn 1.1.   139. Cf. Rom 7.8.
140. Cf. Rom 7.9.
141. Preuschen regards the participle *echōn*, which he prints, to be corrupt. He notes Wendland's emendation: *ei eichen*. We have taken Blanc's conjecture: *echei*.
142. Cf. Rom 5.13.   143. Cf. Jn 15.22.

the Word, and "without him nothing was made,"[144] if we take "nothing" in its more straightforward sense.

(108) And we must not at all blame the Word, if "all things were made through him" and "without him nothing was made,"[145] just as we must not blame the teacher who has shown the student what he ought when the one who errs no longer has any ground for defense as though he were ignorant, because of the teacher's lessons. And this would be so especially if we were to understand the teacher to be inseparable from the student.

(109) For it is as if the Word which exists in the nature of rational beings is a teacher who is inseparable from the student. He always puts forward what must be done, even if we disobey his commands and give ourselves over to pleasures, and disregard his virtuous counsels. But just as we use the eye, which has been made our servant, for things which are better for us and for things which we ought not look at, and in the same way our hearing, when we listen to useless songs and forbidden rumors, so we insult the word which is in us and do not use it as we should. We commit transgression by means of this word which is in sinners for judgment and which, for this reason, judges the man who does not prefer it to all things.[146]

(110) Whence also Jesus says, "The word which I spoke will itself judge you."[147] This is the same as if he had taught, "I, the Word who am always resounding in you, will myself condemn you because you have no ground of defense left at all." This interpretation may, however, appear rather forced, because we have understood the Word who is "in the beginning" and is "with God,"[148] God, the Word, in one way, but we considered him in another way when we declared that the statement, "All things were made through him,"[149] had reference not only to the principal things created, but also to all things done by rational beings, without which Word we commit no sin.

144. Jn 1.3.
145. Ibid.
146. Cf. Jn 9.39.
147. Cf. Jn 12.48.
148. Cf. Jn 1.1.
149. Jn 1.3.

(111) We must also inquire if we must say that the word which is in us is also the same with the Word who is in the beginning, and who is with God, and who is God.[150] This is the case especially since the Apostle seems to teach that this word is not different from the Word who is in the beginning with God when he says, "Say not in your heart, 'Who will ascend into heaven?' that is, to bring Christ down, or, 'Who will descend into the deep?' that is, to bring Christ up from the dead. But what does the Scripture say? 'The word is very near you, in your mouth and in your heart.'"[151]

What was made [in] Him was life,
and the Life was the Light of men.

The Life

(112) The Greeks have certain teachings called paradoxes which they apply with some proof, or what appears to be proof, especially to the man they consider wise.[152] In these paradoxes they say that the wise man alone, and every wise man, is a priest. In addition, they say that the wise man alone, and every wise man, understands the service of God; and the wise man alone, and every wise man, is free because he has received the right of independent action from the divine law, and they define this right as the lawful power of decision.

(113) Why must we now speak of the so-called paradoxes? Because they need much diligent study, and what the Greeks proclaim in paradoxes needs to be compared with the meaning of the Scripture that we may be able to demonstrate that in some cases the word of piety agrees with them and in others, its meaning is opposite to what they say.

(114) Now we were reminded of these paradoxes in our investigation of the statement, "What was made in him was life,"[153] because if someone were to follow the Scripture he could show many such statements in the character of the par-

---

150. Cf. Jn 1.1. 151. Cf. Rom 10.6–8.
152. Cf. Cicero, *Paradoxa Stoicorum*, and especially Paradox 5.
153. Jn 1.4.

adoxes, as it were, and, if one must say it, which are more paradoxical than the statements made by the Greeks. For if we think of the Word in the beginning, the Word who is with God, the Word who is God,[154] perhaps we shall be able to say that he alone who participates in this Word, insofar as he is such, is "rational."[155] Consequently, we could also say that the saint alone is rational.

(115) Again, if we understand the life which was made in the Word, namely him who said, "I am the life,"[156] we will say that no one outside the faith in Christ is alive, [but] that all who are not living for God are dead. Their life is a life of sin and, for this reason, if I may put it this way, a life of death.

(116) But consider if the divine Scriptures do not present this in many places, where, for example, the Savior says, "Or have you not read what was said at the bush: 'I am the God of Abraham, and the God of Isaac, and the God of Jacob?' He is not the God of the dead, but of the living."[157] And, "In your sight no man living will be justified."[158] But which word must we attribute to God himself and which to the Savior? For it is disputed to which of the two the voice belongs which says in the prophets, "As I live, says the Lord."[159]

(117) Let us look first at the statement, "He is not God of the dead, but of the living,"[160] which can be equivalent to, "He is not God of sinners, but of saints." For it was a great gift to the patriarchs that God, instead of a name, applied the designation "their" to his own title "God,"[161] in accordance with which Paul also says, "Therefore God is not ashamed to be called their God."[162]

(118) He is God, therefore, of the fathers and of all the saints; one would not find it recorded anywhere that God is the God of any of the impious If, therefore, he is God of the saints and is said to be God of the living, the saints are living and the living are saints. There is neither a saint outside the

---

154. Cf. Jn 1.1.
155. *Logikos.*
156. Cf. Jn 11.25.
157. Cf. Mk 12.26–27; Ex 3.6.
158. Ps 142.2.
159. Nm 14.28; Ez 34.8.
160. Mk 12.27.
161. Cf. Ex 3.6.
162. Cf. Heb 11.16.

living, nor one called living only, who does not also have with his life the fact that he is also a saint.

(119) Now something similar to this can be seen in the statement, "I will please the Lord in the land of the living."[163] It is as if he said, "in the order of saints," or "in the place of the saints," since the state of being "well-pleasing" in the proper sense is either in the order of the saints or in the place of the saints. No one yet has been completely well-pleasing who has not advanced into the order of the saints. Everyone will have to advance into this state who has previously taken up the shadow, as it were, and image of being truly well-pleasing in this life.

(120) And the statement, "But no one living will be justified before God,"[164] shows that none of the most blessed will be justified with God and with the righteousness in him. It is as if, to use another example, we were also to say something like this: No lamp will give light before the sun. On the one hand, every lamp will give light, but not when it is outshone by the sun. Now everyone living will also be justified, but not before God. They will, however, be justified when they are compared with those below, those who have been conquered by darkness, among whom their light will shine.

(121) And consider if we ought to understand what is said in the gospel in this way too: "Let your light shine before men."[165] It does not [say], "Let your light shine before God," for if he had commanded this, he would have given an impossible command. It would have been as if he had commanded those lights which are alive[166] to let their light shine before the sun.

(122) It is not, therefore, only the ordinary living people who will not be justified before God, but also those among the living who are superior. Or, what is better, the righteousness of all the living together will not be justified in comparison to the righteousness of God. It is as if one should gather all the nightly lights on earth and declare that these cannot give light in comparison to the rays of this sun.

163. Cf. Ps 114.9.
165. Mt 5.16.
164. Cf. Ps 142.2.
166. i.e., the stars.

(123) But to go on from what has been said, we must also consider the words, "As I live, says the Lord."[167] Perhaps living in the proper sense, especially on the basis of what has been said about living, occurs with God alone. And see if the apostle, because he considered the superiority of the life of God to be beyond comparison, and understood the words, "As I live says the Lord," in a manner worthy of God, can for this reason have said of God, "Who alone has immortality,"[168] because none of the living beings with God has the life which is absolutely unchangeable and immutable. And why are we uncertain about the remaining beings, when not even the Christ had the Father's immortality? For he tasted death for all.[169]

(124) At the same time, as we examine the things concerning the living God, and life, which the Christ is, and the things concerning living beings which are in their own region, and living beings which are not justified before God, by quoting, subsequent to these, the statement, "Who alone has immortality,"[170] we shall include in our account what we have assumed, that no rational being whatever possesses blessedness by nature as an inseparable attribute.

(125) For if one should possess blessedness as an inseparable attribute and preeminent life, how would that still be true which is said of God, "Who alone has immortality"?[171] We must know, however, that the Savior has some things not for himself, but for others, and that he has some things for himself and for others. And we must inquire if he has some things for himself and for no one else. It is clear that he is a "shepherd"[172] for others, since he receives no profit for himself from being a shepherd, as those do who are shepherds among men, unless indeed one reckons that the benefit those receive who are shepherded is his benefit because of his love for men.

(126) He is also a "way"[173] for others, and so too a "door,"[174]

---

167. Nm 14.28.
169. Cf. Heb 2.9.
171. Ibid.
173. Cf. Jn 14.6.
168. 1 Tm 6.16.
170. 1 Tm 6.16.
172. Cf. Jn 10.11 and 14.
174. Cf. Jn 10.7 and 9.

and a "rod,"[175] as all would agree. But he is "wisdom"[176] for himself and others, and perhaps this is true also of "Word."[177] And we must inquire, since there is a system of ideas in him insofar as he is "wisdom," if there are some ideas that are incomprehensible to all begotten nature except himself, which he knows for himself.

(127) We must not leave this matter unexamined because of reverence for the Holy Spirit. For that the Holy Spirit also is instructed by him is clear from what is said about the comforter and the Holy Spirit: "Because he will receive from me and will announce it to you."[178] Now we must inquire very carefully if the Spirit, by being instructed, contains all things which the son, who is from the beginning, knows by contemplating the Father.

(128) If, therefore, the Savior has some things for others and, perhaps, some things in some degree for himself and either for no one else, or for one or only a few, we must examine closely, insofar as he is "life"[179] which was made in the Word, whether he is life for himself and others, or for others, and [if] for others, for what others. If indeed "life" and "light of men" are the same—for the Scripture says, "What was made in him was life, and the life was the light of men,"[180]—and the light of men is the light of some, and not of all spiritual beings, but is the light "of men" insofar as[181] the light "of men" is specified, he would be also the life of those men of whom he is also the light. And, insofar as he is life, the Savior would be said to be life not for himself, but for those others of whom he is also the light.

(129) This life indeed comes into existence after the Word, being inseparable from him after it has come into existence. For the Word which purifies the soul must exist in the soul beforehand that, in accordance with this Word and the purification he produces, when all that is dead and weak has

---

175. Cf. Is 11.1.
176. Cf. 1 Cor 1.24 and 30.
177. Cf. Jn 1.1.
178. Jn 16.14.
179. Cf. Jn 1.4.
180. Jn 1.4.
181. Preuschen indicates that there is a textual corruption in the text at this point.

been removed, the pure life might come to be in everyone who has made himself capable of containing the Word insofar as he is God.

(130) We must observe the two occurrences of "in," and examine the difference between them. It occurs first in the statement, The "Word" was "in the beginning," and second in, The "life" was "in the Word."[182] The Word was not made "in the beginning," however, for there was no time when the beginning was without the Word, wherefore it is said, "In the beginning was the Word."[183] On the other hand, life was not in the Word, but life was made, if indeed "life is the light of men."[184] For when man did not yet exist, neither did the "light of men" since the light of men is understood in relationship with men.

(131) Now let no one censure us because he thinks we are describing these things in reference to time. The logical order demands a first, second, and following, even if no time be found when the things put forward by the argument as third and fourth did not exist at all. As, therefore, "all things *were made* through him," not, all things *were* through him, and, "without him nothing *was made*," not, without him nothing *was*, so "what *was made* in him," not what *was* in him, "was life."[185] And again, not what *was made* in the beginning was the Word, but what *was* in the beginning was the Word.

(132) Some copies, however, have, and perhaps not without credibility, "What was made in him is life."[186] Now if life is equivalent to the light of men, no one who is in darkness is alive, and no one who is alive is in darkness, but everyone who is alive is also in light, and everyone who is in light is alive. Consequently only the one who is alive, and everyone who is alive, is a son of light.[187] And he is a son of light whose works shine before men.[188]

182. Cf. Jn 1.1 and 4.   183. Jn 1.1.
184. Cf. Jn 1.4.
185. Cf. Jn 1.3 and 4.
186. Jn 1.3 and 4. This reading appears in codex Sinaiticus and in the Western text.
187. Cf. above, sections 112ff.
188. Cf. Mt 5.16.

The Light

(133) Again, since the opposites which have been passed over can be understood from what is said of their opposites, and the discussion is about the life and light of men, since death is the opposite to life, and the darkness of men to the light of men, it is possible to see that he who is in the darkness of men is in death, and he who does the works of death is nowhere else than in darkness. But he who is mindful of God, if indeed we understand what being mindful of him means, is not in death according to the saying, "He who is mindful of you is not in death."[189]

(134) But whether it is a question of the darkness of men or death, men are not such by nature, since Paul says,[190] "For we were once darkness, but now are light in the Lord,"[191] and this is especially the case if we are now called saints and spiritual men. Just as Paul, although he was darkness, became capable of becoming light in the Lord, so may anyone who was once darkness. I do not know, however, if the fact that the spiritual man was once darkness and later himself became light is maintained by those who think that there are spiritual natures, such as Paul and the holy apostles.

(135) For if the spiritual man was once darkness, what is

---

189. Ps 6.6.
190. Accepting Wendland's emendation, *Paulou legontos*. The text, which Preuschen says is corrupt, has *allou logon*. Blanc accepts Preuschen's suggestion, *allachou legontos*, in her translation. We reject this emendation for the following reasons: (1) It is easier to get from *Paulou* to *allou* than from *allachou*; (2) Origen mentions Paul's name four times in the next several lines in relation to this Scripture. The argument he advances, in fact, depends upon Paul making this statement of himself. The initial verb is second person plural in our biblical MSS rather than first person plural as Origen quotes it. The new 26th edition of the Nestle-Aland *Novum Testamentum Graece* gives no indication of textual variants here. It seems unlikely, however, that Origen would have consciously altered the text for his argument because an opponent could have erased the entire argument by pointing out that the biblical text did not say what Origen indicated it said. It is more likely either than Origen's text had the first person plural verb or that he remembered the text that way. However this may have been, the importance of Paul in relation to this Scripture strongly suggests that Origen would have first introduced it as being said by Paul.
191. Cf. Eph 5.8.

the earthly? And if it is true that darkness has become light, why cannot all darkness become light? For if it were not said in the case of Paul, "We were once in darkness, but are now lights in the Lord,"[192] but were said in the case of those natures which they think are perishing, that they were darkness, or are darkness, the hypothesis about natures would have a basis.

(136) But now Paul says that he was "once darkness, but now is light in the Lord,"[193] so it is possible for darkness to change into light. It is not difficult, however, for one who perceives the possibility of each man changing for the worse and for the better, on the basis of what has been said, to see perceptively the things concerning all human darkness and the death which is in the darkness of men.

(137) But when Heracleon came to the passage, "What was made in him was life,"[194] he took "in him" in a very forced manner to mean "in spiritual men," as though he thought the Word and spiritual men were the same, although he did not say this explicitly. And as if to give a reason, he says, "For he himself furnished their first form at their origin when he brought the things sown by another into form and illumination and their own individuality, and brought them forth."

(138) He did not, however, also observe carefully what Paul says about spirituals, namely that he left unsaid that they are men. "The natural man does not accept the things of the spirit of God, for they are foolishness to him. But the spiritual judges all things."[195] We say that it is no accident that he has not added the noun "man" in the case of the spiritual. For the spiritual is better than "man," since man is characterized either by soul or body or both of these together, but not also by spirit which is more divine than these. The spiritual receives this title in accordance with his predominate participation in the spirit.

(139) At the same time, however, the elements of such an hypothesis are declared without even an apparent proof, nor was he able to arrive at ordinary persuasiveness in his argument concerning these matters. Enough about Heracleon.

(140) But come, let us also examine this: Was the life the light of men only, and not of every creature whatever which experienced blessedness. For if "life" and "light of men" are

---

192. Ibid.
194. Jn 1.4.
193. Eph 5.8.
195. Cf. 1 Cor 2.14 and 15.

the same, and the light of the Christ belongs only to men, the life also belongs only to men. But this is to suppose something that is foolish and, at the same time, impious, since other Scriptures testify against this interpretation, if indeed, when we have advanced, we shall be equal to angels.[196]

(141) We must solve the difficulty before us as follows. If something is predicated of some things, what is predicated does not belong to them alone. So, therefore, if light is predicated of men, it is not the light of men alone. For it were possible to have added, "The life was the light of men 'alone.'"[197] For it is possible that the light of men is also the light of other creatures besides men, as it is possible that these same animals and plants which are the food of men are also the food of other creatures besides men.

(142) This example was drawn from common life; it is fitting to adduce a comparable one for comparison from the inspired words. Here, therefore, we are asking if anything prevents the light of men also being the light of other creatures. We assert that because light is predicated of men, this has not already precluded it also being the light of other creatures which are better than men or similar to men.

(143) God has been recorded indeed to be the God "of Abraham, and the God of Isaac, and the God of Jacob."[198] He indeed who wishes the light to belong to none other than men (because it is said, "The life was the light of men"[199]) will think, according to this analogy, that the God of Abraham, and the God of Isaac, and the God of Jacob, is the God of no one except these three fathers alone. But he is at least also the God of Elias,[200] and, as Judith says, the God of her father, Simeon,[201] and he is God of the Hebrews.[202] Wherefore, according to the analogy, if nothing prevents him from being the God of others also, nothing prevents the light of men from also being the light of other creatures besides men.

(144) But someone else, using the Scripture, "Let us make

---

196. Cf. Lk 20.36.
197. Cf. Jn 1.4.
198. Ex 3.6.
199. Jn 1.4.
200. Cf. 4 Kgs 2.14.
201. Cf. Jdt 9.2.
202. Cf. Ex 3.18; 5.3 and 17; 9.1 and 13; 10.3.

man according to our image and likeness,"²⁰³ will say that everything made "according to the image and likeness of God" is man, adducing countless examples on this subject because, in Scripture, there is no difference between saying man or angel. For the title "angel" and "man" is applied to the same subject, as in the case of the three entertained by Abraham, and the two who came to Sodom.²⁰⁴ In the whole sequence of Scripture, at one time they are said to be men and at another time angels.

(145) But the one who thinks this will say that just as there are angels among those who are admittedly men, as Zacharias, who says, "I am with you as an angel²⁰⁵ of God, says the Lord almighty,"²⁰⁶ and John, of whom it has been written, "Behold I send my angel before your face,"²⁰⁷ so also the angels of God, when they are called "men," are called this because of their work and not because of their nature.

(146) This view will be supported still further because, in the case of the higher powers, the names are not names of the natures of living beings, but of orders of which this or that spiritual nature has been prepared by God. For "throne" is not a form of a living being, nor is "principality," or "dominion," or "power,"²⁰⁸ but they are names of objects over which those thus named were appointed. Their substance is nothing other than man, and to this substance it has chanced to be a throne, or dominion, or principality, or power.

(147) But also the following statement is found in the book of Josue the son of Nun: "A man appeared to Josue in Jericho"²⁰⁹ who says, "I have now come as prince of the power of the Lord."²¹⁰

(148) According to this, therefore, the light of men and the light of every spiritual being will be understood as equivalent in meaning, since every spiritual being which is "according to

---

203. Cf. Gn 1.26. 204. Cf. Gn 18.2; 19.1; Heb 13.2.
205. *Angelos*, "angel," also means "messenger," and is usually so translated in the English versions of the verses Origen cites as examples.
206. Cf. Hg 1.13. Origen is incorrect when he attributes this saying to Zacharias.
207. Cf. Mk 1.2; Mal 3.1. 208. Cf. Eph 1.21.
209. Cf. Jos 5.13. 210. Jos 5.14.

the image and likeness"[211] of God is man. The same thing, however, has been named in a threefold manner: "light of men," and, in general, "light," and "true light." It is the light of men, therefore, either, as we have demonstrated earlier, because nothing prevents us from understanding the light to be the light of other creatures also besides man, or because all spiritual beings are called men because they have been made "according to the image of God."

(149) Now since the Savior here[212] is "light" in general, and in the catholic epistle of the same John, God is said to be light,[213] one thinks it is confirmed from that source too that the Father is not distinct from the son in essence. But another who has observed more accurately and speaks more soundly will say that the light which shines in the darkness and is not overcome by it,[214] and the light in which there is no darkness at all[215] are not the same.

(150) For the light which shines in the darkness comes upon the darkness, as it were, and, although pursued and, if I may so speak, plotted against by it, is not overcome. But the light in which there is no darkness neither shines in the darkness nor is pursued by it at all. Consequently it cannot be recorded to conquer by not being overcome by the darkness which pursues it.

(151) This light which is said to be "true light" was third.[216] Now to the extent that God, the Father of the truth, is more than, and greater than, the truth and, being the Father of wisdom, is greater than and surpasses wisdom, to this extent he transcends being "true light."

(152) We shall know in a more indicative manner that the Father and the Son are two lights through these words from David who says in Psalm 35, "In your light we shall see light."[217] But this light of men itself which shines in the darkness, the true light, is entitled "light of the world" later in the gospel when Jesus declares, "I am the light of the world."[218]

---

211. Cf. Gn 1.26.
212. i.e., in Jn 1.4.
213. Cf. 1 Jn 1.5.
214. Cf. Jn 1.5.
215. Cf. 1 Jn 1.5.
216. Cf. Jn 1.9.
217. Cf. Ps 35.10.
218. Jn 8.12.

COMMENTARY ON JOHN, BOOK 2   135

(153) And let us not fail to notice that while it could have been written, "What was made in him was the light of men, and the light of men was life," John has done the reverse. For he places "the life" before "the light of men," although "life" and "light of men" are the same. In the case of those who share in the life, which is also the light of men, we first encounter the fact that they live the previously mentioned divine life without having been enlightened, for life must be assumed, in order that the one who lives might become enlightened. It would not follow, however, that one not yet considered to be living has been enlightened and that life occurs because he has been enlightened.

(154) For although the life and the light of men are the same, the concepts, nevertheless, are understood in relation to different things. This "light of men" in fact is called also "light of the gentiles" by the prophet Isaias in his statement, "Behold I have set you for a covenant of the people, for a light of the gentiles."[219] And David, confident in this light, says in Psalm 26: "The Lord is my light and my Savior, whom shall I fear?"[220]

(155) It is not pointless, however, to raise these difficulties in reply to those who have invented the mythology concerning aeons in pairs,[221] and who think Word and Life have been produced by Intellect and Truth. For how does Life, the consort of the Word according to them, receive its origin in its consort? For Scripture says, "What was made in him" (that is to say in the previously mentioned Word) "was life."[222] Let them tell us, therefore, how Life, the consort of the Word, has been made in the Word, and how Life, rather than the Word, is the light of men.

(156) Those who are more reasonable, troubled in their investigations and struck by the difficulty, will probably ask us

---

219. Cf. Is 42.6.   220. Ps 26.1.
221. Origen is referring to the Gnostic pleroma which consisted of pairs of male and female deities. See Clement of Alexandria, *Excerpta ex Theodoto* 6; Irenaeus, *Adv. Haer.* 1.1.1; Hippolytus, *Philosoph.* 6.29; Tertullian, *Praescr.* 33.8; *Adv. Valent.* 7.
222. Jn 1.4.

in turn, since we too are afflicted by it, if we have not discovered a reason why the "Word" has not been said to be the "light of men," but the "life" which was made in the Word. To such people we reply as follows. The "life" mentioned there is not that common to rational and irrational beings. It is instead the life which is added to the Word which is completed in us when a share from the first Word is received. Accordingly as we have turned away from what seems to be life but in truth is not, and have yearned to possess life in truth, we first share in it. Once this life exists in us, it also becomes the foundation of the light of knowledge.

(157) And perhaps this life is light potentially and not actually with some who do not earnestly endeavor to examine the objects of knowledge, but with others it becomes light also in actuality. Now it is clear that Paul's command, "Be zealous for the better gifts,"[223] is realized with the latter group. But his command for all, which is the "word of wisdom" and the "word of knowledge" which follows it, is greater[224] than the gifts.[225] But this is not the time to speak of the difference in meaning between "wisdom" and "knowledge" which are adjacent to one another.

And the Light shines in the darkness, and the darkness did not overcome it.

Difference between the light and the shadows

(158) We are still investigating the light of men, since it has been proposed, and, I think, also its opposite which is called "darkness,"—I mean the "darkness of men"—which is examined together with it,[226] for perhaps the "light of men" is a general expression for two individual objects, and likewise also their darkness. For it is possible that one who possesses the light of men and shares in its rays performs the works of

---

223. Cf. 1 Cor 12.31.
224. Accepting Blanc's suggestion to read *meizon* instead of *meizona*.
225. Cf. 1 Cor 12.8.
226. Accepting Preuschen's suggestion to read *hama de touto* for *an de houtō*.

light and knows the light of knowledge[227] because he is enlightened. But we must consider also the analogous case of the opposites, both wicked deeds and the supposed knowledge which is not according to truth. These possess the principle[228] of darkness.

(159) The holy word knows that the ordinances are light, [for] Isaias says, "Because your ordinances are a light upon the earth,"[229] and David says in Psalm 18, "The commandment of the Lord is luminous, enlightening the eyes."[230] We find, however, in one of the twelve prophets that there is some light of knowledge besides the ordinances and commandments: "Sow righteousness for yourselves, eat the fruit of life, enlighten yourselves with the light of knowledge."[231]

(160) It is because there is also another light of knowledge besides the commandments that it is said, "Enlighten yourselves with light," specifying not simply "light," but what sort of light, namely that "of knowledge." For if every light with which man enlightens himself were the "light of knowledge," the statement, "Enlighten yourselves with the light of knowledge," would have been added to no purpose. Again, the same John teaches in the Epistle that darkness is assumed in the case of wicked works, when he declares, "If we say that we have fellowship with him, and walk in darkness, we lie, and do not do the truth."[232] Again he says, "He who says he is in the light, and hates his brother is in darkness even until now,"[233] and further, "He who hates his brother is in darkness and walks in darkness, and does not know where he goes because the darkness has blinded his eyes."[234]

(161) For to walk in darkness indicates blameworthy action; and to hate one's own brother is[235] to fall away from that which is properly called knowledge. But also because he who is ignorant of divine matters, by that very ignorance, walks in

---

227. Cf. Hos 10.12 (LXX). 228. *Logos*.
229. Is 26.9 (LXX). 230. Ps 18.9.
231. Hos 10.12 (LXX). 232. 1 Jn 1.6.
233. 1 Jn 2.9. 234. 1 Jn 2.11.
235. Omitting the negative *ou* with Preuschen. Blanc retains the negative, but treats the sentence as a question: "Does it not constitute . . . ?" which produces the same meaning.

darkness, David says, "They have not known or understood; they walk in darkness."²³⁶

(162) Now consider the statement, "God is light and there is no darkness in him."²³⁷ Is it not for this reason that darkness is not said to be a single entity? There are either two darknesses because of the genre, or there are many, none of which are in God, because there are many wicked actions in relation to each individual, and many false doctrines. It would not be said of the saint to whom the Savior says, "You are the light of the world,"²³⁸ that the saint is "light,"²³⁹ "and there is no darkness in him."

Difference between the light of the Father and that of the Son

(163) But if the statement, "There is no darkness in him,"²⁴⁰ has been applied to the Father, someone will ask how we will say there is something special in him, since we also think the Savior is completely sinless, so that we could also say of him, He "is light and there is no darkness in him."²⁴¹ We have set forth the distinction partially in our previous words. But we shall now more daringly add further to those words that if "him who knew no sin he made sin on behalf of us,"²⁴² that is the Christ,²⁴³ it could not be said of him, "There is no darkness in him."²⁴⁴ For if Jesus condemned sin "in the likeness of sinful flesh"²⁴⁵ by taking up the likeness of sinful flesh, it will no longer be completely accurate to say of him, "There is no darkness in him."²⁴⁶

(164) And we will add that "he himself took our infirmities and bore our diseases,"²⁴⁷ both the infirmities of the soul and the diseases of the hidden man of our heart.²⁴⁸ Because of

---

236. Ps 81.5.
237. 1 Jn 1.5.
238. Mt 5.14.
239. Omitting "of the world" with Preuschen.
240. Cf. 1 Jn 1.5.
241. Cf. 1 Jn 1.5.
242. 2 Cor 5.21.
243. Omitting, with Preuschen, the clause: "If God made him sin on behalf of us."
244. 1 Jn 1.5.
245. Rom 8.3.
246. 1 Jn 1.5.
247. Mt 8.17; Cf. Is 53.4.
248. Cf. 1 Pt 3.4.

these infirmities and diseases which he removed from us, he confesses that his soul is sorrowful and troubled.[249] It is recorded in Zacharias that he has put on filthy garments[250] which are said to be sins when he is about to remove them.[251] Therefore he adds there, "Behold I have taken away your sins."[252]

(165) It is because he took up the sins of the people who believe in him that he says in many ways, "Far from my salvation are the words of my sins,"[253] and, "You know my foolishness, and my offenses are not hidden from you."[254]

(166) But let no one suppose that we say these things impiously against God's annointed. For in the sense that the Father "alone has immortality,"[255] because our Lord, on account of his love for man, took up death on behalf of us, in the same sense the Father alone has the quality expressed in the statement, "There is no darkness in him,"[256] since the Christ, because of the benefit which follows for men, took our darknesses upon himself that by his power he might destroy our death,[257] and completely destroy the darkness in our soul, that what Isaias said might be fulfilled: "The people which sat in darkness have seen a great light."[258]

How the darkness invades the light

(167) This light, indeed, which was made in the Word, which also is life,[259] "shines in the darkness"[260] of our souls. It has come to stay where the world rulers of this darkness live[261] (who by wrestling with the human race struggle to subject those who do not stand firm in every manner to darkness), that, when they have been enlightened, they may be called sons of light. And this light shines in the darkness[262] and is pursued by it, but it is not overcome.

249. Cf. Mk 14.34; Jn 12.27.   250. Cf. Zec 3.3.
251. Cf. Zec 3.4.   252. Ibid.
253. Ps 21.2.   254. Ps 68.6.
255. Cf. 1 Tm 6.16.   256. 1 Jn 1.5.
257. Cf. 2 Tm 1.10.
258. Cf. Is 9.1 (and 2); Mt 4.16. Origen's quotation is almost verbatim with Mt 4.16. It differs considerably from Is 9.1 (and 2).
259. Cf. Jn 1.3 and 4.   260. Cf. Jn 1.5.
261. Cf. Eph 6.12.   262. Cf. Jn 1.5.

(168) Now if someone thinks we have added what has not been written, namely that the light is pursued by the darkness, let him understand that the statement, "The darkness did not overcome it,"[263] is made in vain if the darkness nowhere pursued the light. But John wrote the words, "The darkness did not overcome it,"[264] for those who have the intellectual capacity to understand the things that are commonly passed over subsequent to what has been written. For if it "did not overcome" it, it "did not overcome" it after it had pursued it.

(169) It is clear that the darkness pursued the light on the basis of the things which both the Savior and his own children who received his teaching suffered, since the darkness operated against the sons of light and wished to chase the light away from men. Since, however, if "God be for us" no one will be able to be "against us"[265] even if he wishes, the more they humbled themselves, the greater they became, and they grew extremely powerful.

(170) Now there are two ways that the darkness did not overcome the light. The darkness is either left very far behind it and, because it is slow, cannot keep up with the swiftness of the flight of light even to a limited extent, or, if perhaps the light wished to set an ambush for the darkness and awaited its approach according to its plan, when the darkness drew near the light it was destroyed. In either way, however, the darkness did not overcome the light.

The good shadows; the mystery by which God is enveloped

(171) But while we are occupied in these matters, we must observe that not every time something is named "darkness" is it taken in a bad sense; there are times when it has also been used in a good sense. It is because the heterodox did not make this distinction that they accepted the most irreverent doctrines concerning the creator and withdrew from him, and abandoned themselves to the fictions of myths. We must now point out, therefore, how and when the term darkness is understood in a good sense.

263. Jn 1.5.
264. Ibid.
265. Cf. Rom 8.31.

COMMENTARY ON JOHN, BOOK 2

(172) Darkness, storm clouds, and thunderstorms are said to surround God in Exodus, and in Psalm 17 it says, God "made darkness his hiding-place, his tent around him, dark water in the clouds of the air."[266] For if someone should perceive the mass of speculations about God, and the mass of knowledge which is incomprehensible to human nature, and to other creatures[267] too, perhaps, except Christ and the Holy Spirit, he will know how darkness surrounds God, insofar as we know no word rich enough to be worthy of him. "He made his hiding-place"[268] in this darkness when he ordained that the things which are infinite about himself be unknown.

(173) But if someone takes offense at such interpretations, let him be persuaded both from the dark sayings and the dark, hidden, invisible treasures given to Christ by God,[269] for we do not think that the dark treasures revealed in Christ ("God made darkness his own hiding-place"[270]) have any other meaning than, "The saint shall understand parable and dark saying."[271] Consider if it is for this reason that the Savior says to the disciples, "Because as much as you have heard in darkness speak in the light."[272]

(174) For he commands them, since they are enlightened and, for this reason said to be in the light, to proclaim the difficult and unclear mysteries which have been delivered to them in secret and in the hearing of only a few, to everyone who is made light. I might add more paradoxically in the case of the darkness which is being praised, that this darkness hastens to the light and overcomes it, and it sometimes happens that the darkness, because it is unknown, undergoes such a change for the one who does not perceive its meaning that he who has come to know it declares that what was once known to him as darkness has become light.

---

266. Ps 17.12.
267. *Genētois*. Ancient manuscripts frequently confused *genētos*, "created," and *gennētos*, "begotten" or "generated." Blanc, SC 120.323–5, seems to have taken it in the latter sense when she translates, "*tous les êtres qui . . . sont nés.*"
268. Cf. Ps 17.12. 269. Cf. Col 2.3.
270. Cf. Ps 17.12. 271. Cf. Prv 1.6.
272. Cf. Mt 10.27; Lk 12.3.

> There was a man sent from God,
> whose name was John.

The preexistence

(175) The more acute listener, on hearing the expression "was sent," will ask whence John was sent, and where, because one who has been sent is sent somewhere from somewhere. And since the "where" is clear according to the literal account, namely he was sent to Israel and to those who wished to hear him as he spent time in the wilderness of Judea and baptized at the Jordan river,[273] and according to the deeper meaning he was sent into the world ("world" being taken as the earthly place where there are men), he will examine how one ought to take the "whence." Perhaps, on further close examination of the text he declares also that just as it has been written of Adam,

(176) "And the Lord God sent him out of the paradise of pleasure to work the earth from which he was taken,"[274] so also John was sent, either from heaven, or from paradise, or from whatever other place there may be besides this place on earth, and he was sent "that he might give testimony of the light."[275]

(177) But there is an objection to this explanation which we must not neglect, since it is also written in Isaias, "Whom shall I send, and who will go to this people?", when the prophet answers and says, "Behold, here am I, send me."[276]

(178) The opponent to the implicit deeper sense will say that just as Isaias was sent, not from another place besides this world but, after he had seen "the Lord sitting on a throne high and elevated,"[277] he was sent to the people that he might say, "You shall certainly hear and not understand" etc.,[278] so also John, because the silence regarding the beginning of his mission is analogous to that of Isaias, is sent forth to baptize

---

273. Cf. Mt 3.1.5.
274. Gn 3.23.
275. Jn 1.7.
276. Is 6.8.
277. Is 6.1.
278. Is 6.9.

and to prepare "for the Lord a prepared people"[279] and to give testimony "of the light."[280]

(179) But should these things thus be said against our first explanation, solutions such as the following gain approval when they are brought to bear on the assumed deeper meaning about John. It is added from the very same passage, "This man came for a witness, to give testimony of the light."[281] Now if he came, he came from somewhere. And we must say to him who has difficulty accepting our view what John said in the following verses in reference to having seen the Holy Spirit descending like a dove on the Savior[282] (for he says, "He who sent me to baptize with water, said to me, 'He on whom you see the spirit descending and remaining on him, he is the one who baptizes with the Holy Spirit and fire'[283]"). When did he send him and give him this command? The answer likely to be given to this question is that whenever he sent him to begin baptizing, then he who issued him orders spoke this word.

(180) The fact, however, that John was filled with the Holy Spirit while he was still in his mother's womb is an even more striking argument for John to have been sent from some other region when he was placed in a body with no other purpose for his sojourn in life than his testimony to the light.[284] Gabriel mentions that John was filled with the Spirit while still in his mother's womb when he announces the birth of John to Zachary,[285] when he announces the sojourn of our Savior among men to Mary,[286] and in the statement: "For behold as soon as the voice of your greeting sounded in my ears, the infant in my womb leaped for joy."[287]

(181) He who is careful to do nothing unjustly, or by chance or caprice, must admit that John's soul, being older than his body and subsisting prior to it, was sent to the ministry of

---

279. Lk 1.17.
280. Jn 1.7.
281. Ibid.
282. Cf. Jn 1.32.
283. Cf. Jn 1.33. "And fire" appears in the New Testament MS. C and in Mt 3.11.
284. Cf. Jn 1.7.
285. Cf. Lk 1.15.
286. Cf. Lk 1.35–36.
287. Cf. Lk 1.44.

testimony concerning the light.[288] And in addition, one must also not despise the statement, "He is Elias who is to come."[289]

(182) Now if the general theory concerning the soul prevails, that is, that it has not been sown with the body but exists before it and for various reasons is clothed with flesh and blood, the expression "sent by God"[290] will no longer seem to be exceptional when it is used of John. According to Paul, the worst man of all in effect, "the man of sin, the son of perdition,"[291] has been sent by God, for he says, "Therefore God is sending them the operation of error that they might believe falsehood, that all who have not believed the truth, but have consented to iniquity may be judged."[292]

(183) But see if we shall be able to solve the problem in this way. Every man, in a very general sense, is a man of God by having been created by God. Every man, however, is not called a "[man] of God," but only the one who is devoted to God (as Elias and the men of God recorded in the Scriptures). In the same way, every man can, in the more general sense, have been sent from God but, properly speaking, only the one who appears in life for the divine ministry and service of salvation of the human race can be said to have been sent by God.

(184) We do not find, therefore, the expression "to be sent from God" to be used of anyone other than the saints. It occurs in the case of Isaias, as we stated previously; and in the case of Jeremias, "You shall go to all that I shall send you";[293] and in the case of Ezechiel, "Behold I am sending you to nations which have rebelled and are rebellious against me."[294]

(185) These examples, however, of being sent forth into life which we are investigating will not appear to have direct reference to the problem before us, since they do not speak baldly of being sent forth from outside of life into life. There is some

---

288. Origen believed that souls existed prior to bodies. See *Princ.* 1.8.4; cf. also our note below on section 192. This was a Platonic doctrine (see Plato, *Rep.* 10.617–619e).
289. Mt 11.14.
290. Cf. Jn 1.6.
291. Cf. 2 Thes 2.3.
292. 2 Thes 2.11–12.
293. Jer 1.7.
294. Cf. Ez 2.3.

power in the argument, however, when we apply it to our question in the following manner. Just as God is said to send only the saints, whose examples we supplied, so we must admit this to be the case also of those who are sent into life.

(186) Since we are investigating John's mission in general in our discourse concerning him, it will be appropriate for us to add our own opinion about him. For since we have read the following prophecy about him, "Behold I send my angel before your face, who shall prepare your way before you,"[295] we wonder whether one of the holy angels is sent down for service as forerunner of our Savior.

(187) It is not strange, if the firstborn of all creation[296] assumed a body in accordance with his love for humanity, that there were emulators and imitators of Christ, who desired to minister to his goodness to men through a body like his. And who is not moved when John leaps for joy while he is still in the womb,[297] as though he surpasses the common nature of men?

(188) But if someone also accepts the apocryphal document in circulation among the Hebrews entitled *The Prayer of Joseph,* he will find this doctrine stated outright and clearly there, namely that those who, from the beginning, possessed something superior to men, being much better than the other souls, have descended to human nature from being angels.[298]

(189) Jacob, at least, says, "For I who speak to you am Jacob and Israel, an angel of God and a primal spirit, and Abraham and Isaac were created before any work. But I am Jacob, he who was called Jacob by men, but my name is Israel, he who was called Israel by God, a man who sees God because I am the firstborn of every living being which is given life by God."

(190) And he adds, "And when I was coming from Mesopotamia of Syria, Uriel, the angel of God came out and said,

---

295. Mt 11.10; cf. Mal 3.1.   296. Cf. Col 1.15.
297. Cf. Lk 1.44.
298. On *The Prayer of Joseph* see Emil Schürer. *The Literature of the Jewish People in the Time of Jesus,* tr. P. Christie and S. Taylor (New York: Schocken Books, 1972), 127–9. Origen, according to Schürer, is our main source of information about the document.

'I descended to the earth and dwelt among men,' and, 'I was called Jacob by name.' He was jealous, and fought with me, and wrestled with me,[299] saying that his name preceded my name and that of every angel. And I mentioned his name to him and how great he is among the sons of God: 'Are you not Uriel, my eighth, and I Israel, an archangel of the power of the Lord and chief of the captains of thousands among the sons of God? Am I not Israel, the first minister in the presence of God, and did I not invoke my God by his unquenchable name?'"

(191) For it is likely, if these words were, in fact, spoken by Jacob and have been recorded because of this, that also the statement, "He supplanted his brother in the womb,"[300] occurred in an intelligible manner. Now consider if the famous question about Jacob and Esau has a solution. When "they were not yet born nor had done anything good or bad, that the purpose of God might remain according to election, not of works, but of him who called, it was said, 'the older shall serve the younger.' As it is written, Jacob have I loved, but Esau have I hated. What, then, shall we say? Is there injustice with God? God forbid."[301]

(192) If we, then, do not pursue the works, prior to this life, how is it true that there is no injustice with God when the older serves the younger and is hated, before he has done things worthy of servitude and hatred?[302]

---

299. Cf. Gn 32.24 and 28.   300. Cf. Hos 12.3.
301. Cf. Rom 9.11–14. The MSS. repeat the quotation from the beginning through "it was said." Preuschen has correctly bracketed the repetition.
302. Cf. Origen, *Princ.* 2.9.1–8. Origen believed that God originally created pure spiritual beings without bodies. These beings were all equal, and all possessed free will. Because these beings chose to turn away from good to evil, they were then clothed with various kinds of bodies and set in the various ranks of beings, depending on the extent to which they turned away from the good. This same assumption was used to explain the diversity among human beings. Origen quotes the same passage of Scripture in *Princ.* 2.9.7 for the same reason. There he says that there is no injustice with God in regard to Jacob and Esau "provided we believe that by reason of his merits in some previous life Jacob had deserved to be loved by God to such an extent as to be worthy of being preferred to his brother" (tr. G. W. Butterworth, *Origen: On First Principles* [New York: Harper & Row, 1966], 135). The prob-

But we have digressed far enough by using the story about Jacob and invoking a writing that is worthy of consideration, that our argument about John might be more reliable, which affirms that although he was an angel according to the statement of Isaias, he assumed a body in order to bear testimony to the light. These things we have said about the man John.

*John the Baptist is the voice
which foretells the spoken word*

(193) Now we think that, just as sound and speech[303] differ in us, meaningless sound sometimes indeed being able to be brought forth without speech, and speech also being able to be proclaimed to the mind without sound, as when we meditate in ourselves, so John, who is like sound in relation to Christ who is speech, differs from the Savior who according to one aspect is speech.

(194) John himself suggests this view since he once said in answer to inquirers, "I am the voice[304] of one crying in the wilderness: 'Prepare the way of the Lord; make straight his paths.'"[305] And perhaps it is because Zachary disbelieved in the birth of the voice which makes known the Word of God that he loses his voice and regains it when the voice which is the forerunner of the Word is born.[306] For a voice must be listened to so that the mind can afterwards receive the word revealed by the voice.

(195) It is for this reason that John is also a little older than the Christ so far as his birth is concerned, for we receive our voice before our speech. But John also makes the Christ known,[307] for speech is presented by the voice. And the Christ is also baptized by John who confesses that he needs to be baptized by him,[308] for among men speech is purified by the

---

lem of the righteousness of God in relation to the diversity both among heavenly beings and men was pressed upon Origen by the Gnostics (*Princ.* 2.9.5).
 303. *Logos* is rendered "speech" in this paragraph, which is contrasted with *phōnē*, "sound" or "voice."
 304. *Phōnē*. Cf. note 303. 305. Cf. Mk 1.3; Jn 1.23.
 306. Cf. Lk 1.20 and 64.   307. Cf. Jn 1.29 and 36.
 308. Cf. Mt 3.13–14.

voice, although by nature speech purifies every significant sound. And, in general, when John makes the Christ known, man is making God and the incorporeal Savior known, and a voice is making the Word known.

The significance of the names Zachary, Elizabeth, and John

(196) Now as the precise meaning of names is useful in many cases, so it might also be useful in this passage to see what John and Zachary mean. For, indeed, as there is something worthy of concern in the giving of a name, the relatives want to call him Zachary. They are surprised when Elizabeth wants to name him John. And after Zachary writes, "His name shall be John"[309] he is freed from his wearisome silence.[310]

(197) We find, therefore, in the interpretation of names[311] the name "*Jōa*[n]" without the ending "*ēs*" substituted. We think that this is equivalent to "*Jōannēs*" since the New Testament has hellenized other Hebrew names too, having pronounced them in Greek style, as "*Jakōbus*" instead of "*Jacōb*," and "*Simōn*" instead of "*Symeōn*." Now "Zachary" is said to mean "memory," and "Elizabeth" "oath of my God," or "Sabbath of my God."[312]

(198) John was born as a "gift" from God indeed, from the "memory" concerning God related to the "oath" of our God concerning the Fathers, to prepare "for the Lord a prepared people,"[313] to bring about the completion of the old covenant which is the end of the Sabbath observance. For this reason he could not have been born from the "Sabbath of " our "god," since our Savior created the rest after the Sabbath in accordance with his rest in those who have become conformed to his death and, for this reason, also to his resurrection.[314]

---

309. Cf. Lk 1.63.
310. Cf. Lk 1.64.
311. Omitting *Jōannēs* with Preuschen.
312. For the interpretation of Zachary see Lagarde, *Onomastica*, 82.4, and Wutz *Onomastica* 129. For Elizabeth see Lagarde *Onomastica* 40.2, and Wutz *Onomastica* 40 and 378.
313. Lk 1.17.   314. Cf. Rom 6.5.

This man came for a witness, to give testimony
of the Light, that all might believe through him.

The prophets

(199) Some of the heterodox, who claim to believe in the Christ and do not accept that his sojourn was announced beforehand by the prophets because they invent another [God] besides the creator as the result of their beliefs, attempt to subvert the prophets' testimonies about Christ. They say that the Son of God does not need witnesses since he has what is worthy of belief both in the saving words filled with power which he proclaimed, and in his marvelous works which can immediately astound anyone at all.

(200) And they say, "If Moses has been believed because of his word and mighty works, and did not need any witnesses before him who announced him, and each of the prophets too was received by the people as sent from God, how is it not more so that he who excels Moses and the prophets can accomplish what he wills and benefit the human race without prophets testifying to the things about him?"

(201) They think, therefore, that it is redundant for him to be assumed to have been announced beforehand by prophets who busied themselves with this, as they would say, because they did not want those who believe in Christ to accept the newness of the deity, but wanted them to come to the same God about whom both Moses and the prophets taught before Jesus.

(202) One must say to them, then, that there are many grounds capable of producing faith. Sometimes some are not struck by one proof, but by another. Therefore, God has numerous inducements to present to men that they might accept that the God who is over all created things has become incarnate.

(203) It is possible, therefore, to see clearly some coming to admire the Christ on the basis of the prophetic predictions, struck with amazement at the word of so many prophets before him which established the place of his birth, the country

where he was raised, the power of his teaching, the working of marvelous miracles, and his suffering as a man which was brought to an end by his resurrection.

(204) And we must also consider that the prodigious miracles were able to summon those who lived at the time of the Lord to faith, but that they did not preserve their impressive nature after many years when, by this time, they were also supposed to be myths. For the prophecy which is now being examined with the miracles is more powerful for persuasion than the miracles which took place at that time, even preventing disbelief in them by those who investigate them.

(205) And it may be that the prophetic testimonies not only proclaim the Christ who will come, nor teach us this and nothing else, but that they teach much theology. It may be possible to learn about the relationship of the Father to the Son and of the Son to the Father through the things which the prophets announce about him, no less than from the apostles who describe the greatness of the Son of God.

(206) It is possible, if one dare, to say something like this even apart from these: there are witnesses of Christ who are honored by their witness concerning him, and who do not confer any favor on him at all by their witness concerning the Son of God, as all would admit concerning those who are called witnesses of Christ in this special sense.

(207) What is marvelous, then, if, just as many of the genuine disciples of Christ were honored to be witnesses of Christ, so the prophets who have apprehended him have received the gift from God to announce Christ in advance, teaching not only those after the sojourn of Christ what they must think about the Son of God, but also those in former generations?

(208) [For] just as he who has not known the Son now does not have the Father,[315] so also one must conceive the former situation. Wherefore "Abraham rejoiced that he might see the day of Christ, and he saw it and was glad."[316] He, therefore, who maintains that there is no need for the prophetic witness to Christ wishes to deprive the choir of prophets of their great-

---

315. Cf. 1 Jn 2.23.   316. Cf. Jn 8.56.

est gift. For what would prophecy, which is inspired by the Holy Spirit, have that is so great, if one exclude from it those matters related to the dispensation of our Lord?

(209) For as the religion of those who approach the God of the universe with knowledge[317] has been arranged through a mediator[318] and high priest[319] and advocate,[320] although it would falter should one go in to the Father without going through the door,[321] so also the religion of the ancients was holy and acceptable to God by its understanding of, and faith in, and expectation of Christ. For we have noticed that God confesses that he is a witness,[322] and declares the same thing about the Christ,[323] exhorting all to become imitators of himself and the Christ, insofar as they witness to the things to which it is necessary to witness. For he says, "Become my witnesses; I, too, am a witness, says the Lord God, and the servant whom I chose."[324]

The martyrs

(210) Now everyone who testifies to the truth, whether he presents his testimony in words or deeds or in whatever way, would correctly be called a "witness."[325] But it is already currently the custom of the brotherhood, since they have been amazed at the disposition of those who have struggled to death for truth or courage,[326] to give the name "witnesses" in a special sense only to those who have borne witness to the mystery of godliness[327] by the pouring out of their own blood, although the Savior gives the name "witness" to everyone who bears witness to the things proclaimed about himself.

(211) He says to the apostles, therefore, as he is being taken

---

317. Deleting the conjunction "and" (*kai*). Preuschen thinks the adverb, "with knowledge," is corrupt.
318. Cf. Gal 3.19 and 20.
319. Cf. Heb 7.26–28.
320. Cf. 1 Jn 2.1.
321. Cf. Jn 10.9.
322. Cf. Jer 49.5 (LXX).
323. Cf. Is 43.10.
324. Is 43.10.
325. *Martyr.*
326. Blanc conjectures that the text should read *hagneias*, "purity," instead of *andreias*, "courage."
327. Cf. 1 Tm 3.16.

up: "You shall be my witnesses in Jerusalem and in all Judea and Samaria and to the end of the earth."[328] And further, just as the leper who was cleansed brings the gift prescribed by Moses, doing this "for a testimony"[329] to those who did not believe in the Christ, so also the witnesses testify for a testimony to the unbelievers as do also all the saints whose works "shine before men."[330] For they live to speak boldly in the cross of Christ and to bear witness about the true light.

The six witnesses of John

(212) John too, therefore, came to bear witness concerning the light. He bore witness and "cried out saying," "He who comes after me ranks before me, because he was before me. We all received of his fullness, even grace for grace. For the law was given by Moses; grace and truth came by Jesus Christ. No one has ever seen God; the only begotten God who is in the bosom of the Father has declared him."[331]

(213) This whole speech, therefore, was from the mouth of the Baptist bearing witness to the Christ. This fact escapes the notice of some who think that the speech from the words, "We all received of his fullness" up to "he has declared him" was from the mouth of John the apostle.

(214) In addition to the testimony of the Baptist previously mentioned, which begins with the words, "He who comes after me ranks before me," and stops at "he declared," this testimony too is from John after that second one, when he confesses to those from Jerusalem who sent priests, and Levites (i.e. when the Jews sent them), and does not deny the truth that he himself is not the Christ, or Elias, or the prophet,[332] but "the voice of one crying in the wilderness, 'Make straight the way of the Lord,' as Isaias the prophet said."[333]

(215) After this there is another testimony of the same Baptist about Christ, which further teaches that his preeminent substance extends to all the world in relation to the rational souls, when he says, "He who comes after me has stood in

---

328. Acts 1.8.
330. Cf. Mt 5.16.
332. Cf. Jn 1.19–23.
329. Cf. Mt 8.4.
331. Cf. Jn 1.15–18.
333. Jn 1.23.

your midst, whom you did not know, the strap of whose sandal I am not worthy to loose."[334] And consider if the statement, "He whom you did not know has stood in your midst," can be understood in relation to the reason[335] in each person because the heart is in the midst of every body, and the ruling principle is in the heart.

(216) In addition to these words there is a fourth testimony of John concerning Christ which already alludes to his human suffering, when he says, "Behold the lamb of God who takes away the sin of the world. This is he of whom I said, 'After me comes a man who ranks before me, because he was before me. And I did not know him, but I came baptizing in water that he might be made manifest."[336]

(217) A fifth testimony has also been recorded in the words, "I saw the Spirit descending as a dove from heaven, and it remained upon him. And I did not know him, but he who sent me to baptize in water said to me: 'He on whom you see the Spirit descending and remaining on him, he is the one who baptizes in the Holy Spirit.[337] And I have seen, and I have borne witness that this is the Son of God."[338]

(218) John testifies to the Christ a sixth time to two disciples when he says, after he saw Jesus walking, "Behold, the lamb of God."[339] After this testimony, when the two disciples of John heard and followed Jesus, Jesus turned and saw the two following him and asks them, "What are you seeking?"[340]

The disciples of John seeking Christ and finding him

(219) Perhaps it is not without reason that John stops testifying after six testimonies, and in the seventh place Jesus proposes the question, "What are you seeking?"[341] The speech which addresses the Christ as teacher and confesses the desire

---

334. Cf. Jn 1.26 and 27.   335. *Logon*.
336. Cf. Jn 1.29–31.
337. Preuschen and Blanc mark a lacuna in the text after "Holy Spirit;" Brooke does not. Preuschen correctly notes that Origen usually adds "and with fire" to this verse from Mt 3.11 and Lk 3.16. Cf. above, section 179, note 283.
338. Jn 1.32–34.   339. Jn 1.36.
340. Jn 1.38.   341. Ibid.

to see the dwelling place of the Son of God is fitting for those who have been benefited by John's testimony, for they say to him, "Rabbi (which means, translated, 'Teacher'), where are you staying?"[342] And since "everyone who seeks finds,"[343] he shows John's disciples who asked about Jesus' dwelling, saying to them, "Come and see."[344] Perhaps through the term "come" he is appealing to them on the basis of the active life, and through "see" he subjoins that there will assuredly be contemplation subsequent to the successful completion of acts for those who wish it, contemplation which takes place in the dwelling of Jesus.

(220) Now it was reserved for those who asked where Jesus was staying, who followed the teacher, and saw, to remain with Jesus and to spend that day with the Son of God. And since the tenth number has been observed to be holy, no few mysteries being recorded to have occurred in the number ten, we must think that it is not without reason that in the gospel too the tenth hour is recorded as the time when John's disciples went down with Jesus.[345] Andrew, Simon Peter's brother, was one of these. After he had been benefitted because he remained with Jesus, he found his own brother Simon (for perhaps he had not found him before) and says that he has found the *Messiah*, which is, translated, 'Christ.'[346]

(221) For since "he who seeks finds,"[347] and Andrew sought where Jesus was staying, and after he followed and saw his dwelling, he remained with the Lord in the tenth hour and found the Son of God who is the Word and wisdom, and was ruled by him, for this reason he says, "We have found the Messiah."[348] Now this statement was to be made by everyone who found the Word of God and was ruled by his divinity.

(222) And immediately, as fruit, he introduces his brother to Christ. And Jesus looked favorably on Simon, which means to visit and enlighten his ruling principle by looking. And

342. Cf. Lk 11.10.
344. Jn 1.39.
345. Cf. Jn 1.39.
347. Cf. Lk 11.10.

343. Ibid.

346. Cf. Jn 1.41.
348. Jn 1.41.

because Jesus looked at him, Simon was able to become firm so that he was surnamed and called "Peter" on the basis of his steadfast and firm work.³⁴⁹

John, witness and precursor of the Light

(223) But someone will say, Why have we gone through all these things when it was proposed that we explain the statement, "This man came for a witness, to give testimony to the Light"?³⁵⁰ We must reply that we had to present the testimonies of John about the light and set forth their order and the subsequent benefit to those to whom he testified, which came from Jesus after John's testimony, that the accomplishment of John's testimony might be made manifest.

(224) But even before the testimonies here, the Baptist's leaping in joy in the womb of Elizabeth at Mary's greeting was a testimony about Christ.³⁵¹ He was testifying to the divinity of Christ's conception and birth. For what indeed is John, except everywhere a witness and forerunner of Jesus? He precedes his birth, and dies a little before the death of the Son of God, that, by appearing before the Christ not only to those in birth, but also to those awaiting freedom from death through Christ, he might everywhere prepare for the Lord a prepared people.³⁵² And John's testimony reaches even to Christ's second and more divine coming, for he says, "If you are willing to receive it, he is Elias who is to come. He who has ears to hear, let him hear."³⁵³

(225) Now since there was the beginning in which the Word was (which we proved from Proverbs to be Wisdom³⁵⁴), and since the Word also existed, and life was made in him, and the life was the light of men, I ask why the one who was a "man sent from God, whose name was John, came for a witness to give testimony of the light?"³⁵⁵

(226) Why, then, did he not come "to give testimony of the life," or "to give testimony of the Word," or "of the begin-

349. Cf. Jn 1.42.
351. Cf. Lk 1.44.
353. Cf. Mt 11.14–15.
355. Cf. Jn 1.6–7.
350. Jn 1.7.
352. Cf. Lk 1.17.
354. Cf. Prv 8.22.

ning," or of any other aspect of the Christ whatsoever? Consider if it is not [because] "the people who sat in darkness have seen a great light,"[356] and because "the light shines in the darkness" and is not overcome by it.[357] Those who are in darkness, that is men, need light.

(227) For if the light of men "shines in the darkness"[358]—there is no activity of darkness at all there—we shall share in other aspects of the Christ in which we do not now participate in the proper and accurate sense of the word. For how do we participate in life, who are still clothed with the body of death,[359] whose life "has been hidden with Christ in God"?[360] For "when the Christ, our life, is made manifest, then we too shall be made manifest with him in glory."[361]

(228) The one who came, therefore, could not testify concerning the life which is still hidden with Christ in God. But he did not even come for a witness to testify concerning the Word, if we have in mind the Word with God in the beginning, even the Word which was God, for "the Word became flesh"[362] on earth. His testimony, although it seemed to be concerning the Word, would have been properly called the testimony concerning the Word become flesh, and not the Word which was God. He did not, therefore, come to bear testimony concerning the Word.

(229) And how could there be testimony concerning wisdom to those who, even if they seem to know, do not contemplate the truth in purity but see "through a glass and in a dark manner"?[363] It is likely, however, that before the second and more divine sojourn of Christ shall come, John, or Elias, will be made manifest a little before the Christ, our life, to testify concerning life, and at that time he will testify concerning the Word, and will present his witness concerning wisdom. But we need to investigate if the testimony of John can serve as a

---

356. Mt 4.16; cf. Is 9.2.
358. Jn 1.5.
360. Col 3.3.
362. Jn 1.14.

357. Cf. Jn 1.5.
359. Cf. Rom 7.24.
361. Cf. Col 3.4.
363. Cf. 1 Cor 13.12.

forerunner for each of the aspects of the Christ. This is enough on the statement, "This man came for a witness, to give testimony to the Light."[364] We must consider next what we should understand in the clause, "That all might believe through him."[365]

364. Jn 1.7. 365. Ibid.

BOOK 4

On the Solecisms and Simple Expression of Scripture[1]
(Three pages from the beginning)

HE WHO DISTINGUISHES for himself between the expression, the concepts, and the realities to which the concepts refer, will not take offense at the incorrect use of expressions when he searches and finds that the realities of which the phrases are used are sound. This is especially so when the saints confess that their word and message are "not in the persuasiveness of words of wisdom,[2] but in the demonstration of the Spirit and power."[3]

(Then after speaking of the awkwardness of the Gospel style, he proceeds.)

(2) But because the apostles are aware of those things in which they give offense and the things about which they have not occupied themselves, they say that they are rude "in speech, but not in knowledge."[4] For we must suppose that that was said not only by Paul but also by the rest of the apostles.

---

1. This fragment is preserved in the *Philocalia*, 4. For the most recent critical text of this and the next fragment, along with a French translation and commentary see M. Harl and N. De Lange, *Origène: Philocalie, 1–20*, SC 302.269–305 (1983).

2. *En peithois sophias logōn*. Blanc says that Origen's version is found in a part of the manuscript tradition of 1 Cor 2.4. I, however, can find no manuscript attestation for the text as Origen has it, unless we accept the variant reading Preuschen lists from D (Blanc's text does not even record this variant). D has *peithoi* for *peithois*. This would then agree with the biblical MS. 440, which has *pethoi sophias logōn*. This reading is preferable to what Preuschen has printed as the text, for the text as it stands, with the dative plural adjective *peithois*, needs *logōn* to be in the dative plural rather than the genitive plural.

3. Cf. 1 Cor 2.4.   4. 2 Cor 11.6.

We have also taken the following text in this way: "But we have this treasure in earthen vessels, that the excellency may be of the power of God and not of us,"[5] since "treasure" is used elsewhere of the treasure of knowledge and secret wisdom,[6] and "earthen vessels" of the text of the Scriptures which is simple and easily despised by Greeks, in which the excellency of God's power truly appears. For the mysteries of the truth, and the power of what is said which is not hindered by simple expression, were able to reach the ends of the earth,[7] and to subject not only the foolish things of the world to Christ's word, but sometimes also its wise.[8] For we see our calling, not that there is no one wise according to the flesh, but "that there are not many wise according to the flesh."[9]

But also Paul is a "debtor" when he proclaims the gospel, to deliver the word not only to "barbarians," but also "to Greeks"; and not only "to the foolish" who readily agree, but also "to the wise."[10] For God made him competent to be a "minister of the new testament,"[11] employing the "demonstration of the Spirit and power,"[12] that the assent of those who believe "might not be in the wisdom of men, but in the power of God."[13]

(3) For perhaps if Scripture possessed the beauty and ornament of expression that those works admired by the Greeks possess, someone might suppose that it is not the truth that has grasped men, but that the apparent logical order seen in it, and the beauty of expression have charmed the hearers, and, having deceived them, have taken possession of them.

5. 2 Cor 4.7.
6. Cf. Col 2.3.
7. Cf. Ps 18.5.
8. Cf. 1 Cor 1.26–27.
9. 1 Cor 1.26.
10. Cf. Rom 1.14.
11. Cf. 2 Cor 3.6.
12. 1 Cor 2.4.
13. 1 Cor 2.5.

BOOK 5

What Is the Multitude of Words and the Many Books? And, That All Inspired Scripture Is One Book[1]
(In the Preface)

SINCE YOU ARE NOT CONTENT to have assumed at present the task of God's overseers in relation to us, and you think it proper that while we are absent we devote most of our time to you and to what we owe you,[2] to avoid the toil and circumvent the danger announced by God to those who have devoted themselves to writing on divine subjects, I might take the advice of Scripture to decline to make many books. For Solomon says in Ecclesiastes, "My son, beware of making many books; there is no end, and much study is a weariness of the flesh."[3] For if the text before us did not have some meaning which is hidden and still unclear to us, we would have blatantly transgressed the command, because we have not been careful to avoid making many books.

(Then, after saying that he has completed four volumes on a few words of the gospel, he adds:)

(2) Now so far as the literal sense is concerned, two meanings can be derived from the command, "My son, beware of making many books."[4] One is that one ought not own many books; the other that one ought not compose many books. And if it is not the first, it is by all means the second; but if it is the second, it is by no means the former.[5] But either way

---

1. The fragment is preserved in Harl and De Lange, SC 302.284–298 (*Philocalia*, 5).
2. These remarks are addressed to Ambrose, Origen's patron, who urged him to compose a commentary on John's Gospel. Cf. *Comm. Jn.* 1.9.
3. Cf. Eccl 12.12.   4. Ibid.
5. This statement resembles the fourth and fifth inference schemata of Chrysippus. See *EP* 4.519.

we will appear to learn that we ought not make more books. We could take our stand on what has now occurred to us and send you the saying as an excuse and, having prepared a case from the fact that not even the saints had time for the composition of many books, we could cease dictating the books which are to be sent to you in accordance with the agreements which we made with one another for the future. You, perhaps, struck by the text, might yield to us for the future. But since we must examine the Scripture conscientiously, not hastily crediting ourselves with having grasped the meaning because we have understood the text in its literal sense, I do not dare not present the defense for myself which occurs to me, which you might use against me if I were to break our agreements.

We must address this issue in the first place because history seems to support the literal meaning. None of the saints has produced numerous compositions and set out his understanding in many books. And when I come to the composition of more books, my accuser will say that such a great man as Moses left only five books.

(From Eusebius, Church History *6.25.7–10)*
(And in the fifth volume of the Commentaries on the Gospel according to John
the same man says these things about the apostles.)

(3) Paul, who was made a competent minister of the new covenant, not in the letter, but in the spirit,[6] who completed preaching the gospel from Jerusalem, as far as Illyricum,[7] did not even write to all the churches which he taught. But even to those to which he wrote, he sent few lines. And Peter, on whom the Church of Christ is built, against which the gates of Hades shall not prevail,[8] has left behind one letter which is accepted. Perhaps there is also a second, but it is doubted. Why must I speak of John who leaned on Jesus' breast, who has left one Gospel while confessing that he could compose

6. Cf. 2 Cor 3.6. 7. Cf. Rom 15.19.
8. Cf. Mt 16.18.

so many that the world could not contain them?⁹ He also wrote the Apocalypse after he was commanded to be silent and not to record the sounds of the seven thunders,¹⁰ and an epistle of very few lines. There may also be a second and a third epistle, but not all say that these are genuine. Both, however, are not a hundred lines.

(Then after he has enumerated prophets and apostles, each having written few books or not even a few, he continues after these things.)

(4) Again, after making these remarks, I get dizzy as though I were suffering vertigo, lest perhaps by obeying you I have disobeyed God and have not imitated the saints. Unless I err, therefore, by justifying myself because I love you so much and wish to grieve you in nothing, I find the following defenses for these works.

First of all, we set forth the command from Ecclesiastes: "My son, beware of making many books."¹¹ I juxtapose for comparison with this the saying from the Proverbs of the same Solomon, who says, "In a multitude of words you will not escape sin, but you will be wise if you restrain your lips."¹² And I inquire, therefore, if speaking many words, regardless of what they are, is being loquacious, even if the many words are holy and pertain to salvation? For if this is the way things are, and if he who expounds many beneficial things is loquacious, Solomon himself has not escaped the sin, for he spoke "3000 parables and 5000 odes about the trees from the cedar which is in Libanus even to the hyssop that comes out through the wall; and further also about beasts, and birds, and creeping things, and fish."¹³

For how can teaching accomplish anything without a multitude of words, understood in the simpler sense, since even wisdom herself declares to the perishing, "I stretched out words, and you did not heed."¹⁴ Paul appears to have continued teaching from early morning till midnight, when indeed

9. Cf. Jn 21.25.
10. Cf. Rv 10.4.
11. Cf. Eccl 12.12.
12. Prv 10.19.
13. Cf. 3 Kgs 4.32–33 (Vulg.); 3 Kgs 5.12–13 (LXX).
14. Prv 1.24 (LXX).

Eutychus, overcome with deep sleep, fell down and troubled the audience since they thought he was dead.[15]

(5) If, then, the statement is true, "In a multitude of words you will not escape sin,"[16] and it is also true that Solomon did not sin when he recited the many words about the subjects mentioned earlier, nor did Paul when he extended his teaching until midnight, one must inquire what the multitude of words is, and from there make a transition to see what the many books are.

The complete Word of God which was in the beginning with God is not a multitude of Words, for it is not words. It is a single Word consisting of several ideas, each of which is a part of the whole Word.

Those, however, which are outside of this one, declaring that they contain an exposition and a declaration of whatever sort, even if they are words about truth, as it were—and I will express it paradoxically indeed—no one of them is a word, but each are words. For they are in no way a unit, and in no way are they harmonious and one, but because of disagreement and fighting, they have lost their unity and have become numbers, perhaps even endless numbers. Consequently, according to this understanding, we would say that he who utters anything hostile to religion is loquacious, but he who speaks the things of truth, even if he says everything so as to leave out nothing, always speaks the one Word. The saints are not loquacious since they cling to the goal which accords with the one Word. If, then, a multitude of words is recognized on the basis of the teachings, and not on the basis of the recital of many words, see if we can thus say that all the sacred works are one book, but those outside the sacred are many.

(6) But since I need evidence from the divine Scripture, consider if I can prove this most impressively by establishing that, as we see it, statements about Christ have not been recorded in one book, if we understand books in the more common sense. For they have been recorded in the Pentateuch,

---

15. Cf. Acts 20.7–10.   16. Prv 10.19.

and he has also been mentioned in each of the prophets and in the Psalms, and in general "in all the Scriptures,"[17] as the Savior himself says when he sends us back to the Scriptures and says, "Search the Scriptures for you think you have eternal life in them. And it is they that testify of me."[18]

If then, he refers us to "the Scriptures" as testifying to himself, he does not refer us to this one, but not to that one, but to all which bring tidings of himself, which in the Psalms he calls the "roll of the book" when he says, "In the roll of the book it has been written of me."[19] Let him who wishes to take "in the roll of the book" literally, in reference to some one of those books containing the things about Christ, tell us on what principle he prefers this book over another. For because someone may also suppose that the statement refers us to the book of Psalms itself, we must say to him that it would have had to have been said, "in *this* book it has been written of me." But now he says they are all one roll, by summing up into one the teaching which has come to us concerning himself.

And what book does John see which has writing on the front and back, and is sealed, and which no one could read and loose its seals, except the lion of the tribe of Juda, the root of David who has the key of David, and who opens and no one will close, and closes and no one will open?[20] For the whole Scripture is what is revealed by the book which has writing on the front because its interpretation is easy, and on the back because it is hidden and spiritual.

(7) If it is capable of proof that the sacred works are one book, but the non-sacred many, we must observe in addition that there is one book in the case of the living, from which those who deserve it are blotted out, as it is written, "Let them be blotted out of the book of the living."[21] On the other hand, a plurality of books is brought in the case of those who are reserved for judgment, for Daniel says, "The court convened

---

17. Lk 24.27.
18. Jn 5.39.
19. Ps 39.8.
20. Cf. Rv 5.1–5; 3.7.
21. Ps 68.29.

and the books were opened."²² Moses also testifies to the singleness of the divine book saying, "If you forgive the people's sin, forgive, otherwise strike me out of the book which you have written."²³

I also take what Isaias says in this way, for it is not a peculiarity of his prophecies that the words of the book have been sealed, being read neither by the one who doesn't know how to read because he does not understand the letters, nor by the one who knows how because the book has been sealed.²⁴ This is also true in the case of every Scripture which is in need of the Word which shut it and which will open it, for "he shall shut and no one shall open."²⁵ And whenever he shall open it, no longer can anyone present a difficulty to the clarity which comes from him. For this reason it is said, "He shall open and no one shall close."²⁶

I take it to be similar also in the case of the book mentioned by Ezechiel, in which "had been written lamentation, and a song, and woe."²⁷ For the whole book contains the "woe" of those perishing, and the "song" concerning those being saved, and the "lamentation" concerning those in between. But John, too, who eats one roll on which there is writing "on the back and the front,"²⁸ has considered the whole Scripture as one book, which is thought to be sweet at the beginning, when one chews it, but which is found to be bitter in the perception of himself which comes to each of those who have known it.

In addition, I will add an apostolic saying to this demonstration which has not been understood by Marcion's followers. As a consequence, they reject the Gospels. For when the Apostle says, "According to my gospel in Christ Jesus,"²⁹ and does not say "gospels," they fix their attention on this point and say that the Apostle said "gospel" in the singular because there were not any more gospels. They do not understand that as he is one whom the many preach, so the gospel re-

22. Dn 7.10.
23. Cf. Ex 32.31–32.
24. Cf. Is 29.11–12.
25. Cf. Rv 3.7; Is 22.22 (Sinaiticus and Vaticanus).
26. Ibid.
27. Cf. Ez 2.10.
28. Cf. Rv 10.10; Ez 2.10.
29. Cf. Rom 2.16.

corded by the many is one in power, and there is truly one gospel through the four.

(8) If these things, then, can persuade us about what the one book is and the many, I am more anxious now, not because of the abundance of what I have written, but because of the potential of my thoughts. Perhaps I will fall into transgressing the command if I should set forth as truth something contrary to the truth in even one of my writings, for in that case I shall have written many books.

But even now the heterodox, with a pretense of knowledge, are rising up against the holy Church of Christ and are bringing compositions in many books, announcing an interpretation of the texts both of the Gospels and of the apostles. If we are silent and do not set the true and sound teachings down in opposition to them, they will prevail over inquisitive souls which, in the lack of saving nourishment, hasten to foods that are forbidden and are truly unclean and abominable. For this reason it seems necessary to me that one who is able intercede in a genuine manner on behalf of the teaching[30] of the Church and reprove those who pursue the knowledge falsely so-called.[31] He must take a stand against the heretical fabrications by adducing in opposition the sublimity of the gospel message, which has been fulfilled in the agreements of the common doctrines in what is called the Old Testament with that which is named the New.

Therefore, because of the lack of those interceding for the better things, you yourself, because of your love for Jesus, once devoted yourself to their teachings,[32] since you do not bear a faith that is irrational and unlearned. Later, in good time, having judged them unfavorably by using the understanding which has been given to you, you abandoned them.[33]

Now I am saying these things in accordance with what appears to me, as a defense for those who are able to speak and

---

30. *Logon.*   31. Cf. 1 Tm 6.20.
32. *Logois.*
33. Origen is addressing his patron, Ambrose, whom he had converted from Gnosticism. See Eusebius *H.E.* 6.18.1. Cf. 2 Cor 3.6.

write, and as a defense for myself, lest perhaps by not being of such habit of mind as would be necessary for one made competent by God to be a minister of the new covenant, not of the letter but of the spirit,[34] I devote myself too boldly to dictating.[35]

34. Cf. 2 Cor 3.6
35. Origen is referring to his manner of composition, i.e. dictating to the secretaries provided for him by Ambrose at whose instigation the whole *Commentary* was being written.

BOOK 6

Preamble

Calm which is necessary for the whole structure

EVERY HOUSE, in order to be built as solidly as possible, is built in fair and calm weather that nothing may prevent it from being solidly constructed. The purpose is to make it capable of withstanding the rush of flood,[1] the onslaught of river, and all the other things which are apt to test the weak parts of buildings when a storm occurs, and show those which have been constructed with the excellence proper to them.

(2) This is especially true for that structure which is capable of receiving the principles of the truth, the spiritual structure which consists in proclamation and written characters, as it were. Such a structure is certainly built when the soul is experiencing the peace which passes all understanding,[2] and is calm, and separated from all trouble, and is by no means tossed by waves. At such a time God correctly cooperates in building with the one who has proposed to complete this most excellent work.

(3) It seems to me that because the servants of the prophetic spirit and the ministers of the proclamation of the gospel had understood these things accurately that they made themselves worthy of receiving that hidden peace from him who always gives it to those who are worthy, and who said, "Peace I leave with you, my peace I give to you; not as the world gives peace do I also give peace."[3]

(4) Now consider whether the story about David and Solomon concerning the temple hints at something like this. For

1. Cf. Lk 6.48. 2. Cf. Phil 4.7.
3. Cf. Jn 14.27.

when David, who wages the wars of the Lord and stands firm against many personal enemies and enemies of Israel, wishes to build a temple for God, he is prevented by God through Nathan who says to him, "You shall not build me a house, because you are a man of blood."[4]

(5) Solomon, however, who saw God in a dream and received wisdom in a dream (for the reality [of God] was reserved for him who said, "Behold a greater than Solomon is here"[5]), who enjoyed the profoundest peace so that each man at that time rested under his own vine and under his own fig tree, and who was named after the peace in his time (for Solomon means "peaceful"[6]), because of this peace, has time to construct the famous temple for God. The temple for God is also rebuilt in the times of Esdras, when the truth overcomes wine along with the hostile king and the women.[7]

The interruption of the Commentary

(6) We have said these things as a defense to you, holy Ambrose, wishing, in accordance with your pious encouragement, to construct in writing a tower like that described in the Gospel.[8] We sat down and counted the cost to see if we have what is necessary to complete it, so that we not be mocked by those who see it, despised because we laid a foundation, but cannot complete the work.

(7) After counting up what is at our disposal, we see that we do not possess what is needed to complete the structure. We have, however, trusted in God who enriches us in all speech and knowledge,[9] trusting that he will enrich us as we struggle to keep the spiritual laws. On the basis of what he supplies, we anticipate advancing in the construction even to the parapet of the house. It is this which prevents him who has ascended onto the house of the word from falling. Consequently, those who fall because of unfinished buildings fall

---

4. Cf. 1 Chr 28.3; 2 Kgs 16.8.   5. Mt 12.42.
6. Cf. 1 Chr 22.9; Lagarde, *Onomastica* 208.40.
7. Cf. 1 Ezr 4.36–38 (LXX).   8. Cf. Lk 14.28–30.
9. Cf. 1 Cor 1.5.

only from houses which lack the parapet. Those buildings bear the blame for such slaughters and falls.[10]

(8) Although the storm at Alexandria seemed to oppose us, we dictated the words which were given us as far as the fifth book, since Jesus rebuked the winds and the waves of the sea.[11] But after we had proceeded for a while in the sixth book we were rescued from the land of Egypt, when the God who led his people from Egypt delivered us.

(9) At that time, when the enemy had overrun us most bitterly by his new writings which were truly hostile to the gospel, and when he had stirred up all the perverse winds in Egypt against us, reason summoned me to take a stand in the struggle and to guard my ruling principle, so that wicked thoughts could not also introduce the storm into my soul. I chose to do this rather than continue with the succeeding words of Scripture at an unseasonable time before my mind was tranquil again. In addition, I was hindered because my accustomed stenographers were not present to take the dictations.

Its resumption

(10) Now, however, that the many fiery darts against us have been blunted, for God extinguishes them,[12] and our soul has grown accustomed to what has happened because of the heavenly word, I am compelled to bear more easily the treacheries which have occurred. It is as though we have received a great calm, and, no longer deferring, wish to dictate the subsequent books, praying that God may be present as our teacher to make suggestions in the innermost sanctuary of our soul, that the building of the interpretation of the Gospel according to John might reach its goal.

(11) May God give ear to our prayer, that the body of the whole discourse can be united, and that misfortune, which can cause a break of any kind in the sequence of the Scrip-

---

10. Cf. Dt 22.8.   11. Cf. Mt 8.26; Lk 8.24.
12. Cf. Eph 6.16.

ture, no longer interrupt. And be aware that I make this second beginning of the sixth book very eagerly because what we dictated previously in Alexandria, for some reason or other, has not been brought.

(12) For I thought it better to begin the remaining books now and not await with uncertainty the discovery of what we dictated previously, that this time too might not be lost with me idle from this work. It is no small gain [not][13] to have lost the intervening days. May these words serve as a sufficient preamble. Now let us give ourselves to the text.

And this is the testimony of John.
The verses 16 to 18 are attributed to the Baptist,
the figure of the Old Testament

(13) This is the second recorded testimony of John the Baptist about Christ. The former began with the statement: "This was he who said, 'He who comes after me,' "[14] and ends at the words: "The only begotten God who is in the bosom of the Father, he has declared him."[15]

Now Heracleon does not interpret the statement correctly: "No one has ever seen God,"[16] and what follows, when he declares that this was not said by the Baptist, but by the disciple.

(14) For indeed, according to his view, the words, "Of his fullness we all have received, and grace for grace; for the Law was given by Moses, but grace and truth came by Jesus Christ,"[17] were said by the Baptist. If this is so, why has he, who has received of the fullness of Christ even second grace for former grace, and who confesses that the Law has been given by Moses but that grace and truth have come by Jesus Christ, not understood, from the things which have come to him from the fullness, how "no one has ever seen God," and that the only begotten who is in the bosom of the Father has delivered the explanation to him and to all who have been recipients of his fullness?

13. I am assuming either (1) the negative *ouk* from the introductory clause was understood to negate the infinitive as well or (2) the negative *mē* has dropped out of the text preceding the infinitive.
14. Cf. Jn 1.15.
15. Jn 1.18.
16. Cf. Jn 1.18.
17. Jn 1.16–17.

The ancient patriarchs and prophets have known Christ

(15) For "[he who is] in the bosom of the Father"[18] did not now for the first time make the declarations which he made to the apostles, as though there had been no one fit to receive them previously, since, indeed, in his existence before Abraham was, he teaches us that Abraham rejoiced that he might see his day and was glad.[19] As we have said in our preceding discussion, both the statement, "And of his fullness we have all received," and the phrase, "Grace for grace,"[20] reveal that the prophets too have received their gift from the fullness of Christ, and that they have received the second grace for the former, for they too, being led by the Spirit, arrived at the vision of truth after they were initiated in types.

(16) Wherefore not all the prophets, but "many" desired to see what the apostles saw,[21] for if there were a difference between prophets, those who had been perfected and who excelled did not desire to see what the apostles saw, for they had seen them. Those, however, who have not, like these, succeeded in ascending to the sublimity of the Word, have longed for the things known by the apostles through Christ. We have taken "to see" not to have been used in a literal sense, and we have understood "to hear" to be declared spiritually, since he alone who has acquired ears to hear[22] has been prepared to hear the words of Jesus. This does not happen very quickly.

They have known the lessons of the living

(17) Further on this same subject, it is also possible to conclude from these words that the saints who preceded Jesus' bodily sojourn, who had a somewhat greater mental grasp than the majority of believers, perceived the mysteries of divinity, because the Word of God was teaching them even before he became flesh (for he was always working, being an

---

18. Jn 1.18.
20. Jn 1.16.
22. Cf. Mk 4.9.

19. Cf. Jn 8.58 and 56.
21. Cf. Mt 13.17.

imitator of his Father of whom he says, "My Father works until now"[23]).

(18) He says, perhaps to the Sadducees who do not believe in the doctrine of the resurrection, "Have you not read what was said by God at the bush: 'I am the God of Abraham, and the God of Isaac, and the God of Jacob?' But he is not God of the dead, but of the living."[24] If, therefore, God "is not ashamed to be called the God"[25] of these men, and they are numbered among the living by Christ, and all the believers are sons of Abraham,[26] since all the nations are blessed in faithful Abraham[27] whom God appointed father of the nations,[28] are we hesitant to accept that the living have known the lessons of the living, since they were instructed by Christ, who has existed before the morning star,[29] before he became flesh?

(19) They lived because they shared in him who said, "I am the life."[30] And, as heirs of such great promises, they received a manifestation, not only of angels but also of God in Christ. And perhaps because they saw the image of the invisible God,[31] since he who has seen the Son has seen the Father,[32] they have been recorded to have seen God and to have heard him, in that they have perceived God and heard God's words in a manner worthy of God.

(20) I think, however, that those who are perfectly and genuinely sons of Abraham are sons of his deeds understood spiritually, and of the knowledge which was made known to him, since the things he knew and did occur in those who are called sons of the patriarch, in relation to which he teaches those who have ears[33] when he says: "If you were sons of Abraham, you would do the works of Abraham."[34]

23. Jn 5.17.
24. Cf. Mt 22.31–32; Mk 12.26–27; Lk 20.37–38.
25. Cf. Heb 11.16.   26. Cf. Rom 4.11.
27. Cf. Gal 3.8.   28. Cf. Gn 17.5.
29. Cf. Ps 109.3.   30. Cf. Jn 11.25.
31. Cf. Col 1.15.   32. Cf. Jn 14.9.
33. Cf. Mt 11.15.   34. Cf. Jn 8.39.

*They have understood the mysteries concealed in
their visions, their speech, and their deeds*

(21) And if "a wise man shall understand the words from his own mouth, and shall bear knowledge on his lips,"[35] we must either declare rashly that the prophets were not wise, if they have not understood "the words from their own mouth," or admit that the prophets were wise, because they have received what is correct and true and have understood "the words from their own mouth" and borne knowledge on their lips.

(22) It is clear that Moses saw in his mind the truth of the Law and the allegorical meanings related to the anagogical sense of the stories he recorded, and that Josue understood the true distribution of land which took place after the overthrow of the twenty-nine kings,[36] since he could see better than us that the things accomplished through himself were shadows of certain realities.

(23) It is clear that Isaias also saw the mystery of the one seated on the throne and of the two seraphim and their wings, and of the altar and tongs, and of the concealment of their face and feet by the seraphim,[37] and that Ezechiel saw the cherubim and their course, and the firmament above them, and the one seated on the throne.[38] What could be more glorious and exalted than these things?

(24) Now, so as not to prolong the discussion excessively by speaking of situations one by one, when I have added a few further examples, I will leave it to the readers to decide and to examine what they wish about these matters. I wish to prove that those who have been perfected in former generations have known no less than the things which were revealed to the apostles by Christ, since the one who also taught the apostles revealed the unspeakable mysteries of religion to them.

(25) For Paul says in the Epistle to the Romans, "Now to

---

35. Cf. Prv 16.23.
37. Cf. Is 6.1–6.
36. Cf. Jos 12.7–24.
38. Cf. Ez 1.4–28.

him who is able to establish you, according to my gospel, according to the revelation of the mystery which has been kept secret for eternal times, but now has been made manifest both through the writings of the prophets and the appearance of our Lord Jesus Christ."[39] If the mystery which was kept secret long ago has been made manifest to the apostles through the writings of the prophets, and the prophets understood "the words from their own mouth"[40] because they were "wise," the prophets knew the things which have been made manifest to the apostles.

(26) But because it was not revealed to many, Paul says, "In other generations it was not made known to the sons of men as it has now been revealed to his holy apostles and prophets in the spirit, that the gentiles should be fellow heirs and of the same body."[41]

Difference between the recognition of a mystery and the prospect of its realization

But consider (since, indeed, it is thus possible that an objection will be raised by those who do not accept our argument in respect to this text to understand "revealed" in this way) whether it is possible to see "revealed" in two ways. In one way, a thing is revealed when it is understood; in the other, if this thing should be[42] prophesied, it is revealed on the condition that it has occurred and been fulfilled, for it is revealed at that time when it is completely fulfilled.

(27) The prophets knew, therefore, that "the gentiles" were to be "fellow heirs, and of the same body, and participants" in the promise in Christ,[43] insofar as it pertains to their knowledge that "the gentiles" will be "fellow heirs, and of the same body, and participants." They knew when they will be, and why, and what they will be, and how those who were

39. Cf. Rom 16.25–26; 2 Tm 1.10.   40. Cf. Prv 16.23.
41. Eph 3.5–6.
42. Preuschen thinks the text is corrupt here. Brook suggests substituting *telētai to* for *ē touto*, which would read, "if what is prophesied has been completed . . ." Blanc substitutes *toiouto* for *touto* and translates, "*lorsque la chose prophétisée est telle qu'elle peut se réaliser. . . .*"
43. Cf. Eph 3.6.

strangers to the covenant and aliens from the promise[44] were later to be "of the same body and participants."

(28) This much was revealed to the prophets. But the things which will be have not been revealed in the same manner to those who understand but do not see what is prophesied accomplished, as to those who see their fulfillment with their own eyes. This happened in the case of the apostles. For in their way, in my opinion, they understood the events no more than the fathers and the prophets. It is true of them, however, that "what in other generations was not revealed as it has now been revealed to the apostles and prophets, that the gentiles should be fellow heirs, and of the same body, and participants in the promise in Christ,"[45] insofar as the apostles understand the mysteries and perceive the self-evident truth through the completed event.

(29) It is also possible to interpret in the same way the saying, "Many prophets and just men desired to see the things that you see, and did not see them, and to hear the things that you hear and did not hear them"[46] as if those too desired to see the mystery of the incarnation of the son of God effected, and his descent to accomplish the plan of his suffering which brings salvation to so many. We could also take something else like this as an example: Grant that there is some apostle who understands "the unutterable words which man is not permitted to speak."[47] Although he will not see the second glorious bodily sojourn of Jesus which has been proclaimed by the believers, he desires to see it. Some other person, however, who not only has [not] thoroughly understood and perceived the same things with the apostle, but also clings to the divine hope much less than he does, happens to experience the second sojourn of our Savior. Let the apostle, in our example, have desired this sojourn of the Savior, but let him not have seen it.

(30) We will not be wrong, indeed, in saying that these two[48] have seen what the apostle, or even apostles, desired to

---

44. Cf. Eph 2.12. 45. Cf. Eph 3.5–6.
46. Cf. Mt 13.17. 47. 2 Cor 12.4.
48. Preuschen marks a corruption in the text here. He suggests in place of "these two," "these indeed."

see. By no means must we then say that they have more understanding or are more blessed than the apostles. So, too, the apostles are not wiser than the fathers or Moses and the prophets.[49] And it is especially true that they are not wiser than those who, because of their virtue, were further considered worthy of divine appearances and manifestations and revelations of great mysteries.

The Christians must defend the Old Testament against heretics

(31) We have spent time, however, examining these matters at greater length because some, in the fantasy of glorifying Christ's sojourn, say that the apostles were much wiser than the fathers and the prophets, and have fashioned another God who is greater. Others, not daring to go so far as this in their argument, because of the unexamined nature of their teachings, minimize the gift given to the fathers and the prophets from God through Christ, through whom "all things were made."[50] If all things were made through him, however, it is clear that both the good things which were revealed to them, and their actions, symbols of the holy mysteries of godliness, were included.

Resumption of the discussion of the attribution of verses 16–18

(32) But come, let us consider these matters, since the true soldiers of Christ[51] must, in every way, form a fortification for truth and nowhere permit an opening for persuasive falsehood, so far as they are able.

(33) Perhaps they will say that the earlier testimony about Christ comes from John: "He who comes after me was preferred before me, because he was before me."[52] On the other hand, the saying, "Because of his fullness we all have received, and grace for grace,"[53] and what follows was spoken by the disciple.

49. Cf. Lk 16.29.
51. Cf. 2 Tm 2.3.
53. Jn 1.16.
50. Cf. Jn 1.3.
52. Jn 1.15.

(34) Now we must expose this interpretation as forced and inconsistent in the following manner. It is very forced to suppose that the word of the Baptist is suddenly and unseasonably, as it were, broken off by the word of the disciple. The sequence of the text is clear to everyone who knows how just to listen for a while to the context of what is being said: "This was he who said, 'He who comes after me was preferred before me, because he was before me.'"[54]

(35) But by the statement, "Because of his fullness we all have received,"[55] the Baptist is teaching how Jesus was preferred before him by being before him (since he is the firstborn of all creation[56]). It is for this reason that he says, "He was preferred before me, because he was before me."[57] And I think he existed before me and is more honored with the Father, because both I and the prophets before me have received the more divine and greater prophetic grace from his fullness for the grace we received from him in relation to our free choice.

(36) In addition, "he was preferred because he was before me,"[58] since, when we have received of his fullness, we have also understood that the Law has been given "through Moses," not "by Moses," but that grace and truth have not only been given through Jesus Christ, but have also come into existence through him, since his God and Father has both given the Law through Moses and[59] has produced through Jesus Christ the grace and truth which have come to men.

Truth in itself and truth of God's creatures

(37) Once we have understood more correctly the text which declares, "Grace and truth came through Jesus Christ,"[60] we will not be troubled as though the statement, "I am the way, and the truth, and the life,"[61] were a contradiction to this statement. For if it is Jesus who declares, "I am

---

54. Cf. Jn 1.15.
55. Jn 1.16.
56. Cf. Col 1.15.
57. Jn 1.15.
58. Cf. Jn 1.15.
59. Omitting the repetition of the next phrase which Preuschen brackets.
60. Jn 1.17.
61. Jn 14.6.

the truth," how does the truth come into existence through Jesus Christ?

(38) For one does not himself come into existence through himself. We must understand, however, that the ultimate truth itself and, if I may put it this way, the archetype of the truth in rational souls, from which images of that truth, as it were, have been impressed on those who understand the truth, did not come through Jesus Christ nor through anyone at all, but came through God. Just as the Word which was in the beginning with God[62] did not come through someone, and wisdom, which "God created as the beginning of his ways,"[63] did not come through someone, so neither did the truth come through someone.

(39) The truth in men, however, came through Jesus Christ, as the truth in Paul and in the apostles came through Jesus Christ. It is not strange to say that although there is one truth, many truths, as it were, have flowed from it. The prophet David, at any rate, knows many truths when he says, "The Lord seeks out truths."[64] For the Father of truth does not seek out the one truth, but the many, because of which those who possess them are saved.

Justice, Life, Christ—justices, lives, Christs

(40) We find something similar to the teaching about truth and truths said about justice and justices. The ultimate justice itself is Christ, "who was made wisdom for us from God, and justice, and sanctification, and redemption."[65] The justice in each person, however, is formed from that justice, so that many justices come into existence in those who are saved; wherefore it has also been written, "The Lord is just and has loved justices."[66] For we found the text this way in the accurate copies and in the translations other than the Septuagint,[67] and in the Hebrew.

62. Cf. Jn 1.2.
63. Cf. Prv 8.22.
64. Ps 30.24.
65. 1 Cor 1.30.
66. Ps 10.7.
67. Modern editions of the Septuagint have the plural, though Rahlfs notes that Sinaiticus has the singular.

(41) Now consider if it is likewise possible that the other things, too, in which Christ is said to be in the singular are multiplied in a similar manner and named in the plural, such as "Christ is our life," as the Savior himself says: "I am the way and the truth and the life,"[68] and the apostle, "When Christ, your life, appears, then you also shall appear with him in glory."[69] And, again, it is written in the Psalms: "Your mercy is better than lives."[70] For lives are multiplied because of Christ who is life in each one.

(42) It is perhaps in this way that we should also seek the meaning of the words, "Do you seek a proof of Christ who speaks in me?"[71] It is as though Christ is found in each saint, and because of the one Christ, there are many Christs who are imitators of him who have also been formed according to him who is the image of God, whence God says through the prophet, "Touch not my Christs."[72] What, then, we seemed to have passed over as we were explaining the saying, "Grace and truth came through Jesus Christ,"[73] we have now unfolded according to what came to mind, and at the same time we have demonstrated that it is still the voice of John the Baptist testifying to the son of God through these words too.

The next two testimonies

The historical account

(43) Now, therefore, let us consider John's second testimony. Jews from Jerusalem send priests and Levites to inquire who John might be,[74] since they are kinsmen of the Baptist who happens to be from the priestly race.[75] When he says, "I am not the Christ,"[76] by this very word he has made a confession of truth. He has not, as someone might suppose, made a denial by saying, "I am not the Christ." It is not a denial to say to the glory of Christ that he is not the Christ.

68. Jn 14.6.
69. Col 3.4.
70. Ps 62.4.
71. Cf. 2 Cor 13.3.
72. Cf. Ps 104.15.
73. Jn 1.17.
74. Cf. Jn 1.19.
75. Cf. Lk 1.5.
76. Jn 1.20.

(44) Once the priests and Levites who were sent from Jerusalem have heard that he is not the awaited Christ, they inquire if he might be Elias, the person who held the second rank in honor as an object of their hope. He says that he is not Elias, again confessing the truth through the expression, "I am not."[77]

(45) And inasmuch as there were many prophets in Israel—there was one in particular, who had been prophesied by Moses, who was especially expected in accordance with the saying, "The Lord our God shall raise up a prophet like me for you from your brothers; him you shall hear. And it shall be that every soul that will not hear that prophet shall be destroyed from his people"[78]—they ask a third time, not if he is a prophet, but if he is "the prophet."[79]

(46) They do not apply this title to the Christ, but suppose that he is another in addition to the Christ. Because John knows that he of whom he is the forerunner is both the Christ and this prophet who was prophesied, he says, "No."[80] He might have answered, "Yes," if they had asked their question without using the article, for he was not unaware that he was a prophet.

(47) Even in all these answers the second testimony of John has not yet been completed until he has made himself known from the prophetic text of Isaias: "The voice of one crying in the desert, 'Prepare the way of the Lord,' "[81] to those who ask for an answer which they will relate to those who sent them.

(48) It is worthwhile to ask whether the second testimony has been completed, and the statement, "I baptize in water, but one has stood in your midst whom you do not know; he is the one who comes after me, the thong of whose shoe I am not worthy to loose,"[82] is a third testimony to those sent from the Pharisees and who wish to learn why he baptizes when he is neither the Christ, nor Elias, nor the prophet. Is this a third testimony, or is it part of the second, even that which is reported to the Pharisees?

77. Jn 1.21.
79. Jn 1.21.
81. Jn 1.23; cf. Is 40.3.
78. Cf. Acts 3.22–23; Dt 18.15.
80. Ibid.
82. Cf. Jn 1.26–27.

(49) I would say, so far as it is possible to conjecture from the text, that the word to those sent from the Pharisees is a third testimony. We must observe nevertheless that the first testimony presents the divinity of the Savior; the second destroys the opinion of those who were uncertain whether John might be the Christ; and the third proclaims the one who is invisibly present among men, who will presently come.

Attitude of the interlocutors of Jesus

(50) But before considering the next testimonies in which he points to (the Christ) and testifies of him, let us look at each phrase of the second and third testimony. Note first that two embassies come to the Baptist. One consists of "priests and Levites" sent from Jerusalem by the Jews "to ask him, 'Who are you?'"[83] The other comes from the Pharisees who send also because they are in doubt about the answer which had been given to the priests and Levites.[84]

(51) Observe carefully, therefore, how, in accordance with the character of priests and Levites, things are said with gentleness and curiosity: "Who are you?" and, "What then? Are you Elias?" and, "Are you the prophet, then?" and in addition to these questions, "Who are you, that we may give an answer to them that sent us? What do you say of yourself?"[85] There is nothing self-willed or rash in the inquiry of these men; everything is appropriate to scrupulous servants of God.

(52) But those sent by the Pharisees, who had no interest in what was said [by] the Levites and priests, address the Baptist with arrogant and rather senseless words: "Why, then, do you baptize, if you are not the Christ, nor Elias, nor the prophet?"[86] Perhaps they send their embassy, not wishing to learn as the priests and Levites previously mentioned, but to prevent him from baptizing. Perhaps they think that baptizing is the work of no one else except Christ, Elias, and the prophet.

83. Jn 1.19.
85. Cf. Jn 1.19–22.
84. Cf. Jn 1.24.
86. Jn 1.25.

(53) The one who will read Scripture accurately must pay attention everywhere, to observe, when necessary, who is speaking and when it is spoken, that we may discover that words are appropriately matched with characters throughout the holy books.

Then the Jews sent priests and Levites from Jerusalem to ask him: 'Who are you?' And he confessed and did not deny; and he confessed: 'I am not the Christ.'

Comparison between the questions posed by the Jews to John and by John to Jesus

(54) What ambassadors had to be sent to John from the Jews and whence, except those men assumed to excel according to God's election, sent from Jerusalem, the place chosen above all the earth which is called good, where the temple of God was? They interrogate John, therefore, with the greatest respect. Nothing like this, however, has been recorded to have been done by the Jews concerning Christ. It is John who does to Christ what the Jews do to him, when he inquires through his own disciples, "Are you he that is to come, or should we expect another?"[87]

(55) After John has confessed and has not denied, he later declares to those who have come, "I am the voice of one crying in the wilderness."[88] Christ, on the other hand, since he has a testimony which is greater than John, makes his response in words and deeds when he declares, "Go and relate to John what you see and hear. The blind see, the lame walk, the lepers are cleansed, the deaf hear, the poor have the gospel preached to them."[89] We will take these matters up more opportunely in their appropriate places, if God grants.

The awaiting of the Messiah

(56) Someone may, perhaps, reasonably raise the question why in the world, when the priests and Levites inquire of John, not if he is the Christ, but, "Who are you?", the Baptist

87. Mt 11.3.   88. Jn 1.23.
89. Cf. Mt 11.4–5.

does not answer, "I am the voice of one crying in the wilderness," which the question, "Who are you?" demanded. His answer would have been appropriate had they inquired, "Are you the Christ?"[90] For the answer, "I am not the Christ," fits the question, "Are you the Christ?"[91] But the answer, "I am the voice of one crying in the wilderness," fits the question, "Who are you?"[92]

(57) We must say to this, however, that, as is likely, John saw from the question the reverence of the priests and Levites. Their question suggested their secret suspicion that he who baptizes might be the Christ, but they were cautious about asserting this more boldly that they might not seem rash. This is why he declares with good reason that he is not the Christ, to remove all their false suspicion about him first, then, in this way, to present the truth.

(58) Their second question, and further the third, reveal that they had suspected something such as this. As a matter of fact, since they consider Elias to be second in honor, the object of their hope and esteem after Christ, when John declares that he is not the Christ, they ask, "What then? Are you Elias? And he says, 'I am not.'"[93]

(59) In the third place they want to learn if he is the prophet. When he answers "no," since they no longer have of themselves a name of one expected to visit them to mention, they say, "Who are you? That we may give an answer to those who sent us. What do you say about yourself?"[94] Their question reveals the following: On the one hand, you are not these persons who are awaited and expected to make an appearance to Israel but, on the other hand, although you are someone we do not know, you baptize. Therefore teach us this, that we may be able to report back to those who sent us to you for this reason.

(60) We shall also add this which relates to our foregoing discussion. The people were disturbed that the time of Christ's sojourn might already be imminent from the time slightly

90. Jn 1.19, 20 and 23.
92. Jn 1.23 and 19.
94. Jn 1.22.
91. Jn 1.20.
93. Cf. Jn 1.21.

preceding the birth of Jesus up to the manifestation of his preaching.

(61) Wherefore, in all probability, since the scribes and lawyers were already expecting the one awaited, deriving his time from the divine Scriptures, Theodas[95] had sprung up, who had gathered no small crowd by claiming to be the Christ, I think, and after him, "Judas of Galilee, in the days of the enrolling."[96] Since, therefore, Christ's sojourn is rather heatedly expected and discussed, it is with good reason that the Jews send priests and Levites from Jerusalem to John, wishing to learn by the question, "Who are you?",[97] if he will admit to being the Christ.

And they asked him, 'What then?
Are you Elias?' And he says, 'I am not.'
The coming of Elias before that of Christ

(62) Who of those who hear Jesus say of John, "If you wish to receive it, he is Elias who is to come,"[98] would not inquire how John says to those who ask, "Are you Elias?", "I am not"?[99] Will he not also inquire how one ought to consider John himself to be Elias who is to come according to Malachias' statement which is as follows: "And behold, I am sending you Elias the Thesbite before the great and renowned day of the Lord comes, who will restore the heart of the father to his son and the heart of a man to his neighbor, lest I come and smite the earth utterly"?[100]

(63) In addition the word of the angel of the Lord which appeared to Zachary, which stood on the right of the altar of incense,[101] indicated to Zachary something similar to what Malachias said, in these words: "And your wife Elizabeth will bear you a son and you shall call his name John."[102] And after a few words, "He shall go before him in the spirit and power

95. Cf. Acts 5.36.
96. Cf. Acts 5.37.
97. Jn 1.19.
98. Mt 11.14.
99. Jn 1.21.
100. Mal 3.22–23 (LXX), 4.5–6 (Vulgate).
101. Cf. Lk 1.11.
102. Lk 1.13.

of Elias, to turn the hearts of the fathers to the children and the disobedient to the wisdom of the just, to prepare a prepared people for the Lord."[103]

Use of this text by the believers of the reincarnation

(64) On the first point, at least, someone will say that John was not aware that he was Elias. They too, perhaps, will use this, who defend the doctrine of transmigration from these words,[104] since the soul changes bodies and by no means remembers its former lives. These same people will also say that some of the Jews who agreed with the doctrine about the Savior have said that he, therefore, is one of the ancient prophets who has risen,[105] not from the tombs, but from birth.

(65) For when his mother Mary is clearly indicated, and Joseph the carpenter is supposed to be his father, how could they think that he, being one of the prophets, had arisen from the dead? These same people, by employing what has been recorded in Genesis, "I will destroy every resurrection,"[106] will perplex the ones who take their stand on the doctrine and have devised deceptively persuasive arguments which are introduced from the Scriptures to solve the problem.

Difference between the soul, the spirit, and power

(60) But one who belongs to the Church[107], who repudiates the doctrine of transmigration as false, and does not admit that the soul of John was ever Elias, will use the previously mentioned statement of the angel who did not mention the soul of Elias at John's birth, but his spirit and power, through

---

103. Lk 1.17.
104. *Metensōmatoseōs*. Origen's reference may be to Basilides and his school. Cf. *Excerpta ex Theodoto*, 28; Clement, *Str.* 4.83.2.
105. Cf. Lk 9.19.   106. Gn 7.4.
107. Origen may be referring to himself in the "one who belongs to the Church." He calls himself *aner ekklesiastikos* in *Hom. in Luke*, 16.6. The view presented here, at least, is presented as his view in his fourth homily on Luke (*Hom. Lk* 4, GCS 49.99–109 [1959], ed. M. Rauer, p. 27) and Frag. 17 on Luke (ibid., pp. 233–234).

the saying, "And he will go before him in the spirit and power of Elias, to turn the hearts of the fathers to their children."[108] He can demonstrate through countless Scriptures that the spirit is different from the soul and that the power which is mentioned differs from the spirit and the soul. This is not the right time to present many examples of these things lest we divert our discourse excessively.

(67) The statement, "The Holy Spirit will come upon you and the power of the most High will overshadow you,"[109] will be enough for the present for the distinction between power and spirit. And the statement, "The spirits of prophets are subject to prophets,"[110] and, "The spirit of Elias has rested upon Eliseus,"[111] will be enough to distinguish the spirits in the prophets, inasmuch as they have been given to them by God as though they were called their possessions. For so there will be nothing strange, he says, in John who in the spirit and power of Elias turns the hearts of the fathers to the children,[112] because of this spirit which is said to be Elias who is to come.[113]

(68) But to solve these matters he will also use the following argument: If the God of the universe, having been made familiar to the saints, becomes their God, the being named the God of Abraham, and the God of Isaac, and the God of Jacob,[114] by how much more will it be possible for the Holy Spirit, having been made familiar to the prophets, to be called their spirit, that the Spirit might thus be said to be the spirit of Elias and the spirit of Isaias?

(69) This same churchman will say that, on the one hand, it is possible that those who have supposed that Jesus was one of the prophets who had arisen from the dead were mistaken both concerning the previously mentioned teaching and concerning their suppositions that he was one of the prophets. But, on the other hand, it is possible that they make a mistake in regard to their belief that he is one of the prophets, and

108. Lk 1.17.
109. Lk 1.35.
110. 1 Cor 14.32.
111. Cf. 2 Kgs 2.15.
112. Cf. Lk 1.17.
113. Cf. Mt 11.14.
114. Cf. Ex 3.6.

hold a false view also related to their ignorance of his so-called father and actual mother, and think that he has arisen from the tombs.

(70) In relation to the statement in Genesis about the resurrection, the churchman will reply by using the saying, "For God has raised up for me another seed, for Abel whom Cain killed,"[115] since "resurrection" occurs also in the case of "generation." This man indeed, because of what we have just now demonstrated, responds to the first difficulty differently than the one who assumes transmigration, and will say that John is Elias who is to come, in one sense, but that he responded to the priests and Levites, "I am not,"[116] because he had the intention of their inquiry in mind.

(71) For the earlier question to John from the priests and Levites was not intended to ascertain if the same spirit was in both men, but if John were that very Elias who had been taken up, now appearing without a birth according to the Jewish expectation, for those who had been sent from Jerusalem may have been ignorant of John's birth. He appropriately answers this question, "I am not," for Elias who had been taken up had not come, having changed his body and being named John.

Impossibility of the Jews ignoring the birth of John

(72) The first man, however, whose understanding we presented, who thinks transmigration is proven from this text and occupies himself with the touchstone of the letter, will say to the second that it is not consistent that the son of such a great priest as Zachary, who had been born contrary to all human expectation when both parents were old, was unknown to so many Jews in Jerusalem and to those Levites and priests they sent, who do not know that he was born [in this manner]. And this is especially the case, since Luke testifies, "Fear came upon all who lived around them" ("them" clearly being Zachary and Elizabeth) "and all these things were discussed in all the hill country of Judea."[117]

---

115. Gn 4.25.
116. Jn 1.21.
117. Lk 1.65.

COMMENTARY ON JOHN, BOOK 6   189

(73) If, however, the birth of John from Zachary was not unknown, and the Jews from Jerusalem sent through the Levites and priests to inquire, "Are you Elias?", it is clear that they said this, thinking the doctrine about transmigration to be true, since it was derived from their fathers and was not alien to their secret teaching. John says, therefore, "I am not Elias," because he is not aware of his own former life.

Impossibility of John ignoring his former existence

(74) Because there is a persuasiveness in these arguments that is not to be despised, the churchman will again raise a problem for the former. Is it fitting for a prophet who is enlightened by the Spirit[118] and prophesied by Isaias,[119] and whose birth is predicted by such a great angel before he is born,[120] who had received from the fullness of Christ,[121] who had partaken of such great grace,[122] who had understood that truth came through Jesus Christ, who had related so many things about God and the only begotten in the bosom of the Father,[123] to lie and not to have suspended his judgment[124] when he did not know what he was?

(75) It would have been fitting to withhold his opinion about things that were rather unclear, and neither to affirm nor deny the proposed question. But would it not have been reasonable, if this teaching had been held by many, for John to have been in doubt concerning whether his soul ever was in Elias?

The Jews believe that perhaps the
end of the world is imminent

(76) As far as the historical meaning is concerned, the churchman will challenge the former to ask those acknowledged by the Hebrews to know their secret teachings if there is any such teaching among them. For if there appears not to

---

118. Cf. Lk 1.35.
119. Cf. Is 40.3.
120. Cf. Lk 1.11 and 13.
121. Cf. Jn 1.16.
122. Ibid.
123. Cf. Jn 1.18.
124. I have accepted Brooke's emendation of *mēd'* for *kan*.

be such a teaching, it is clear that the argument of the former man has been dissipated.

(77) The churchman, therefore, will use the solution which was related before no less, and, in addition, will himself further demand that attention be given to the intention of the things asked. For if, as he has established, those who sent knew that John had been born of Zachary and Elizabeth, and even more so those who were sent, since they belonged to the priestly house and would not be unaware of the incredible good offspring of so renowned a fellow kinsman as Zachary, what did they have in mind when they asked, "Are you Elias?" since they were men who had read that he was taken up as though into heaven, and who awaited his coming?

(78) Perhaps, then, since they expect Elias before Christ at the consummation, and Christ after him, they seem to ask figuratively, as it were, "Are you the one who announces in advance the word which will precede Christ at the consummation?" He wisely responds to this: "I am not."[125]

Many have ignored the birth of Jesus

(79) Furthermore, the churchman, in opposition to the questions raised by his adversary when he attempted to demonstrate that the priests would not have been unaware of John's remarkable birth because "all these things" were discussed "in the hill country of Judea,"[126] will say that a similar error occurred among many also concerning the Savior when "some said he was John the Baptist, and others Elias, and others Jeremias, or one of the prophets,"[127] as even the disciples had said to the Lord when he asked them when he was in the regions of Cesarea Philippi.

(80) Herod, too, when he says of the Christ, "John whom I beheaded is himself risen from the dead,"[128] seems not to have known what was said by those who asked, "Is not this the carpenter's son? Is not his mother called Mary, and his

125. Jn 1.21.
126. Cf. Lk 1.65.
127. Cf. Mt 16.14.
128. Cf. Mk 6.16; Mt 14.2.

brothers James, and Joseph, and Simon, and Jude? And are not all his sisters with us?"[129]

(81) It is not strange, therefore, that, just as in the case of the Savior, although many knew of his birth from Mary, others were deceived, so also in the case of John, some were aware of his birth from Zachary, but others were in doubt whether the awaited Elias had appeared after the fashion of John (and the perplexity about whether John was Elias has no more place than that about whether the Savior was John).

(82) Of these men, the physical appearance of Elias could not be recovered[130] from personal experience, but only from the text, "A hairy man with a girdle of leather about his loins."[131] The figure of John, on the other hand, may have been previously known; it was not similar to Jesus' appearance. Nonetheless, the suspicion had occurred to some that John had perhaps arisen from the dead with his name changed to Jesus.

The false identification of Elias and Phinees perhaps explains that of Elias and John

(83) Indeed concerning a change of name, I do not know for what reason the Hebrews have a tradition as related in their secret teachings that Phinees, the son of Eleazar, who admittedly prolonged his life under many judges, as we have read in the book of Judges,[132] is himself Elias. They have also promised immortality to him in Numbers through the peace which is mentioned, because, being zealous and moved with a divine zeal, he pierced the Madionite woman and the Israelite man, and stopped the so-called wrath of God according to what has been written: "Phinees the son of Eleazor the son of Aaron has stopped my wrath because he was zealous with my zeal."[133]

---

129. Mt 13.55–56.
130. Reading *apolabesthai* with Blanc. Preuschen prints *apoballesthai* and marks it as a corruption.
131. Cf. 2 Kgs 1.8.   132. Cf. Jgs 20.28.
133. Cf. Nm 25.11. On the identification of Phinees and Elias by the Jews

(84) It is not strange, therefore, if those who suppose Phinees and Elias to be the same (whether they speak correctly or not, for I do not propose to make a study of this question now) think John and Jesus are the same. Or were they in doubt indeed about this and wished to learn if John and Elias were the same man?

Question on the destiny of the soul

(85) But first of all we must investigate more carefully and inquire further, among other things, about the doctrine concerning the essence of the soul, the origin of its existence, its entrance into the earthly body, the distributions of the life of each soul, its release from the body, and see if it is possible or not that it enter a second time in a body, and in the same cycle and the same order or not,[134] and if it enters the same body or another. Further, if it is the same body we must inquire whether it remains the same in substance but changed in quality, or if it will be the same both in substance and quality, and if it will always use the same body or will change it.

(86) We will also have to investigate what transmigration is in the strict sense, in what way it differs from incarnation,[135] and if it follows that the one who speaks of transmigration maintains the world as incorruptible. In these investigations it will also be necessary to compare the arguments of those who wish, in accordance with the Scriptures, the soul to be sown together with the body and the consequences which follow these arguments.

(87) In general, since the doctrine of the soul is vast and difficult to interpret, being gathered from words occurring here and there in the Scriptures, it needs its own systematic

---

see L. Ginzberg, *The Legends of the Jews* (Philadelphia: The Jewish Publication Society of America, 1909–1938), 3.114, 389; 6.316.

134. Blanc, SC 120.190–191, notes that the terms used here appear in Stoicism of the periodical reordering of the universe.

135. The terms compared here are *metensōmatosis* (transmigration) and *ensōmatōsis* (incarnation).

'Are you the Prophet?' And he answered, 'No.'

John is a prophet, not the prophet who is Christ

(88) If the Law and the prophets were until John,[136] what else indeed might we say John to be than a prophet? As also his father, Zachary, filled with the Holy Spirit, prophesies and says,[137] "And you, child, shall be called the prophet of the Highest, for you shall go before the Lord to prepare his ways."[138] Unless, then, one shall understand the words, "you shall be called," not to be equivalent to, "you shall be," John was a prophet. This is especially so because of what the Savior said to those who thought he was a prophet: "But what did you go out to see? a prophet? yes, I say to you, and more than a prophet."[139]

(89) Now we must observe that by saying "Yes, I say to you," he affirms that John is a prophet. But if, in addition to being a prophet the Savior also says he is "more than a prophet," how then, if he is a prophet, did he answer "no" to the priests and Levites when they asked, "Are you the prophet?"[140] We must say to this that it is not the same to ask, "Are you the prophet?" and, "Are you a prophet?" We made the same observations when we investigated the differences between "the God" and "God," and between "the Word" and "Word."[141]

(90) Since, then, it is written in Deuteronomy, "[The Lord] your God will raise up a prophet like me for you from your brothers; you shall hear him; and it shall be that every soul which will not hear that prophet shall be destroyed from his people,"[142] some prophet was specially expected who would be similar to Moses in some respect, to mediate between God

---

136. Cf. Mt 11.13.
137. Cf. Lk 1.67.
138. Lk 1.76.
139. Mt 11.9.
140. Jn 1.21.
141. See Book 2.13–15.
142. Cf. Acts 3.22–23; Dt 18.15, 18 and 19; Lv 23.29.

and men, and, who would receive the covenant from God and give the new covenant to those who became disciples. And the people of Israel knew so far as each of the prophets was concerned that no one of them was the one announced by Moses.

(91) As, therefore, they were in doubt about whether John was the Christ, so also they were in doubt whether he was "the prophet." It is not strange if those who were in doubt about whether John was the Christ did not understand thoroughly that the Christ and the prophet are the same. For not knowing that Christ and the prophet are the same is the consequence of uncertainty about John.

(92) The distinction, however, between "the prophet" and "a prophet" eludes most people, as it also eludes Heracleon, who says in these very words: "So, therefore, John confessed that he was not the Christ, but neither was he a prophet nor Elias." Since he took the words in this way, he should have examined them in relation to their contexts, whether John tells the truth or not when he says he is neither a prophet nor Elias. But Heracleon did not give attention to the contexts. In the books which he has left he passed over such important things without examination, having said very few things and those not investigated scientifically in their sequences. We shall speak of these matters soon.

Therefore they said to him, 'Who are you? That we may give an answer to those who sent us. What do you say about yourself?'

Questions of the priests and Levites

(93) This is the meaning of what those who were sent say: Although we surmised what you are, we have come to learn. We have learned that you are not what we surmised. It remains, consequently, to hear from you who you are, that we may report your answer about yourself to those who sent us.

* *143

---

143. The remainder of the commentary on verse 22 is lost.

He said: 'I am the voice of one crying in the wilderness, "Make straight the way of the Lord," just as Isaias the Prophet said.'

John is the voice

(94) Just as he who is the Son of God strictly speaking uses a word when he is none other than the Word (for he himself was the Word in the beginning, the Word with God, the Word which was God[144]), so John, the servant of that Word, uses voice to point to the Word when he is none other than the voice if we understand Scripture in the proper sense.

(95) Because he understood the prophecy about himself spoken by Isaias, he does not say that he is a voice "crying in the wilderness," but a voice "of one crying in the wilderness,"[145] of one who stood and cried, "If anyone thirst, let him come to me and drink,"[146] of one also who said, "Prepare the way of the Lord; make straight his paths; every valley shall be filled, and every mountain and hill shall be brought low, and all the crooked places shall be made straight."[147]

(96) Just as it is written in Exodus that God says to Moses, "Behold I have made you the God of Pharaoh, and Aaron your brother shall be your prophet,"[148] so one must understand the situation of God the Word in the beginning and John to be somewhat analogous to these although not alike in every way. For John was the voice of that Word, capable of pointing him out and revealing him.

(97) For this reason, when Zachary says to the angel, "How shall I know this? For I am an old man, and my wife is advanced in her days,"[149] he is very appropriately visited with no other punishment than the loss of his voice because of his disbelief in the birth of the voice, according to Gabriel's statement to him: "Behold, you shall be dumb and unable to speak

---

144. Cf. Jn 1.1.
145. Jn 1.23.
146. Jn 7.37.
147. Cf. Lk 3.4–5; Jn 1.23; Is 40.3–4.
148. Ex 7.1.
149. Lk 1.18.

until the day in which these things come to pass, because you did not believe my words which will be fulfilled in their time."[150] This Zachary indeed received his voice back when "he asked for a writing tablet and wrote saying, 'His name is John,' and all marveled. For immediately his mouth was opened, and his tongue loosed, and he began to speak blessing God."[151]

(98) Now just as in explaining how we must understand the son of God to be the Word we have made known the thoughts which were presented, so in the appropriate sequence must we understand that John was the voice which alone was able, in a worthy manner, to contain the Word which was announced, since John "came for a witness," as "a man sent from God," "that he might bear testimony of the light, that all might believe through him."[152]

(99) We will understand this especially if, as we explain the clause, "That all might believe through him,"[153] we recall what we set forth about the verse, "This is he of whom it is written, 'Behold I am sending my angel before your face, who will prepare your way before you.'"[154] It is also said correctly that he is not the voice "of one speaking in the wilderness," but "of one crying in the wilderness." For he who cries "Prepare the way of the Lord," also says it, but the same one could say it while not crying it.

Necessity and nature of the "cry"

(100) But he cries and shouts that both those who are afar may hear him speaking and those who are hard of hearing may understand the greatness of what is said since it is proclaimed with a loud voice, helping both those who have departed from God and those who have lost the keenness of their hearing. For this reason too "Jesus stood and cried saying, 'If anyone thirsts, let him come to me and drink.'"[155] It

---

150. Cf. Lk 1.20. 151. Cf. Lk 1.63–64.
152. Jn 1.7, 6 and 7.
153. Jn 1.7. Origen's discussion of this portion of the verse is lost. Book 2 closes by proposing to discuss this statement.
154. Mt 11.10. 155. Jn 7.37.

is for this reason that "John testifies of him and cries out saying."[156] For this reason too God commands Isaias to cry with the voice "of one saying, 'Cry.' And I said, 'What shall I cry?'"[157]

(101) But if the mental voice of those who pray should not be extremely loud, though it is not weak, and should they not raise a cry and shout, God still hears those who pray thus, for it is he who says to Moses, "Why do you cry out to me?"[158] when he had not cried out audibly (for this is not recorded in Exodus), but through prayer he had cried loudly in that voice which is heard by God alone.[159] For this reason also David says, "I cried to the Lord with my voice, and he hearkened to me."[160]

(102) Now the necessity of the voice of one crying in the wilderness is that the soul which is devoid of God and destitute of truth (for what other wilderness is harder to deal with than a soul that is bereft of God and of all virtue?) because it is still going in a crooked manner and is in need of teaching, might be exhorted to make straight the way of the Lord.[161] He who in no way imitates the crookedness of the serpent's path makes this way straight, but he who acts in a contrary manner perverts it. Wherefore such a man is rebuked together with those like him by the statement, "Why do you pervert the straight ways of the Lord?"[162]

The way of the Lord

(103) Now the way of the Lord is made straight in two ways: by contemplation which is clarified by truth unmixed with falsehood, and by activity which follows sound contemplation of the appropriate action to be taken which is conformed to the correct sense of these things to be done. And to understand more accurately the words, "Make straight the way of the Lord,"[163] it will be timely to juxtapose what is said in Prov-

---

156. Jn 1.15.
157. Cf. Is 40.6.
158. Ex 14.15.
159. Cf. Origen, *Ex. Hom.* 5.4.
160. Cf. Ps 76.2.
161. Cf. Is 40.3.
162. Cf. Acts 13.10.
163. Jn 1.23.

erbs: "Decline not to the right hand nor to the left."[164] He who declines to either side has lost the straightness, no longer being worthy of providential care when he oversteps the straightness of the path, "for the Lord is just, and has loved justice, and his countenance has beheld straightness."[165] And what he sees, he illuminates.

(104) This is why the one who is observed and who perceives the benefit of this attention says, "The light of your countenance, Lord, is marked upon us."[166] Let us stand on the roads, therefore, as Jeremias has said,[167] and look and ask for the ancient paths of the Lord. Let us see what the good way is, and follow it just as the apostles stood and asked the patriarchs and the prophets for the ancient paths of the Lord. Later, after they had interrogated their writings and had come to understand them, they saw the good way, Jesus Christ, who said, "I am the way,"[168] and they walked in it.

(105) For that way is good which leads the good man to the good Father, the man who brings forth good things from his good treasure, even the good and faithful servant.[169] But this way is narrow; the majority and those who are very carnal cannot travel it. But the way is also constricted by those who use force to pass through it, since it is not said that it "constricts," but "is constricted."[170]

(106) For he who has not loosed the sandals from his feet and does not genuinely recognize that "the place" on which he stands, or even on which he treads, "is holy ground"[171] constricts the way which is living and perceptive of the unique features of the traveler. But this way will lead to the life since he is the one who said, "I am the life."[172]

(107) The Savior, who contains all virtue, is multiple in his aspects. For this reason he is the way for the one who has not yet arrived at the goal but is still advancing, but for him who has already put off all that is dead, he is life. He who travels

---

164. Cf. Prv 4.27.
165. Cf. Ps 10.7.
166. Ps 4.7.
167. Cf. Jer 6.16.
168. Jn 14.6.
169. Cf. Mt 7.14; Lk 6.45; Mt 25.21.
170. Cf. Mt 7.13–14.
171. Cf. Ex 3.5.
172. Cf. Jn 14.6.

this way is instructed to carry nothing on him since it provides bread and the items necessary for life; he has no need for a staff because enemies can do nothing on this way,[173] and since it is holy, there is no need for sandals.[174]

(108) It is possible, however, that the words, "I am the voice of one crying in the wilderness,"[175] and what follows is equivalent to saying, I am the one of whom it is written, "The voice of one crying," since John is the one who cries, and his voice cries out in the wilderness: "Make straight the way of the Lord."[176]

The interpretation of Heracleon: the Savior is the Word, John the voice, the prophets a noise

Heracleon, however, holding a rather slanderous view of John and the prophets, says: "The Word is the Savior, the voice in the wilderness is that signified by John, and the whole prophetic order is a noise."

(109) But we must say to him that just as it is the case that "if the trumpet give an uncertain sound no one prepares for battle,"[177] and he who has knowledge of mysteries or has prophecy, without love, has become as sounding brass or a clanging cymbal,[178] so if the prophetic voice is nothing more than noise, how does the Savior say, as he refers us to it: "Search the Scriptures, because you think you have eternal life in them, and they are those who testify,"[179] and, "If you believed Moses you would believe me, for he wrote of me,"[180] and, "Well did Isaias prophesy of you saying, 'This people honors me with their lips' "?[181]

(110) For I do not know if anyone will admit that an unintelligible noise is reasonably commended by the Savior, or if it is possible to prepare oneself for battle with the opposing forces from the Scriptures to which we are referred, as from the sound of a trumpet, if the sound should be an unclear noise. And if the prophets did not have love, and for this reason were sounding brass or a clanging cymbal,[182] how does the Lord refer those who are to be benefited to their noise, as those interpreters have understood it?

(111) I do not know how, without any explanation, he asserts that the voice which belongs to the Word becomes the Word, as also the

---

173. Cf. Mk 6.8.
174. Cf. Ex 3.5.
175. Jn 1.23.
176. Ibid.
177. Cf. 1 Cor 14.8.
178. Cf. 1 Cor 13.1 and 2.
179. Jn 5.39.
180. Jn 5.46.
181. Mt 15.7–8; cf. Is 29.13.
182. Cf. 1 Cor 13.1.

woman is changed into a man.[183] And, as though he has the authority to lay down a doctrine and to be believed and to advance, he says that the sound will change into voice, giving the position of a disciple to the voice which changes into the Word, and that of servant to the change from noise to voice. If he had brought any kind of plausible argument to bear to establish these points, we would have struggled to refute them, but as it is, an unsupported denial is sufficient for their refutation.

Difference between John and his attributes

(112) But come, let us now take up what we set aside when we examined the words preceding these, namely how John has been discussed. For the Savior, according to Heracleon, says John is both a prophet and Elias, but he himself denies that he is either of these. When the Savior says he is both a prophet and Elias he is indicating, Heracleon says, not John himself but his attributes; but when he says he is greater than the prophets and greatest among those born of women,[184] then he is characterizing John himself. But John, he says, when asked about himself answers concerning himself and not concerning his attributes.

(113) How we have tested these things to the best of our ability! We have permitted none of the terms mentioned to be unsupported in order to examine what Heracleon affirmed, since he does not have the right to say what he wishes. For he does not even attempt to demonstrate in any way how it is that John is Elias and the prophet so far as his attributes are concerned, and the voice of one crying in the wilderness so far as he himself is concerned. He does, however, use an example. He says that his attributes, being like clothes, were other than himself, and when he was asked if he himself were the clothes, he would not answer, "Yes."

(114) I do not quite perceive how, in his view, being the Elias who is to come is John's clothes. Perhaps it accords with our view when we explained, to the best of our ability, the words, "In the spirit and power of Elias."[185] Perhaps it can be said that this spirit of Elias is the clothing of John's soul.

Reason for the choice of priests and Levites

(115) But when he wishes in addition to explain why those sent from the Jews to question him are priests and Levites, his answer is not bad: "Because it was fitting for these who are devoted to God to

---

183. For a discussion of the Gnostic doctrine about the woman becoming a man see Blanc, SC 120.27–31.
184. Cf. Lk 7.28; Mt 11.11.   185. Lk 1.17.

be curious about these matters and to inquire." But it is not quite with deliberate precision that he says: "Because he too was from the Levitical tribe." We raised problems with this idea previously when we examined it:[186] If those who were sent knew John and knew about his birth, what place did they have to ask if he were Elias? And again on the question, "Are you the prophet?"[187] because he thinks nothing special is signified by the addition of the article, he says, "They asked if he were a prophet, wishing to learn this rather common thing."

John would be older than the Prophets

(116) And furthermore, not only Heracleon, but also, so far as I can see, all the heterodox, because they have not been able to distinguish a simple ambiguity, have assumed that John is greater than Elias and all the prophets because of the statement, "Among those born of women, no one is greater than John."[188] They do not see that the statement, "Among those born of women, no one is greater than John," is true in two ways. It is true not only in his being greater than all, but also in some being equal to him. For it is true that although many prophets are equal to him, no one is greater than he in relation to the grace which has been given to him.[189]

(117) Heracleon, however, thinks it is proven that John was greater by the fact that Isaias prophesies of him[190] since no other prophet was considered worthy of this honor by God. But he has ventured to say this because he truly disdains what is called the Old Testament and has not observed that even Elias himself is the subject of prophecy. For Elias too is the subject of prophecy by Malachias when he says, "Behold I am sending Elias the Thesbite to you, who will restore the heart of the father to his son."[191]

(118) And Josias too, as we have read in the third book of Kings,[192] is prophesied of by name by the prophet who had come from Juda who says, when Jeroboam also was present, "O altar, thus says the Lord: 'Behold a son is to be born to the house of David. His name will be Josias.'"[193] And some say that Samson too is prophesied of by Jacob when he says, "Dan shall judge his people, as if Israel too were one tribe,"[194] because Samson, who was from the tribe of Dan, judged Israel. But let these things be said as a rebuke of his rashness who declared that no one but John is the subject of prophecy. He said these things when he wished to explain the meaning of the statement, "I am the voice of one crying in the wilderness."[195]

186. See Book 6.72–73.
187. Jn 1.21.
188. Lk 7.28; Mt 11.11.
189. Cf. Rom 12.6.
190. Cf. Is 40.3.
191. Cf. Mal 3.22–23 (LXX); 4.5–6 (Vulgate).
192. Cf. 1 Kgs 13.2.
193. Ibid.
194. Gn 49.16.
195. Jn 1.23.

And those who were sent were of the Pharisees. And they asked him and said to him: 'Why then do you baptize, if you are not the Christ, nor Elias, nor the Prophet?'

Hypocrisy and boasting of the Pharisees

(119) Those from Jerusalem, on the one hand, who sent priests and Levites who questioned John, once they had learned both who John was not and who he was, maintained a most dignified tranquility. It is as though they tacitly agree, and indicate their acceptance of what was said, that it is fitting for the voice of one crying in the wilderness to baptize to make straight the way of the Lord.

(120) The Pharisees, on the other hand, since in accordance with their name they are a separated and factious people,[196] show the Jews in the metropolis and the ministers of the service of God, the priests and Levites, that they do not agree, by sending those who ask in a manner that is rebuking and, so far as in their power, preventive of his baptizing: "Why then do you baptize if you are not the Christ, nor Elias, nor the prophet?"[197] Perhaps, if we were to spin what is written in the Gospels into one account by consolidating it, we would say that they say these things now, but later, I know not how, when they have delivered themselves to be baptized by John, heard him say, "Brood of vipers, who warned you to flee from the wrath to come? Therefore produce fruit worthy of repentance."[198]

(121) These words are spoken by the Baptist in Matthew when he sees many of the Pharisees and Sadducees coming for baptism, though they clearly do not possess the fruits of repentance and are boasting pharisaically in themselves on the basis that they have Abraham as their father.[199] This is why they are rebuked by John who, according to the fellowship of the Holy Spirit, possesses the zeal of Elias. For this statement is rebuking: "Think not to say within yourselves, 'We have

---

196. Cf. Lagarde, *Onomastica* 61.20. 197. Jn 1.25.
198. Mt 3.7–8. 199. Cf. Mt 3.9.

Abraham for our father.'"²⁰⁰ And that statement is instructive which concerns the possibility, by the power of God, of changing even those called faithless stones because of their stoney heart, from stones into children of Abraham, since they were present in the prophet's eyes and did not escape his divine vision. For this reason he says, "I say to you that God is able of these stones to raise up children to Abraham."²⁰¹

(122) And since they come to baptism when they have not produced fruit worthy of repentance, he says to them most appropriately, "But already the axe is laid to the root of the trees. Every tree that does not produce good fruit is cut down and cast into the fire."²⁰² It is as if he says to them outright, Since you have come to baptism and have not produced the fruit of repentance, you are the tree which does not produce good fruit, which is cut down by the sharpest and most active axe of that Word which is living and effectual and more piercing "than any two edged sword."²⁰³

(123) Luke also presented the boast of the Pharisees in the passage, "Two men went up into the temple to pray, the one a Pharisee and the other a publican. And the Pharisee stood and prayed thus with himself: 'God, I thank you that I am not as the rest of men, extortioners, unjust, adulterers, or even as this publican.'"²⁰⁴ Consequently the publican goes down to his house, justified, rather than the Pharisee because of these words, and Jesus says in relation to this that everyone who exalts himself is humbled.²⁰⁵

Their question is, "What is the truth of baptism?"

The Pharisees approach baptism, therefore, as hypocrites (according to the Savior's reproving words to them).²⁰⁶ The Baptist, however, is not unaware that they still have the poison of snakes and asps under their tongues, for the "poison of asps is under their lips."²⁰⁷

(124) And truly "their madness in the likeness of a ser-

---

200. Mt 3.9.
201. Cf. Mt 3.9.
202. Cf. Mt 3.10.
203. Cf. Heb 4.12.
204. Cf. Lk 18.10–11.
205. Cf. Lk 18.14.
206. Cf. Mt 23.13.
207. Cf. Ps 13.3; 139.4; Rom 3.13.

pent,"[208] was revealed by their bitter question, "Why then do you baptize, if you are not the Christ, nor Elias, nor the prophet?"[209] I would say to these men, since they suppose that Christ, and Elias, and the prophet baptize, but the voice of him who cries in the wilderness has not received this right, "You there, you inquire harshly of the angel who has been sent before the face of Christ to prepare his way before him,[210] while you are ignorant of all the mysteries that pertain to his position. For the Christ, who is Jesus, even if you do not wish him to be, does not himself baptize, but his disciples,[211] although he himself is "the prophet."[212]

(125) And what is the source of your belief that Elias who is to come will baptize? He did not even baptize the wood on the altar in the times of Achab, when it needed a bath that it might be burned up when the Lord appeared in fire.[213] He commanded the priests to do this, and not only once, for he says, "Do it a second time, when also they did it a second time," and "Do it a third time, when also they did it a third time."[214] How, then, will he who did not himself baptize at that time, but gave the task to others, baptize when he has come in fulfillment of the things said by Malachias?[215] Christ, therefore, does not baptize in water, but his disciples.[216] He reserves for himself the act of baptizing with the Holy Spirit and fire.[217]

(126) Since Heracleon accepted the statement made by the Pharisees to be correct, that it was appointed to Christ and to Elias and to every prophet to baptize, he says in these very words, "who alone were appointed to baptize." He is refuted by what we have just said, but especially because he has understood "prophet" in the more general sense, for he is not able to show that any of the prophets baptized. His statement is convincing, however, that the Pharisees inquire out of malice and not out of a desire to learn.

208. Ps 57.5.
210. Cf. Mk 1.2.
212. Cf. Jn 1.21.
213. Cf. 1 Kgs 18.21–38.
214. Cf. 1 Kgs 18.34.
216. Cf. Jn 4.2.

209. Jn 1.25.
211. Cf. Jn 4.2.

215. Cf. Mal 4.5–6.
217. Cf. Mt 3.11; Lk 3.16.

Comparison with the Synoptic Gospels

(127) Since we think it is necessary to compare texts from the Gospels which resemble the words under consideration, and to do this for each passage to the end (of our work) to demonstrate the harmony in things which seem to clash, and to explain the things which are similar in each individual passage, let us do this here too.

(128) The statement, "The voice of one crying in the wilderness: Make straight the way of the Lord,"[218] is placed in the mouth of the Baptist by John, the disciple. In Mark, however, it is recorded as the beginning of the gospel of Jesus Christ according to the writing of Isaias as follows: "The beginning of the gospel of Jesus Christ, just as it is written in Isaias the prophet: 'Behold I send my angel before your face, who will prepare your way, the voice of one crying in the wilderness: Prepare the way of the Lord, make his paths straight.'"[219]

(129) The words, "Make straight the way of the Lord," which John[220] quotes do not occur, however, in the prophet. Perhaps John, then, to shorten the saying, "Prepare the way of the Lord, make straight the paths of our God," wrote, "Make straight the way of the Lord,"[221] since Mark, by bringing together two prophesies spoken by two prophets in different places has produced the saying, "Just as it is written in Isaias the prophet, 'Behold, I send my angel before you, who will prepare your way. The voice of one crying in the wilderness: Prepare the way of the Lord, make his paths straight.'"[222]

(130) For the saying, "The voice of one crying in the wilderness"[223] follows immediately after the story about Ezechias when he arose from his illness,[224] but the saying, "Behold, I send my angel before you," is said by Malachias.[225]

218. Jn 1.23.
219. Cf. Mk 1.1–3; Mal 3.1; Is 40.3.
220. The MSS. have Mark. Preuschen correctly treats it as a scribal error.
221. Is 40.3; Jn 1.23. 222. Mk 1.2–3.
223. Is 40.3. 224. Cf. Is 39.
225. Cf. Mal 3.1.

(131) What John did, however, by shortening the saying which he quoted, Mark himself, too, has exhibited in another text. For, on the one hand, the prophet says, "Prepare the way of the Lord, make the paths of our God straight."[226] But Mark says, "Prepare the way of the Lord, make his paths straight."[227] He has made a similar abridgement also in the case of the saying, "Behold, I send my angel before your face, who will prepare your way."[228] For he has not quoted the "before me" which precedes.[229]

(132) In addition, when we examined the statement, "They had been sent from the Pharisees, and they asked him,"[230] we placed the question of the Pharisees first, since it has been passed over in silence by Matthew, * *[231] before what is recorded to have happened, that "when John saw many of the Pharisees and Sadducees coming to baptism he said to them, 'Generation of vipers' "[232] etc., for the natural order is to have inquired first, then to have come.

(133) We must observe also that Matthew says that those who went out to John to be baptized in the Jordan river, confessing their sins, namely Jerusalem and all Judea and all the country around the Jordan, heard no rebuking and critical word from the Baptist,[233] but only those many Pharisees and Sadducees who were seen to have come heard the words, "Generation of vipers," etc.[234] Mark, however, mentions no rebuke to have been spoken by John to those who came, who consisted of all Judea and all those of Jerusalem, and who were baptized by him in the Jordan and confessed their sins. Accordingly, neither are the Pharisees and Sadducees mentioned.[235]

226. Is 40.3.
227. Mk 1.3.
228. Cf. Mk 1.2.
229. Origen's meaning here is obscure, for no such phrase occurs in the LXX text of either Mal 3.1 or Is 40.3. He perhaps has the phrase in mind as it is quoted in Mt 11.10 and Lk 7.27, although here, too, it is "before you" and not "before me."
230. Jn 1.24.
231. Lacuna in the text. I have accepted Preuschen's conjecture that *pro* has been lost.
232. Cf. Mt 3.7.
233. Cf. Mt 3.5–6.
234. Mt 3.7.
235. Cf. Mk 1.5.

(134) Further, we must also mention that both Matthew and Mark say that all Jerusalem and all Judea and all the country around the Jordan, or all the country of Judea and all those of Jerusalem are baptized confessing their sins. Matthew, however, introduces the Pharisees and Sadducees who come for baptism, although they do not at all confess their sins. It is likely, therefore, that it is just this which is the reason that they heard the words, "Generation of vipers".[236]

(135) Do not suppose, however, that our comparison of the materials from the other Gospels was untimely in the course of our examination of the words of those of the Pharisees who were sent to John and who questioned him. For if we have accurately referred the question of the Pharisees, which is recorded by John the disciple, to their baptism which occurs in Matthew, it was the natural consequence to examine the words in their passages and to compare the observations which were found.

(136) Like Mark, Luke too has recalled the words, "The voice of one crying in the wilderness,"[237] from his own personal viewpoint as follows: "The Word of God came upon John, the son of Zachary, in the wilderness. And he came into all the country around the Jordan preaching the baptism of repentance for the remission of sins, as it is written in the book of the words of Isaias the prophet: 'The voice of one crying in the wilderness: Prepare the way of the Lord, make his paths straight.'"[238]

(137) But Luke added also the following words of the prophecy: "Every valley shall be filled, and every mountain and hill shall be brought low, and the crooked shall be made straight, and the rough ways smooth. And all flesh shall see God's salvation."[239] Like Mark, he wrote, "Make his paths straight,"[240] abbreviating, as we mentioned earlier, the saying, "Make straight the paths of our God."[241]

(138) And in place of the statement, "All the crooked shall

---

236. Mt 3.7.
238. Lk 3.2–4.
240. Lk 3.4; Mk 1.3.

237. Is 40.3.
239. Cf. Lk 3.5–6; Is 40.4–5.
241. Is 40.3.

be made straight,"[242] he presented the text without the "all," along with having written the plural in place of the singular "straight."[243] Further, also in place of the phrase, "the rough ways plain," he wrote, "the rough ways smooth,"[244] and having omitted, "and the glory of the Lord will appear," he employed what follows: "And all flesh shall see God's salvation."[245] These observations are useful as an indication of the fact that the evangelists abbreviate the prophetic words.

Comparison of different addresses to crowds and Pharisees

(139) And further, we must also observe that Matthew says that the words "Generation of vipers, etc."[246] were addressed to the Pharisees and Sadducees coming to baptism, being a different group from those confessing their sins and hearing no such word. Luke, however, records that these words were addressed to the crowds coming out to be baptized by John,[247] since he did not make two ranks of those being baptized which we found in Matthew.[248]

(140) But he, too, since the crowds are not ranked in order of praise, as will be clear to those who are observant, suitably introduces the Baptist saying to the crowds, "Generation of vipers," etc.[249] And further, he says to the Pharisees and Sadducees, "Produce fruit," in the singular, "worthy of repentance,"[250] but to the crowds, "Produce fruits," in the plural, "worthy of repentance."[251]

(141) Perhaps the Pharisees are demanded to produce the fruit of repentance *par excellence,* which is nothing other than the Son and faith in him, but the crowds, since they do not even possess a beginning of good deeds, are demanded to produce all the fruits of repentance, for which reason the plural is addressed to them.

242. Is 40.4.
243. Lk 3.5; Is 40.4. The editors of the 26th edition of the Nestle-Aland Greek text of the New Testament have opted for the singular in Lk 3.5 and placed the plural in the apparatus. Vaticanus has the plural and Sinaiticus the singular.
244. Lk 3.5; Is 40.4.
246. Mt 3.7.
248. Cf. Mt 3.5 and 7.
250. Mt 3.8.
245. Is 40.5; Lk 3.6.
247. Cf. Lk 3.7–9.
249. Lk 3.7.
251. Cf. Lk 3.8.

(142) He says to these Pharisees, "Think not to say within yourselves, 'We have Abraham for our father.'"[252] The crowds now have a beginning, thinking that they are introduced into the divine Word in order to approach the truth, wherefore they begin to say within themselves, "We have Abraham for our Father."[253] The Pharisees, on the other hand, are not beginning, but have thought this for a long time. Both, however, hear John say that children can be raised up to Abraham from the previously mentioned stones which he points to,[254] which will be raised from their lack of sensation and deadness.

The fruit or fruits men have clamored for

(143) Now observe that he says to the Pharisees who have fruit, [but] a false kind according to what is said in the prophet: "You ate false fruit":[255] "Every tree, therefore, which does not produce good fruit, is cut down."[256] To the crowds, on the other hand, who are producing no fruit at all, he says, "Every tree, therefore, which does not produce fruit is cut down."[257] The one tree which has no fruit does not have good fruit; therefore, it deserves to be felled. The other, however, although it has fruit, does not have fruit that is completely good; therefore, it too is appropriately cast out by the axe.

(144) If we should inquire more carefully into matters concerning fruits, we will find that it is impossible for a tree, which is beginning to be cultivated now, to bear good fruit first even if it should bear. The husbandman is pleased for it to bear fruit proper to the beginning of cultivation at first. Later in the course, by means of the prunings proper to the agricultural art, after he has received mediocre fruits he will, at length, also receive good fruits. The Law too testifies to our interpretation when it says that he who plants must permit what is planted to produce unclean fruit for three years, its

---

252. Mt 3.9.
253. Cf. Lk 3.8.
254. Cf. Mt 3.9; Lk 3.8.
255. Hos 10.13.
256. Mt 3.10.
257. Cf. Lk 3.9. New Testament manuscripts are divided on whether the text of Lk 3.9 should contain the word "good." The word is printed in modern critical texts of the New Testament. Its inclusion in the MSS., however, could easily be accounted for from the parallel in Mt.

fruits not being eaten. For it says, "The unclean fruit shall not be eaten by you for three years, but in the fourth year all the fruit shall be holy, as praise to the Lord."[258]

(145) He says appropriately, therefore, to the crowds without the addition of "good": "Every tree, therefore, which does not produce fruit is cut down and cast into the fire."[259] Furthermore, the tree which continues to bear fruit like that in the beginning "is cut down and cast into the fire,"[260] because it is a tree which does not produce good fruit when it does not produce fruit as praise to the Lord once the three year period is past and it has entered the fourth year.[261]

*The necessary view on the whole
of the diverse attitudes towards the Baptist*

(146) Now although all these things appear to be a digression as we cite the words from the other Gospels, they do not appear to be untimely or foreign to our present consideration. For after the priests and Levites were sent from Jerusalem to ask John who he was, Pharisees send to him asking, "Why then do you baptize if you are not the Christ, nor Elias, nor the prophet?"[262] After they have examined him, they are next present to be baptized, as Matthew records,[263] and hear words appropriate to their imposture and hypocrisy.

(147) And because what was said to them was similar to what is said to the crowds, we had to consider a comparison of the statements and their precise meaning. The natural sequence demanded that we consider more than what was present. Furthermore, we shall also, of necessity, add the following remarks to what has been said: Two ranks of those who send are recorded in John. One is the Jews from Jerusalem who send priests and Levites;[264] the other, Pharisees who raise the question of why he baptizes.[265]

258. Cf. Lv 19.23–24.
259. Cf. Lk 3.9. See note 257.
260. Mt 3.10; Lk 3.9.
261. Cf. Lv 19.24.
262. Jn 1.25. Preuschen's text has omitted the "nor" between "Elias" and "the prophet." Both Blanc and Brooke have it. Since none of the three mentions a textual problem here, I have assumed that it was a printing error in Preuschen's text.
263. Cf. Mt 3.7.
264. Cf. Jn 1.19.
265. Cf. Jn 1.24.

(148) We have explained that, after the question, the Pharisees come to be baptized. Perhaps, then, those Jews who sent from Jerusalem before the Pharisees, also came to be baptized before them, once they received John's words, since they sent to him before the Pharisees.

(149) For Jerusalem, all Judea and consequently all the country around the Jordan were being baptized in the Jordan river by him confessing their sins;[266] or as Mark[267] says, "All the country of Judea went out to him in the Jordan river, and all the people of Jerusalem, and were baptized by him in the Jordan river, confessing their sins."[268] Matthew, therefore, does not introduce the Pharisees and Sadducees, to whom the words are addressed, "Generation of vipers, etc."[269] nor does Luke introduce the crowds who hear the same rebuke,[270] as confessing their sins.

(150) It is worthwhile to raise the question, when all the city of Jerusalem and all Judea and all the country around the Jordan are being baptized by John in the Jordan, how the Savior says, "John the Baptist has come neither eating nor drinking, and you say, 'He has a demon.'"[271] And to those who inquire, "By what authority do you do these things?" he says, "I also will ask you one word which, if you tell me, I too will tell you by what authority I do these things. Whence was the baptism of John? From heaven, or from men?"[272] And when they discuss the matter they say: "If we say, 'From heaven,' he will say, 'Why did you not believe him?'"[273]

(151) The difficulty is solved as follows. The Pharisees, as we have observed previously, who heard the words, "Generation of vipers, etc."[274] although they have not believed him, probably come for baptism because they fear the crowd and, in accordance with their hypocrisy towards them, consider it proper to let themselves be washed that they might not seem to be opposed to such people.

266. Cf. Mt 3.5.
268. Mk 1.5.
270. Cf. Lk 3.7.
272. Cf. Mt 21.23–25.
274. Cf. Mt 3.7.

267. The MSS. have Luke.
269. Mt 3.7.
271. Cf. Lk 7.33.
273. Cf. Mt 21.25.

(152) Thinking, then, that he has his baptism from men and not from heaven, they are afraid to say what they think because of the crowd, for fear of being stoned.[275] Consequently, what the Savior says to the Pharisees is not contrary to what has been recorded in the Gospels about the multitude of those who are baptized by John. It was the insolence of the Pharisees that caused them to say that John had a demon, and to declare that Jesus had performed his miracles by Beelzebub, the prince of demons.[276]

John answered them, saying: 'I baptize with water; he has stood in your midst, whom you do not know, he who comes after me, the latchet of whose shoe I am not worthy to loose.'

Pertinence of the response of John

(153) Heracleon thinks John does not answer what those sent by the Pharisees asked, but what he himself wished. He does not notice that he is accusing the prophet of stupidity, if indeed when he is asked one thing he answers about another. This is something that must be guarded against since it is a common fault in a consultation.

(154) We say, however, that the answer is especially to the point. For what else would be appropriate to say to the question, "Why, then, do you baptize, if you are not the Christ?"[277] than to show that his own baptism is more corporeal? For "I," he says, "baptize with water."[278] And after he said this in response to the words, "Why then do you baptize?" he responds to the second part, "If you are not the Christ," by glorifying the preeminent essence of Christ, whose power is such that although he is invisible in his deity, he is present with every man and is coextensive with everything, including the whole universe. This is revealed by the words, "He has stood in your midst."[279]

275. Cf. Lk 20.6.
277. Jn 1.25.
279. Ibid.
276. Cf. Lk 7.33; 11.15.
278. Jn 1.26.

Grandeur of Jesus

(155) Since the Pharisees who expected the sojourn of the Christ saw nothing so great about him, supposing him to be only a perfectly holy man, he rebukes their ignorance about his preeminence suitably by adding to the words, "He has stood in your midst," the words, "whom you do not know."[280]

(156) And, so that no one might suppose that the one who is invisible and extends to every man and the whole universe is other than the one who became incarnate and appeared on the earth and associated with men, he joins to the words, "He has stood in your midst, whom you do not know," the words, "Who comes after me,"[281] i.e. who will be made manifest after me.

(157) And because he understood the preeminence of the Christ which surpassed his own nature, a subject that some were in doubt about since they asked if he might be the Christ, wishing to show how far he fell short of Christ's greatness so that no one should think more about him than what he sees in him or hears from him[282] he adds, "the latchet of whose shoe I am not worthy to loose."[283] He is hinting that he is not sufficient to loose and explain the word about his incarnation which has been bound, as it were, and hidden to those who do not understand, so as to say anything worthy of so great a sojourn which was compressed into so short a time.

Parallel passages of the Synoptics

(158) It is not untimely for us, since we are investigating the words, "I baptize with water,"[284] to juxtapose the similar texts on this subject from the evangelists and compare them with the one before us.

(159) Matthew says, therefore, "when he saw many of the Pharisees and Sadducees coming for baptism,"[285] after the rebuking words which we investigated, "I baptize you in water

---

280. Ibid.
282. Cf. 2 Cor 12.6.
284. Jn 1.26.
281. Jn 1.27.
283. Jn 1.27.
285. Mt 3.7.

unto repentance; but he who comes after me is mightier than I, whose shoes I am not worthy to bear; he will baptize you in the Holy Spirit and fire."[286] This is in agreement with the word in John which speaks of the avowal of his baptism in water to those sent from the Pharisees.[287]

(160) Mark says, "John preached saying, 'He who is mightier than I comes after me, the latchet of whose shoes I am not worthy to stoop down and loose. I baptized you with water, but he will baptize you with the Holy Spirit.'"[288] He is teaching that these things have been proclaimed to the masses and to all who hear.

(161) Luke says, "While the people were in suspense and all were reasoning in their hearts about John, whether he might be the Christ, John answered, saying to all, 'I baptize you with water, but he who is mightier than I, the latchet of whose shoes I am not worthy to loose, he will baptize you with the Holy Spirit and fire.'"[289]

Discussion of the text of Matthew

(162) Since, then, we have the parallel texts of the four Gospels in hand, let us see, to the best of our ability, the intention of each individually and the differences, beginning from Matthew who is also related in tradition to have published his Gospel before the others for the Hebrews, i.e. for those of the circumcision who believe.[290] "I," he says, "baptize you in water unto repentance,"[291] purifying you, as it were, and turning you away from worse ways and exhorting you to repentance. For I have come "to prepare for the Lord a prepared people,"[292] and, by the baptism of repentance, to make ready a place for the one who will come after me, and who, for this reason, will benefit you in better ways and much more mightily than I am able. For his baptism is not corporeal, since the Holy Spirit fills the one who repents, and a more divine fire removes everything material, and utterly destroys every-

286. Cf. Mt 3.11.
287. Cf. Jn 1.24–26.
288. Cf. Mk 1.7–8.
289. Lk 3.15–16.
290. Cf. Eusebius *H.E.* 6.25.4; 3.39.15–17; Irenaeus *Adv. Haer.* 3.1.2.
291. Cf. Mt 3.11.
292. Lk 1.17.

thing earthly, not only from the one who contains it but also from the one who hears those who possess it.

(163) But he who comes after me is so much mightier than I that I am not even sufficient to bear the parts of the garment of the lowest powers around him, which are not set forth in a naked manner so that just anyone can understand them, nor am I sufficient to bear him who submits to them.

(164) I do not know which of the two subjects I should address, whether my great weakness which cannot bear the paltry things of the Christ in comparison with the greater things around him, or his deity which surpasses and is greater than the whole universe. If indeed I, who received so great a grace that I was even thought worthy of prophecy which foretells the events related to my coming into the life of men in the words, "I am the voice of one crying in the wilderness,"[293] and, "Behold I send my angel before your face."[294] I, whose birth "Gabriel, who has stood before God,"[295] announced, contrary to expectation, to my father who was advanced in age,[296] I, at whose name Zachary regained, at the same time, his voice and the ability to prophesy by it,[297] I who received testimony from my Lord that no one, therefore, among those born of women is greater than me,[298] I am not even worthy to bear his shoes. If, indeed, I cannot bear his shoes, what must we say about his garments? Who is this who will be able to preserve his garment complete? Who is it who can grasp with his understanding the tunic which is seamless from above because it is woven throughout,[299] and contains a teaching?

(165) We must note that although the Four Gospels have said that John confesses that he has come to baptize in water, only Matthew adds to this the phrase "unto repentance."[300] He is teaching that the benefit of baptism depends on the choice of the one who is baptized. It is a benefit for the one who repents, but it will result in a more grievous judgment for the one who does not approach baptism in this way.

293. Jn 1.23.
294. Mt 11.10.
295. Lk 1.19.
296. Accepting Wendland's correction of *gegenēmenō* for *gegennēmenou*.
297. Cf. Lk 1.64.
298. Cf. Mt 11.11.
299. Cf. Jn 19.23.
300. Mt 3.11.

(166) We must know that, although the prodigious miracles in relation to the healings performed by the Savior are symbols of those always being set free from every disease and sickness by the Word of God, and though they were physical, they have no less profited those who experienced the kindness by summoning them to faith. In the same way also, the washing through the water, which is a symbol of the soul's purification as it washes from itself all the filth which comes from evil, is no less also in itself the beginning and source of divine gifts to the one who hands himself over to the divinity of the power of the invocation of the venerable Trinity, "For there are diversities of gifts."[301]

(167) The history recorded in the Acts of the Apostles bears witness to my word concerning the fact that the Spirit resided so manifestly at that time in those who were baptized,[302] the water having prepared the way for him in advance in those who approached it genuinely. So even Simon the magician was astonished and wished to receive this gift from Peter, but he wanted to receive that which is most just by means of unjust mammon.[303]

(168) We must note that John's baptism was inferior to Jesus' baptism which was given through his disciples.[304] Those, therefore, in Acts who have been baptized into John's baptism, who have not even heard that there was a Holy Spirit, are baptized a second time by the Apostle.[305]

(169) For the washing of regeneration did not come about at the hands of John, but at the hands of Jesus through his disciples, and the so-called bath of rebirth takes places with the renewal of the Spirit,[306] which even now is borne above the water,[307] since it is from God, but it does not appear in everyone after the water. These words complete our examination of the statements in the Gospel according to Matthew.

301. Cf. 1 Cor 12.4.
302. Cf. Acts 8.16–17.
303. Cf. Acts 8.18–20; Lk 16.9.
304. Cf. Jn 4.2.
305. Cf. Acts 19.2–5.
306. Cf. Ti 3.5.
307. Cf. Gn 1.2.

The text of Mark

(170) Let us now consider Mark's words. He has recorded that when John preached, he said the same[308] things in this way: "One who is mightier than I is coming after me."[309] These words are equivalent to, "He who comes after me is mightier than I."[310] But he no longer says the same things in the statement, "I am not worthy to stoop down to loose the latchet of his shoes."[311]

(171) It is one thing to bear the shoes which obviously have already been loosed from the feet of the wearer, but another to stoop down to loose the latchet of shoes. Consequently, since no one of the evangelists errs or lies, as those who believe would say, the Baptist has made both statements, but at different times, moved in his understanding now in one way, now in another.

(172) For those whose records differ have not, as some think, reported about the same things, as if they remembered inaccurately each of the things which were said or happened.

Spiritual interpretation of the shoes of Jesus

It is a great thing, then, to bear the shoes of Jesus, but it is also great to stoop down to his bodily aspects which have occurred somewhere below, in order to contemplate his image below, and to loose each difficulty related to the mystery of the Incarnation, as if each were the latchet of his shoes.

(173) For one is the bond of obscurity just as the key of knowledge[312] is also one. Not even he who is greatest among those born of women[313] is sufficient in himself to loose or open[314] these difficulties, since he alone who bound and locked[315] grants to whom he wishes to loose and to open the latchet of his shoes and the things that have been locked.

---

308. Accepting Blanc's accenting of *tauta*. Preuschen accents the word so as to mean "these things."
309. Mk 1.7.
310. Mt 3.11.
311. Mk 1.7.
312. Cf. Lk 11.52.
313. Cf. Lk 7.28.
314. Cf. Rv 5.2.
315. Cf. Rv 3.7.

(174) If the passage about the shoes possesses a hidden meaning we ought not pass over it. I think, therefore, that the Incarnation, when the Son of God takes up flesh and bones, is one of the shoes; and the descent into the house of Hades, whoever Hades is, and the journey into prison with the Spirit is the other.[316]

(175) It is said in Psalm 15 of the descent into the house of Hades: "You will not leave my soul in Hades."[317] And Peter, in the Catholic Epistle, says of the journey in prison with the Spirit, "Having been put to death in the flesh, but enlivened in the spirit, in which also he went and preached to the spirits in prison which were once disobedient when God's patience waited in the days of Noe while the Ark was being built."[318]

(176) He, therefore, who is able to show the meanings of both sojourns in a worthy manner is sufficient to loose the latchet of Jesus' shoes. He himself, by stooping down in his understanding and descending with the one who has descended into Hades, descends both from heaven and from the mysteries of Christ's divinity to his sojourn which necessarily took place among us when he put on man like a shoe.

(177) But when he put on man he also put on death. "For to this end Jesus died and arose, that he might be Lord both of the dead and of the living."[319] And for this reason he put on the living and the dead, that is the one on earth and the one in Hades, "that he might be Lord of both the dead and the living."

(178) Who, then, is sufficient to stoop down and loose the latchet of such great shoes, and after he has loosed them, not to let them be, but by virtue of a second sufficiency, to take them up and bear them by carrying about in memory what has been perceived?

(179) We must not leave unexamined, however, the fact that the statement is made in the same way in Luke and John without the expression, "stooped down."[320] Perhaps it is possible, on the one hand, for one who has stooped down to loose

---

316. Cf. 1 Pt 3.18–19.
318. Cf. 1 Pt 3.18–20.
320. Cf. Lk 3.16; Jn 1.26.

317. Cf. Ps 15.10.
319. Cf. Rom 14.9.

the shoes in relation to what was said previously. But it is also possible that one preserve the majesty of the exaltation of the Word and discover the loosing of the shoes which were bound in the course of the investigation, so that once he has loosed these shoes, he beholds the Word as he actually is, without the shoes, stripped of inferior things, the son of God.

Comparison of John and the Synoptics

(180) Now not to be "sufficient"[321] is not the same as not being "worthy"[322] which John writes. For it is possible for one to be sufficient although he is not worthy, and it is possible for one who is worthy not yet to be sufficient.

(181) For if indeed the gifts are given for the common good[323] and not only "in proportion to our faith,"[324] it would be the work of a God who loves man, and who foresees the harm from the accompanying self-conceit or pride, sometimes not to give sufficiency even to one who is worthy. And it is a proper quality of the goodness of God to conquer the one who is being benefitted while he is benefitting him, taking in advance the one who will be worthy and, before he becomes worthy, adorning him with sufficiency that, after the sufficiency he might reach the point of being worthy. It is not at all the case that on the basis of his worthiness he should reach the point of being sufficient, anticipating the giver and having received his gifts in advance.

(182) John says, therefore, in the Synoptics that he is not "sufficient,"[325] but in John that he is not "worthy."[326] He is not excluded, however, who at least has said that although he is not yet sufficient he should become sufficient, even if he was not worthy up to this time; and again he is not excluded who at least has said that he is not worthy, and although he is not worthy he might reach the point of becoming worthy.[327]

(183) This is true, then, unless someone should say that the

---

321. Cf. Mt 3.11.
322. Cf. Jn 1.27.
323. Cf. 1 Cor 12.7.
324. Rom 12.6.
325. Cf. Mt 3.11; Mk 1.7; Lk 3.16.
326. Cf. Jn 1.27.
327. The point of this sentence lies in Origen's distinction between the ideas of "being" and "becoming."

mortal nature is never capable of coming to the point of worthily loosing [and] bearing the shoes, since John truly says he was never able to become sufficient to loose the latchet of the shoes and to become worthy of the same.[328] But however much we may advance, there are still things left behind not yet understood, since according to the wisdom of Jesus Son of Sirach, "When a man has finished, then he begins, and when he has ceased, then he shall be at a loss."[329]

The shoes and the shoe

(184) Let us discuss further the shoes which are thus specified by the three evangelists, comparing them with the one specified in the singular by the disciple John. For he says, "I am not worthy to loose the thong of his shoe."[330]

(185) Perhaps, then, he was overcome by the grace of God which he had freely received[331] when he was not yet worthy in himself of so much as to loose the thong of the other's shoes when he considered his sojourn among men about which he also testifies. Since he also lacked knowledge of the events which followed, as he did not know whether Jesus was the one who also comes to that place where he was to go from prison after he was beheaded, or it was necessary to await another,[332] for this reason, he alludes even now to the problem which was later revealed more clearly to us, and says, "I am not worthy to loose the latchet of his shoe."[333]

(186) But he who thinks this discussion rather superfluous will combine the statement about the shoes and the one about the shoe into the same account so that he says, as it were, I am by no means worthy to loose the latchet, not even to make a beginning of even one shoe. Or, it is also possible that what is said in the four Gospels be combined into a single account as follows.

(187) If John understands the things concerning his sojourn here, but is in doubt about the events which come next, he is

---

328. The construction of the passage is very obscure.
329. Sir 18.5.
330. Jn 1.27.
331. Cf. Mt 10.8.
332. Cf. Mt 11.3.
333. Jn 1.27.

speaking the truth when he says that he is not sufficient to loose the latchet of his shoes, for he does not loose both latchets when he has loosed that of one shoe. But he is also speaking the truth in reference to the latchet of the shoe, since, as we have said before, he is still in doubt about whether he is the coming one or there is another, who is also to be expected there.[334]

The presence of the Word

(188) Concerning the statement, "He whom you do not know has stood in your midst,"[335] we must take these words of the Son of God, the Word, through whom all things were made,[336] who subsists in his essence insofar as the substance is concerned, and is identical with wisdom. For he has permeated all creation,[337] that the things which are made through him may always be made, and it may always be true of everything, whatever it be, that "all things were made through him and without him nothing was made,"[338] and "You made all things in wisdom."[339]

(189) But if he has permeated all creation, it is obvious that he has also permeated those who asked, "Why then do you baptize, if you are not the Christ, nor Elias, nor the prophet?"[340] The same one has stood "in the midst," being also a firm word, confirmed everywhere by the Father. Or, let the saying, "He has stood in your midst" be taken in the sense that "he has stood in your midst" means you men because you are spiritual beings, since it is demonstrated that the ruling principle is located in the midst of every body, being in the heart according to the Scriptures.

(190) These, therefore, who have the Word in their midst but have no knowledge of his nature, knowing neither his source and origin, nor how he has existed in them, did not know him although they had him in their midst. But John

---

334. Cf. the discussion above in section 185 and, for the general setting of the discussion, section 174.
335. Jn 1.26.
336. Cf. Jn 1.3.
337. Cf. Col 1.16–17.
338. Jn 1.3.
339. Ps 103.24.
340. Jn 1.25.

knows him. For the words, "Whom you do not know,"[341] which are spoken reproachfully to the Pharisees, show that he has known very well what is not known by them, namely the Word.

How Christ will come after the Baptist

(191) And because he knows him, the Baptist knows that the one who is in their midst is coming after him, i.e. by sojourning in those who are washed in their understanding[342] after him and the teaching given by him in baptism. The same thing is not meant, however, by the word "after" as it is used here, and when Jesus sends us *after* himself.[343]

(192) In the latter case we are commanded to come after him, that by going in his steps we might come to the Father; here, [however], it is used to show that after John's teachings (since he has come "that all might believe through him"[344]), the perfect Word sojourns in those who have prepared themselves in advance, and have purified themselves in advance through the inferior means.

Strength of the attitude of Christ

(193) In the first place, then, the Father stands, being immutable and unchangeable. His Word, however, also always stands, even if in the act of saving he becomes flesh and is in the midst of men, neither comprehended,[345] nor even seen. He stands, however, and teaches, inviting all to drink from his plentiful spring, for "Jesus stood and cried saying, 'If any man thirst, let him come to me and drink.'"[346]

The interpretation of Heracleon: he does not believe in the visible presence of the Savior

(194) But Heracleon says the statement, "He stands in your midst"[347] is the equivalent of: He is already present and is in the world and among men, and is already manifest to all of you. In this way he nullifies what we have shown about him permeating the whole world.

---

341. Jn 1.26.
343. Cf. Mk 1.17 and 20.
345. Cf. Jn 1.5.
347. Cf. Jn 1.26.

342. *Kata logon.*
344. Jn 1.7.
346. Jn 7.37.

(195) We must reply, When is he not present? And when is he not in the world? Even the gospel says as much: "He was in the world, and the world was made through him."³⁴⁸ It is for this reason too that these to whom the Word is he "whom you do not know,"³⁴⁹ do not know him, because they have not yet gone out of the world, and "the world did not know him."³⁵⁰

(196) At what time did he interrupt his sojourn among men? Was he not in Isaias when he said, "The spirit of the Lord is upon me, because he has anointed me,"³⁵¹ and "I became manifest to those who were not seeking me"?³⁵² Let them say if he was not also in David when he said, not on his own, "But I was appointed king by him over Sion his holy mountain,"³⁵³ and as many other words as have been recorded in the Psalms in the person of Christ.

(197) And why must I demonstrate in detail that he was always among men? The statements which are capable of showing this clearly would be difficult to enumerate. Must I refute what was not stated correctly—namely "He is already present and is in the world and among men"—as Heracleon's interpretation of the words: "He has stood in your midst"?³⁵⁴

John confesses his unworthiness in the face of Jesus

His statement, however, is not unconvincing that the words, "who comes after me,"³⁵⁵ reveal that John is the forerunner of the Christ. For he is truly like a servant running before his master.

(198) Heracleon has, however, taken the statement, "I am not worthy to loose the thong of his shoes,"³⁵⁶ much too simply, in the sense that the Baptist confesses through these words that he is not worthy even of the lowliest service to the Christ. But after this interpretation he has suggested rather plausibly this view: I am not sufficient that for my sake he should descend from his greatness and receive flesh as a shoe, of which I can give no account or description or explain the plan concerning it.

The Baptist as the symbol of the Creator

(199) The same Heracleon, after taking the shoe as the world in a very powerful and ingenious manner, changed his position to declare very impiously that all these words must be understood also about that person who is indicated by John. For he thinks that the

---

348. Jn 1.10.
349. Jn 1.26.
350. Cf. Jn 1.10.
351. Is 61.1.
352. Is 65.1; cf. Rom 10.20.
353. Ps 2.6.
354. Jn 1.26.
355. Jn 1.27.
356. Ibid.

224   ORIGEN

Creator of the world, who is inferior to Christ, acknowledges this fact through these words. This is the greatest of all impieties. For the Father who sent him, the God of the living, as Jesus himself testifies, being God of Abraham, and of Isaac, and of Jacob,[357] the Lord of heaven and earth because he has made them, is alone good and greater than the one who was sent.

The shoe, figure of the world

(201) But even if, as we said previously, Heracleon has taken all the world in a very powerful manner to be the shoe of Jesus, I do not think we must agree. For how will the saying, "Heaven is my throne and the earth my footstool,"[358] which Jesus attested to be said of the Father, be retained with such an interpretation? For "swear not by heaven," he said, "because it is the throne of God, nor by the earth, for it is his footstool."[359]

(202) And how will it be possible to set the text, "'Do not I fill heaven and earth?' says the Lord,"[360] side by side with the whole world understood as Jesus' shoe? It is worthwhile, however, to give attention to whether we must understand the words in relation to the fact that the Word and Wisdom have permeated the whole world, and the Father is in the Son, as we presented it, or he who first girded himself with all creation, because the Son was in him, granted to the Savior, since he was second after him and God the Word, to pervade the whole creation.

(203) It will be especially worthwhile for those who can comprehend the ceaseless movement of so great a heaven which brings so great a multitude of stars around with itself from east to west to inquire into what immanent power is so great and ancient in all the world. It may, perhaps, be impious to dare say that this power is different from the Father and the Son.

These things were done in Bethabara beyond the Jordan where John was baptizing.

Necessity of replacing Bethany with Bethabara

(204) We are not unaware that "these things were done in Bethania" occurs in nearly all the manuscripts. It seems likely too that, in addition, this was the earlier reading.

And, to be sure, we have read "Bethania" in Heracleon.

---

357. Cf. Mt 22.32.
359. Cf. Mt 5.34–35.

358. Is 66.1; Acts 7.49.
360. Jer 23.24.

COMMENTARY ON JOHN, BOOK 6

But since we have been in the places, so far as the historical account is concerned, of the footprints of Jesus and his disciples and the prophets, we have been convinced that we ought not to read "Bethania," but "Bethabara."

(205) For, as the same evangelist says, Bethania, the country of Lazarus and Martha and Mary, is about fifteen stades from Jerusalem.[361] The Jordan river is about 188 stades, roughly speaking, beyond Bethania. There is, however, no place in the vicinity of the Jordan with the same name as Bethania. They say, however, that Bethabara is pointed out on the bank of the Jordan. There they say John baptized.

(206) In addition, the meaning of the name Bethabara is appropriate for the baptism of the one who prepares for the Lord a prepared people, for it is translated, "house of preparation." Bethania, however, means "house of obedience."[362] Where else would it be appropriate for the one sent as an angel before the face of Christ to prepare his way before him[363] to baptize than in the "house of preparation"?

(207) And what sort of country is more suitable for Mary who chose the good part which is not taken from her, and for Martha who is disturbed because she is entertaining Jesus,[364] and their brother Lazarus who is said to be loved by the Savior,[365] than Bethania, "the house of obedience"? We must not, therefore, despise precision concerning names if we wish to understand the Holy Scriptures perfectly.

(208) The following examples in the Gospels, however, may persuade us that matters related to names are incorrect in the Greek manuscripts in many places. The business about the swine which were thrown down from a cliff by demons and drowned in the sea is recorded to have occurred in the country of the Gerasens.[366]

(209) Gerasa, however, is a city of Arabia which has neither a sea nor a lake nearby. The evangelists would not have said

---

361. Cf. Jn 11.1 and 18.
362. Cf. Lagarde, *Onomastica* 201.55; 175.8.
363. Cf. Mal 3.1.   364. Cf. Lk 10.41–42.
365. Cf. Jn 11.3.
366. Cf. Mt 8.28–32; Mk 5.1–13; Lk 8.26–33.

something so clearly false and easy to refute since they were men who knew the regions around Judea thoroughly.

(210) And since we have found the words, "Into the country of the Gadarenes," in a few manuscripts,[367] we must also say something about this name. Gadara is a city of Judea around which there are famous hot springs, but there is no lake [or] sea lying beside the cliffs.

(211) But Gergesa, from which comes the name the Gergesenes, is an ancient city in the vicinity of the lake which is now called Tiberias. There is a cliff lying beside this lake from which they point out the swine were cast down by the demons. Gergesa means the "lodging of those who have cast out,"[368] which is perhaps a name prophetically significant of what the citizens who owned the swine did in regard to the Savior when they urged him to depart from their borders.

(212) It is possible to see the same inaccuracy in many passages of the Law and prophets, as we have investigated them thoroughly after we learned from the Hebrews and compared our manuscripts with theirs, which are confirmed by the translations of Aquila and Theodotion and Symmachus which have not yet been corrupted.

(213) We will present a few things, therefore, that those who are eager for learning might become more attentive about these matters. One of the sons of Levi, the first, is named Geson[369] in most of the manuscripts instead of Gerson, which is the same name as that of the first-born of Moses.[370] The name was appropriate since both were born because of a sojourn in a foreign land.[371]

(214) Again, we say Juda's second son to be Aunan, but the Hebrews say he is Onan, "their toil."[372] In addition to these,

---

367. The confusion of the name of the place in this story is well attested in the apparatus of the 26th edition of the Nestle-Aland New Testament text.
368. Cf. Lagarde, *Onomastica,* 202.61; 189.10.
369. Preuschen thinks "Gedson" should be written in place of "Geson."
370. Cf. Ex 6.16; Nm 3.17; Ex 2.22.
371. See Blanc SC 120.293, note 3, for the Hebrew etymology of the name "Gerson."
372. Cf. Gn 46.12.

in the departures of the sons of Israel in Numbers we found that "they departed from Soccoth and camped in Bouthan."[373] But the Hebrew says "Aiman"[374] instead of Bouthan.

(215) Why should I spend more time presenting examples since it is easy for one who wishes to investigate and come to know what is true in relation to the names? But we must especially suspect those passages of the Scriptures where there is a catalogue of several names together, as the names concerning the distribution of land in Josue, and in the first book of Paralipomenon from the beginning up to somewhere near the mention of Anan.[375] And likewise also in Esdras.

(216) We must not despise the proper names, since they indicate facts useful for the interpretation of the passages. This, however, is not the time to abandon what lies before us and investigate the science[376] of the study of names.

In Jordan, translated "a descent," is the figure of the Word made flesh

(217) Let us, therefore, observe the names that occur in the Gospel text. Jordan is translated by "their descent."[377] The name of Jared resembles this, if I may say so. It too is translated "descending,"[378] since, as it is written in Enoch, if one wants to accept this book as sacred Scripture, he was born to Maleleel in the days of the descent of the sons of God to the daughters of men.[379] Some have supposed that this descent intimates the descent of souls to bodies, having assumed that the daughters of men is a figurative expression for the earthly tent.

(218) But if this is so, what river would be "their descent," to which one must come to be purified, which has not descended with its own descent, but that of men, if not our Savior

---

373. Nm 33.6.
374. Preuschen thinks this is incorrect since the Hebrew has "Etham."
375. Cf. 1 Chr 9.44. 376. *Logos*.
377. Cf. Lagarde, *Onomastica* 206.70.
378. Cf. Lagarde, *Onomastica* 167.36.
379. Cf. Enoch 37.1; 6.1–7.2; 86.1–6; Gn 6.2.

who separates those who are endowed with their inheritance by Moses from those who receive their own portions through Jesus?[380]

(219) "The streams" of this "river" which has descended "make glad the city of God,"[381] as we have found in the Psalms. This is [not] the Jerusalem perceptible to the senses (for it does not have a river lying beside it), but the blameless Church of God which is built "upon the foundation of the apostles and prophets, Christ Jesus "our Lord" being the chief cornerstone."[382]

(220) Nevertheless, we must understand the Jordan to be [the] Word of God which became flesh and dwelt among us.[383] This is Jesus who distributed as an inheritance the humanity which he took up, wherefore he is also the "chief cornerstone." He too is baptized, although he was in the divinity of the Son of God which he had assumed. It is at the time of his baptism that he receives the pure and guileless dove of the Spirit, which has been bound to him and can no longer fly away, for he says, "Upon whom you see the Spirit descending and remaining upon him, he it is who baptizes with the Holy Spirit."[384] He, therefore, received the Spirit which remained on him that he might be able to baptize those who come to him with that very Spirit which remained.

(221) John, however, baptizes "beyond the Jordan"[385] in the regions lying outside Judea in Bethabara, since he is the forerunner of him who has come to call, not the "just but sinners,"[386] and who teaches that the strong have no need of physicians, but those who are sick,[387] since indeed, baptism is given "for the remission of sins."[388]

---

380. i.e. Josue. The Greek spelling of Josue is *Jesus*. Origen often plays on this identity of name between Josue and Jesus.
381. Cf. Ps 45.5.
382. Cf. Eph 2.20.
383. Cf. Jn 1.14.
384. Cf. Jn 1.33.
385. Cf. Jn 1.28.
386. Cf. Mt 9.13.
387. Cf. Mt 9.12.
388. Mk 1.4.

The different aspects of the Savior concerning the different states of the soul

(222) It is likely, however, that someone who has not understood the different aspects of the Savior will take offense at the interpretation which was rendered concerning the Jordan, because John says, "I baptize in water, but he who comes after me is mightier than I; he will baptize you in the Holy Spirit."[389]

(223) We must say to him that while the Word of God is a drink,[390] to some he is water, but to others he is wine which gladdens the heart of man,[391] and to others he is blood because of the saying: "Unless you drink my blood, you do not have life in yourselves."[392] But also, while he is said to be food, he is not understood to be the living bread and flesh[393] at the same time. In the same way, the same one is a baptism of water, and of spirit, and of fire,[394] and for some, even of blood.

(224) Now he speaks of this last baptism, in the view of some, in the saying: "And I have a baptism with which to be baptized, and how distressed I am until it is accomplished!"[395] In agreement with this, the disciple John has recorded in his Epistle that the three, the Spirit, and the water, and the blood, became one.[396] And to be sure,[397] if one acknowledges that he is a way and a door,[398] it is clear that he is not yet a door for the person for whom he is still a way, and that he is no longer a way for the person for whom he is already a door.

---

389. Cf. Mt 3.11.
390. Cf. Jn 4.10.
391. Cf. Ps 103.15.
392. Cf. Jn 6.53.
393. Cf. Jn 6.51 and 53.
394. Cf. Lk 3.16; see also Crouzel, *Origène*, 291.
395. Lk 12.50. Preuschen punctuates the saying as a question.
396. Cf. 1 Jn 5.8.
397. I have emended *de pou* of the texts to *dēpou*. The indefinite adverb *pou*, "somewhere" or "perhaps" does not fit the sentence. Origen certainly knew the location of Jesus' statements that he is the "door" and the "way." *Pou*, however, would suggest that he was uncertain of the location of the sayings, or, if we take the meaning "perhaps" it puts an indefiniteness in the clause that does not fit the rest of the sentence.
398. Cf. Jn 14.6; 10.7.

(225) Let all, then, who are being instructed in the beginning principles of the oracles of God,[399] who come to the voice of the one crying in the wilderness: "Make straight the way of the Lord,"[400] which is "beyond the Jordan"[401] at the "house of preparation,"[402] be prepared through the previous preparation, so that they can receive the spiritual word which is born in them through the enlightenment of the Spirit.

(226) As a consequence of this exposition, because we have collected the materials about the Jordan, we will have a more accurate understanding of the river. God, then, leads the people across the Red Sea, by Moses, the water itself having made a wall for them on the right and on the left,[403] and, by Jesus,[404] he leads them across the Jordan.[405]

A spiritual interpretation of the crossing of the Red Sea

(227) When Paul, however, read the Scripture, since he no longer waged war according to the flesh[406] (for he knew that "the Law is spiritual"[407]), he teaches us to understand the facts of this very crossing at the Red Sea spiritually, saying in the First Epistle to the Corinthians: "For I do not wish you to be ignorant, brothers, that our fathers were all under the cloud, and all passed through the sea. And all were baptized into Moses in the cloud in the sea, and all ate the same spiritual food and all drank the same[408] spiritual drink, for they drank of the rock which followed them, and the rock was Christ."[409]

(228) In conformity with these words, let us also ask God to grant us the ability to understand spiritually the crossing of the Jordan through Jesus.[410] We say that Paul would have said also of this crossing, "I do not wish you to be ignorant, brothers, that our fathers all passed through the Jordan, and all were baptized into Jesus[411] in the Spirit and in the river."

---

399. Cf. Heb 5.12.
400. Jn 1.23.
401. Jn 1.28.
402. See section 206 above.
403. Cf. Ex 14.22.
404. i.e. Josue.
405. Cf. Jos 3.15–16.
406. Cf. 2 Cor 10.3.
407. Rom 7.14.
408. Preuschen thinks *auto* should be inserted here with V. Blanc inserts it in her text.
409. Cf. 1 Cor 10.1–4.
410. Josue.
411. Josue.

(229) Jesus,[412] who succeeded Moses, was a type of Jesus the Christ who succeeded the dispensation through the Law with the gospel proclamation. This is why, although they are all baptized into Moses in the cloud and in the sea, their baptism has a bitter and briny element, for they still fear their enemies and cry out to the Lord and to Moses saying, "Did you bring us out to die in the wilderness because there were no graves in Egypt? Why did you do this to us, having brought us out of Egypt?"[413]

(230) But the baptism into Jesus[414] in the truly sweet and fresh river has many elements superior to that baptism, since the religion has by this time been clarified and received a proper order. The Ark of the covenant of the Lord our God and the priests and Levites lead the way; the people follow the servants of God,[415] which means that they follow those who are capable of understanding the commandment about purity. Jesus[416] says to the people, "Purify yourselves tomorrow; the Lord will do wonders among us."[417]

(231) And he commands the priests to go before the people with the Ark of the covenant. It is then, too, that the mystery of the dispensation of the Father with the Son is manifested, since the Son is highly exalted by him who grants "that in the name of Jesus every knee should bow, of those that are in heaven, on earth, and under the earth; and that every tongue should confess that Jesus Christ is Lord, to the glory of God the Father."[418]

(232) These matters are revealed through the following words which have been recorded in the book of Josue: "And the Lord said to Jesus,[419] 'In this day I will begin to exalt you before the sons of Israel.'"[420] We must also hear our Lord Jesus saying to the sons of Israel, "Come here and hear the Word of the Lord our God. In this you shall know that the living God is among you."[421] For by being baptized into Jesus we will know that the living God is among us.

412. Josue.
414. Josue.
416. Josue.
418. Phil 2.10–11.
420. Cf. Jos 3.7.

413. Cf. Ex 14.11.
415. Cf. Jos 3.3.
417. Cf. Jos 3.5.
419. Josue.
421. Cf. Jos 3.9–10.

A new Passover made at the crossing of the Red Sea

(233) After they observed the Passover in Egypt they begin the exodus.[422] In the book of Josue, however, after the crossing of the Jordan, on the tenth day of the first month they encamped in Galgal. At this time it was necessary for the first time to take the uncircumcised[423] and give them a name as men who were to feast after Jesus' baptism. And all the sons of Israel who were formerly uncircumcised and who had come out of Egypt are circumcised by Jesus[424] with a sharp stone.[425] And the Lord acknowledges that he removed the reproach of Egypt on the day of the baptism into Jesus, when Jesus[426] purified the sons of Israel.

(234) For it is written: "And the Lord said to Jesus the son of Nun, 'This day I have taken away from you the reproach of Egypt.'"[427] Then the sons of Israel observed the Passover on the fourteenth day of the month much more cheerfully than the one in Egypt, seeing that they also "ate unleavened bread and fresh from the grain of the holy land,"[428] a food better than the manna.

(235) For God does not feed them on lesser foods when they have received the land according to promise, nor do they obtain inferior bread through Jesus[429] who is so great. This will be clear to the one who has perceived the true holy land and the Jerusalem above.

(236) For this reason the assertion occurs also in the same Gospel: "The fathers ate manna in the wilderness, and died. He who eats this bread will live forever."[430] The manna, although given by God, was the bread of progress, bread supplied to those still being attended, bread most appropriate for those under guardians and administrators.[431] But the new

---

422. Cf. Ex 12.21–37.
423. Accepting Preuschen's suggestion to substitute "uncircumcised" for "sheep." See Jos 4.19–5.8. Lk 1.59 and 2.21 suggest that a person was named at the time of his circumcision.
424. Josue. 425. Cf. Jos 5.2–3.
426. Jesus, in this sentence and the next, is Josue.
427. Jos 5.9. 428. Cf. Jos 5.11.
429. Josue. 430. Cf. Jn 6.49 and 51.
431. Cf. Gal 4.2.

bread in the holy land—reaped from the grain of the land when Jesus procured it, others having labored, but his disciples reaping it[432]—was a bread more life-giving than that. It is the bread which is given to those capable of receiving the inheritance of the fathers because of their perfection.

(237) This is why he who is still instructed by that former bread is subject to spiritual[433] death, but he who has arrived at the bread which succeeds it will live forever[434] when he has eaten it.

I think the presentation of all these matters was timely in our examination of the baptism at the Jordan performed by John in Bethabara.

Elias and Eliseus

(238) We must note in addition that when Elias was about to be taken up in a whirlwind as into heaven, he took his sheepskin and rolled it up and struck the water, and it was divided on this side and that, and both crossed, that is to say himself and Eliseus.[435] He was better prepared to be taken up after he was baptized in the Jordan, since Paul, as we explained previously, called the more incredible passage through water a baptism.[436]

(239) It is because of this same Jordan that Eliseus is capable of receiving the gift which he has desired through Elias, for he said, "Let a double portion come upon me in your spirit."[437] Perhaps he received the gift in the spirit of Elias in a double measure upon himself because he crossed the Jordan twice, once with Elias, and a second time when he took the sheepskin of Elias and struck the water and said: "Where is the God of Elias *aphpho*?[438] And he struck the waters, and they divided on this side and that."[439]

---

432. Cf. Jn 4.38.
433. Preuschen indicates that the text is corrupt here. It reads *to logō thanaton*. Wendland suggested substituting *tō logikō*, in agreement with the preceding *tō artō*. I have substituted *ton logikon*, in agreement with *thanaton*.
434. Cf. Jn 6.49 and 51.   435. Cf. 4 Kgs 2.1 and 8.
436. Cf. 1 Cor 10.2.   437. 4 Kgs 2.9.
438. *Aphpho* is written in the text of the LXX. It is a transliteration of the Hebrew '*aph hu*'.
439. Cf. 4 Kgs 2.14.

(240) But if someone should take offense at the expression, "He struck the water," because of our assertion that the Jordan was a type of the Word who condescended to our descent, we must say that in the Apostle the rock clearly was Christ, which was struck twice with the rod that they might be able to drink from the "spiritual rock which followed."[440]

(241) There is also, therefore, a kind of smiting in the objection of those who are fond of bringing forth ideas contrary to the conclusion of the Word[441] before they have learned what is being investigated. God delivers us from these. Where they thirst, he gives a drink, and where what is sought is impenetrable for us and inaccessible because of its depth, he makes it penetrable by the dividing of the Word, since most things are clarified for us by the Word which is capable of division.

Naaman the Syrian

(242) But in addition, that we may accept the interpretation of the Jordan, that river which is so fresh and grants so much grace, it is useful to present both Naaman the Syrian who was cleansed from leprosy, and the comments made about the rivers by the enemies of religion.

(243) It is written of Naaman, therefore: "He came with his horse and chariot, and stood at the doors of the house of Eliseus. And Eliseus sent a messenger to him saying, 'Go and wash seven times in the Jordan, and your flesh will return to you and you will be cleansed.'"[442] Then Naaman becomes angry because he does not perceive that it is our Jordan, and not the prophet, which removes the uncleanness of those who are unclean because of leprosy and heals them. For the work of a prophet is to send one to that which heals.

(244) Since, therefore, Naaman does not understand the great mystery of the Jordan, he says, "Behold I said that he will assuredly come out to me and will stand and call upon the name of the Lord his God and will place his hand upon

---

440. 1 Cor 10.4; cf. Ex 17.5–6; Nm 20.7–11.
441. Perhaps "reason." The text is *tou logou*.
442. Cf. 4 Kgs 5.9–10.

the place and the leprosy will recover,"[443] for placing the hand on leprosy and cleansing it was the work of my Lord Jesus alone. To the man who asked with faith, "If you will, you can make me clean, he not only said "I will, be made clean," but in addition to the word which he spoke, he also touched him, and he was cleansed from his leprosy.[444]

(245) Naaman who is still in error and does not see how inferior the other rivers are to the Jordan for healing the suffering, praises the rivers of Damascus, Abana and Pharphar, saying, "Are not the Abana and the Pharphar, rivers of Damascus, better than all the waters of Israel? Shall I not go and wash in them and be cleansed?"[445]

The Jordan, salvific river

For just as "no one is good but one, God"[446] the Father, so among rivers, none is good and able to release him from leprosy who washes his soul with faith in Jesus, except the Jordan.

(246) I think it is for this reason that those who sit by the rivers of Babylon, who remembered Sior, are recorded in Scripture to weep.[447] For when those who are captives because of evil have tasted other waters after the holy Jordan, they remember and long for their own saving river. This is why they say of the rivers of Babylon, "There we sat," namely because they could not stand, "and wept."[448]

(247) Jeremias too rebukes those who desire to drink the water of Egypt, and forsake the water which descends from heaven and is named water "of the descent,"[449] that is the Jordan, when he says: "And what have you to do with the way of Egypt, to drink the water of Geon, and to drink the water of rivers?"[450] Or, as the Hebrew has it: "To drink the water of Sior," of which this is not the time to speak.

---

443. Cf. 4 Kgs 5.11.
445. Cf. 4 Kgs 5.12.
446. Mk 10.18.
448. Ps 136.1.
449. Cf. above, paragraphs 217–18.
450. Cf. Jer 2.18.

444. Cf. Mt 8.2–3.

447. Cf. Ps 136.1.

Jordan, domain of God

(248) But that the foregoing word by the Spirit which speaks in the inspired Scriptures is not about rivers perceptible to the senses can be seen also from the things prophesied in Ezechiel to Pharaoh, king of Egypt, which goes as follows: "Behold, I am against you Pharaoh, king of Egypt, the great dragon seated in the midst of his rivers saying, 'The rivers are mine, and I made them.' And I will set traps in your jaws, and stick the fish of the river to your fins, and I will bring you up out of the midst of your river, and all the fish of the river, and I will cast you down swiftly, and all the fish of the river. You will fall upon the face of the earth, and you will not be gathered and you will not be buried."[451]

(249) What sort of physical dragon has ever been reported to have been seen in the actual river of Egypt? But perhaps the river of Egypt, which could not even kill the little child Moses, is the region of our enemy, the dragon. And just as the dragon is in the Egyptian river, so God is in the river which makes glad the city of God,[452] for the Father is in the Son.

(250) For this reason those who come to wash themselves in him put away the reproach of Egypt,[453] and become more fit to be taken up. They are cleansed from the most abominable leprosy,[454] and receive a double portion of gifts, and are prepared to receive the Holy Spirit, since the dove of the Spirit has not flown to another river.[455]

(251) Since, therefore, we have considered the Jordan in a manner more worthy of God, and the baptism in it, and Jesus who was baptized in it, and the "house of preparation,"[456] let us draw from the river as much of such aid as we need.

---

451. Cf. Ez 29.3–5. 452. Cf. Ps 45.5.
453. Cf. Jos 5.9.   454. Cf. 4 Kgs 5.9–14.
455. Cf. Mk 1.10. In section 250 Origen alludes to various conclusions he has drawn earlier in his discussion of the Jordan: Elias (238), Naaman (243–245), Eliseus (239), Jesus (220).
456. Cf. above, section 206.

The next day he sees Jesus coming to him.
The first meeting of Jesus and John the Baptist

(252) Earlier, Jesus' mother, as soon as she conceived, visited John's mother, and the latter was pregnant herself.[457] At this time the one infant who was being formed granted his semblance very precisely to the other infant who was being formed, causing him to be conformed to his glory.[458] Consequently because of their common appearance, John is thought to be Christ, and Jesus is supposed to be John risen from the dead[459] by those who do not distinguish the image from the one according to the image.[460] But now the Baptist sees Jesus himself coming to him after John's testimony about him which was examined previously.

(253) We must note, however, that on that first occasion the infant John leaped in his mother's womb because of the sound of Mary's greeting which reached Elizabeth's ears who at that time received the Holy Spirit from the voice, as it were. For "it came to pass," the Scripture says, "when Elizabeth heard Mary's greeting, the infant leaped in her womb, and Elizabeth was filled with the Holy Spirit, and she cried out with a loud voice and said."[461] But on this occasion, "John sees Jesus coming to him, and says, 'Behold the lamb of God who takes away the sin of the world.'"[462] One is instructed first by hearing about higher things; after this he becomes an eyewitness of them.

(254) Nevertheless, that John was benefited in his formation by the infant still being formed when the Lord came to Elizabeth in his mother, will be clear to one who has understood the comments we have made about John being the voice, but Jesus the Word.[463] For there is a loud voice in Elizabeth when she is filled with the Holy Spirit because of Mary's greeting,

---

457. Cf. Lk 1.39–41.
458. Cf. Phil 3.21.
459. Cf. Lk 9.5; Mt 14.2; Mk 6.14.
460. Cf. Gn 1.26.
461. Lk 1.41–42.
462. Jn 1.29.
463. See above, 6.94–100.

as the text itself shows which goes as follows: "And she (that is, Elizabeth) cried out with a loud voice and said."[464]

(255) When the sound of Mary's greeting reached Elizabeth's ears it filled her own John. This is why John leaps, and the mother becomes the mouth, as it were, and prophetess of the Son when she cries out with a loud cry and says, "Blessed are you among women, and blessed is the fruit of your womb."[465]

(256) Consequently, Mary's hasty journey into the hill country and entrance into Zachary's house, and the greeting with which she greets Elizabeth can now become clear to us.[466] For all these things occurred that Mary might share with John, who was still in his mother's womb, some of the power she had after she conceived, and that he might share some of the prophetic grace he received with his mother.

(257) Such dispensations were accomplished most reasonably in the hill country, since nothing great is received by those who will be called valleys because of their lowliness.

Progression and chronology of testimonies of John

At this point, therefore, after John's testimonies—the first being spoken by him who cried out and spoke of God,[467] the second to the priests and Levites who were sent from Jerusalem by the Jews,[468] and the third addressed to those of the Pharisees who examined him rather sharply,[469]—the one who testified now sees Jesus coming to him as he continues to advance and improve. The use of the expression "the next day" is a symbol of John's progress and improvement. For Jesus comes, in the subsequent illumination, as it were, and on the day following what had preceded. He is not only known as having stood in the midst even of those who knew him not,[470] but now also when he is seen as having come to him who earlier made these declarations.

---

464. Lk 1.42.
465. Ibid.
466. Cf. Lk 1.39–41; on the symbolism of "the hill country" cf. Crouzel, *Origène*, 177.
467. Cf. Jn 1.15–18.
468. Cf. Jn 1.19.
469. Cf. Jn 1.24.
470. Cf. Jn 1.26.

(258) On the first day, then, the testimonies occur, and on the second Jesus comes to John. But on the third day John stood with two of his disciples, and saw Jesus walking, and said, "Behold the lamb of God."[471] He urges those present to follow the Son of God. On the fourth day when he wished to go out into Galilee, he who came to seek the lost "finds Philip and says to him, 'Follow me.' "[472]

(259) And on the third day after the fourth, which is the sixth from the beginning of those enumerated by us, the wedding occurs in Cana of Galilee. We will go into this when we come to the passage. We must, however, also note this: Mary, who is superior, goes to Elizabeth, who is inferior, and the Son of God goes to the Baptist. These facts encourage us to be helpful without hesitation to those who are in a lower position, and to be moderate.

Complementary reports of the different Gospels

(260) But inasmuch as the disciple John does not say whence the Savior comes to the Baptist, we learn this from Matthew who wrote, "Then Jesus comes from Galilee to the Jordan, to John to be baptized by him."[473]

(261) Mark also added the place in Galilee when he said, "And it came to pass in those days Jesus came from Nazareth of Galilee and was baptized in the Jordan by John."[474]

(262) Luke, however, made no mention of the place from which Jesus comes, having left it to those who have mentioned the matter. He does teach us, however, what we have not learned from the others, that immediately after the baptism heaven was opened to him as he prayed, and the Holy Spirit descended in bodily form as a dove.[475]

(263) Again no one had added to Matthew's account that John hindered the Lord when he said to the Savior, "I have need to be baptized by you, and do you come to me?",[476] that they might not repeat what had been said. It is also only Mat-

---

471. Jn 1.36.
473. Mt 3.13.
475. Cf. Lk 3.21–22.
472. Cf. Jn 1.43.
474. Mk 1.9.
476. Mt 3.14.

thew who has recorded what the Lord replied to John: "Suffer it to be so now, for so it is fitting for us to fulfill all righteousness."⁴⁷⁷

And he says, 'Behold the Lamb of God who takes away the sin of the world.'

The diverse sacrifices of the Jews: images and spiritual realities

(264) There are five animals which are offered on the altar, three being land animals and two winged.⁴⁷⁸ It seems worthwhile to me to ask why the Savior is said to be a "lamb" by John and none of the rest. But also, in the case of the land animals, since three ages are offered according to each species, why did he name the lamb from the species of sheep? Now these are the five animals: a young bull, a sheep, a goat, a turtle-dove, a pigeon.

(265) And these are the three ages of each of the land animals: a young bull, a bull, a calf; a ram, a lamb, a little lamb; a he-goat, a she-goat, a kid. And of the winged animals, a pair of nestling pigeons only; a faultless pair of turtle-doves. Therefore, he who desires to understand accurately the spiritual meaning⁴⁷⁹ concerning the sacrifices must investigate for what heavenly things these animals served as an example and shadow, and for what reason the Word ordains that each of the animals be sacrificed, and in particular, he must collect the things said about the lamb.

(266) The apostle says somewhere that the discussion about the sacrifices ought to be understood about certain heavenly mysteries, "Which serve for an example and shadow of heavenly things."⁴⁸⁰ And again, "It is necessary, therefore, that the patterns of heavenly things should be cleansed with these; but the heavenly things themselves with better sacrifices than these."⁴⁸¹

---

477. Mt 3.15.
479. *Logos*.
481. Heb 9.23.

478. Cf. Lv 5.6–7; 18.
480. Heb 8.5.

(267) But once one has discovered each of these, it is a task which far surpasses human nature to be able to understand the truth of the spiritual law which has come through Jesus Christ.[482] This is a task for none other than the perfect man who has "by practise his senses exercised to the discerning of good and evil,"[483] who is able to say from his truthful disposition, "But we speak wisdom among the perfect."[484] It is possible to say truthfully of these matters and matters like them: "Which none of the princes of this world knew."[485]

The lamb offered in perpetual sacrifices

(268) We find the lamb, however, offered in the perpetual sacrifices. Thus it is written: "And these are what you shall offer upon the altar: two blameless lambs a year old daily upon the altar continually, a perpetual offering. You shall offer the one lamb in the morning and the second lamb you shall offer in the evening. With the one lamb a tenth part of flour mixed with beaten oil, the fourth part of a hin, and a libation of wine, the fourth part of a hin.

(269) And you shall offer the second lamb in the evening according to the first sacrifice and its libation, you shall offer a pleasing odor, an offering to the Lord, a perpetual sacrifice unto your generations at the doors of the tent of testimony before the Lord, where I will command the children of Israel, and I will be sanctified in my glory, and I will sanctify the tent of testimony."[486]

(270) What other perpetual sacrifice can be spiritual to a spiritual being than the Word in his prime, the Word symbolically called "lamb," which is sent down at the same time the soul is illuminated (for this would be the perpetual morning sacrifice), and is again taken up at the end of the mind's time spent among things more divine? For it cannot always continue to be among the higher things insofar as it has been ordained that the soul be yoked with a body that is earthly and weighed down.

482. Cf. Jn 1.17.
484. 1 Cor 2.6.
486. Cf. Ex 29.38–44.

483. Cf. Heb 5.14.
485. Cf. 1 Cor 2.8.

(271) But if someone should ask what the saint will do between dawn and evening, let him infer the principle from those matters related to the cult, and then follow it in these matters too. For there, too, the priests offer the perpetual sacrifice as the beginning of sacrifices, but next, before the perpetual evening sacrifice,[487] they offer the other sacrifices according to the Law, such as those concerning transgression, or involuntary sins, or salvation, or a vow, or jealousy, or the Sabbath, or the new moon, and the rest,[488] which would be too long to discuss at the present moment.

(272) In the same way, then, we too, after we have begun our offering with an explanation of the image, which is the Christ, will be able to comprehend many things that are very beneficial. And again, when we have left off in the matters regarding Christ, we shall arrive at evening, as it were, and night, coming also to corporeal matters.

The Lamb of God: the man Jesus

(273) But if we examine the declaration about Jesus who is pointed out by John in the words, "This is the Lamb of God who takes away the sin of the world,"[489] from the standpoint of the dispensation itself of the bodily sojourn of the Son of God in the life of men, we will assume that the lamb is none other than his humanity. For he "was led as a sheep to the slaughter, and was dumb as a lamb before its shearer,"[490] saying, "I was as an innocent lamb being led to be sacrificed."[491]

(274) This is why in the Apocalypse, too, a little lamb is seen "standing as though slain."[492] This lamb, indeed, which was slain in accordance with certain secret reasons, has become the expiation of the whole world.[493] In accordance with the Father's love for man, he also submitted to slaughter on behalf of the world, purchasing us with his own blood from him who bought us when we had sold ourselves to sins.

487. Cf. Ex 29.38–39.
488. Cf. Lv 6.1–6 and 17; Nm 15.25; Lv 3.1–16; Nm 6.14; 5.15, 18 and 25; 28.10 and 11; 29.6.
489. Jn 1.29.
491. Cf. Jer 11.19.
493. Cf. Rv 5.9.
490. Cf. Is 53.7.
492. Cf. Rv 5.6.

(275) He, however, who led this lamb to the sacrifice was God in man, the great high priest,[494] who reveals this through the saying, "No one takes my life from me, but I lay it down of myself. I have power to lay it[495] down, and I have power to take it up again."[496]

The martyrs

(276) The remaining sacrifices, of which those relating to the law are a symbol, are akin to this sacrifice. But in addition, the other sacrifices akin to this sacrifice seem to me to be the shedding of the blood of the noble martyrs. It was not in vain that the disciple John saw them standing beside the heavenly altar.[497] "But who is wise, that he shall understand these things? Or intelligent, and he shall know them?"[498]

(277) Now to comprehend, even if to a limited extent, the more spiritual sense[499] of such sacrifices which cleanse those for whom they are offered, one must understand the sense of the sacrifice of the daughter of Jephte who was offered as a holocaust because of the vow of him who conquered the children of Ammon.[500] She who was offered as a holocaust consented to this vow, for, when her father said, "I have opened my mouth to the Lord against you," she said to him, "And if you have opened your mouth to the Lord against me, perform your vow."[501]

(278) Such accounts give an appearance of great cruelty to God to whom such sacrifices are offered for the salvation of men. We need a generous and perceptive spirit in order to refute the reproaches made against providence and, at the same time, to make a defense of all the sacrifices insofar as they are rather mysterious and beyond human nature. "For

---

494. Cf. Heb 8.1. Origen is making a contrast here between the divine side of Christ's nature which functioned as the high priest who made the offering, and the human side which was the lamb that was offered. Cf. Origen, *Gn Hom* 8.9.
495. The "it" (*autēn*) is missing from the MSS.
496. Cf. Jn 10.18.   497. Cf. Rv 6.9.
498. Cf. Hos 14.10.   499. *Logos*.
500. Cf. Jgs 11.29–39.
501. Cf. Jgs 11.35–36.

the judgments of God are great and hard to narrate; for this reason uneducated souls went astray."⁵⁰²

(279) But, it has also been attested among the pagans that many delivered themselves as victims for the common good when destructive diseases were rampant. The faithful Clement, of whom Paul testifies when he says, "With Clement and the rest of my fellow laborers whose names are in the book of life,"⁵⁰³ accepts, and not without reason, that these things happened in this way because he believed in the histories.⁵⁰⁴

(280) The things prescribed concerning the martyrs also have a similar absurdity in the judgment of one who wishes to denounce the mysteries which elude most people. For it pleased God that we submit to all the most painful tortures while confessing his divinity rather than that we be delivered from what are thought to be such great evils for a short time by accommodating ourselves in speech to the will of the enemies of the truth.

(281) We must hold, therefore, that a dissolution of maleficent powers occurs through the death of the holy martyrs. The martyrs' endurance and confession until death, and zeal for godliness blunts, as it were, the sharpness of their treachery against the sufferer. Consequently, when their power is blunted and exhausted there are many others, in addition, who have already been conquered who are set at ease because they are freed from the weight with which the attacking evil powers were oppressing and harming them.

(282) In addition, those who would have suffered if those who inflict wicked things on others had not been exhausted, no longer experience suffering since he who has offered such a sacrifice has conquered this adverse power. The following illustration is useful, at least in part, in relation to what I have just said. He who destroys a venomous animal or lulls it to sleep with a charm, or by some power empties it of venom, benefits many who would later suffer something from it, if it had not been destroyed, or lulled to sleep, or emptied of its venom.

502. Cf. Wis 17.1.   503. Cf. Phil 4.3.
504. Cf. 1 Clement 55.1.

(283) Moreover, if one who had earlier been bitten should become aware that there is a deliverance from the harm caused by the bite if he should fix his gaze on the animal which injured him dying, or tread on its corpse, or touch it when it is dead, or taste some part of it, the healing and kindness from him who destroyed the harmful animal would affect him also who had suffered earlier. We must conceive that something like this occurs in the death of the most godly martyrs, since many are benefited from their death by some ineffable power.

Efficacy of the sacrifice of Christ

(284) Now we have occupied ourselves with the discussion about the martyrs and the account concerning those who have died because of a state of pestilence, in order to see the distinctive character of him who was led as a sheep to slaughter and was dumb as a lamb before its shearer.[505] For if these stories are not told in vain by the Greeks, and if the stories about the martyrs who became the refuse of the world, and about the apostles who were called the "offscourings of all"[506] for the same reason, have been related correctly, what must we understand, and of what magnitude, about the Lamb of God who was sacrificed that he might take away the sin, not of a few, but of the whole world,[507] for which also he has suffered?

(285) For if "anyone sin, we have an advocate with the Father, Jesus Christ the just, and he is the propitiation for our sins, and not for[508] ours only, but also for the whole world,"[509] since "he is the Savior of all men, especially of the faithful."[510] It is he who "blotted out the handwriting against us" with his own blood and removed it from our midst, that no traces even of the sins which have been expunged might be found, and "having fastened it to the cross," who "after he had despoiled

---

505. Cf. Is 53.7. 506. Cf. 1 Cor 4.13.
507. Cf. Jn 1.29.
508. The text has *ouk epi* instead of *ou peri* which appears in the text of the New Testament. Preuschen thinks *ou peri* should be read.
509. 1 Jn 2.1–2. 510. Cf. 1 Tm 4.10.

the principalities and powers, exposed them boldly after he had triumphed over them "in the cross."[511]

(286) We are taught, therefore, to be of good cheer when we are afflicted in the world. We learn that the reason for being of good cheer is this: the world has been conquered[512] and, of course, subjected to him who conquered it. For this reason, all the nations, set free from those who formerly controlled them, serve him, because "he delivered the poor from the mighty" through his own passion, "and the needy who had no helper."[513]

(287) This Savior, indeed, after he humbled the denouncer by humbling himself, remains from generation to generation[514] with the spiritual sun before the splendor of the Church, figuratively called the moon.[515]

He needs purification from the Father

But after he had destroyed his enemies through his passion, the Lord, who is mighty in battle and strong,[516] needing the cleansing for his manly deeds which can be given to him by the Father alone, prevents Mary from touching him saying, "Do not touch me, for I have not yet ascended to the Father. But go and say to my brethren, 'I am going to my Father and your Father, and to my God and your God.'"[517]

(288) When he goes, however, bearing victory and trophies, with the body which arose from the dead (for how else are we to understand, "I have not yet ascended to my Father"? and, "But I am going to my Father"?), then certain powers say, "Who is this that is coming from Edom, with scarlet garments from Bosra, so beautiful?"[518] And those escorting him say to those stationed at the gates of heaven, "Lift up your gates, and the king of glory will come in."[519]

(289) And they inquire further, as it were, if I may speak

---

511. Cf. Col 2.14–15.
513. Cf. Ps 71.12.
515. Cf. Origen, *Gn. Hom.* 1.5–6.
517. Cf. Jn 20.17.
519. Ps 23.7.

512. Cf. Jn 16.33.
514. Cf. Ps 71.4–5.
516. Cf. Ps 23.8.
518. Is 63.1.

in this way, when they see his blood-stained right hand and his whole body filled with the works of prowess: "Why is your apparel red and your garments like the residue of a full wine-vat which has been trampled down?"[520] To which he answers, "I have crushed them in pieces."[521]

(290) It is truly for these reasons that he needed to wash "his robe in wine, and his garment in the blood of the grape."[522] For after he took our infirmities and bore our diseases,[523] and after he took away the sin of the whole world,[524] and benefited so many, perhaps then he received the baptism which is greater than any which could be imagined by men, concerning which I think he said, "And I have a baptism with which to be baptized, and how distressed I am until it be accomplished."[525]

(291) That I might oppose the opinions of the majority by examining the account more daringly, let those who suppose his martyrdom to be the greatest baptism beyond which another cannot be conceived tell us why in the world after this event he says to Mary, "Do not touch me."[526] He ought rather to have handed himself over to her touch since he had received the perfect baptism through the mystery of his passion.

(292) But since, as we said before, after he had performed manly deeds against his adversaries he needed to wash "his robe in wine, and his garment in the blood of grapes,"[527] he went up to the Father,[528] the husbandman of the true vine, that, having washed there after the ascent to the height when he led captivity captive, he might descend bearing various gifts.[529] Among these gifts were the tongues as of fire which were distributed to the apostles,[530] and the holy angels who will be present in their every act and will deliver them.[531]

---

520. Cf. Is 63.2–3.
521. Is 63.3.
522. Gn 49.11.
523. Cf. Mt 8.17; Is 53.4.
524. Cf. Jn 1.29.
525. Lk 12.50.
526. Jn 20.17.
527. Gn 49.11.
528. Cf. Jn 15.1.
529. Cf. Eph 4.8; Ps 67.19.
530. Cf. Acts 2.3.
531. Cf. Ps 33.8.

Christ alone consents to dwell with the fishermen

(293) Before these dispensations, since they had not yet been cleansed, they could not receive the visitation of angels among them; perhaps the angels did not even wish to be present with those who had not been prepared and cleansed by Jesus.

(294) For to eat and drink with sinners and publicans,[532] and to offer his own feet to the tears of a repentant sinner,[533] and to descend to death for the ungodly[534] not thinking equality with God a thing to be grasped, and to empty himself taking the form of a servant,[535] was unique to Jesus' love for man.

Redemption is the work of the Father

(295) In accomplishing all these things it was the will of the Father who delivered him up for the ungodly[536] that he was accomplishing rather than his own will, for the Father is good,[537] and the Savior is an image of his goodness. And when he shows kindness to all the world, since God in Christ is reconciling the world to himself,[538] which had formerly become an enemy because of evil, he performs his acts of kindness methodically and orderly, not all at once taking all his enemies as the footstool of his feet.[539] For the Father says to him who is Lord of each of us, "Sit at my right hand, until I make your enemies the footstool of your feet."[540]

(296) These things go on until death, the last enemy, is destroyed by him.[541] And if we understand what it means to be subjected to Christ primarily from the saying, "And when all things shall be subjected to him, then the Son himself shall be subject to him who subjected all things to him,"[542] we will

---

532. Cf. Mk 2.16.
534. Cf. Rom 5.6.
536. Cf. Rom 8.32.
538. Cf. 2 Cor 5.19.
540. Ps 109.1.
542. Cf. 1 Cor 15.28.

533. Cf. Lk 7.38.
535. Cf. Phil 2.6–7.
537. Cf. Mt 19.17; Wis 7.26.
539. Cf. Heb 10.13; Ps 109.1.
541. Cf. 1 Cor 15.26.

understand the Lamb of God who takes away the sin of the world[543] in a manner worthy of the goodness of the God of the universe.

Sufferings inflicted upon sinners

(297) But the sin of all men is not taken away by the Lamb, if they neither grieve nor are tormented till it be taken away. For since thorns have not only been sown, but have also taken deep root in the hands of everyone who has become drunk because of evil, and has lost sobriety, according to what is said in Proverbs, "Thorns grow in the hand of the drunkard,"[544] what must we say in addition regarding the extent of distress they produce in him who has received such plants into the body of his own soul? For he who has admitted evil into the depth of his own soul to such an extent that he has become thorn-producing earth has to be cut down by the living and effectual word of God which is more piercing than any two-edged sword and more capable of burning than any fire.[545]

(298) That fire which discovers thorns, and which, because of its own divinity, will stop them and not in addition set the threshing floors or fields of grain on fire, will need to be sent to such a soul.

The ways of that lamb who takes away the sin of the world,[546] beginning with his own slaughter, are many, some of which can be clear to a large number of people, but others escape the notice of most and are known to those alone who are considered worthy of the divine wisdom.

(299) Why must we say how many ways there are among men by which one comes to believe, since he who is still present in such a body observes it for himself? But one way to believe and for sin to be removed is by scourges, and evil spirits, and very difficult diseases, and very painful sicknesses.

(300) Who knows, then, the things that come after these? But it was necessary, that the apparent conclusion from our

543. Cf. Jn 1.29.
545. Cf. Heb 4.12; Sir 48.1.
544. Prv 26.9.
546. Cf. Jn 1.29.

examination of the saying, "Behold the Lamb of God who takes away the sin of the world,"[547] not be destroyed, to have a more complete understanding of these matters, that once we know that it is possible both to be reproved by God's anger and chastened by God's wrath, since he leaves no one at all unconvicted and unchastened as the result of his excessive love for man, we might do all things so that we [not] need such reproofs and chastisement that come through the most painful trials.

Sense of the word "cosmos" in this verse

(301) The reader must consider what we have said in our earlier books about the meaning of the term "world" in Scripture supplemented with numerous examples, for I have not thought it reasonable to repeat it.[548] We are not ignorant, however, that someone has taken world to mean the Church alone, it being the adornment of the world,[549] since it is also said to be the light of the world, for Scripture says, "You are the light of the world."[550] And the Church is the adornment of the world, since Christ, who is the first light of the world, is its adornment.

(302) But we must consider whether Christ and his disciples are said to be the light of the same world. When Christ is the light of the world, perhaps he is the light of the Church, and when his disciples are the light of the world, perhaps they are the light of those who are summoned, who are other than the Church, as Paul has said concerning these in the opening of the earlier Epistle to the Corinthians, when he writes, "To the Church of God with all who called upon the name of the Lord Jesus Christ."[551] If, [therefore], someone should suppose that the Church is said to be the light of the world, as it were, of the rest of the race of men and the unbelievers, if he will understand this prophetically because of the doctrine[552] about

---

547. Jn 1.29.
548. Blanc, SC 157.359, correctly notes that if the reference is to the *Comm. Jn.*, the section has been lost.
549. *Kosmon, tou kosmou.* 550. Mt 5.14.
551. Cf. 1 Cor 1.2.
552. *Logos.*

the end, the assertion perhaps has a place. But if it is taken as already occurring, let them show how the rest of the race is being enlightened by the Church as it sojourns in the world, since the light of something enlightens the object of which it is the light.

(303) But if they cannot show this, let them give attention to whether we have correctly taken the Church to be the light, and those who call upon (the name of the Lord) to be the world. The next saying occurring in the Gospel according to Matthew will commend our interpretation to one who searches the Scriptures[553] very carefully. For he says, "You are the salt of the earth."[554] The rest of men, of whom those who have believed are salt, are perhaps, understood as the earth. The believers, through their faith, are the reason the world is preserved. For "if the salt should go flat,"[555] and no longer be that which salts and preserves the earth, at that time the end will occur, since it is clear that if lawlessness be multiplied, and love grow cold upon the earth[556] (since even the Savior himself uttered a doubtful word concerning conditions at his own coming, when he said, "But when the Son of man comes, will he find faith on the earth?"[557]) then the end of the former[558] age will occur.

(304) Let the Church, therefore, be said to be the world when it is enlightened by the Savior. But we ask if one would correctly conceive of the Church as the world in relation to the statement, "Behold, the Lamb of God who takes away the sin of the world,"[559] the sin being taken away being limited to the Church alone?

(305) For how will we explain what the same disciple says in the epistle about the Savior being the propitiation for sins? The statement goes as follows: "And if anyone sin, we have an advocate with the Father, Jesus Christ the just. And he is

---

553. Cf. Jn 5.39.
554. Mt 5.13.
555. Cf. Mt 5.13.
556. Cf. Mt 24.12.
557. Lk 18.8.
558. The text has the strange expression: *tou pro aiōnos*. Both Blanc and the ANF translation ignore the preposition in their translation. Blanc gives a literal rendering in a footnote: "la fin de ce qui précède l'*éon*."
559. Jn 1.29.

the propitiation for our sins, and not for ours only, but also for those of the whole world."[560] And I think what Paul says is similar to this, which goes as follows: "Who is the Savior of all men, especially of the faithful."[561]

The interpretation of Heracleon

(306) Again, although he has no evidence and cites no witnesses, Heracleon declares on this passage [that John says, "Lamb of God," as a prophet, but, "He who takes away the sin of the world,"[562] as more than a prophet]. He thinks the former is said of his body, but the second is said of him who was in the body, because the lamb is imperfect in the species of sheep, and so also is the body in comparison with him who dwells in it.

(307) But he says, if he had wished to ascribe perfection to the body, he would have spoken of a ram about to be sacrificed. After our examinations, however, which have been so extensive, I do not think it necessary for us to be concerned about the passage, struggling with what Heracleon has said in such a paltry manner. But we must note this one thing: just as the world scarcely contained him who had emptied himself,[563] so it needed a lamb, and not a ram that its sin might be taken away.[564]

* *

560. 1 Jn 2.1–2.   561. 1 Tm 4.10.
562. Jn 1.29.   563. Cf. Phil 2.7.
564. Preuschen notes that the end of this book is missing.

BOOK 10

Introduction

Text commented on in Book 10

"AFTER THIS he went down to Capharnaum, he, and his mother, and brothers, and disciples, and they remained there not many days. And the pasch of the Jews was at hand, and Jesus went up to Jerusalem. And he found in the temple those selling oxen, and sheep and doves, and the money-changers sitting. And when he had made, as it were, a scourge of small cords, he drove them all out of the temple, both the sheep and the oxen, and he poured out the coins of the money-changers, and overturned their tables. And he said to those selling doves, 'Take these things from here. Do not make my Father's house a market.' Then his disciples remembered that it was written, 'Zeal for your house will devour me.' Therefore the Jews answered and said to him, 'What sign do you show us, since you do these things?' Jesus answered and said, 'Destroy this temple, and in three days I will raise it up.' Therefore the Jews answered, 'This temple was built in forty-six years. Will you raise it up in three days?' But he was speaking of the temple of his body. When, therefore, he was raised from the dead, his disciples remembered that he said this, and they believed the Scripture and the word which Jesus spoke. Now when he was in Jerusalem at the pasch at the feast, many believed in his name because they saw the signs which he did. But Jesus himself did not entrust himself to them, because he knows all men, and because he had no need that anyone testify about man, for he himself knew what was in man."[1]

---

1. Cf. Jn 2.12–25.

254 ORIGEN

(1) * * * *[2] the numbers have been considered worthy of being recorded in it in accordance with a certain analogy which belongs to each object of Scripture. We must examine whether that book of Moses which is entitled *Numbers* teaches the doctrine concerning numbers in a special way to those who are able to investigate such things.

(2) I make these remarks to you at the beginning of the tenth book because I see that the number ten holds a privileged position in many passages of Scripture, as you yourself are capable of perceiving with careful consideration, since you hope to receive something additional from God in this book also. That such may be the case, let us attempt, to the best of our ability, to put ourselves into the power of God who wishes to give the best gifts.

(3) Our point of departure for beginning this book is the words, "After this he went down to Capharnaum, he, and his mother, and brothers, and disciples, and they remained there not many days."[3] The other three authors of the Gospels say that after the Lord's struggle with the devil, he withdrew into Galilee.[4]

(4) Matthew and Luke, however, say that he was in Nazareth first after these events, and that he left there[5] and went to settle in Capharnaum.[6] Matthew and Mark also mention a reason for his withdrawal from there: he had heard that John had been delivered up.[7]

---

2. The opening page of this book has been lost. Preuschen proposes that the quotation from Jn 2.12–25 with which Book 10 begins was added as a replacement by someone else after the loss of the opening page. He correctly observes that nowhere else does Origen quote in one place the entire text for a book of the *Commentary*.

3. Cf. Jn 2.12.

4. Cf. Mt 4.12; Mk 1.14; Lk 4.14.

5. *Auta*. Nazareth in this sentence, and again in section 9 below is neuter (or masculine), dative, plural. A. Menzies, ANF 10.381, comments in a footnote that "Nazara is with Origen a neuter plural." This seems to be the only solution to the puzzling use of the neuter plural here. Menzies' statement is problematical, however, for Origen writes Nazara with a feminine singular article in section 50 below where he is paraphrasing Mt 4.13.

6. Cf. Mt 4.13; Lk 4.16.31.   7. Cf. Mt 4.12; Mk 1.14.

Descent to Capharnaum

(5) Matthew's words are as follows: "Then the devil left him, and behold angels came and ministered to him. And when Jesus had heard that John was delivered up, he withdrew into Galilee. And when he left Nazareth, he came and settled in Capharnaum on the sea coast, in the borders of Zabulon and of Nephthalim, that the word of the prophet Isaias might be fulfilled, who said, 'Land of Zabulon,'"[8] And after the words in Isaias, he says, "From that time Jesus began to preach, and to say, 'Repent, for the kingdom of heaven is at hand.'"[9]

(6) Mark says, "And he was in the desert forty days being tempted by Satan; and he was with beasts, and the angels ministered to him. And after John was delivered up Jesus came into Galilee preaching the gospel of God: 'The time is fulfilled, and the kingdom of God is at hand; repent, and believe the gospel.'"[10]

(7) Then, after telling about Andrew and Peter, and James and John,[11] he records these words: "And he entered Capharnaum, and immediately on the sabbath he began teaching in the synagogue."[12]

(8) And Luke says, "And when he had ended the temptation, the devil departed from him for a time. And Jesus returned in the power of the spirit into Galilee. And a report about him went out through the whole country. And he was teaching in their synagogues, being glorified by all. And he came into Nazareth where he had been raised, and he entered the synagogue according to his custom on the sabbath day."[13]

(9) And after he has related what Jesus said in Nazareth, and the wrath against him of those in the synagogue when they cast "him out of the city" and brought him "to the brow of the hill on which their city was built, that they might cast

---

8. Mt 4.11–15.
10. Cf. Mk 1.13–15.
12. Cf. Mk 1.21.
9. Mt 4.17.
11. Cf. Mk 1.16–20.
13. Cf. Lk 4.13–16.

him down headlong," and that the Lord "passed through their midst and went his way,"[14] he subjoins these words: "And he went down into Capharnaum, a city of Galilee, and was teaching them on the sabbath."[15]

Necessity of spiritual sense for resolving contradictions of the Gospels

(10) * * * [We must, however, set before the reader] that the truth of these accounts lies in the spiritual meanings, [because] if the discrepancy is not solved, [many] dismiss credence in the Gospels as not true, or not written by a divine spirit, or not successfully recorded. The composition of these Gospels, in fact, is said to have involved both. Let those who accept the four Gospels and who think the apparent discrepancy is not to be solved through the anagogical sense tell us when the Lord came to Capharnaum in relation to the difficulty we mentioned earlier concerning the forty days of temptation which can have no place at all in John. For if it occurred six days after the time when he was baptized, since his ministry at the marriage in Cana of Galilee took place on the sixth day,[16] it is clear that he has not been tempted, nor was he in Nazareth, nor had John yet been delivered up.

(11) After Capharnaum, then, where he remained not many days because the pasch of the Jews was at hand, he went up to Jerusalem, when he casts both the sheep and the oxen out of the temple, and pours out the coins of the money-changers.[17]

(12) And Nicodemus, a ruler of the Pharisees, seems likely to have come to him at night in Jerusalem, and to have heard those words which can be found in the Gospel:[18] "And after these things Jesus and his disciples came into the land of Judea, and there he remained with them, and baptized."[19] At this time also John was "baptizing in Ennon near Salim because there was much water there, and they came and were

---

14. Cf. Lk 4.28–30.
15. Lk 4.31.
16. Cf. Jn 2.1.
17. Cf. Jn 2.12–15.
18. Cf. Jn 3.1–2.
19. Jn 3.22.

COMMENTARY ON JOHN, BOOK 10   257

baptized. For John had not yet been cast into prison."[20] And when "a questioning arose from John's disciples with the Jews about purification, and they came to John,"[21] saying of the Savior, "Behold, he is baptizing, and all are going to him,"[22] they heard words from the Baptist which can be found with all their precision in the Scripture itself.

(13) But perhaps, when we ask when the Christ was first in Capharnaum, they will say, following the text of Matthew and the other two, "After the temptation, when he left Nazareth and went and settled in Capharnaum beside the sea."[23] If they say this, how will they say that both what is said in Matthew and Mark are true at the same time that he withdrew into Galilee because he had heard about John who had been delivered up,[24] and what occurs in John after even other ministries in addition to that in Capharnaum alone,[25] namely, the ascent to Jerusalem[26] and the descent from there into Judea,[27] when John had not yet been cast into prison, but was baptizing in Ennon near Salim?[28]

(14) On the basis of numerous other passages also, if someone should examine the Gospels carefully to check the disagreement so far as the historical sense is concerned—we shall attempt to show this disagreement in individual cases, insofar as we are able—, he would grow dizzy, and would either shrink from really confirming the Gospels, and would agree with one of them at random because he would not dare reject completely the faith related to our Lord, or, he would admit that there are four [and would say] that their truth is not in their literal features.

Parable for the different narrators

(15) But to grasp some notion of the evangelists' intention concerning such matters, we must also say the following. Assume that God, his words to the saints, and his presence,

20. Jn 3.23–24. 21. Cf. Jn 3.25–26.
22. Cf. Jn 3.26.
23. Cf. Mt 4.13; Mk 1.13–21; Lk 4.13–31.
24. Cf. Mt 4.12; Mk 1.14.
25. Cf. Jn 2.12. 26. Cf. Jn 2.13.
27. Cf. Jn 3.22. 28. Cf. Jn 3.23–24.

which is present with them when he reveals himself at special times in their progress, are set before certain people who see in the Spirit. Since there are several and they are in different places, and by no means all receive the same benefits, assume that each one individually reports what he sees in the Spirit about God, his words, and his manifestations to the saints. The result would be that one man would report about these things which were said and done by God to this just man at this place, and another would report about the things that were prophesied and accomplished for another, and another would want to teach us about a third man besides the two previously mentioned. And assume that there is also a fourth man who acts in a way that is analogous to the three concerning something. Now let these four men agree with one another concerning certain things suggested to them by the Spirit, and let them differ a little concerning other things, so that their accounts are like this: God appeared to so-and-so at this time in this place, and he has done these things to him as follows; he appeared to him in a form such as this, and led him to this place where he did these things.

(16) Let the second man report that God appeared at the same time with what is said to have happened in the first report, in some city, to one whom he also perceives, a second person who is in a place far separated from the place of the former, and let him record that other words were spoken at the same time to him whom, according to our hypothesis, we have taken to be a second man. And we must understand similar things concerning the third, and the fourth man.

(17) But let these men agree with one another, as we have said previously, in reporting the truth about God and his benefits to certain people in some of the narratives they report. To one, then, who thinks that the writing of these men is history, which would proceed to present the deeds through an historical image, and who supposes that God is in space with its limitation, not being able to produce several appearances of himself at the same time to several people in several places, and to say several things at the same time, it will seem impossible that the four men, whom I presented, are telling

the truth. For it is impossible, in this view, for God to be in some prescribed time, since he is also thought to be in space with its limitation, and to say different things to different people, and to do these things and their opposites, and, let us say, to be sitting and standing at the same time, if one should say that he has said or done certain things when he stood at this time in this place, and another should say he was sitting.

Spiritual nature of the contents of the Gospels

(18) In the case of these four narrators, therefore, whom I have assumed, who wanted to teach us by a type the things they had seen in their mind, if they should be wise, the meaning of their historical accounts would be found to be harmonious once it was understood. We must conceive that it is this way also in the case of the four evangelists who made full use of many things done and said in accordance with the prodigious and incredible power of Jesus. In some places they have interwoven in Scripture something made clear to them in a purely intellectual manner, with language as though it were something perceptible to the senses.

(19) But I do not condemn, I suppose,[29] the fact that they have also made some minor changes in what happened so far as history is concerned, with a view to the usefulness of the mystical object of [those matters]. Consequently, they have related what happened in [this] place as though it happened in another, or what happened at this time as though at another time, and they have composed what is reported in this manner with a certain degree of distortion.

(20) For their intention was to speak the truth spiritually and materially at the same time where that was possible but, where it was not possible in both ways, to prefer the spiritual to the material. The spiritual truth is often preserved in the material falsehood, so to speak. It is as if we were also to say, on the basis of the story, that Jacob was telling the truth in

---

29. *De pou*, "but . . . I suppose." I think it is possible that Origen may have written *dēpou*, "to be sure," and that *de pou* is a scribal error. Cf. my note 396 in Book 6.

the spiritual sense when he declared to Isaac, "I am Esau your firstborn son,"[30] because he had a share of the birthright which was already perishing in his brother.[31] And by means of the robe and the kid's skin[32] he took up Esau's outer character and became Esau, apart from the voice praising God, that Esau might receive a place to be blessed later. For perhaps if Jacob had not been blessed as Esau, Esau would not have been able to receive the blessing by himself.

Agreement of Scriptures

(21) Therefore Jesus too is many things in his aspects. It is likely that the different evangelists took their thoughts from these aspects and wrote the Gospels, sometimes also being in agreement with one another concerning certain things. For example, opposite statements concerning our Lord, so far as the literal meaning is concerned, are true: "He was born of David," and, "He was not born of David."

(22) For, on the one hand, the statement, "He was born of David," is true, if we understand his material part, as also the apostle says: "Who was born of the seed of David, according to the flesh."[33] But this very statement is false if we should take it that he was born of the seed of David in the case of his more divine power, for he was appointed son of God in power.[34]

(23) And perhaps for this reason the holy prophecies proclaim him here as servant, and there as son. He is called servant because of the "form of a servant,"[35] and because he is "of the seed of David,"[36] but son in accordance with his power as firstborn.[37] So it is true to say that he is man and that he is not man. He is man insofar as he is capable of death; not man insofar as he is more divine than man.

(24) I also think that Marcion, by misconstruing sound ideas,[38] when he rejects his birth from Mary so far as his

---

30. Cf. Gn 27.19.
32. Cf. Gn 27.15–16.
34. Cf. Rom 1.4.
36. Cf. Rom 1.3.
38. *Logous.*

31. Cf. Gn 25.31–34.
33. Rom 1.3.
35. Cf. Phil 2.7.
37. Cf. Col 1.15; Rom 1.4.

divine nature is concerned, declared that consequently he was not born of Mary, and for this reason he has dared to exclude these passages from the gospel. Those who have annulled his humanity and have accepted only his deity appear to have suffered something like this, as have those too who, contrary to the latter, exclude his deity, but confess the man as holy and the most righteous of all men.

(25) Likewise those who introduced the docetic heresy, since they did not consider him who humbled himself "unto death" and became obedient unto the cross,[39] but imagined only impassiveness and superiority to every such occurrence, wish to deprive us, so far as it is in their power, of the most righteous man of all men, although we cannot be saved through that being of theirs.

(26) For as "through one man" came "death," so also through one man came the justification of life.[40] Without the man, we would have received no benefit from the Word, if he had remained God as he was in the beginning with the Father,[41] and not taken up the man who was first of all men, and more precious than all, and purer than all, being able to receive him. After that man we too shall be able to receive him, each to the extent and in such a way as the quality and size of place we make for him in our soul.

(27) I have made all these comments about the manifest disagreements of the Gospels wishing to present their [agreements] by way of spiritual interpretation.

(28) On the same subject we must also use the following example: Paul says that as the man of flesh he was sold under sin,[42] and was able to judge nothing, "but the spiritual man judges all things" and "is judged by no one."[43] The words of the man of flesh are, "For what I will, this I do not do; but what I hate, this I do."[44] The words of the spiritual man, however, are: "What I will, I do; and what I hate, I do not do." But also he who was caught up "to the third heaven" and

---

39. Cf. Phil 2.8.
41. Cf. Jn 1.1.
43. 1 Cor 2.15.
40. Cf. Rom 5.12 and 18.
42. Cf. Rom 7.14.
44. Rom 7.15.

heard "secret words"[45] was a different man than the one who says "I will boast about such a one, but I will not boast on behalf of myself."[46]

(29) But if he also became as a Jew to Jews that he might gain Jews, and to those under law as under law [that] he might gain [those under law], and to those without law, as without law, "not being without the law of God, but in the law of Christ," that he might gain those without law, and to the weak he became weak, that he might gain the weak,[47] it is clear that we must examine his words in one way in respect to his attitude to the Jews, and in another when he is under the law, and sometimes when he is as one without the law, and other times when he becomes weak.

(30) For example, what he says "by way of concession, not as a command,"[48] he says when he is weak. For he says "Who is weak, and I am not weak?"[49] But when he shaves and offers an offering,[50] or circumcises Timothy,[51] he becomes a Jew. And when he says to the Athenians, "I found an altar on which was written, 'To the unknown God.' What, therefore, you worship ignorantly, this I proclaim to you,"[52] and, "As also some of your own poets have said, 'For we are also his offspring,'"[53] he becomes as one without law to those without law, bearing testimony to religion to the most irreligious people and applying to his own purpose him who said, "We have our beginning from Zeus, for we are also his offspring."[54] And perhaps there are places where he is under law to those who are not Jews, but are under law.

(31) Now these examples are useful for us, not only regarding matters concerning the Savior, but also regarding matters concerning the disciples about whom also there is some disagreement according to the literal meaning. For perhaps Simon who is found by his own brother Andrew, and

---

45. Cf. 2 Cor 12.2 and 4.
46. Cf. 2 Cor 12.5
47. Cf. 1 Cor 9.20–22.
48. 1 Cor 7.6.
49. 2 Cor 11.29.
50. Cf. Acts 21.24 and 26.
51. Cf. Acts 16.3.
52. Cf. Acts 17.23.
53. Acts 17.28.
54. Cf. Aratus *Phaenomena* 5; Acts 17.28.

hears the words, "You shall be called Cephas,"[55] is different in aspect from the man who is seen, together with his brother, by Jesus as he walks beside the sea of Galilee, and who, together with that Andrew, hears the words, "Follow me, and I will make you fishers of men."[56]

(32) For it was fitting that the evangelist whose announcement of the Word which became flesh[57] is made in a more theological manner,[58] and who, for this reason did not record the birth of the Word in the beginning with God,[59] did not mention the one found beside the sea and called from there, but the one who is found by his brother who remained with Jesus at the tenth hour,[60] and, because he is found in this manner, immediately receives the name "Cephas."

(33) For it is unlikely that he who is seen by the Savior as he walks beside the sea of Galilee is also the recipient of the statement, "You are Peter, and upon this rock I will build my church."[61]

(34) In John, the Pharisees know that Jesus baptizes—he baptizes among his disciples in addition to his other remarkable activities.[62] The Jesus in the Synoptics, however, does not baptize at all.

(35) Furthermore, John the Baptist, in the evangelist with the same name, continues for a long time before he is cast into prison. In Matthew, however, he is cast into prison at about the time of Jesus' temptation. For this reason too, Jesus withdraws into Galilee, to avoid being put in prison. But in John, the Baptist is not even found to be delivered to prison.

Explication of the text of John

(36) But who is so wise, and has such competence as to learn everything in regard to Jesus from the four evangelists,

---

55. Cf. Jn 1.40–42.
56. Cf. Mt 4.18–19; Mk 1.16–17.
57. Cf. Jn 1.14.
58. Accepting Brooke's suggestion, *theologikōteron*, with Blanc. Preuschen prints [theo] *logikōteron*.
59. Cf. Jn 1.2.
60. Cf. Jn 1.39.
61. Mt 16.18.
62. Cf. Jn 3.22; 4.1.

and to be capable of understanding each thing by himself, and to keep in sight all his visits and words and works in each place?

(37) Nevertheless, in relation to the passage before us, we think that subsequently on the sixth day the Savior, when he has performed his ministry at the wedding in Cana of Galilee, went down, together with his mother and brothers and disciples, to Capharnaum, which means "field of exhortation."[63]

(38) For after the good cheer with the wine it was necessary that the Savior, together with his mother and disciples, enter the "field of exhortation," to exhort, with reference to the fruits which will be in the plentiful[64] field, those who were disciples, and that soul which had conceived him of the Holy Spirit, or those who were benefited there.

The powers descending with him

(39) We must ask, however, why his brothers are not invited to the wedding, (nor were they present, for they are not mentioned), but they go down to Capharnaum with him and his mother and the disciples. And we must examine further why they do not now go into Capharnaum, nor go up to it, but go down.

(40) Consider, then, if here we should understand the brothers to be the powers which came down with him, which are not invited to the wedding in accordance with the explanations we have already given, but receive benefits more humbly and differently in places inferior to those called disciples of Christ. If his mother is invited, some are bearing fruit to whom also the Lord himself goes down with the servants and disciples of the Word, to benefit such, and his mother is with him.

---

63. See Lagarde, *Onomastica*, 193.27. Blanc, SC 157.406 calls attention to the same interpretation of Capharnaum in Origen's *Comm.Mt.* 13.11.
64. Accepting the emendation, *plērei*, with Huet, Delarue, Brooke, Koetschau, and Blanc. Preuschen prints *plēthei* and marks it as corrupt. He does not mention *plērei* in his apparatus. For the phrase, cf. Gn 27.27.

Duration of Christ's sojourn with the crowds and the saints

(41) Those called Capharnaum seem, indeed, not to have room for the full sojourn of Jesus and those who come down with him among them. Consequently they remain among them not many days indeed.[65] For the lower "field of exhortation" does not have the capacity for illumination concerning many teachings, being capable of only a few.

(42) But to contemplate the differences between those who receive Jesus in a greater or lesser degree, we must compare with the statement, "They remained there not many days,"[66] what he who arose from the dead says to those who have been disciples and who are being sent to make disciples of all the nations, "Behold I am with you all days until the end of the age."[67] For to those, on the one hand, who will know everything which human nature can know while it is still here, it is said categorically, "Behold I am with you." And as every dawn[68] among those things to be contemplated multiplies the days for those who are most blessed, he says, "All days until the end of the age." On the other hand, it is said of those in Capharnaum, to whom not only Jesus, but also his mother, and his brothers and disciples go down as to inferior men, "they remain there not many days."[69]

(43) It is probable, however, that there will be some who will ask, and not without reason, if after all the days of this age he will no longer be present who said, "Behold I am with you," i.e. with those who received him, "until the end of the age,"[70] for the word "until" indicates some temporal limit, as it were.

(44) But we must also say to this question that the expression, "I am with you," is not the same [as the expression, "I am in you"].[71] Perhaps, then, we might say more legitimately that the Savior is not "in" those who are disciples, but is

---

65. Cf. Jn 2.12.
67. Mt 28.20.
69. Jn 2.12.
66. Jn 2.12.
68. *Anatolē*. Lit. "rising."
70. Mt 28.20.
71. The bracketed portion appears in MS. V.

"with" them to the extent that they have not arrived at the end of the age in their intellect.

(45) But whenever they see pending the end of that age which has been crucified to them, so far as their preparation is concerned, then, because Jesus is no longer with them, but is in them, they will say, "I no longer live, but Christ lives in me,"[72] and, "Do you seek proof of Christ who speaks in me?"[73]

(46) We make these comments while somehow privately preserving for ourselves and defending the interpretation that "all days" means those days "until the end of the age"[74] in relation to things human nature is capable of grasping while it is still here. For it is possible also, if that interpretation be preserved, to fasten attention on the "I," so that the one who is with those sent to make disciples of all the nations until the end[75] is the one who emptied himself and took the form of a servant.[76]

(47) But being different in condition from this one, as it were, before he emptied himself, he has come to be with them after the end of the age, until all "his enemies are made his footstool"[77] by the Father. Afterwards, when the son delivers "the kingdom to God and the Father,"[78] the Father will say to them: "Behold I am with you." But whether it is all days until this time, or simply all days, or not even all, but every day, is left with him who wishes to consider it. For the questions we are discussing do not require us at this point to digress to such an extent from the subject-matter.

Exegesis of Heracleon

(48) Heracleon, however, in explaining the statement, "after this he went down into Capharnaum,"[79] says that once more the beginning of another dispensation is revealed, since "[he went] down" is not said without meaning. He says Capharnaum means these most remote places of the cosmos, these material realms into which he descended. And because the place is alien, he says, he is not said to have done or said anything in it.

---

72. Cf. Gal 2.20.
73. Cf. 2 Cor 13.3.
74. Mt 28.20.
75. Cf. Mt 28.20.
76. Cf. Phil 2.7.
77. Cf. Heb 10.13; Ps 110.1.
78. 1 Cor 15.24.
79. Jn 2.12.

The Synoptics refute him

(49) Had our Lord then not have been recorded to have done or said anything in Capharnaum in the rest of the Gospels, perhaps we would have been in doubt about admitting his interpretation.

(50) But, as it is, Matthew says our Lord left Nazareth and came and settled in Capharnaum by the sea,[80] and from that time began to preach saying, "Repent, for the kingdom of heaven is at hand."[81]

(51) And Mark relates that the Lord came into Galilee preaching the Gospel of God beginning with his temptation with the devil, after John was delivered up.[82] And after the selection of the four fishermen for apostleship, "they enter Capharnaum, and immediately he began teaching in the synagogue on the Sabbaths, and they were astonished at his teaching."[83]

(52) In addition, Mark records his action which took place in Capharnaum. For "immediately," he says, "there was a man in their synagogue with an unclean spirit. And he cried out saying, 'Ha, what have we to do with you, Jesus of Nazareth? Have you come to destroy us? We know who you are, the Son of God.'

(53) And Jesus rebuked him saying, 'Be silent, and depart from him.'" And when he had torn "him and cried out with a loud voice, the unclean spirit departed from him. And they were all amazed."[84] Simon's mother-in-law, also, is released from a fever in Capharnaum.[85]

(54) In addition to these, Mark says when it was evening in Capharnaum "all who were ill and demon-possessed" were healed.[86]

(55) Luke also reports things similar to Mark concerning Capharnaum when he says, "And he went into Capharnaum, a city of Galilee, and was teaching them on the Sabbaths. And

---

80. Cf. Mt 4.13.
81. Mt 4.17.
82. Cf. Mk 1.13–14.
83. Cf. Mk 1.21–22.
84. Cf. Mk 1.23–27.
85. Cf. Mk 1.30–31.
86. Cf. Mk 1.32.34.

they were astonished at his teaching, because his speech was with authority.

(56) And there was a man who had a spirit of an unclean demon in the synagogue, and he cried out with a loud voice, 'Ha, what have we to do with you, Jesus of Nazareth? I know who you are, the holy one of God.' And Jesus rebuked him saying, 'Be silent, and depart from him.' Then also, after the demon had thrown him into the midst, he departed from him, not having hurt him at all."[87]

(57) And after these things he reports that the Lord, "having risen from the synagogue, entered Simon's house,"[88] and, having rebuked the fever in his mother-in-law, released her from the sickness. After she was healed, he says, "And when the sun had set, all who had any sick with various diseases brought them to him. And he laid his hands on each one of them and healed them. And demons also departed from many, crying out and saying, 'You are the Son of God.' And he rebuked them and did not permit them to speak because they knew that he was Christ."[89]

(58) But we have presented all this information about what the Savior said and did in Capharnaum to refute the interpretation of Heracleon who says, "For this reason he is not said to have done or said anything in it."

(59) Let him either grant that there are two meanings of Capharnaum and let him present the evidence and persuade us of which one he speaks, or if he cannot do this, let him refrain from saying that the Savior has visited any place for no reason.

(60) We too, if God grants it, when we come to such passages in our comparative reading where it would seem that when he visited some places he accomplished nothing, will attempt to make clear that his visit was not in vain.

(61) And further, when the Lord entered Capharnaum, Matthew says the centurion came to him saying, "My servant lies in the house paralyzed suffering terribly."[90] And, after other words were spoken by the Lord, the centurion heard

---

87. Cf. Lk 4.31–35.
88. Cf. Lk 4.38.
89. Cf. Lk 4.40–41.
90. Cf. Mt 8.5–6.

him say, "Go, and let it be done for you as you have believed."[91] He has also presented the story about Peter's mother-in-law in agreement with the other two Gospels.[92]

Synthesis of the accounts

(62) We think it is an honorable task, and one appropriate for one eager for knowledge in Christ, to gather from the four Gospels everything which has been recorded concerning Capharnaum; the words and works of the Lord in it, how often he resided in it, when he is said to have gone down into it, when to have entered it, and from where. When these things have been compared with one another, they will prevent us from making mistakes in our interpretation concerning Capharnaum.

(63) But if the sick are healed there, and other miracles occur there, and the preaching, "The kingdom of heaven is at hand,"[93] begins from there, it is probable, as we indicated at the beginning, that it is a symbol of some inferior "place of exhortation,"[94] the place becoming the "place of exhortation" perhaps because Jesus exhorted those whom he taught and for whom he performed works there. For we also know the names of places which are named after occurrences related to Jesus. Take Gergesa, where the fellow-countrymen of the swine urged him to depart from their borders. It is interpreted to mean "residence of those who have cast out."[95]

(64) In addition, the following observation has also been made about Capharnaum: not only did he begin to preach there, "The kingdom of heaven is at hand,"[96] but [also], according to the three evangelists, he performed his first miracles there.

(65) None of the three, however, in relation to the wonders he recorded to have occurred first in Capharnaum, has made the comment of the disciple John in relation to the first work,

---

91. Cf. Mt 8.13.
92. Cf. Mt 8.14–15.
93. Cf. Mt 4.17.
94. Cf. sections 37 and 42 above.
95. Cf. Lagarde, *Onomastica*, 202.62.
96. Cf. Mt 4.17.

when he says, "This beginning of signs did Jesus in Cana of Galilee."[97]

(66) What occurred in Capharnaum was not the beginning of the signs, for good cheer is the essential characteristic of the signs of the Son of God. But because of the critical circumstances which have befallen men, the Word exhibits his special beauty not so much by his service in healing those who have suffered, as in cheering with his sober drink those who, because of their health, are also able to participate in feasting.

And the Pasch of the Jews was near.

Human celebrations, celebrations of the law, and celestial celebrations

(67) In examining the precision of the most wise John, I asked myself what the addition "of the Jews" means for him. For what other nation has a feast of the pasch? For this reason it would have been sufficient if he had said, "And the pasch was near."

(68) But perhaps, since there is a human pasch of those who do not celebrate it according to the intention of the Scripture, and a divine one which is the true one which is executed in spirit and truth by those who worship God in spirit and truth,[98] he has contrasted the one said to be "of the Jews" with the divine one.

(69) Let us, therefore, listen to the Lord when he ordains the pasch by law. What does he say when it is first mentioned in Scripture? "And the Lord spoke to Moses and Aaron in the land of Egypt saying, 'This month is the beginning of months for you; it is the first in the months of the year for you.

(70) Speak to the whole congregation of the children of Israel saying, "On the tenth day of this month let each man take a sheep in accordance with their paternal houses."[99] And

---

97. Cf. Jn 2.11.
98. Cf. Jn 4.24.
99. Cf. Ex 12.1–3.

after a few words in which the pasch has not as yet been mentioned by name, he adds, "And thus shall you eat it: with your loins girded, your sandals on your feet, and your staffs in your hands; and you shall eat it in haste. It is the pasch of the Lord.'"[100]

(71) He does not say, "It is your pasch." And after a few words he mentions the feast a second time in this way: "And it shall be if your sons say to you, 'What is this service?' And you shall say to them, 'It is the sacrifice of the pasch of the Lord, when he protected the houses of the children of Israel.'"[101] And again, after a few words, "And the Lord spoke to Moses and Aaron saying, 'This is the law of the pasch: no foreigner shall eat of it.'"[102]

(72) And again, after a few words, "But if some proselyte should come to you and celebrate the pasch of the Lord, every male of his house shall be circumcised."[103]

(73) We must observe that in the legislation it is nowhere called "your pasch." Once in the passages which we quoted it is mentioned without any addition, and three times it appears as "the pasch of the Lord." To admit that this is the case concerning the distinction between the "pasch of the Lord" and the "pasch of the Jews," let us consider also what is said in Isaias as follows: "I will not abide your new moons and sabbaths and your great day. My soul hates your fasting and abstention and your new moons and feasts."[104]

(74) The Lord does not say that these things which are celebrated by sinners, which are hated by his soul, if one can speak of such, are his own—neither the new moons, nor the sabbaths, nor a great day, nor fasting, nor the feasts.

(75) The following words, however, are said in the legislation of Exodus about the Sabbath: "And Moses said to them, 'This is the word which the Lord spoke: The Sabbath rest is holy to the Lord.'"[105] And after a few words, "And Moses said, 'Eat, for today is the Sabbath for the Lord.'"[106]

---

100. Cf. Ex 12.11.
102. Ex 12.43.
104. Is 1.13–14.
106. Cf. Ex 16.25.

101. Ex 12.26–27.
103. Ex 12.48.
105. Cf. Ex 16.23.

(76) And in Numbers, before the sacrifices for each feast, since each day is a feast according to the law of the perpetual sacrifice, these words are written: "And the Lord said to Moses, 'Proclaim to the children of Israel, and you shall speak to them saying, "You shall observe to offer to me my gifts, my offerings, my fruit-offering for a pleasing odor in my feasts." And you shall say to them, "These are the fruit-offerings which you shall offer to the Lord.'"[107] He mentioned his own feasts, and his gifts, and his offerings, and not those which lie outside those ordained by law in the Scripture.

(77) Now something like this has also been recorded in Exodus concerning the people whom God says are his own when they do not sin, but when they renounced him by making the calf, he called them the "people of Moses." On the one hand, he says to Pharaoh, "You shall say, Thus says the Lord: 'Send forth my people that they may worship me in the wilderness.

(78) But if you are not willing to send my people forth, behold I will send the dog-fly upon you and your servants, and upon your people and your houses, and the houses of the Egyptians shall be filled with the dog-fly, even to the land on which they dwell.

(79) And in that day I will make the land of Gessen wonderful, on which land my people dwell. There will be no dog-fly upon it,[108] that you may know that I am Lord, the Lord of all the earth. And I will put a division in the midst of my people.'"[109] But, on the other hand, the Lord spoke to Moses saying, "Go, descend quickly, for your people whom you brought out of the land of Egypt have transgressed."[110]

(80) Therefore, just as the people are God's when they do not sin, but are no longer said to be his when they sin, so also the feasts are the feasts of sinners when they are hated by the Lord's soul, but when they are ordained by the Lord, they are called the Lord's.

---

107. Cf. Nm 28.1–3.
108. Accepting the feminine relative pronoun which Preuschen suggests in his apparatus. The feminine dative, he notes, agrees with the reading of the LXX in Codex Alexandrinus on this verse.
109. Cf. Ex 8.16–19.   110. Cf. Ex 32.7.

(81) Now the pasch is also one of the feasts. In the text of the gospel before us it is not said to be of the Lord, but of the Jews. But Scripture also says elsewhere, "These are the feasts of the Lord which you shall call holy convocations."[111]

(82) On the one hand, therefore, on the basis of the Lord's word it is not possible to oppose what we have presented.

Celestial Passover

But, on the other hand, someone will plausibly raise a question on the basis of the apostle who writes in the Epistle to the Corinthians, "For also Christ our pasch is sacrificed."[112] He does not say, "Christ the pasch of the Lord is sacrificed."

(83) Now we must reply either that he has said simply, "our pasch is sacrificed," meaning it was sacrificed because of us, or that every feast which is truly the Lord's, of which the pasch is one, will be celebrated, not in this age nor upon the earth, but in the coming age and in heaven, when the kingdom of heaven is present.

(84) Concerning those feasts, one of the twelve prophets says, "What will you do in the days of festal assembly, and in the days of the feast of the Lord?"[113] And Paul says in the Epistle to the Hebrews, "But you have come to mount Sion, and to the city of the living God, the heavenly Jerusalem, and to thousands of angels, to a festal assembly, and to the church of the firstborn who are recorded in the heavens."[114] And in the Epistle to the Colossians, "Let no man, therefore, judge you in food and in drink, or in respect of a feast, or new moon, or Sabbaths, which are a shadow of things to come."[115]

(85) It is the task, however, of the wisdom which has been hidden in mystery[116] to make manifest in what manner we, who were formerly guided under the true law by guardians and stewards until the fullness of time should be present[117] and we should receive the perfection of the Son of God, shall keep festival in the heavenly places of which there was a

---

111. Cf. Lev 23.2.
113. Cf. Hos 9.5.
115. Col 2.16–17.
117. Cf. Gal 3.24; 4.2 and 4.

112. 1 Cor 5.7.
114. Heb 12.22–23.
116. Cf. 1 Cor 2.7.

shadow among the corporeal Jews.[118] It is also the task of this wisdom to contemplate the things established by law concerning foods, which are symbols of the things which will maintain and strengthen our souls there.

(86) Now it is likely that someone who has a mental image of the sea of such great thoughts, and who wishes to consider[119] how the service in a place is an example and shadow of heavenly services, and who wishes to reflect on the sacrifices and the sheep, has taken offense even at the apostle who, on the one hand, wished to raise our thoughts from the earthly teachings concerning the law, but, on the other hand, did not at all indicate how these things will be.

(87) But if there are both feasts, of which the pasch is one, and they are referred anagogically to the age to come, this is even more reason we must consider how, "Christ our pasch is sacrificed"[120] now, and later will be sacrificed.

Spiritual interpretation of Jewish celebrations

(88) But we must add a few words on the difficulty of these teachings, which need their own special and voluminous study. There is need of a study of every mystical teaching in the law, and separately a study of matters related to the feasts, and, in an even more specialized sense, concerning the pasch.

(89) The pasch of the Jews, therefore, is a sheep which is sacrificed, being taken by each man according to his paternal house. It is celebrated by the slaughter of tens of thousands of lambs and kids, the mass proportionate to the number of houses of the people. But "Christ our pasch is sacrificed."[121]

(90) And again, unleavened bread is a part of their pasch, since all leaven is removed from their houses.[122] But we feast not "with the old leaven," nor "with the leaven of malice and wickedness, but with the unleavened bread of sincerity and truth."[123]

(91) And we must investigate very carefully if there is some

---

118. Cf. Heb 8.5.
119. Accepting Wendland's emendation of *sōsai* to *skopēsai*.
120. 1 Cor 5.7.   121. Ibid.
122. Cf. Ex 12.15.   123. Cf. 1 Cor 5.8.

third beyond the two mentioned, namely the pasch of the Lord and the feast of unleavened bread, because those serve as an example and shadow of those heavenly things. It is not only foods, and drinks, and new moons, and sabbaths, but the feasts too are a shadow of things to come.

Ordinances concerning the Lamb and sacrifices on the cross

(92) In the first place, when the apostle says, "Christ our pasch is sacrificed,"[124] someone will raise the following objections. If the sheep sacrificed by the Jews is a type of sacrifice of Christ, it is necessary either that they sacrifice one, and not many, sheep just as there is one Christ, or since many sheep are sacrificed, we must seek many Christs, as it were, who are sacrificed in conformity with the type.

(93) But, to dismiss this objection, how does the sheep which is sacrificed contain an image of Christ, when the sheep is sacrificed by those who are observing the law, but Christ is killed by those who are transgressing it? And further how, in the case of Christ, "shall they eat the flesh that night roasted with fire, and eat the unleavened bread with bitter herbs"?[125] We must also interpret the command, "You shall not eat thereof anything raw or boiled in water, but only roasted with fire. You shall eat the head with the feet and the entrails. You shall not leave any of them until morning, and you shall not break a bone of them; but you shall burn that which is left from them until morning."[126]

(94) John seems to have used the command, "You shall not break a bone of it,"[127] in his gospel, as referring to the plan concerning the Savior, even when they are commanded in the law as they eat the sheep not to break a bone of it.

(95) He speaks as follows: "Therefore the soldiers came, and they broke the legs of the first, [and of the] other who was crucified with him. But after they came to Jesus, when they saw that he was already dead, they did not break his legs. But one of the soldiers opened his side with a spear, and

124. 1 Cor 5.7.
126. Cf. Ex 12.9–10.

125. Cf. Ex 12.8.
127. Ex 12.10.

immediately blood and water came out. And he who saw it has borne testimony, and this testimony is true. And he knows that he speaks the truth, that you also may believe. For these things happened that [the] Scripture might be fulfilled: 'You shall not break a bone of him.' "[128]

(96) There are also ten thousand other matters besides these which could be investigated and examined concerning the pasch and the unleavened bread in relation to the text of the apostle, but [they need], as we said before, a general, voluminous work.

(97) But now, as though in an abridgement, by citing these things because of the text before us, we shall attempt to solve the apparent difficulties in as few words as possible, as follows, having recalled also the statement, "This is the lamb of God who takes away the sin of the world,"[129] since it says also in the pasch, "You shall partake of the lambs and the kids."[130]

(98) For the evangelist too, since he is in agreement with Paul, will seem to be entangled in difficulties such as this concerning those matters which we have examined.

Eating of the Word

(99) But we must say that if the Word became flesh,[131] and the Lord says, "Unless you eat the flesh of the Son of man and drink his blood, you do not have life in yourselves; he who eats my flesh and drinks my blood has eternal life, and I will raise him up in the last day; for my flesh is real food and my blood is real drink; he who eats my flesh and drinks my blood remains in me, and I in him,"[132] perhaps this is the flesh of the lamb which takes away the sin of the world, and perhaps this is the blood from which one must put some on the two doorposts and on the lintel in the houses in which we eat the pasch. And perhaps we must eat of the meat of this lamb in the time of the world, which is night. And we must eat the meat roasted with fire with unleavened bread.[133] For the Word of God is not only flesh. He says, indeed, "I am the

---

128. Cf. Jn 19.32–36.
130. Cf. Ex 12.5.
132. Jn 6.53–56.
129. Cf. Jn 1.29.
131. Cf. Jn 1.14.
133. Cf. Ex 12.8.

bread of life,"¹³⁴ and "This is the bread which comes down from heaven that one may eat of it and not die. I am the living bread which came down from heaven. If anyone eat of this bread he shall live forever."¹³⁵

(100) We must not, however, fail to remark that all food is loosely said to be bread, as it is written in the case of Moses in Deuteronomy: "He did not eat bread for forty days, and he did not drink water,"¹³⁶ instead of saying, he partook of neither dry nor wet nourishment.

(101) Now I have noted this because it is also said in the Gospel According to John, "And also the bread which I shall give for the life of the world is my flesh."¹³⁷

(102) But we eat the flesh of the lamb and the unleavened bread with bitter herbs¹³⁸ either by being grieved with a godly grief because of repentances for our sins, a grief which produces in us a repentance unto salvation which brings no regret,¹³⁹ or, by seeking and being nurtured from the visions of the truth which we discover because of our trials.

(103) One must not, therefore, eat the flesh of the lamb raw, as the slaves of the letter do in the manner of animals which are irrational and quite savage. In relation to men who are truly rational through their desire to understand the spiritual aspects of the word, the former share the company of wild beasts.

(104) We must strive, however, in transforming the rawness of Scripture into boiled food, not to transform what has been written into what is flaccid, watery, and limp. This is what they do who "have itching ears and" turn them away "from the truth,"¹⁴⁰ and transform the anagogical meanings so far as they are concerned to the carelessness and wateriness of their manner of life.

(105) But let us, by means of the boiling spirit and the fiery words given by God, such as Jeremias received from the one who said to him, "Behold I have placed my words in your

---

134. Jn 6.48.
135. Jn 6.50–51.
136. Dt 9.9; Ex 34.28.
137. Jn 6.51.
138. Cf. Ex 12.8.
139. Cf. 2 Cor 7.9–10.
140. Cf. 2 Tim 4.3–4.

mouth as fire,"[141] roast the meat of the lamb so that those who partake of it say, as Christ speaks in us,[142] "Our heart was burning in the way as he opened the Scriptures to us."[143] But we will have[144] to roast the meat of the lamb in order to seek such a goal.[145] We must compare the confession of what Jeremias had suffered for the words of God when he said, "And it was as a fire burning, blazing in my bones, and I am weak from every side and am not able to bear it."[146]

(106) We must begin eating from the head, that is from the most important and principal teachings about heavenly things, and we must end at the feet, that is the final elements of the lessons which investigate the uttermost nature in the things which exist, either that of material things, or things under the earth, or evil spirits and unclean demons.

(107) For the teaching[147] concerning them, being different than themselves, can, since it is stored up in the mysteries of Scripture, be named figuratively "feet" of the lamb. We must also not abstain from the entrails and the inner and hidden parts. We must, however, approach all the Scripture as one body, and not break or cut through the most vigorous and firm bonds in the harmony of its total composition. This is what they have done who have, so far as it is in their power, broken the unity of the Spirit in all the Scriptures.

(108) Let this prophecy of the lamb, however, which has been mentioned, nurture us only for the duration of the night of darkness in this life. For we must leave nothing of this nourishment, which shall thus be useful to us only in the present time, until the dawn of the day of those things which follow this life.

(109) For when the night is past and the following day has come, we shall eat unleavened bread, having no bread at all made from that which is older and leavened from below.[148]

141. Cf. Jer 5.14. 142. Cf. 2 Cor 13.3.
143. Cf. Lk 24.32.
144. Accepting *deēsei* for *de ēxei*.
145. The text of this sentence is corrupt.
146. Jer 20.9. 147. *Logos*.
148. Cf. 1 Cor 5.7.

This unleavened bread will be useful to us until the manna, which follows the unleavened bread, be given. This is the food of angels, and not of men.[149] Let the sheep, therefore, be sacrificed for each of us in every house of our fathers. And let it be possible that one man transgresses by not sacrificing the sheep, and another observes all the law by sacrificing, and by boiling it thoroughly, and not breaking a bone of it.[150]

(110) And thus, as in a few words, let Christ, our pasch which has been sacrificed, be rendered in harmony with the interpretation of the apostle,[151] and with the lamb in the gospel.[152] For we must not suppose that historical things are types of historical things, and corporeal of corporeal. Quite the contrary: corporeal things are types of spiritual things, and historical of intellectual.

(111) It is not necessary now that we ascend in our discourse[153] also to the third pasch which will be celebrated with ten thousand angels in a most perfect assembly and a most blessed exodus. Even what we have said is fuller and goes beyond what the text demands.

Proximity of the sojourn at Capharnaum and the Passover of the Jews

(112) We must not leave unexamined how "the pasch of the Jews was at hand,"[154] when the Lord was in Capharnaum together with his mother, and brothers, and disciples.

(113) In the Gospel According to Matthew, then, after the devil left him, and the angels came and ministered to him, and he had heard that John had been arrested,[155] "he withdrew into Galilee, and when he left Nazareth he came and dwelt in Capharnaum."[156] Then, after he has begun to preach, and has chosen the four fishermen as apostles, and has taught in the synagogues of all Galilee, and has healed those who were brought to him, he goes up into the mountain and delivers the beatitudes and those words connected with them.[157]

149. Cf. Ps 77.25.
151. Cf. 1 Cor 5.7.
153. *Logō*.
155. Mt 4.11–12.
157. Cf. Mt 4.17–7.29.

150. Cf. Ex 12.10.
152. Cf. Jn 1.29.
154. Jn 2.13.
156. Mt 4.12–13.

And when he completed that teaching, and came down from the mountain, he entered Capharnaum a second time, and from there he embarked in a boat and crossed into the country of the Gerasens.[158] And when he was urged to pass over from their borders, "he embarked in a boat and crossed over and came into his own city."[159] When he had performed certain cures there,[160] "he went about all the cities and villages teaching in their synagogues."[161]

(114) Many other things also occur after these before Matthew notes the time of the pasch.[162] In the other evangelists, too, one does not find it said that the pasch is at hand after the time he spent in Capharnaum.

(115) It is possible, however, to preserve the intention of the men by considering what we said earlier about the time spent[163] in Capharnaum which was near the pasch of the Jews. This time was a little preferable and a little better than it, especially since those selling oxen and sheep and doves were found in the temple at the pasch of the Jews.[164] The presence of these merchants is even more cause to propose that this pasch is not of the Lord, but of the Jews. For as the Father's house had become a house of merchandise with those who did not sanctify it, so also the pasch of the Lord had become the pasch belonging to men and to the Jews at the hands of those who took it in a lowly and corporeal way.

(116) It will be easier, however, in other places to view the statements which are made about the time of the pasch, which takes place around the spring equinox, and whether any other problem demands investigation.

(117) Heracleon, however, says, "This is the great feast, for it was a type of the Savior's passion, when the sheep was not only killed, but also provided rest when it was being eaten. In being sacrificed,

---

158. Cf. Mt 8.1–28. 159. Mt 9.1.
160. Cf. Mt 9.2–6; 18–25; 27–30.
161. Cf. Mt 9.35.
162. Cf. Mt 26.2.
163. The text is uncertain here. I have accepted the text printed in Blanc which emends *endiatribē* to *diatribēs*, and inserts the relative pronoun *he* immediately after it.
164. Cf. Jn 2.13–14.

it signified the passion of the Savior in the world, but in being eaten it signified the rest at the wedding."

(118) We have quoted his text that we might despise him when we see how frivolously and feebly, with no proof beyond himself, the man behaves with such great themes.

And Jesus went up to Jerusalem, and He found in the Temple those who sold oxen and sheep and doves, and the money-changers sitting, and when He had made a scourge of little cords, he cast the sheep and the oxen out of the Temple and poured out the money of the money-changers, and overturned the tables. And He said to those selling doves: 'Remove these things from here. Do not make my Father's House a house of merchandise.' Then his Disciples remembered that it was written: 'Zeal for your house has devoured me.'

Parallel passages of Synoptics

(119) We must note that John records as Jesus' second work that which involved those whom he found in the temple selling oxen, sheep and doves. The other evangelists, however, related a similar work nearly at the end, at the time of the mystery of his passion.

(120) Matthew has it as follows: "And when he entered Jerusalem, the whole city was moved saying, 'Who is this?' And the crowds said, 'This is Jesus the prophet from Nazareth of Galilee.' And Jesus entered the temple and cast out all those selling and buying in the temple. And he overturned the tables of the money-changers and the chairs of those selling doves. And he says to them, 'It is written, My house shall be called a house of prayer, but you are making it a den of thieves.'"[165]

(121) Mark says, "And they enter Jerusalem. And when he entered the temple he began to cast out those selling and buying in the temple, and he overthrew the tables of the

---

165. Mt 21.10–13.

money-changers and the chairs of those selling doves. And he did not permit anyone to carry a vessel through the temple. And he taught them and said, 'Is it not written: My house shall be called a house of prayer for all nations? But you have made it a den of thieves?'"[166]

(122) Luke has, "And as he drew near, when he saw the city he wept over it, saying, 'If you also had known the things that pertain to your peace in this day; but now they are hidden from your eyes. For the days shall come upon you and they will encircle and constrain you from every side, and they will dash you and your children to the ground, and they will not leave a stone upon a stone in you because you did not know the time of your visitation.' And when he entered the temple he began to cast out those selling, saying to them, 'It is written: And my house shall be a house of prayer, but you have made it a den of thieves.'"[167]

They attach the episode of the money changers in the temple to that of the triumphal entrance into Jerusalem

(123) In addition we must also observe that John has recorded that events similar to those mentioned in the Synoptics at the time of the Lord's ascent to Jerusalem when he performed these works in the temple, occurred after many others on another visit of his to Jerusalem in addition to the present one.

(124) Consequently, we must observe what has been said, and begin with what is said in Matthew. "And when he drew near Jerusalem, and came into Bethphage to the mount of Olives, then Jesus sent two disciples, saying to them, 'Go into the village opposite you; and immediately you will find an ass tied, and a colt with her. Loose them and bring them to me. And if anyone should say to you, What are you doing?, you shall say, The Lord has need of them; And immediately he will send them.' Now this was done to fulfill what was spoken through the prophet, saying, 'Say to the daughter of Sion, Behold your king comes, meek and mounted on an ass, and the foal of a beast of burden.' And the disciples went and did

166. Cf. Mk 11.15–17.   167. Cf. Lk 19.41–46.

as Jesus commanded them. They brought the ass and the colt and placed their garments upon them, and he sat upon them. And a great multitude spread their garments in the way. * * *[168] And the multitudes preceding and following him cried out, 'Hosanna to the son of David. Blessed is he who comes in the name of the Lord. Hosanna in the highest.' "[169]

(125) And there follows these words: "And when he entered Jerusalem the whole city was moved,"[170] which we presented in the previous discussions.

(126) In the second place, we consider Mark's words, "And when they were drawing near to Jerusalem, to Bethphage and Bethania at the mount of Olives, he sends two of his disciples and says to them, 'Go into the village opposite you, and immediately when you enter it, you will find a colt tied, on which no man has yet sat. Loose it and bring it. And if anyone should say to you, Why are you doing this?, say, The Lord has need of it; and immediately he will send it here.' And they went and found a colt tied at the gate, outside on the street, and they loosed it. And some of those standing there said to them, 'What are you doing loosing the colt?' And they spoke to them just as Jesus said, and they permitted them. And they brought the colt to Jesus, and placed their garments on it. And others cut boughs from the fields and strewed them in the way. And those preceding and those following cried out, 'Hosanna, blessed is he who comes in the name of the Lord. Blessed is the kingdom of our father David which is coming. Hosanna in the highest.' And he entered into Jerusalem, into the temple. And when he had viewed all things round about, since the hour was already late, he went out to Bethania with the twelve. And the next day, when they departed from Bethania, he was hungry."[171] Then after the affair of the withered fig tree, "they entered Jerusalem. And when he entered the temple he began to cast out those selling,"[172] etc. * *[173]

---

168. Preuschen thinks the next clause in the text of Matthew has fallen out by homoioteleuton.
169. Cf. Mt 21.1–9.   170. Mt 21.10.
171. Cf. Mk 11.1–12.   172. Mk 11.15.
173. Preuschen thinks some words have been lost here which closed this sentence and began the next.

(127) [And in] Luke we have it in this way, "And it came to pass as he approached Bethphage and Bethania, to the mount which is called Olives, he sent two of the disciples, saying, 'Go into the village opposite. When you enter it you will find a colt tied on which no man has ever sat. Loose it and bring it. And if anyone should ask you, Why are you loosing it? You shall say thus: The Lord has need of it.' And the disciples departed and found it as he said to them. But as they were loosing the colt, its owners said to them, 'Why are you loosing the colt?' And they said, 'The Lord has need of it.' And they brought it to Jesus; and they cast their garments upon the colt and set Jesus on it. And as he went, they spread their garments in the way. And when he now approached the descent of the mount of Olives, a multitude of disciples began to meet him, rejoicing and praising God in a loud voice for all the mighty works they had seen, saying, 'Blessed be the king in the name of the Lord. Peace in heaven, and glory in the highest.' And some of the Pharisees from the multitude said to him, 'Teacher, rebuke your disciples.' And he answered and said, 'I say to you that if these be silent, the stones will cry out.' And as he drew near, when he saw the city he wept over it"[174] and the following, which we quoted.

This same entry in John

(128) John, however, after a large number of events, describes an ascent of the Lord to Jerusalem different from the one described in the words, "And Jesus went up to Jerusalem, and found in the temple those selling oxen and sheep."[175] He makes the following statements after the supper in Bethania which was six days before the pasch, at which Martha served and Lazarus reclined at the table:[176] "And on the next day a great multitude which had come to the feast, when they heard that Jesus was coming to Jerusalem, took branches of palm trees, and went out to meet him, and cried out, 'Hosanna, blessed in the name of the Lord be the king of Israel.' And

---

174. Cf. Lk 19.29–41.   175. Jn 2.13–14.
176. Cf. Jn 12.1–2.

Jesus found a young ass and sat upon it, as it is written: 'Fear not, daughter of Sion, behold, your king is coming, sitting upon an ass's colt.' "[177]

Contradictions between the evangelists

(129) Although I have quoted the text of the Gospels at very great length, I think this has been done of necessity to show the disagreement according to the literal meaning. The Synoptics relate what most people assume to be the same things that are written also in John, to have occurred in one and the same visit of the Lord to Jerusalem. But John reports that the things related occurred in two ascents to Jerusalem separated by many acts revealed between them, and by visits of the Lord to different places.

(130) I, therefore, assume that it is impossible for those who understand nothing beyond the historical meaning in these passages to show that the apparent disagreement is an agreement. And if anyone thinks that we have not understood it correctly, let him intelligently write a rebuttal to such a view as ours.

Spiritual interpretation of the episode of the money-changers in the temple

(131) Now we shall set forth in the same manner, according to the ability given to us, the things which move us to the harmony of these texts, as we have asked him who gives to everyone who asks and struggles intensely to seek, and we are knocking, that the hidden things of Scripture may be opened to us by the keys of knowledge.[178] Let us consider first the text of John which begins, "And Jesus went up to Jerusalem."[179] Jerusalem, then, as the Lord himself teaches in the Gospel According to Matthew, is the "city of the great king,"[180] which lies not in a valley or somewhere below, but which is built on a high mountain, and "mountains are around it,"[181] "which is

---

177. Cf. Jn 12.12–15.
179. Jn 2.13.
181. Cf. Mt 5.14; Ps 124.2.

178. Cf. Mt 7.7–8; Lk 11.52.
180. Cf. Mt 5.35.

compact together,"¹⁸² and "there did the tribes of the Lord go up, a testimony to Israel."¹⁸³

(132) And this city, to which none of those on earth ascends or enters, is also called Jerusalem. And every soul which has a natural exaltation and sees spiritual things clearly and sharply is a citizen of this city. It is possible even for a resident of Jerusalem to be in sin, for even the best natural dispositions can sin, destroying their goodness of disposition and not only sojourning in one of the foreign cities of Judea, but also being enrolled as a citizen there, unless they turn back quickly after the sin.

(133) Jesus, [therefore], goes up to Jerusalem after he has helped those in Cana of Galilee,¹⁸⁴ and after he has gone down to Capharnaum,¹⁸⁵ that he might perform the works which are recorded among those in Jerusalem. He found in the temple, which is also said to be the house of the Savior's Father, that is, in the church or in the proclamation of the sound message of the church, some who were making his Father's house a house of merchandise.¹⁸⁶

The traders

(134) Jesus always finds some such in the temple. For when, in what we call the church, which is the house "of the living God, the pillar and ground of the truth,"¹⁸⁷ are there not some money-changers sitting, needing stripes from the whip Jesus made from ropes, and money-changers needing their coins poured out and their tables overturned?¹⁸⁸

(135) And when are there not those who are selling oxen commercially? These ought to be kept for the plow, that by putting their hands to it and not turning back they might become fit for the kingdom of God?¹⁸⁹ And when are there not those who prefer the mammon of iniquity to the sheep which provide them the material to adorn themselves?¹⁹⁰

182. Ps 121.3.
184. Cf. Jn 2.1–11.
186. Cf. Jn 2.14–16.
188. Cf. Jn 2.14–15.
190. Cf. Lk 16.9.

183. Cf. Ps 121.4.
185. Cf. Jn 2.12.
187. 1 Tm 3.15.
189. Cf. Jn 2.14; Lk 9.62.

(136) There are always many, too, who despise what is honest and pure and devoid of all bitterness and gall. For the sake of miserable gain, they abandon the care of those who are figuratively called doves.

(137) Therefore, whenever the Savior finds in the temple, the house of the Father, those who are selling oxen and sheep and doves, and the money-changers sitting, he drives them out, together with their commercial sheep and oxen, using the whip he has made from ropes. He also pours out the coins as not worth keeping, since he has shown their uselessness. And he overturns the tables in the souls of those fond of money, saying also to those selling doves, "Take these hence,"[191] that they might no longer trade in the temple of God.

Jesus repeals the sacrifices in the temple

(138) I think, in addition, that he has also performed a more profound sign through what has been said, so that we recognize that these events have occurred as a symbol of the fact that no longer will the ministry related to that temple still be able to be performed by the priests so far as the sacrifices perceptible by the senses are concerned, nor will the law still be able to be observed even as the corporeal Jews would wish.

(139) For when Jesus once and for all casts out the oxen and the sheep, and commands that the doves be removed from there,[192] no longer indeed were oxen, sheep, and doves destined to be sacrificed according to the customs of the Jews for a long time.

(140) It is also likely that the money which was poured out[193] belonged to that which is stamped with the images of material money and not the image of God, since, after Jesus came and used his whips against the people, the legislation according to the letter which kills,[194] which appears to be august, was about to be nullified and poured out. Its office was to be given

---

191. Jn 2.16.
192. Jn 2.15–16.
193. Cf. Jn 2.15. 194. Cf. 2 Cor 3.6.

instead[195] to those from the gentiles who believe in God through Christ. The kingdom of God, too, was to be taken from them and given to a nation performing its fruits.[196]

Jesus purifies the soul

(141) It is also possible that the soul which has a naturally intelligent disposition, which is higher than the body because of the intelligence which is united with it is, by nature, a temple to which Jesus humbly ascends from Capharnaum which lies somewhere below. Emotions, which are earthly, senseless and harmful, and things which are supposed to be good but are not, are found in this soul prior to the discipline which comes from Jesus. Jesus drives these out with his word which has been plaited of demonstrative [and] reproving doctrines, that no longer might his Father's house be a [house] of merchandise, but that it might receive the worship of God performed according to the laws which are heavenly and spiritual, for its own salvation and that of many people.

(142) Now the ox is a symbol of earthly things, for it is a worker of the earth. The sheep is a symbol of unintelligent and beastly things, since the animal is more servile than most irrational animals. The dove is a symbol of vain and unstable reasonings, and the coins, of things thought to be good.

Literal interpretation

(143) But if someone should take offense at such an interpretation because the animals used in Scripture are pure, we must say that the Scripture which is reported to have taken place according to the accepted historical sense would have been unconvincing. For it was not possible to report that a herd of other animals besides the pure had been introduced in the temple of God, and that it was for commerce in other animals besides those which were sacrificed.

(144) Wherefore, in my opinion, the evangelist used what was customarily done by the merchants at the times of the

---

195. Cf. Acts 1.20; Ps 109.8.
196. Cf. Mt 21.43.

Jewish feasts, when they brought these animals in addition into the outer court of the temple, and availed himself also of an act which had occurred.

Prodigious character of the intervention of Jesus

(145) And indeed he who is concerned about a more accurate insight will consider if it was in accordance with Jesus' position in this life, since he was supposed to be the son of a carpenter, to venture to do so great a thing as to drive out a multitude of merchants who had come up to the feast to sell to such a multitude the sheep which were to be sacrificed according to their ancestral houses.[197] The sheep numbered many thousands; there were also oxen to be sold to those who were wealthier and who had vowed such large animals; and there were doves which many would purchase since they would be feasting at the festal assembly. And when the moneychangers[198] saw their money being poured out and their tables overturned did they not accuse Jesus of an outrage?

(146) And who, if he is struck with a whip of cords and is being driven out by one they supposed to be worthless, would not seize him and cry out and work vengeance with his own hand, especially since he has so large a multitude of those who seemed to be insulted as well to cooperate in such acts against Jesus?

(147) And let us consider if [the fact that] the Son of God takes cords and weaves a whip for himself and drives them out of the temple does not point to one who is self-willed, and rather rash, and undisciplined in nature.

(148) One who wants to preserve the historical sense also has one escape left as a defense for these deeds: the divine power of Jesus who was able, when he wished to quench the inflamed anger of his enemies, and to prevail over tens of thousands with divine grace, and to bring to nought clamoring arguments. "For the Lord will bring to nought the counsels of nations, and he rejects the arguments of peoples; but the

---

197. Cf. Ex 12.3.
198. Preuschen marks a lacuna at this point in the text; Brooke does not.

counsel of the Lord abides forever."[199] Consequently, the historical meaning in our passage, if indeed it even occurred, indicates that a miracle was executed no less than any which he performed most incredibly and which summoned those who saw them to faith through his divinity.

(149) And it is possible to show that this miracle is greater than that which occurred in relation to the water which was changed into wine in Cana of Galilee. In that case it was soulless matter which was changed; in this, the governing faculties of so many thousands enslaved.

Presence of the disciples

(150) We must note, however, that Jesus' mother is said to be at the wedding, and Jesus and his disciples are said to have been invited, [and he and his mother and brothers and his disciples are said] to have gone down to Capharnaum, but no one except Jesus is related [to have gone up to Jerusalem].[200]

(151) But the disciples also appear to be present later, since they remembered, "The zeal of your house will devour me."[201] Perhaps Jesus was going up to Jerusalem in each of the disciples, and this is why it is not said that "Jesus and his disciples went up to Jerusalem," as it is said that "he and his mother and brothers and his disciples went down to Capharnaum."[202]

Literal interpretation of the entry into Jerusalem in Matthew

(152) But now we must consider the remarks found in the other Gospels which are parallel to the passage on the expulsion from the temple of those who were making it a house of merchandise.

(153) Take those in Matthew first. He says when the Lord entered Jerusalem the whole city was moved, saying, "Who is this?"[203]

---

199. Cf. Ps 32.10–11.
200. Cf. Jn 2.1–12. Origen's statement, as it stands in the MSS. does not agree with Jn 2.12, for it says that no one but Jesus went down to Capharnaum. Section 151 shows clearly that Origen has made some remark concerning Jesus being in Jerusalem alone. Preuschen thinks the bracketed words were lost by homoioteleuton.
201. Jn 2.17. 202. Jn 2.12.
203. Mt 21.10.

(154) But before this he narrates the events related to the ass and the colt, which were taken at the Lord's command by two disciples whom he sent from Bethphage to the village opposite it where also the ass, which was previously tied, was loosed by the two disciples. They had been commanded that if anyone should ask them why they were doing this, to answer, "The Lord has need of them, and immediately he will send them."[204]

(155) And Matthew reports that the prophecy was fulfilled through these events which says, "Behold the king is coming, meek and mounted on an ass and a colt, the foal of a beast of burden,"[205] which we found in Zacharias.[206]

(156) And as the disciples went and did as Jesus commanded them and "brought the ass and the colt, they placed," Matthew says, "their garments upon them and" the Lord "sat upon them"[207] (now it is clear that both the ass and the colt are meant). At this time also "a very great multitude spread their garments in the way, and others cut branches from the trees and spread them in the way,"[208] while the crowds which went before and that which followed had cried out, "Hosanna to the son of David; blessed is he who comes in the name of the Lord; hosanna in the highest."[209]

(157) But, as though because of these events, "when he entered Jerusalem the whole city was moved, saying, 'Who is this?'"[210] The crowds, that is to say those who went before him and those who followed, answered the people who asked who he was: "'This is Jesus the prophet, from Nazareth of Galilee.'

(158) And Jesus entered the temple and cast out all those selling and buying in the temple, and he overturned the tables of the money-changers and the chairs of those selling doves. And he says to them, 'It is written, My house shall be called a house of prayer, but you are making it a den of thieves.'"[211]

(159) At this point we will inquire of those who think that Matthew set forth nothing beyond the historical meaning

204. Cf. Mt 21.1–3.
206. Zec 9.9.
208. Cf. Mt 21.8.
210. Mt 21.10.
205. Cf. Mt 21.5.
207. Cf. Mt 21.6–7.
209. Mt 21.9.
211. Mt 21.11–13.

when he wrote his gospel: What was the urgency that two of the disciples be sent into the village opposite Bethphage to find an ass tied and a colt with her, to loose and bring to him?

(160) And what happened worth recording in an ass and a colt having been sat upon and having entered the city? And why does Zacharias prophesy of the Christ and say, with a view to these matters, "Rejoice greatly, daughter of Sion; proclaim it, daughter of Jerusalem; behold, your king is coming to you, just and saving; he is meek and mounted on a beast of burden and a young colt"?[212]

(161) For if this prophecy foretells only the bodily event which is revealed in the Gospels, let those who stop at the literal meaning maintain for us the sequence of the prophecy which goes like this: "And he will destroy the chariots out of Ephraim, and the horse out of Jerusalem, and the bow for war will be destroyed, and a multitude and peace from the gentiles, and he will rule the waters to the sea, and the springs[213] of the rivers of the earth,"[214] and what follows.

(162) We must see, however, that Matthew did not cite the text as it is found in the prophet. For in place of "Rejoice greatly, daughter of Sion; proclaim it, daughter of Jerusalem," he has written, "Say to the daughter of Sion," thus abbreviating the prophecy. And he also omitted the words, "just and saving, he," and said as it is found, "meek and mounted." Instead of "upon an ass and a colt, the foal of a beast of burden."[215]

(163) The Jews too, when they examine with us the connection of this prophecy with the things recorded about Jesus, exert no negligible pressure on us when they demand how Jesus destroyed the chariots out of Ephraim, and the horse out of Jerusalem, and how he destroyed the bow for war and

---

212. Zec 9.9; cf. Mt 21.5.
213. The text of the LXX which Origen follows here appears to be corrupt. The word translated "springs" is in the wrong case to be the object of "rule." Blanc, who thinks the text of the LXX here is unintelligible, notes that the translation Origen gives of the Hebrew in the *Hexapla* (PG 16.3007) is *apo potamōn heōs tōn peratōn tēs gēs*, which would make the second clause mean: he will rule "from the rivers to the ends of the earth."
214. Zec 9.10.   215. Cf. Zec 9.9 and Mt 21.5.

has done the things which follow. But this is enough about the prophecy.

(164) But if they should allege that it is the length of the way, since they find nothing worthy of the dispensation of the Son of God in the story[216] about the ass and colt, in the first place, those who use fifteen stades, which is a short distance, do not provide any reasonable defense of the way at all, and second, let them tell us how he needed two beasts for so short a journey, for it says, "He sat upon them."[217]

(165) And further, I also do not think the statement, "If anyone should say to you, you shall say that the Lord has need of them, and immediately he will send them,"[218] is worthy of the greatness of the Son of God's divinity. Such a statement says that so great a nature acknowledges that he has need of an ass to be loosed from its bonds, and of a colt which comes with it. For everything which the Son of God needs must be great and worthy of his goodness.

(166) And in addition to these matters, the large crowd scatters their garments in the way. While Jesus puts up with these actions and does not rebuke them as is clear from the words found in the other Gospels: "If these should be silent, the stones will cry out,"[219] I do not know if they do not manifest a certain stupidity on the part of one who takes delight at such things if nothing else is revealed by them. And also the fact that they cut branches from the trees to scatter in the way of the asses passing by would seem to be more a hindrance of him who is being crowded than a planned reception.

(167) We must raise here all the questions we raised [about] those he cast out of the temple, and more in addition.

(168) For, on the one hand, in the Gospel According to John he casts out those who buy,[220] but Matthew says, "He cast out all those selling and buying in the temple."[221] Now it is likely that the number of buyers was much larger than that of sellers.

216. *Logon*.
217. Cf. Mt 21.7.
218. Cf. Mt 21.3.
219. Cf. Lk 19.40.
220. Cf. Jn 2.14–16. This is surely a scribal error, for the text of John speaks only of sellers.
221. Mt 21.12.

(169) And we must give attention to whether casting out all those selling and buying in the temple would have been beyond the position of one thought to be the son of a carpenter, unless perhaps, as we also said there, he subjected them all by divine power, for according to the other evangelists, they heard harsher words than John uses.

House of God or prayer—house of trade or den of thieves

(170) For John says that Jesus said to them, "Do not make my Father's house a house of merchandise."[222] But in the other Gospels they are rebuked for having made the house of prayer a "den of thieves."[223] The Father's house could not become a den of thieves, but it was being defiled by sinners to the extent that it had become a house of merchandise.

(171) And since it is only a house of prayer, by no means being the Father's house, once it has been neglected it will even receive thieves, although it does not become their house, but their den, a thing not made by architectural and intellectual skill.

Spiritual interpretation of entry into Jerusalem

(172) To perceive the meaning in these matters, therefore, belongs to that true understanding which has been given to those who say, "But we have the mind of Christ, that we may see the things that are given to us by God."[224]

(173) We are convinced that it is beyond our ability, for our ruling principle is not untroubled, nor are our eyes such as the eyes of Christ's beautiful bride must be, of which eyes the bridegroom says, "Your eyes are doves."[225] He is hinting, perhaps, at the perceptive power of spiritual people, because the Holy Spirit came upon the Lord [Jesus] as a dove,[226] and the Lord is in each one. Nevertheless, even in our condition, we will not hesitate to examine the words of life which have been spoken, and to attempt to grasp their power which streams forth into him who has apprehended them with faith.

222. Jn 2.16.
223. Cf. Mt 21.13; Mk 11.17; Lk 19.46.
224. Cf. 1 Cor 2.16 and 12.   225. Song 1.15.
226. Cf. Mt 3.16; Mk 1.10; Lk 3.22; Jn 1.32.

Entry of the Word into the soul

(174) Jesus, therefore, is the Word of God who enters the soul, which is called Jerusalem, riding on an ass which has been loosed from its bonds by the disciples. Now by the ass I mean the artless letters of the Old Testament which are clarified by the two disciples who loose them. One of these disciples is the person who refers the things which have been written anagogically to the service of the soul and who interprets them allegorically for it, and the other is the one who presents the good and true things which are to be through those things which are found in the shadow.

(175) Now he is also riding the young colt, which is the New Testament. For it is possible to find in both Testaments the word of truth[227] which cleanses us and drives out all the arguments which are buying and selling in us.

(176) But he does not enter the soul, which is Jerusalem, alone; neither does he enter with a certain few. For there must be many things present in us which precede the Word of God who perfects us, and many others which follow him. All, however, praise and glorify him, and place their own adornment and garment under him, that his mounts might not touch the earth[228] since they have the one who has come down from heaven resting upon them.

(177) And that the old and new words of the Scriptures which carry him might be even higher above the earth, branches must be cut from the trees that they may walk on things which are set forth reasonably. And the multitudes which go before and follow him can indicate the cooperation of angels, some which prepare the way for him in our souls, through which activities they themselves have been adorned, but others follow his presence in us. Since we have frequently spoken about this presence we have no need of testimonies on it now.

(178) And perhaps [someone] might reasonably compare the sounds which envelop the word which brings them into

227. Cf. 1 Cor 6.7.   228. Cf. Dn 8.5.

the soul to an ass, for the beast is a burden bearer, and a great burden and a heavy load are revealed from the text, especially from the Old Testament, as is clear to one who has given attention to the things which are done by the Jews.

(179) The colt, however, is not a burden bearer as the ass. For although every burden of the letter is heavy for those who cannot receive the ascending and very light burden of the spirit, yet at least the new letter is less heavy than the old.

(180) Now I know some who have understood the ass which was bound to be those from the circumcision who believe, and who are released from many bonds by those who have been instructed by the Word in a truly spiritual manner. And they take the colt to be those from the gentiles, who were free and without any imposed yoke so far as rebelliousness and delight in pleasure are concerned before they received the word of Jesus.

Jesus pursues enemies of his people

(181) Although these have not mentioned the multitudes which precede and which follow, it is not unconvincing to apply those who precede to Moses and the prophets, and those who follow to the holy apostles, all of whom enter the city of Jerusalem. We must investigate Jerusalem in relation to this meaning, for it has many selling and buying who are driven out by the Son of God.

(182) Perhaps "the Jerusalem which is above"[229] is now meant, into which the Lord will ascend conducting those of the circumcision and those of the gentiles who believe, while either prophets and apostles or the angels who minister to him—for these too can be indicated by those who precede and those who follow him—precede him and follow. Before his ascent this city had the so-called "spirits of wickedness in high places,"[230] or the Chanaanites and the Hethites and the Amorrhites, and the other enemies of the people, and, in general, foreigners. And perhaps it was possible there for the prophecy to be fulfilled which says, "Your land is desolate,

---

229. Cf. Gal 4.26.   230. Eph 6.12.

your cities are burned, foreigners devour your country before you."[231]

(183) For it is these who defile the heavenly house of the Father, the holy Jerusalem, the house of prayer, and have made it a "den of thieves,"[232] who are none other than themselves. It is these who have money that is not legal tender, and who give those who approach obols and small change, coins that are cheap and contemptible.

(184) These are those who take the more precious things from souls as they wrestle with them, and strip off the better things that they might give them worthless things.

The ass and the colt

(185) But the disciples go and find the ass tied, and release it. It does not have Jesus because of the veil which is placed on it in the law.[233]

(186) And the colt is also found with her, since both had been lost before Jesus. Now I mean those of the circumcision and those from the gentiles who believed later.

(187) But there is danger in mentioning how these beasts are sent back immediately after Jesus has been placed on them and has gone up into Jerusalem. It involves the mystery of the change of the saints into angels, who will be sent in the age after this one, in a similar manner to those ministering spirits who were sent to minister because of those who will inherit eternal life,[234] thanks to these things.

(188) But if the ass and colt should be the Old and New Scriptures on which the Word of God is borne, it will not be difficult at all to show how they are sent away once the Word has appeared in them. After the Word has entered Jerusalem, they do not remain among those who have rejected all the arguments which are buying and selling.

(189) I do not think it is without significance that this place, in which were the ass which was tied and the colt, is a village, and that it is nameless. For the whole earth, where the ass is

---

231. Is 1.7.
233. Cf. 2 Cor 3.15.
232. Cf. Mt 21.13.
234. Cf. Heb 1.14.

found tied and the colt, is a village, viewed in relation to the whole cosmos in heaven, and it is sufficiently designated as a village without the addition of another name.

(190) Matthew says that those who were to fetch the ass and the colt were sent from Bethphage, which was a priestly place which means "house of jaws."[235]

(191) We have had to make these comments, in accordance with our ability, on the events in Matthew. An account that is complete and more detailed than these words will be related more opportunely whenever it is granted to us to comment on the Gospel According to Matthew.[236]

(192) Now Mark and Luke say that the two disciples, in accordance with the Lord's command, found a colt tied on which no man had ever sat, which they loosed and brought to the Lord.[237]

(193) Mark adds that "they found the colt tied at the door outside in the street."[238] And who is outside? Those from the gentiles who were "strangers to the covenants" and aliens from the promise of God,[239] who were on the street and not resting under a roof or house, bound by their own sins and loosed by the twofold understanding of Jesus' pupils which was mentioned earlier.

(194) But the bonds of the colt which was tied, and the sins which have been committed against the sound Word, which are reproved by him who is the door of life, were not inside, but outside in relation to it (I mean, of course, the door). For it may be that there can be no bond of wickedness inside the door.

(195) And there were some standing beside the bound colt, as Mark says,[240] (I think they that had bound it), [and] as Luke writes, "The owners of the colt said to the disciples, 'Why are you loosing the colt?'"[241] For the lawbreakers who have subjected and bound the sinner are owners who cannot look the

---

235. Or, "house of cheeks." See Lagarde, *Onomastica*, 188.75.
236. Origen discusses Mt 21.1–13 in his *Commentary on Matthew* 16.14–23.
237. Cf. Mk 11.2; Lk 19.30. 238. Cf. Mk 11.4.
239. Cf. Eph 2.12. 240. Cf. Mk 11.5.
241. Cf. Lk 19.33.

true owner in the face who is dragging the colt away from their bonds.

(196) It is for this reason that the disciples say, "The Lord has need of him."[242] When the evil owners could make no response, the disciples bring the colt to Jesus bare. They throw their own adornment on it, that when the Lord is seated on it he may rest on the disciples' garments which were thrown upon it.

Differences between the Gospels

(197) The remaining matters, however, will not be obscure at all, based on what has been said in Matthew: how "they enter Jerusalem, and when he entered the temple he began to cast out those selling and buying in the temple,"[243] or, "As he drew near, when he saw the city he wept over it. And when he entered the temple he began to cast out those who were selling."[244]

(198) There are some who have the temple within themselves in whom he casts out all those who are selling and buying in the temple. But there are others who do not obey the Word of God very much, in whom he only begins to cast out those who sell and buy. And there is a third group besides these in whom he has begun to cast out only those who sell, and not also those who buy.

(199) In John, however, everyone, along with the sheep and oxen, is cast out with the whip plaited from cords. Now consider carefully if it is possible that the variations at least of what is written, and the disagreements are to be solved by the anagogical method of interpretation, each evangelist describing different activities of the Word in souls with different dispositions, which produce not identical, but similar results.

(200) The apparent discrepancy between Jesus' ascents to Jerusalem in the writer of the Gospel in our hands and the Synoptics, as we have quoted their texts, can only be rescued in this manner. While John encountered similar actions, in

---

242. Lk 19.34.
244. Lk 19.41 and 45.
243. Cf. Mk 11.15.

place of branches which were cut from the trees,²⁴⁵ or leafy branches from the fields, and scattered in the way,²⁴⁶ he says the large crowd had taken palm branches to go out to the feast, and they went out to meet him crying out, "Blessed is he who comes in the name of the Lord, even the king of Israel."²⁴⁷

(201) In addition he says the young ass on which the Christ sits is found by Jesus himself.²⁴⁸ In this way he has presented something additional concerning the figurative significance of the young ass which received a greater benefit that was "not from men nor through men, but through Jesus Christ."²⁴⁹

(202) Neither did John quote the exact words of the prophet. Instead he has, "Fear not, daughter of Sion, behold your king is coming seated," * * * instead of "mounted * * upon the foal of an ass * * upon a beast of burden and a young colt."²⁵⁰ And the expression "Fear not, daughter of Sion" does not appear at all.²⁵¹

The prophecy of Zachary

(203) Since the saying of the prophet is quoted by all, however, let us see if it was not necessary that the daughter of Sion rejoice greatly, and that the daughter of Jerusalem, who is superior to her, not only rejoice greatly, but also proclaim it, since her king was coming, just and saving and meek, mounted on a beast of burden and a young colt.

(204) Everyone, then, who has welcomed him will no longer be frightened by the heterodox armed with captious arguments, the so-called chariots of Ephraim which are destroyed by the Lord,²⁵² nor will they be frightened by the horse which is vain for salvation,²⁵³ the mad desire for women²⁵⁴ which is

---

245. Cf. Mt 21.8.   246. Cf. Mk 11.8.
247. Jn 12.13.   248. Cf. Jn 12.14.
249. Gal 1.1.
250. Cf. Jn 12.15; Zec 9.9. Preuschen thinks several short phrases have been lost from the text.
251. Cf. Zec 9.9, which begins, "Rejoice greatly, daughter of Sion."
252. Cf. Zec 9.10.   253. Cf. Ps 32.17.
254. Cf. Jer 5.8.

identified with things perceptible to the senses and which harms many of those who wish to dwell in Jerusalem and to give attention to sound teaching.[255]

(205) And it is fitting to rejoice at every "bow for war"[256] being destroyed by him who is borne on the beast of burden and the young colt, since the fiery darts of the enemy[257] no longer prevail against the one who has received Jesus into his own temple.

(206) And there will also be a "multitude" with "peace" from the gentiles[258] in the Savior's visit [to] Jerusalem, when he rules over the waters, that he may crush the heads of the dragons on the water,[259] and may tread on the waves of the sea, reaching as far as the mouths of all the rivers on earth.[260]

(207) Mark, however, writing that the Lord said of the ass, "On which no man had yet sat,"[261] seems to me to be hinting that those who later believed had themselves never yet been subjected to reason[262] before Jesus' arrival among them.

(208) For perhaps no man had ever sat upon the colt, but some beasts or power hostile to reason sat upon it, since the wealth of the opposing powers is also said in the prophet Isaias to be borne on asses and camels in these words, "In affliction and distress the lion and the cub, there also is the offspring of flying asps, which carry their wealth on asses and camels."[263]

(209) We must inquire again of those devoted to the literal meaning, if, according to them, the clause, "on which no man had ever sat,"[264] would not appear to have been written to no purpose. For who, besides a man, sits on a colt? These words complete our interpretation.

---

255. *Logō*.
257. Cf. Eph 6.16.
259. Cf. Ps 73.13.
261. Mk 11.2.
263. Cf. Is 30.6.

256. Zec 9.10.
258. Cf. Zec 9.10.
260. Cf. Zec 9.10.
262. *Logō*.
264. Mk 11.2.

Interpretation of Heracleon

(210) But let us also consider Heracleon's words. He says the ascent [to] Jerusalem indicates the Lord's ascension from material things to the psychic[265] region which is an image of Jerusalem.

(211) And he thinks the expression, "He found in the temple,"[266] and not "in the shrine,"[267] is used that it might not be thought that the mere calling, apart from the Spirit, is aided by the Lord. For he considers the holy of holies to be the temple, which the high priest alone may enter.[268] He says, I think, that the pneumatics advance to that place. The forecourt of the temple, where the Levites too are found, he considers to be a symbol of the psychics who attain salvation outside the pleroma.

(212) In addition to these, he understood those found in the temple selling oxen and sheep and doves, and the money-changers sitting,[269] to represent those who give nothing away free, but suppose the entrance of foreigners into the temple to be a matter of merchandise and profit. They furnish the sacrifices for the service of God for the sake of their own profit and greed.

(213) And he expounds in his own peculiar way the fact that the whip was made from cords by Jesus,[270] who did not receive it from another, when he says that the whip is an image of the power and activity of the Holy Spirit who blows away the wicked. And he adds that the whip, the cord, the linen, and all such things are an image of the power and activity of the Holy Spirit.

(214) Then he has added on his own what has not been written, namely that the whip was tied to a piece of wood. By taking the wood to be a type of the cross, he says that the gamblers, the merchants and all evil have been nailed upon and destroyed by this wood.

(215) And when he investigates what Jesus did, babbling, I do not know in what manner, he says the whip was prepared from these two things. For he did not make it, he says, from dead leather, that he might no longer construct the church as a den of thieves and merchants,[271] but as the house of his Father.

The response of Origen

(216) We must, however, address a most necessary point concerning the deity to him also from these words. If Jesus says that the temple in Jerusalem is the house of his own

---

265. *Psychikos.* 266. Jn 2.14.
267. The distinction is between *hieron* and *naos.*
268. Cf. Heb 9.7. 269. Cf. Jn 2.14.
270. Cf. Jn 2.15.
271. Cf. Mt 21.13.

Father, and this temple was constructed for the glory of him who created the heaven and the earth,[272] are we not taught openly to consider the Son of God to be a Son of none other than the creator of heaven and earth?

(217) Since it is a house of prayer, the apostles of Christ, too, are commanded by the angel to enter this house of Jesus' Father (as we have found in the *Acts of the Apostles*), and to stand and speak "to the people all the words of this life."[273]

(218) But also, because they are entering a "house of prayer"[274] to pray there, they approach through the beautiful gate.[275] They would not have done this had they not have known that he was the same God with the one worshipped by those who consecrated that shrine.

(219) This is why both Peter and the apostles, who obey God rather than men,[276] say, "The God of our fathers raised Jesus, whom you killed by hanging him on a tree."[277] They know that Jesus had been raised from the dead by no other God than the God of the Fathers. This is the one Christ also glorifies and says that he is the God of Abraham, and Isaac, and Jacob, who are not "dead, but living."[278]

(220) Furthermore, if the house of Christ's God were not the house of the same God, how would the disciples have remembered what is said in Psalm 68: "The zeal of your house has devoured me"?[279] For that is what is stated in the prophet, and not 'devours me.'

(221) Now Christ is especially jealous for the house of God in each of us, not wishing it to be a house of merchandise,[280] nor that the house of prayer become a den of thieves,[281] since he is son of a jealous God.[282] This is the case if we understand such words from the Scriptures in a reasonable manner, which were spoken metaphorically from the human viewpoint to set forth the fact that God wishes nothing alien to his will to be

---

272. Cf. Rv 10.6.
273. Acts 5.20.
274. Cf. Mt 21.13.
275. Cf. Acts 3.2.
276. Cf. Acts 5.29.
277. Acts 5.30.
278. Cf. Mt 22.32.
279. Ps 68.10.
280. Cf. Jn 2.16.
281. Cf. Mt 21.13.
282. Cf. Ex 20.5.

mingled with the soul of any men, but especially with the soul of those who wish to receive [the teachings of the] most divine faith.

(222) However, we must know that Psalm 68, which contains the statement, "The zeal of your house has devoured me,"[283] and a little later "They gave me gall for my food, and in my thirst they gave me vinegar to drink,"[284] both having been recorded in the Gospels,[285] is placed in the mouth of Christ, indicating no change in the person of the speaker.

(223) It is especially careless of Heracleon, however, to think that the statement, "The zeal of your house will devour me"[286] is placed in the mouth of the powers which were cast out and destroyed by the Savior, since he is not able to preserve the sequence of the prophecy in the Psalm when he supposes that it was placed in the mouth of the powers which were cast out and destroyed.

(224) Now it follows, from his viewpoint, that the statement, "They gave me gall for my food,"[287] which is recorded in the same Psalm, was also spoken by them. The phrase, "shall devour me" probably bothered him, because he thought it impossible for Christ to say such a thing, since he is not aware of the custom of using words with human feelings of God and Christ.

The Jews, therefore, answered and said to him, 'What sign do you show us, seeing that you do these things?' Jesus answered and said to them, 'Destroy this temple, and in three days I will raise it up.'

(225) The Jews now seem to me to signify those who are corporeal and friends of sense perceptions, who, in addition to those expelled by Jesus, make the Father's house a "house of merchandise."[288] Because they are angered [in the interest

---

283. Ps 68.10. 284. Ps 68.22.
285. Cf. Mt 27.34 and 48; Lk 23.36; Jn 19.28–29.
286. Jn 2.17. 287. Ps 68.22.
288. Cf. Jn 2.16.

of the things]²⁸⁹ he²⁹⁰ mistreated, they demand a sign, by which the Word, whom they do not accept, will appear to have acted properly in these matters.

(226) The Savior, however, by joining as one the saying²⁹¹ about his own body with that about that temple, answers the question, "What sign do you show us, seeing that you do these things?"²⁹² with "Destroy this temple, and in three days I will raise it up."²⁹³

(227) For although he could have shown them as many as 10,000 other signs, this was by no means the case in relation to the clause, "Seeing that you do these things." He responded appropriately with matters concerning the temple in place of other signs unrelated to the temple.

Temple and body of Jesus, figures of the Church

(228) Both, however, (I mean the temple and Jesus' body) according to one interpretation, appear to me to be a type of the Church, in that the Church, being called a "temple,"²⁹⁴ is built of living stones, becoming a spiritual house "for a holy priesthood,"²⁹⁵ built "upon the foundation of the apostles and prophets, Christ Jesus being the chief corner stone."²⁹⁶

(229) And through the saying, "Now you are the body of Christ and members in part,"²⁹⁷ (we know) that even if the harmony of the stones of the temple appear to be destroyed, [or,] as is written in Psalm 21,²⁹⁸ all the bones of Christ appear to be scattered in persecutions and afflictions by the plots of those who wage war against the unity of the temple by persecutions, the temple will be raised up and the body will arise on the third day after the day of evil²⁹⁹ which threatens it and

---

289. *Pragmasin*. Preuschen brackets this word and Blanc omits it. Brooke retains the word.
290. Accepting the singular which Brooke proposes. Preuschen and Blanc have the plural.
291. *Logon*.
292. Jn 2.18.
293. Jn 2.19.
294. Cf. Eph 2.21.
295. Cf. 1 Pt 2.5.
296. Cf. Eph 2.20.
297. 1 Cor 12.27.
298. Cf. Ps 21.15.
299. Cf. Eccl 7.15.

the day of consummation which follows. For the third day will dawn in the new heaven and the new earth,[300] when these bones, the whole house of Israel,[301] shall be raised up on the great day of the Lord, once death has been conquered.[302] Consequently, the resurrection of Christ too, which followed from his passion on the cross, contains the mystery of the resurrection of the whole body of Christ.

(230) Just as that perceptible body of Jesus has been crucified, buried, and afterwards raised up, so the whole body of the saints of Christ have been crucified with Christ and now no longer live.[303] For each of them, like Paul, boasts in nothing else than "in the cross of our Lord Christ Jesus," through whom he has been crucified to the world and the world to him.[304]

(231) He has, therefore, not only been crucified with Christ, and crucified to the world, but he is also buried with Christ, "for we were buried with Christ," Paul says.[305]

(232) And as if he has attained some pledge of the resurrection, he says, "We were raised with him," since he walks in a certain newness of life,[306] inasmuch as he has not yet arisen so far as concerns that anticipated blessed and perfect resurrection. He has, therefore, either now been crucified, and, after these things, is buried, or he is now buried, having been removed from the cross, and at some time, insofar as he has now been buried, he will arise.

Resurrection of the body, which is the Church

(233) The mystery of the resurrection, however, is great, and difficult for many of us to understand. It is mentioned also in many other passages of the Scriptures, and is proclaimed no less through these words in Ezechiel: "And the hand of the Lord was upon me, and brought me out in the spirit of the Lord, and set me in the midst of a plain, and this plain was full of human bones. And he led me about through

---

300. Cf. Rv 21.1.
302. Cf. 1 Cor 15.54.
304. Cf. Gal 6.14.
306. Cf. Rom 6.4–5.
301. Cf. Ez 37.11.
303. Cf. Gal 2.20.
305. Cf. Rom 6.4.

them on every side, and lo, they were very numerous on the face of the plain, and lo, they were very dry. And he said to me, 'Son of man, shall these bones live?' and I said, 'Lord, Lord you know these things.' And he said to me, 'Prophesy to these bones, and say to them, 'Dry bones, hear the word of the Lord.' "[307]

(234) And a little later, "And the Lord spoke to me saying, 'Son of man, these bones are the whole house of Israel. And they say, 'Our bones have become dry; our hope has perished; we are lost.' "[308]

(235) To what sort of bones are the words spoken, "Hear the word of the Lord,"[309] as though they perceive the word of the Lord, because they are the house of Israel or the body of Christ? Concerning the latter, the Lord said, "All my bones have been scattered,"[310] although his physical bones were not scattered. In fact, none of them was even broken.[311]

(236) But when this[312] resurrection of Christ's true and more perfect body takes place, then the members of Christ, the bones which at present are dry as seen in relation to what will be, will be brought together, bone to bone and joint to joint,[313] for none of those who have been deprived of joint will attain to the perfect man, "to the measure of the stature of the fullness" of the body "of Christ."[314]

(237) And then the many members will be one body, when all who are the many members of the body become one body.[315] It is the prerogative of God alone, who will mix the body together, to make the distinction of foot and hand and eye and hearing and sense of smell of those who complete the head in the one case, and the feet in the other, and the rest of the members, the weaker and humbler, and the shameful and the honorable.[316]

(238) At that time, rather than now, he gives greater honor

---

307. Cf. Ez 37.1–4.
308. Ez 37.11.
309. Ez 37.4.
310. Ps 21.15.
311. Cf. Jn 19.36.
312. Reading *hautē* with Blanc. Preuschen and Brooke print *autē*.
313. Cf. Ez 37.7.
314. Cf. Eph 4.13.
315. Cf. 1 Cor 12.12.
316. Cf. 1 Cor 12.15–24.

to the one who lacks, that by no means "might there be schism in the body, but that the members might be mutually concerned for one another."³¹⁷ And if a member has some happiness, all the members share a feeling of well-being, or if one member is glorified, they all rejoice together.³¹⁸

Death precedes resurrection

(239) What I have said is not unrelated to the temple and those who were driven out by the Savior who says of the event, "The zeal of your house will devour me."³¹⁹ Nor are my words unrelated to the Jews who ask for a sign to be shown to them, and the Lord's response to them, when he joins a word about the temple with one about his own body, and declares, "Destroy this temple and in three days I will raise it up."³²⁰

(240) For these irrational and commercial things must be driven away from this temple which is the body of Christ, that it might no longer be a house of merchandise.

(241) This temple, too, must be destroyed by those who plot against the Word of God, and after it has been destroyed, be raised up on the third day which we mentioned previously. At this time also the disciples will remember what³²¹ God's Word said before the temple of God was destroyed, and will believe, not in the Scripture only, but also in the word which Jesus spoke, their faith also being perfected with their knowledge at that time.

(242) Each person likewise, when Jesus cleanses him, by putting aside those things which are irrational and which engage in business, will be destroyed because of the zeal for the word which is in him, to be raised up by Jesus, not on the third day so far as the text before us is concerned, for it is not written, "Destroy this temple, and on the third day I will raise it up," but "in three days."³²²

(243) For the structure³²³ of the temple is raised on the first

---

317. 1 Cor 12.25. 318. Cf. 1 Cor 12.26.
319. Jn 2.17. 320. Jn 2.19.
321. Accepting Koe's emendation, *hou*, with Blanc. Preuschen has *ho te*.
322. Jn 2.19.
323. *Kataskeuē*, Wendland's conjecture. There is a lacuna in the text.

day after it is destroyed, and on the second, but its erection is completed in the full three days. For this reason also there both has been a resurrection and will be a resurrection, if indeed we were buried with Christ and arose with him.[324]

(244) And since the expression, "We arose with," is not sufficient for the resurrection in its entirety, "in Christ all shall be made alive, but each in his own order, Christ the firstfruits, then those who are of Christ in his coming, then the end."[325]

(245) For what occurred on the first day in the paradise of God[326] belonged to the resurrection; it was also a part of the resurrection when he appeared and said, "Do not touch me, for I have not yet ascended to the Father";[327] but the resurrection was completed when he went to the Father.

Incorrect interpretations of this text

(246) Those, however, who are confused on the subject of the Father and the Son bring together the statement, "And we are also found false witnesses of God, because we have testified against God that he raised up Christ, whom he did not raise,"[328] and words like these which show him who raises to be different from him who has been raised, and the statement, "Destroy this temple, and in three days I will raise it up."[329] They think that these statements prove that the Son does not differ from the Father in number, but that both being one, not only in essence, but also in substance,[330] they are said to be Father and Son in relation to certain differing aspects,[331] not in relation to their reality.[332] For this reason, we must first quote to them the texts capable of establishing definitely that the Son is other than the Father, and we must say that it is necessary that a son be the son of a father and that a father be the father of a son.

(247) After this we must say to them that it is not strange for him, who admits that he can do nothing except what he

---

324. Cf. Rom 6.4.
326. Cf. Lk 23.43.
328. 1 Cor 15.15.
330. *Hypokeimenō*.
332. *Hypostasin*.

325. 1 Cor 15.22–24.
327. Jn 20.17.
329. Jn 2.19.
331. *Epinoias*.

sees the Father doing, and who says that whatever the Father does, the Son likewise also does,[333] to have raised the dead[334] (which was the body), since the Father, who we must say emphatically has raised the Christ from the dead, grants this to him.

Heracleon's interpretation

(248) Heracleon, however, says, "in three days" is used in place of "on the third day" without asking, although he has understood in the expression "in three days," how the resurrection is accomplished in three days.

(249) Furthermore, he says the third day is the spiritual day, in which they think the resurrection of the Church is indicated.

(250) It follows, then, to say that the first day is material, and the second psychic, since the resurrection of the Church has not occurred on them.

The trial of Jesus

(251) It is likely, moreover, that what has been recorded in the Gospels According to Matthew and Mark in the name of[335] the false witnesses who accuse our Lord Jesus Christ at the end of the gospel,[336] contains a reference to the saying, "Destroy this temple and I will raise it up in three days."[337]

(252) For he, on the one hand, was speaking about the temple of his body,[338] but they, supposing that the things said here were said about the temple built from stones, accused him and said, "This man said, 'I am able to destroy the temple of God and after three days to rebuild it.'"[339] Or, as Mark has it, "We heard him say, 'I will destroy this temple made with hands, and after three days I will build another not made with hands.'"[340] At this time also the high priest stood up and said to him, "'Do you have no answer? What are these testifying

---

333. Cf. Jn 5.19.   334. Cf. Jn 11.43–44.
335. I have emended *hypo* to *hyper*. Something is wrong in the text at this point. Koe suggested altering *hypo* to *peri*; Wendland omitted it.
336. Cf. Mt. 26.61; Mk 14.58.   337. Cf. Jn 2.19.
338. Cf. Jn 2.21.   339. Cf. Mt 26.61.
340. Mk 14.58.

against you?' But Jesus was silent."³⁴¹ Or, as Mark³⁴² says, "And the high priest stood up in the midst and asked Jesus, saying, 'Do you not have an answer? What are these testifying against you? But he was silent and answered nothing."³⁴³

(253) I think I had to cite these texts because they contain a reference to the text in hand.

The Jews then said, 'This Temple was built in forty-six years, and will you raise it up in three days?'

The temple of Jerusalem

(254) We are not able to say how the Jews declare that the temple was built in forty-six years, if we follow the literal sense.³⁴⁴

(255) For it is written in the third book of the Kings that "they prepared the stones and the wood in three years."³⁴⁵ "And in the fourth year, in the second month, when king Solomon was ruling over Israel, the king commanded, and they brought great precious stones for the foundation of the house, and unhewn stones. And the sons of Solomon and the sons of Hiram hewed them and laid them in the fourth year, and they laid the foundation of the house of the Lord in the month Nisan and the second month. In the eleventh year, in the month Baal, which was the eighth month, the house was completed in its whole plan and in its whole arrangement."³⁴⁶

(256) If,³⁴⁷ then, we take the period of preparation into account also in the time of construction, a full eleven years were not completed in the construction of the temple.

(257) How, then, do the Jews say, "This temple was built in

---

341. Mt 26.62 and 63.
342. The text has Luke, but the verses cited are from Mark.
343. Mk 14.60–61.
344. Origen takes the statement to be made about the building of the temple by Solomon, not about the temple built by Herod, as the discussion which follows makes clear.
345. Cf. 3 Kgs 5.32 (LXX).
346. Cf. 3 Kgs 6.1–1d (LXX).
347. Emending *hina to ean*. A purpose clause makes no sense in this context. Blanc says nothing about *hina* in her text, but translates it "si."

forty-six years"?³⁴⁸ Unless, perhaps, someone shall strive to prove in a way that does violence to the text that the forty-six years are fulfilled in relation to the time from which David, deliberating about the construction of the temple, says to Nathan the prophet, "Behold, I dwell in a house of cedar, and the ark of God sits in the midst of a tent."³⁴⁹ For although as a man of blood, he was prevented from constructing it,³⁵⁰ he seems, at least, to have been occupied concerning the gathering of the material of the temple.

(258) David, the king, therefore, says to all the assembly in the first book of Paralipomenon, "Solomon my son, whom the Lord has chosen, is young and tender, and the work is great, because the building is not for man, but for the Lord God. According to all my ability, I have prepared for the house of my God gold, silver, bronze and iron, wood, stones of Soom and of filling, and various expensive stones, and every precious stone, and much Parian marble. Further, in that I take pleasure in the house of my God, I have gold and silver which I have acquired, and lo, I have given it to the house of my Lord for its grandeur, beyond the things which I prepared for the house of the saints, 3,000 talents of gold from Suphir, and 7,000 talents of refined silver, that the houses of God may be overlaid with them by the hand of craftsmen."³⁵¹

(259) For David ruled seven years in Hebron and thirty-five in Jerusalem.³⁵² If, therefore, someone can show that the beginning of the preparation of the temple, when he was gathering the necessary material, occurred in the fifth year of his reign, he will be able, in a forced manner, to speak about the forty-six years. But someone else will say that the temple indicated is not that built by Solomon, [for] that one was destroyed in the times of the captivity, but the one built in the time of Esdras,³⁵³ of which we cannot prove clearly that the statement about forty-six years is accurate.

348. Jn 2.20.
349. Cf. 2 Kgs (Sam) 7.2.
350. Cf. 1 Chr 22.8; 2 Kgs (Sam) 16.8.
351. Cf. 1 Chr 29.1–5 (LXX)   352. Cf. 3 Kgs 2.11.
353. Cf. Ezr 6.

(260) It also appears that at the time of the Maccabees a great deal of disorder occurred concerning the people and the temple.³⁵⁴ I do not know if the temple was rebuilt in so many years at that time.

(261) Heracleon, however, not having understood the literal sense, says that Solomon constructed the temple, which is an image of the Savior,³⁵⁵ in forty-six years. He refers the number six to matter, that is the formed object, and the number forty "which is the Tetrad," he says, "which does not admit union," to the infusion, and the seed in the infusion.

(262) But see if it is possible to understand forty with reference to the four elements of the world which are introduced in the things set apart³⁵⁶ for the temple, and the six with reference to the fact that man came to be on the sixth day.

But he spoke of the temple of his Body. When, therefore, He was raised from the dead, His Disciples remembered that He had said this, and they believed the Scripture and the Word which Jesus had spoken.

Body of Jesus and the Church: dwellings of the glory of God

(263) If the body of Jesus is said to be his temple, it is worth asking whether we must take this in a singular manner, or must endeavor to refer each of the things recorded about the temple anagogically to the saying about the body of Jesus, whether it be the body which he received from the Virgin, or the Church, which is said to be his body, since we too are called members of his body by the apostle.³⁵⁷

354. Cf. 1 Mc 1.21–29.
355. It is unclear in the text precisely what this participial clause modified. It could, as well, modify Solomon. This would make Origen and Heracleon agree. (See below 266, where "the son of David who builds the temple is a type of Christ.") W. Foerster, *Gnosis: A Selection of Texts*, 168, translates, "Heracleon says 'the fact that Solomon completed the temple in forty-six years is an image of the Saviour.'"
356. Accepting Koe's emendation *aphōrismenois*, with Blanc. Preuschen prints *agōnismenois* and marks it as corrupt.
357. Cf. Eph 5.30.

(264) One will, therefore, have recourse to the singular view, freeing himself from problems when he despairs of being able to refer each of the statements made in reference to the temple to the body, whatever it might be. He will say that the body, understood in either way, has been called the temple because as the temple had the glory of God dwelling in it,[358] so the first born of all creation,[359] being the image and glory of God, is properly said to be the temple bearing the image of God in respect to his body or the Church.

Comparison of the Church and the temple

(265) We are, however, deferring a discussion of the details about the temple in the third book of Kings, seeing that it is difficult to explain, and goes far beyond our text and, above all, is not directly related to our present Scripture.

(266) We are persuaded, however, that the distinctive character of inspired Scripture is made manifest in such matters in a special way, since Scripture has shown that they are beyond human nature and are in accordance with the wisdom of God, a wisdom which is hidden, which none of the princes of this world knew.[360] And since we grasp the fact that we ourselves need the wisdom of the special Spirit to understand such great matters in a way fitting a sacred subject, we shall attempt to describe as briefly as possible our understanding of the things in the passage. We learn from Peter that the Church is a body and a house of God built from living stones, a spiritual house for a holy priesthood.[361] Consequently, in accordance with this, the son of David who builds the temple is a type of Christ, when he builds the temple for the glory of God in the earthly Jerusalem when the most profound peace[362] has followed the wars. This temple was built that the service might no longer be celebrated in a tent, a movable object.

(267) We shall attempt, however, to refer each of the statements which have reference to the temple anagogically to the Church. For perhaps, if all Christ's enemies become his foot-

---

358. Cf. Jn 1.14.
360. Cf. 1 Cor 2.7 and 8.
362. Cf. 4 Mc 3.20.

359. Cf. Col 1.15.
361. Cf. 1 Pt 2.5.

stool, and the last enemy, death, be destroyed,[363] there will be the most perfect peace, when Christ will be Solomon, which means "peaceful,"[364] the prophecy being fulfilled in him, which says, "I was peaceful with those who hated peace."[365]

The living stones

(268) Then each of the living stones,[366] will be a stone of the temple according to the worth of its life here. One will be an apostle or prophet in the foundation, supporting those which rest upon it; another, after those in the foundation, being supported by the apostles, on the one hand, will himself also with the apostles support those who are weaker.[367] And one will be a stone of the innermost parts where the ark and the cherubim and the mercy seat are located.[368] Another will be a stone of the surrounding wall, and still another will be outside of the surrounding wall of the Levites and priests, a stone of the altar of whole burnt offerings.

(269) The holy powers will be entrusted with their administration and service. These powers are the angels of God, which are, on the one hand, certain dominations, or thrones, or principalities, or authorities,[369] but, on the other hand, they are those which have been subordinated to these, of whom the 3,600 chief overseers appointed over the works of Solomon are types. These include also the 70,000 who bear the burden, and the 80,000 stone-cutters on the mountain, who carry out the tasks and prepare the stones and wood.[370]

(270) Now we must note that those recorded to bear the burden are related to the number seven. But the stone-cutters and those who shape the stones that they might be fitted to the temple are associated with the number eight. The overseers, however, who are 3,600, are connected with the perfect number six, which is multiplied, as it were, by itself. The tasks, however, of the preparation of the stones which are carried

363. Cf. 1 Cor 15.25–26.
364. See Lagarde, *Onomastica*, 204.31.
365. Ps 119.7.
366. Cf. Hermas, *Vis.* 3.5; 1 Pt 2.5.
367. Cf. Eph 2.20.
368. 3 Kgs 6.19 and 27.
369. Cf. Col 1.16.
370. Cf. 3 Kgs 5.15–16.

and made ready for the building, which were completed in three years, seem to me to signify the duration of the interval which is akin to the Triad in eternity.

(271) These things will come to pass when peace is achieved, 430 years after the dispensation of the affairs related to the exodus from Egypt,[371] and the affairs relating to Egypt were accomplished 430 years after God's covenant with Abraham. Consequently, there are two Sabbatical numbers from Abraham to the beginning of the building of the temple: 770.[372] At this time Christ, our king, will order the 70,000 porters not to take ordinary stones for the foundation of the house, but great stones, precious and unhewn, that they might be hewn, not by just any workers, but by the sons of Solomon. For we have found this written in the third book of Kings.[373]

(272) Because of the profound peace at that time, Hiram, king of Tyre, also cooperates in the building of the temple, giving his own sons to the sons of Solomon to hew the great and precious stones for the holy place. And the stones were set in the foundation of the house of the Lord in the fourth year.[374] The house was completed, however, in an ogdoad of years, in the eighth month of the eighth year from the foundation.[375]

(273) It will not be out of place, however, in the interest of those who think these words signify nothing more than the literal meaning to introduce parenthetically some persuasive arguments in search of a meaning in these words worthy of the Spirit, since they are writings of the Spirit.

(274) Did the sons of the kings devote themselves to the hewing of great and precious stones, taking up a craft foreign to their royal and noble birth? And has the number of porters, stone-cutters, overseers, and the amount of time involved in

---

371. Cf. 3 Kgs 6.1.
372. Blanc, SC 157.550, suggests that perhaps one of the 430s should be replaced with 340.
373. Cf. 3 Kgs 5.15–18 (6.1a–1b LXX).
374. Cf. 3 Kgs 6.1b–1c (LXX); 6.37.
375. Cf. 3 Kgs 6.38; 6.1d (LXX).

the preparation of the stones, and the indication of similar things been recorded as it happened?[376]

(275) It was necessary that the holy house which was being prepared for God in a time of peace be built without hammer and axe and any iron tool, so that nothing noisy be heard in the temple of God.[377]

(276) Again I raise a difficulty for those who are slaves to the letter: how is it possible, when there are 80,000 stonecutters, for the house of God to be built with gleaming smooth stones, although no hammer, axe, or any iron tool is heard in his house while it is being built?[378] Perhaps, however, the stones which are hewn out, being living stones,[379] are hewn out noiselessly and quietly outside the temple area, that they might come prepared to the place of the building fitted to them.

(278) And there was also a stairway around the house of God with curved lines which had no angles. For it is written, "And a winding stairway went up to the middle room, and from the middle to the third."[380] The ascent in the temple of God had to be winding, since the spiral in the ascent is an imitation of the perfect[381] circle.

(279) And that this house might be solid, bondings five cubits in height[382] are built into it as much as possible through the whole house to show that the ascent from objects perceptible by the senses to those perceptions called divine, an ascent which leads to the comprehension of spiritual realities, takes place in the height.

(280) The place of the more fortunate stones, however, seems to be that which is called *dabir*, where the ark of the covenant of the Lord was, [which], if I may put it this way, contained the handwriting of God, the tablets which were written with his finger.[383]

376. Cf. 2 Chr 2.2.
377. Cf. 3 Kgs 6.7.
378. Cf. 3 Kgs 5.15; 6.7.
379. Cf. 1 Pt 2.5.
380. 3 Kgs 6.8.
381. Literally, most equal (*isaitaton*).
382. Cf. 3 Kgs 6.10.
383. Cf. 3 Kgs 6.16; Ex 31.18.

(281) The whole house is gilded, for Scripture says, "He overlaid the whole house with gold, as far as the completion of all the house."[384]

(282) There were, moreover, two cherubim in the *dabir*. Those who translate the words of the Hebrews into Greek have not been able to translate this word properly.

(283) Some have said rather imprecisely that it is the temple itself, while it is more honorable than the temple.[385] Nevertheless, everything related to the house is gold, symbolizing the mind which is completely perfected for the accurate examination[386] of spiritual matters.

(284) The curtains of the court are fashioned because there are some things that are absolutely inaccessible and unknown, inasmuch as the inmost parts are not revealed to most of the priests and Levites.[387]

Solomon and Hiram

(285) Now it is worthwhile to ask how Solomon is said also to build the temple as king, and "Hiram of Tyre, the son of a widow," whom Solomon sent and took, as master-builder. Hiram was "from the tribe of Nephtali; his father was a Tyrian, an artificer of brass, and filled with understanding and knowledge to do all work in brass. He was brought to king Solomon, and did all the works."[388]

(286) I am focusing, however, on whether Solomon can be taken for the firstborn of all creation,[389] and Hiram for the man which he assumed who, as a consequence of the unity of men (for Tyrians mean those who unite),[390] belongs to our race by nature. This man, filled with all skill and understanding and knowledge, was brought in to cooperate with the firstborn of all creation that he might build the temple. Hidden

---

384. Cf. 3 Kgs 6.22 (LXX).
385. Blanc, SC 157.556, notes that the LXX translates *dabir* with *naos* (temple) in Ps 27.2, and that Aquila and Symmachus translate it with *chrēmatistērion*, "sanctuary."
386. Accepting Wendland's suggestion to read *exetasin* instead of *apotaxin*.
387. Cf. 3 Kgs 6.36a (LXX).
388. Cf. 3 Kgs 7.1–2.   389. Cf. Col 1.15.
390. Cf. Origen, *Comm. Mt.* 11.16; Lagarde, *Onomastica*, 199.90.

oblique windows[391] are also prepared in the temple to enable it to receive the illuminations of the light of God in a saving manner, and (Why must I mention each thing?) that the body of Christ, the Church might be found having an understanding[392] of the spiritual house,[393] even the temple of God. As I said before, we need the wisdom which has been hidden in a mystery,[394] which is contained only in him who can say, "But we have the mind of Christ,"[395] that we might understand spiritually each of the things which have been said, in accordance with the will of him who ordained that these things be written.

(287) Our present passage, however, does not require that we explain each detail. These explanations, therefore, are sufficient for us to see how "he spoke of the temple of his body."[396]

The destruction and restoration of the temple

(288) It is worthwhile following these discussions, to see if it is possible that the things recorded as occurring in relation to the temple have ever happened, or will happen concerning the spiritual house.

(289) The argument, however, will appear to raise problems on either side. For if we shall say that something analogous[397] to the events in the historical account of the temple can happen, or has happened, our hearers will be unwilling to admit to a change of such great good things, first because they are unwilling, and second because a change of good things will be absurd.

(290) But if we wish to preserve unchanged the good things once given to the saints[398] and will not adapt the events of the historical account, we will, in such action, appear to do something like the heretics do by not preserving the harmony of the narrative of the Scriptures from beginning to end.

---

391. Cf. 3 Kgs 6.4 (LXX). 392. *Logon.*
393. Cf. 1 Pt 2.5. 394. Cf. 1 Cor 2.7.
395. 1 Cor 2.16. 396. Jn 2.21.
397. Accepting Preuschen's suggestion to read *ti analogon* instead of *tina logon.*
398. Jude 3.

(291) If, however, we are not to understand the promises recorded in the prophets, and especially in Isaias, like old women and Jews, as being about the Jerusalem on earth; if it is said that after the captivity and the destruction of the temple certain notable events have occurred in the building of the temple and the restoration of the people from captivity, we must say in addition that there has been a temple and the people have been in captivity, and will return to Judea and Jerusalem, and Jerusalem will be built with precious stones.[399]

(292) I do not know, however, if the same events can recur in long revolving cycles of time, although in an inferior state.

(293) But the words of the promises in Isaias are as follows: "Behold I am preparing carbuncle for you as your stone, and sapphire as your foundations, and I will make your battlements jasper, and your gates stones of crystal, and your enclosing wall choice stones, and all your sons shall be taught of God, and your children shall enjoy much peace, and you shall be built in justice."[400]

(294) And, a little later, he says to Jerusalem itself, "And the glory of Libanus shall come to you with cypress and pine and cedar; together they shall glorify my holy place. And the dreaded sons of those who have humbled and provoked you will come to you, and you will be called the city of the Lord, Sion of the holy one of Israel, because you had become forsaken and hated, and there was none who helped you. And I will make you an eternal joy, gladness from generation to generation. And you shall suck the milk of the gentiles, and devour the wealth of kings, and you shall know that I am the Lord who saves you and chooses you, the God of Israel. And for brass I will bring you gold, and for iron I will bring you silver, and for wood I will bring you brass, and for stones iron. And I will establish your rulers in peace, and your overseers

---

399. This, it seems to me, is the most natural way to read the text. Blanc takes it this way, but notes the translation of R. Gögler, which agrees with that in ANF, X, 406: "we must say that we are now the temple and the people which was carried captive, but is to come up again to Judea and Jerusalem, and to be built with the precious stones of Jerusalem."

400. Is 54.11–14.

in justice. And injustice will no longer be heard in your land, nor affliction and hardship in your borders, but salvation shall be called your walls, and your gates a signet. And you shall no longer have the sun for the light of the day, nor shall the rising of the moon enlighten the night for you, but Christ[401] shall be your everlasting light, and God your glory. For the sun shall not set for you, and the moon shall not wane for you. For the Lord shall be an everlasting light for you, and the days of your mourning shall be completed."[402]

(295) These words are clearly prophecies of the coming age addressed to the sons of Israel who are in captivity, to whom he who says, "I was not sent except to the lost sheep of the house of Israel,"[403] came when he was sent. But if, in spite of the fact that they are captives, they will be the recipients of things in their fatherland, at which time proselytes also will come to them through the Christ and will flee to them for refuge, according to the statement, "Behold proselytes will come to you through me, and will flee to you for refuge,"[404] it is obvious that those who were taken captive had once been around the temple, and that they will again return there when they will be rebuilt, having become the most precious of stones. For one who conquers in the Apocalypse of John, too, has the promise that he will be a pillar in the temple of God which will not go out.[405]

(296) I have made all these comments that we might have understanding, even if limited, of the matters related to the temple, and the house of God, and the Church, and Jerusalem, "of which things it is not possible now to speak separately."[406]

(297) We must, however, make the most accurate and careful examination possible concerning these matters for those who do not faint in the toils while reading the prophecies [and] in seeking the spiritual meaning in them. These words are sufficient about the temple of his body.[407]

---

401. *Christos.* The LXX has *kyrios.*
402. Cf. Is 60.13–20.
403. Mt 15.24.
404. Is 54.15.
405. Cf. Rv 3.12.
406. Heb 9.5.
407. Cf. Jn 2.21.

Partial faith and perfect faith

(298) Since, however, "when he was raised from the dead, his disciples remembered that he had said this, and they believed the Scripture, and the word which Jesus spoke,"[408] we must admit, as far as the literal meaning is concerned, that after the Lord was raised from the dead that the disciples understood that the things said about the temple refer to his passion and resurrection, and they recalled that the saying, "In three days I will raise it up"[409] indicated the resurrection. It was then that "they believed both the Scripture and the word which Jesus spoke,"[410] since there is no earlier testimony that they have believed the Scripture or this word which Jesus spoke. For faith is, strictly speaking, the acceptance with one's whole soul of the object of faith at baptism.

(299) But as for the anagogical meaning, since we previously mentioned the resurrection from the dead of the whole body of the Lord, we must know that the disciples, once they were reminded through the fulfilments of the Scripture which they had not thoroughly understood when they were in this life,[411] once it was brought before their eyes and made manifest that it contained an example and shadow of certain heavenly things,[412] believe what they formerly did not believe, and believe the word of Jesus as he who spoke it intended, which they had not understood before the resurrection.

(300) For how can one be said to believe the Scripture in the proper sense, when he does not perceive the meaning of the Holy Spirit in it, which God wants to be believed rather than the intent of the letter? According to this we must say that none of those who walk according to the flesh[413] believe in the spiritual meanings of the law whose first principle they do not even imagine.

(301) But they say that those who have not seen and have

---

408. Jn 2.22. 409. Jn 2.19.
410. Jn 2.22.
411. Blanc, SC 157.566, correctly notes that he probably meant while Jesus was in this life.
412. Cf. Heb 8.5. 413. Cf. 2 Cor 10.2.

believed are more blessed than those who have seen and have believed, because they have misconstrued what the Lord said to Thomas at the end of John's Gospel: "Blessed are those who have not seen, and have believed."[414] For [it is] not [possible] that those who have not seen and have believed are more blessed than those who have seen and believed.

(302) According to their interpretation at least then, those who come after the apostles are more blessed than the apostles, which is the most ridiculous of all things. He who will be blessed as the apostles must see with his mind the things believed, being able to hear, "Blessed are your eyes because they see, and your ears because they hear"[415] and, "Many prophets and just men have desired to see what you see, and have not seen them, and to hear what you hear, and have not heard them."[416]

(303) But one must be content also to receive the inferior blessing which says, "Blessed are those who have not seen and have believed."[417]

(304) And how are the eyes which have been pronounced blessed by Jesus for the things they have seen not more blessed than those who have not attained the vision of such things? Now Simeon is contented when he has received God's salvation into his arms, and when he beheld it he said, "Now, Lord, you may release your servant, according to your word in peace, because my eyes have seen your salvation."[418] Wherefore we must endeavor to open our eyes, according to Solomon, that we may be filled with bread, for he says, "Open your eyes, and be filled with bread."[419] Let these be my words in explanation of the statement, "They believed the Scripture and the word which Jesus spoke,"[420] that, from the things we have examined about faith, we may grasp that we will be given the perfection of faith in the great resurrection from the dead of the whole body of Jesus, his holy Church.

(305) For what has been said in the case of knowledge, "Now

414. Jn 20.29.
416. Mt 13.17.
418. Lk 2.29 and 30.
420. Jn 2.22.
415. Cf. Mt 13.16.
417. Jn 20.29.
419. Prv 20.13.

I know in part,"⁴²¹ follows also, I think, in the case of every good thing, and faith is one of these other things.

(306) Consequently, "Now I believe in part," but when "the perfection" of faith comes "that which is in part will be abolished."⁴²² Faith which comes through sight is much better, if I may put it this way, than faith "through a mirror and in a riddle"⁴²³ like our present knowledge.

Now when He was in Jerusalem at the Pasch on the feast day, many believed in his Name, seeing his signs which He did. But Jesus Himself did not trust Himself to them, because He knows all men, and because He had no need that someone give testimony concerning man, for He knew what was in man.

To believe in him and in his Name

(307) Someone may ask how it is that Jesus did not trust himself to those who were attested to believe. We must reply to this that it is not to those who believe in him that Jesus does not entrust himself, but to those who believe in his name, for believing in him differs from believing in his name.

(308) He, at least then, who will not be judged because of his faith, escapes judgment because he believes in him, not because he believes in his name, for the Lord says, "He who believes in me is not judged."⁴²⁴ He does not say, "He who believes in my name is not judged."

(309) And he no longer says, "He who believes in me has already been judged,"⁴²⁵ for perhaps the one who believes in his name believes, and for this reason does not deserve to have been judged already, but he is inferior to the one who believes in him. This is why Jesus does not trust himself to one who believes in his name.

(310) We must cling, therefore, to him rather than to his name, that, when we perform miracles in his name, we may not hear the words which were spoken of those who boasted

---

421. 1 Cor 13.12.
423. Cf. 1 Cor 13.13.
425. Ibid.

422. 1 Cor 13.10.
424. Cf. Jn 3.18.

in his name alone,[426] but that, becoming imitators of Paul,[427] we may have the courage to say, "I can do all things in Christ Jesus who strengthens me."[428]

Now we must observe this too: John says above, "The pasch of the Jews was at hand."[429] Here Jesus was not at the pasch of the Jews, but at the pasch in Jerusalem.[430] In the earlier passage, when the pasch is said to be "of the Jews," it is not said to be a feast day. Here, however, Jesus is recorded to be "at the feast." For he was in Jerusalem at the pasch and the feast when many believed even in his name.

(311) We must note, indeed, that many are said to believe, not in him, but "in his name."[431] Those, however, who believe in him are those who travel the narrow and strait way which leads to life, so far as it is found by the few.[432]

(312) It is possible, however, that many of those who believe in his name recline with Abraham, Isaac, and Jacob in the kingdom of heaven, since "many will come from the east and the west, and will recline with Abraham, Isaac and Jacob in the kingdom of heaven,"[433] which is the Father's house in which there are many mansions.[434]

(313) And we must observe that many who believe in his name do not believe as Andrew, Peter, Nathanael and Philip;[435] they are persuaded by the testimony of John who says, "Behold, the Lamb of God,"[436] or by the Christ found by Andrew,[437] or by Jesus who said to Philip, "Follow me,"[438] or by Philip who declares, "We have found him of whom Moses and the prophets wrote, Jesus the son of Joseph from Nazareth."[439]

(314) These, however, "believed in his name, seeing his signs which he did."[440] And because[441] they believe, not in him, but

426. Cf. Mt 7.22–23.
427. Cf. 1 Cor 4.16; 11.1.
428. Phil. 4.13.
429. Jn 2.13.
430. Cf. Jn 2.23.
431. Cf. Jn 2.23.
432. Cf. Mt 7.13–14.
433. Mt 8.11.
434. Cf. Jn 14.2.
435. Cf. Jn 1.40–45.
436. Jn 1.36.
437. Cf. Jn 1.41.
438. Cf. Jn 1.43.
439. Cf. Jn 1.45.
440. Jn 2.23.
441. My conjecture. Something is wrong in the text at this point which has *sēmeia* ("signs") as the object of believe.

"in his name," Jesus "did not trust himself to them, because he knows all men, and had no need that someone give testimony concerning man," because he knows what is in each man.[442]

(315) We must make good use of the saying, "He had no need that someone give testimony concerning man"[443] to show that the Son of God is able, of himself, to see concerning each man, and by no means needs testimony from anyone.

(316) But we must contrast the saying, "He had no need that someone give testimony concerning man"[444] with, "He had no need that someone give testimony concerning anyone." For if we take the word "man" to have reference to everyone who is according to the image of God, or every spiritual being, he will have no need that anyone give testimony for his sake concerning any spiritual being whatever, since he knows all men from himself in accordance with the power which has been given him by the Father.

(317) But, if we restrict the word "man" to the mortal spiritual being alone, we will say that he had need that someone give testimony concerning those beings above man, since he was not sufficient to know the things pertaining to them too, on a par with human things.

(318) But another will say that the one who emptied himself[445] had no need that anyone give testimony concerning man, but that he had need of testimony concerning those better than humanity.

(319) We must also investigate this question: How many of his signs did the many see when they believed in him? For he is not recorded to have performed signs in Jerusalem, unless signs occurred but they have not been recorded. Consider, however, if it is possible that the making of a whip from cords, and casting everyone out of the temple, along with the sheep and the oxen, and pouring out the coins of the money-changers, and overturning the tables, be reckoned as signs.[446]

(320) We must say, however, to those who would suppose

---

442. Cf. Jn 2.23–25.
444. Ibid.
446. Cf. Jn 2.15. See above, sections 148–149.
443. Cf. Jn 2.25.
445. Cf. Phil 2.7.

that he has no need of witnesses concerning men alone, that the evangelist has rendered a twofold testimony to him: that he knows all, and that he has no need that anyone give testimony concerning man.[447]

(321) Now if he knew all, he knew not only men, but also the things which are above man, and all who are outside of bodies such as these. He knew what was in man since he was greater than those who reprove and judge by prophesying, and who bring to light the secrets of the hearts of all, which the Spirit whispers to them.[448] But the statement, "He knew what was in man,"[449] can be taken also with reference to the lower or higher[450] powers which work in men.

(322) For if someone gives "place to the devil,"[451] Satan enters him, just as Judas gave place when the devil had put it into his heart to betray Jesus, wherefore also Satan entered him after the morsel.[452]

(323) But if one gives place to God, he becomes blessed. For "blessed is he whose help is from God, and the ascent in his heart is from God."[453] The Son of God, therefore, who knows all things, knows "what was in man."[454]

Since the tenth volume has now received a sufficient conclusion, we shall bring the book to a close at this point.

447. Cf. Jn 2.25.
448. Cf. 1 Cor 14.24–25.
449. Jn 2.25.
450. Literally, worse or better.
451. Cf. Eph 4.27.
452. Cf. Jn 13.2 and 27.
453. Cf. Ps 83.6.
454. Jn 2.25.

INDICES

INDEX OF PROPER NAMES

Aaron, 33, 34, 191, 195, 270, 271
Abel, 188
Abraham, 12, 37, 77, 125, 132, 133, 145, 150, 172, 173, 187, 202, 203, 209, 224, 303, 316, 325
Acasius, 9
Achab, 204
Adam, 56, 58, 78, 142
Aiman, 227
Alexandria, 4–6, 34, 170, 171
Ambrose, 5, 6, 33, 95, 160, 161, 167, 169
Ammon, 243
Amos, 95
Andrew, 40, 154, 255, 262, 263, 325
Antioch, 4
Aquila, 226, 318
Arabia, 225
Aristotle, 56
Aunan, 226

Babylon, 235
Balthasar, H. U. von, 28
Basil, 9
Basilides, 186
Beelzebub, 212
Beeri, 95, 96
Bethabara, 224, 225, 233
Bethania, 224, 225, 283, 284
Bethel, 17
Bethphage, 282–284, 291, 292, 298
Blanc, C., 7, 27, 28, 35, 40, 49, 55, 56, 63, 70, 71, 75, 83, 94, 102, 115, 117, 122, 130, 136, 137, 141, 151, 153, 158, 175, 191, 192, 200, 210, 217, 226, 230, 250, 251, 263, 264, 280, 292,

305, 307, 308, 311, 313, 316, 318, 320, 322
Blesilla, 7
Bosra, 246
Bouthan, 227
Brooke, A., 9, 26–28, 33, 35, 37, 40, 49, 70, 83, 102, 115, 117, 153, 175, 189, 210, 263, 289, 305, 307

Cadiou, R., 92
Caesarea, 4, 5, 9
Cain, 188
Campenahusen, H. Von, 3
Cana, 11, 239, 256, 264, 270, 286, 290
Capharnaum, 253–257, 264–270, 279, 280, 286, 288, 290
Celsus, 6
Cesarea Philippi, 190
Chrysippus, 104, 105, 160
Cicero, 124
Clement of Alexandria, 3, 23, 101, 135, 186
Clement of Rome, 244
Cleophas, 40, 44
Corsini, E., 27, 28
Courcelle, P., 9
Crouzel, H., 4, 229, 238

Daly, R., 28
Dan, 31, 201
Daniel, 164
Daniélou, J., 10, 14, 15, 24
David, 37, 44, 49, 63, 77, 83, 87, 94, 106, 107, 112, 134, 135, 137, 164, 168, 169, 179, 197, 201, 260, 283, 291, 312, 314
Delarue, 27, 115, 264
Demetrius, 4

331

INDEX

Edom, 246
Egypt, 110, 170, 231, 232, 235, 236
Eleazar, 191
Elias, 132, 144, 152, 155, 156, 181, 182, 184–194, 200–202, 204, 210, 221, 233
Eliseus, 233, 234
Elizabeth, 81, 148, 155, 185, 188, 190, 237–239
Ennon, 256, 257
Enoch, 227
Ephraim, 292, 300
Esau, 146, 260
Esdras, 169, 312
Esther, 119
Eusebius, 3, 4, 6, 9, 161, 166, 214
Eutychus, 163
Euzoius, 9
Ezechias, 205
Ezechiel, 63, 144, 165, 174, 236, 306

Faye, E. de, 24
Ferrarius, A., 27
Foerster, W., 23

Gabriel, 143, 195
Gadara, 226
Galgal, 232
Galilee, 239, 254–257, 263, 264, 267, 270, 279, 281, 282, 286, 290, 291
Geerasa, 225
Geerson, 226
Gergesa, 226, 269
Geson, 226
Ginzberg, L., 192
Gögler, R., 14, 28, 320
Gorday, P., 10
Grant, R., 10
Gregory of Nazianzus, 9
Gregory of Nyssa, 105
Grobel, K., 23

Hades, 16, 77
Hanson, R., 10, 15, 17
Harl, M., 9, 10, 20, 84, 95, 158, 160
Harnack, A. von, 3
Hatch, E., 34

Hebron, 312
Heine, R., 4, 10, 13, 38
Heracleon, 6, 7, 20, 22–26, 113, 120, 121, 131, 171, 194, 199–201, 204, 212, 222–224, 252, 266, 268, 280, 302, 304, 310, 313
Hermas, 55, 315
Hippolytus, 23, 135
Hiram, 311, 316, 318
Huet, P., 27, 264

Iao, 96
Illyricum, 161
Irenaeus, 6, 23, 93, 135, 214
Isaac, 77, 125, 132, 145, 173, 187, 224, 260, 303, 325
Isaias, 44, 47, 50, 51, 61, 63, 66, 77, 79, 95–97, 101, 114, 115, 135, 137, 139, 142, 144, 147, 152, 165, 174, 181, 187, 189, 195, 197, 199, 201, 205, 207, 255, 271, 301, 320
Israel, 31, 32, 40, 61, 63, 72, 79, 80, 86, 87, 119, 142, 145, 146, 169, 181, 184, 194, 201, 227, 231, 232, 235, 270, 271, 286, 300, 307, 311, 320, 321

Jacob, 61–63, 77, 80, 86, 87, 125, 132, 145–148, 173, 187, 201, 224, 259, 303, 325
James (apostle), 255
James (brother of Jesus), 191
Janssens, Y., 23, 24
Jared, 227
Jephte, 243
Jeremias, 61, 95–97, 101, 107, 144, 198, 235, 277, 278
Jericho, 133
Jeroboam, 201
Jerome, 6, 7, 9
Jerusalem, 16, 40, 41, 47, 95, 96, 152, 161, 181–183, 188, 189, 202, 206, 207, 210, 211, 225, 228, 232, 238, 253, 256, 257, 273, 281–286, 290–292, 295–297, 299–302, 311, 314, 320, 321, 324–326
Jesse, 63

INDEX 333

Jesus, 14, 35–40, 42–51, 62, 68–70, 79, 82, 83, 88, 90, 100, 103, 112, 113, 115, 116, 123, 134, 138, 149, 154, 155, 161, 165, 170–172, 175, 176, 178, 179, 185, 191, 192, 196, 198, 203–205, 212, 216–218, 220, 222, 224, 225, 227, 228, 230–233, 235–239, 241, 245, 248, 250, 251, 253, 255, 256, 259, 260, 263, 265–270, 275, 281, 283–303, 304, 305, 306, 308, 310–311, 313, 322–327
Jesus son of Sirach, 220
Job, 53
John the Apostle, 31, 32, 37, 38, 42, 57, 62, 64, 66, 97, 105, 110, 116, 134, 135, 137, 152, 161, 164, 165, 170, 206, 207, 210, 218, 219, 229, 243, 255, 263, 269, 270, 275, 277, 281, 282, 284, 285, 293, 294, 299, 300, 321, 323, 325
John the Baptist, 16, 20, 33, 39, 50, 62, 81, 82, 133, 142–145, 147, 148, 152–156, 171, 177, 178, 180–197, 199, 200–203, 205–212, 214–217, 220–224, 228, 229, 237–240, 252, 254, 255, 257, 263, 267, 279, 325
Jordan, 14, 142, 206, 207, 211, 225, 227–230, 232–236, 239
Joseph, 75, 145, 186
Joseph, husband of Mary, 325
Joseph, brother of Jesus, 191
Josias, 201
Josue, 13, 133, 227, 228, 230–232
Juda, 31, 62, 63, 72, 86, 164, 201, 226
Judas, 48, 327
Judas of Galilee, 185
Jude, 191
Judea, 95, 96, 142, 152, 188, 190, 206, 207, 211, 226, 228, 256, 257, 286, 320
Judith, 132
Justin, 15, 16

Koch, H., 17
Koe, 308, 310, 313

Koetschau, 264

Lagarde, P. de, 96, 148, 169, 202, 225–227, 264, 269, 298, 315, 318
Lange, N. de, 9, 10, 20, 158, 160
Lazarus, 225, 284
Levi, 226
Libanus, 162
Lommatzach, 27, 28, 70, 102
Lubac, H. de, 10
Lucifer, 49
Luke, 37, 64, 203, 207, 208, 211, 214, 218, 239, 254, 255, 267, 282, 284, 298

MacRae, G., 23
Malachias, 185, 201, 204, 205
Maleleel, 227
Marcion, 85, 165, 260
Mark, 37, 49, 50, 205–207, 211, 214, 217, 239, 254, 255, 257, 267, 281, 283, 298, 301, 310, 311
Martha, 225, 284
Mary, 14, 38, 81, 143, 155, 186, 190, 191, 237–239, 260, 261
Mary Magdalene, 246, 247
Mary, sister of Martha, 225
Matthew, 37, 63, 202, 206–208, 210, 211, 213–216, 239, 251, 254, 255, 257, 263, 267, 268, 279–282, 285, 290–293, 298, 299, 310
Mates, B., 97, 111
Melchisedech, 33, 34
Menzies, A., 27, 28
Mesopotamia, 145
Migne, 27
Mordochai, 119
Moses, 13, 35, 40, 41, 66, 107, 119, 149, 152, 161, 165, 171, 174, 177, 178, 181, 193–195, 197, 199, 226, 227, 230, 231, 236, 254, 270–272, 277, 296, 325
Moss, C., 28
Munich, 26

Naaman, 234, 235
Nardoni, E., 13

Nathan, 169, 312
Nathanael, 40, 325
Nautin, P., 4, 5, 8, 34
Nazareth, 239, 254–257, 267, 279, 281, 291, 325
Nephtali, 318
Nephtalim, 255
Nicodemus, 256
Noe, 218

Onan, 226
Origen, 3–28, 33, 34, 36, 37, 44, 53, 56, 63, 67, 75, 83, 89, 93–95, 97, 104–106, 111, 113, 115, 116, 118, 121, 122, 130, 133, 135, 139, 144–147, 158, 160, 166, 167, 186, 196, 197, 206, 219, 228, 236, 243, 246, 254, 259, 264, 290, 292, 298, 311, 313, 318
Osee, 95–97, 101

Pagels, E., 6, 25, 26
Palestine, 4
Pamphilus, 9
Paul, 14, 17, 18, 35–39, 42, 44, 46, 48, 50, 54, 56, 62, 66, 73, 76, 112–115, 125, 130, 131, 136, 144, 158, 159, 161–163, 174, 175, 179, 230, 233, 250, 252, 261, 273, 276, 306, 325
Peter, 39, 40, 42, 67, 154, 155, 161, 216, 218, 255, 262, 263, 267–269, 303, 314, 325
Philip, 40, 51, 239, 325
Philo, 34
Phinees, 191, 192
Photius, 23
Pilate, 60
Plato, 37, 55, 107, 118, 144
Preuschen, E., 7–10, 27, 28, 35, 40, 49, 54, 62, 63, 70, 75, 77, 83, 87, 94, 97, 99, 101, 102, 115, 117, 122, 128, 130, 136–138, 146, 148, 151, 153, 158, 175, 176, 178, 191, 205, 206, 210, 217, 226, 227, 229, 230, 232, 233, 245, 254, 263, 264, 272, 283, 289, 290, 300, 305, 307, 308, 313, 319

Ps.-Tertullian, 23
Ptolemaeus, 23, 24
Puech, H., 24

Quispel, G., 24, 26, 122

Rauer, M., 8
Rebecca, 12
Redpath, H., 34
Rist, J., 97
Ruben, 31
Rudolph, K., 6
Rufinus, 9

Sabai, 76
Salim, 256, 257
Samaria, 152
Samson, 201
Satan, 53
Schürer, E., 145
Severus, A., 4
Simeon, 132, 323
Simon, 148
Simon, brother of Jesus, 191
Simon, and Cleophas, 40, 44
Simon, magician, 82, 216
Sion, 47
Soccoth, 227
Sodom, 133
Solomon, 18, 56, 71, 72, 160, 162 163, 168, 169, 311–313, 315, 316, 318, 323
Symmachus, 226, 318
Syria, 145

Tanner, T., 9
Tertullian, 23, 135
Thabor, 116
Theodas, 185
Theodore of Mopsuestia, 8
Theodotion, 226
Theodotus, 24
Thomas, 323
Tiberias, 226
Timothy, 43, 262
Torjesen, K., 10, 11
Trigg, J., 4, 7, 13
Tyre, 316, 318

Ullmann, W., 10, 11, 18

INDEX

Uriel, 145, 146

Valentinus, 6, 23, 24, 120

Wendland, P., 122, 130, 215, 233, 274, 308, 310, 318
Wiles, M., 3, 4, 11, 17, 20
Wutz, F., 96, 148

Zabulon, 255
Zacharias, 16, 139, 291, 292
Zachary, 81, 143, 147, 148, 185, 188–191, 193, 195, 196, 207, 215, 238
Zandee, J., 122
Zebedee, 50
Zeus, 262

INDEX OF HOLY SCRIPTURE

(Books of the Old Testament)

Genesis
1.1: 53, 103, 104
1.2: 216
1.3,6: 56
1.6,9: 104
1.26: 100, 133, 134, 237
1.27: 55
3: 58
3.23: 142
4.25: 188
6.2: 227
7.4: 186
17.5: 173
18.2: 133
19.1: 133
25.15–16: 260
25.25: 86
25.31–34: 260
27.19: 260
27.27: 264
32.24,28: 146
43.34: 75
46.12: 226
49.8: 86
49.8–9: 63
49.10: 63
49.11: 247
49.16: 201

Exodus
2.22: 226
3.2,6: 77
3.5: 198, 199
3.6: 125, 132, 187
3.14: 119
3.18: 132

5.3,17: 132
6.16: 226
7.1: 195
8.16–19: 272
9.1,13: 132
10.3: 132
12.1–3: 270
12.3: 289
12.5: 276
12.8: 275–277
12.9–10: 275
12.11: 271
12.15: 274
12.21–37: 232
12.26–27: 271
12.43: 271
12.48: 271
14.11: 231
14.15: 197
14.22: 230
16.23: 271
16.25: 271
17.5–6: 234
20.5: 303
25.17–19: 82
29.38–39: 242
29.38–40: 241
31.18: 317
32.7: 272
32.31–32: 165
34.28: 277

Leviticus
3.1–16: 242
5.6–7.18: 240
6.1–17: 242
6.15: 14

19.23–24: 210
23.2: 273
23.29: 193

Numbers
3.17: 226
4.28: 125
5.15,18,25: 242
6.14: 242
14.28: 127
15.25: 242
20.7–11: 234
25.11: 191
27.17: 31
28.1–3: 272
28.10–11: 242
29.6: 242
33.6: 227

Deuteronomy
4.19–20: 101
9.9: 277
18.15: 181
18.15,18–19: 193
22.8: 170
30.12–14: 89
32.4: 107

Joshua
3.3: 231
3.5: 231
3.7: 231
3.9–10: 231
3.15–16: 230
5.2–3: 232
5.9: 232, 236

336

INDEX

5.11: 232
5.13–14: 133
12.7–24: 174

Judges
11.29–39: 243
20.28: 191

1 Samuel
25.28: 87

1 Kings
13.2: 201
18.21–38: 204
18.34: 204

2 Kings
1.8: 191
2.15: 187
7.2: 312
16.8: 169, 312
19.20: 94

3 Kings
2.11: 312
4.32–33: 162
5.12–13: 162
5.15: 317
5.15–16: 315
5.15–18: 316
5.32: 311
6.1: 311, 316
6.4: 319
6.7: 317
6.8: 317
6.10: 317
6.16: 317
6.19,27: 315
6.22: 318
6.36: 318
6.37: 316
6.38: 316
7.1–2: 318

4 Kings
2.1,8: 233
2.9: 233
2.14: 132, 233
5.9–10: 234

5.9–14: 236
5.11: 235
5.12: 235

1 Chronicles
9.44: 227
22.8: 312
22.9: 169
28.3: 169
29.1–5: 312

2 Chronicles
2.2: 317

Ezra
6: 312

Esther
4: 119

Job
3.8: 53
25.5: 86
40.14: 53
40.20: 53

Psalms
2.6: 223
2.7: 74
4.7: 198
6.6: 130
10.7: 179, 198
13.3: 203
15.10: 77, 218
17.12: 141
18.5: 159
18.9: 137
19.8: 91
21.2: 139
21.15: 305, 307
21.16: 58
23.7: 246
23.8: 246
26.1: 135
30.24: 179
32.6: 93
32.10–11: 290
32.27: 91, 300
33.8: 247
35.7: 59, 72

35.10: 134
39.8: 164
43.25: 49
44.2: 64, 91
44.2–3: 92
44.3,8: 93
44.6: 88
44.8: 72
44.11: 93
45.5: 228, 236
48.13: 59
49.1: 76, 99
57.5: 204
62.4: 180
67.12: 44
67.19: 247
68.6: 139
68.10: 303
68.22: 304
68.29: 164
71.1–2: 72
71.4–5: 246
71.12: 246
73.13: 301
76.2: 197
77.25: 279
81.5: 138
83.6: 327
87.5–6: 77
88.33: 87
88.34: 87
103.4: 49
103.15: 74, 229
103.24: 57, 83, 94, 117, 221
104.15: 180
109.1: 248
109.3: 173
109.8: 288
110.1: 266
113.12: 101
114.6–7: 49
114.9: 126
117.22: 88
117.22–23: 64
119.7: 315
121.3: 286
121.4: 286
124.2: 285
135.2: 76

Psalms (*continued*)
136.1: 235
139.4: 203
141.6: 88
142.2: 108, 125, 126
148.5: 56, 121

Proverbs
1.6: 141
1.24: 162
4.27: 198
8.9: 42, 110
8.22: 45, 54, 56, 57, 77, 83, 94, 155, 179
10.19: 162, 163
16.7: 52, 53
16.23: 174, 175
20.13: 323
22.20–21: 11
24.54: 71
26.9: 249
30.6: 120

Ecclesiastes
7.15: 305
12.12: 18, 160, 162

Song of Songs
1.15: 294
2.5: 79
2.9: 17

Isaiah
1.7: 297
2.1: 95, 101
6.1: 142
6.1–6: 174
6.8: 142
6.9: 142
9.1–2: 139
9.2: 156
9.5: 77, 91
11.1: 87, 128
11.1–3: 64
22.22: 165
26.9: 137
29.11–12: 165
29.13: 199
30.6: 301

35.10: 110
39: 205
40.3: 181, 189, 197, 201, 205–207
40.3–4: 195
40.4: 208
40.4–5: 207
40.5: 208
40.6: 197
40.9: 47
42.1–4: 63
42.6: 135
43.10: 151
48.16: 115
49.1–3: 61
49.2: 79, 88
49.2,3,6: 61, 79
49.3: 88
49.3,6: 80
49.5–6: 61, 80, 86
49.6: 65, 66
52.6–7: 47
52.7: 44
53.4: 138, 247
53.7: 51, 80, 242, 245
54.11–14: 320
54.15: 321
60.13–20: 321
61.1: 47, 223, 224
63.1: 246
63.2–3: 247
65.1: 223

Jeremiah
1.7: 144
2.18: 235
5.8: 300
5.14: 278
6.16: 198
11.19: 61, 242
14.1: 95, 101
20.9: 278
23.24: 224
49.5: 151

Lamentations
4.20: 107

Ezekiel
1.4–28: 174
2.3: 144
2.10: 165
29.3–5: 236
34.8: 125
34.23: 63
37.1–4: 307
37.7: 307
37.11: 306, 307

Daniel
7.10: 165
8.5: 295
12.2: 49

Hosea
1.1: 95, 101
9.5: 273
10.12: 137
10.13: 209
12.3: 146
14.10: 243

Joel
2.11: 66

Zephaniah
1.14: 66

Haggai
1.13: 133

Zechariah
3.3: 139
3.4: 139
9.9: 88, 242, 291, 300
9.10: 292, 300, 301

Malachai
1.6: 74
3.1: 133, 145, 205, 225
3.22–23: 185, 201
4.5–6: 204

1 Ezra
4.36–38: 169

Judith
9.2: 132

INDEX 339

Wisdom
  7.26: 248
  17.1: 244

Sirach
  18.5: 220
  48.1: 249

1 Maccabees
  1.21–29: 313

2 Maccabees
  7.28: 55

4 Maccabees
  3.20: 314

Enoch
  6.1–7.2: 227
  37.1: 227
  86.106: 227

(Books of the New Testament)

Matthew
  1.1: 37
  3.1,5: 142
  3.5: 211
  3.5–6: 206
  3.5,7: 208
  3.7: 206–208, 210, 211, 213
  3.7–8: 202
  3.8: 208
  3.9: 202, 203, 209
  3.10: 203, 209, 210
  3.11: 204, 214, 215, 217, 219, 229
  3.13: 239
  3.13–14: 147
  3.14: 239
  3.15: 240
  3.16: 294
  3.17: 172
  4.11–12: 279
  4.11–15: 255
  4.12: 254, 257
  4.12–13: 279
  4.13: 254, 257
  4.13–14: 267
  4.16: 139, 156
  4.17: 255, 267, 269
  4.17–7.29: 279
  4.18–19: 263
  5.13: 251
  5.14: 68, 138, 250, 285
  5.14,16: 66
  5.16: 96, 126, 129, 152
  5.34–35: 224
  5.35: 285
  5.45: 47
  7.7–8: 285
  7.13–14: 325
  7.22–23: 325
  8.1–28: 280
  8.2–3: 235
  8.4: 152
  8.5–6: 268
  8.11: 325
  8.13: 269
  8.14–15: 269
  8.17: 138, 247
  8.26: 170
  8.28–32: 225
  9.1: 280
  9.2–6: 280
  9.12: 59, 228
  9.13: 228
  9.18–25: 280
  9.27–30: 280
  9.35: 280
  10.8: 220
  10.10: 70
  10.27: 141
  10.34: 79
  11.3: 35, 39, 183, 220
  11.4–5: 183
  11.5: 44
  11.9: 193
  11.10: 145, 196, 215
  11.11: 200, 201, 215
  11.13: 193
  11.14: 144, 185, 187
  11.14–15: 155
  11.15: 173
  11.19: 96
  11.27: 52, 91
  12.17,19: 63
  12.18–21: 63
  12.32: 114, 115
  12.42: 169
  12.50: 117
  13.16: 323
  13.17: 176, 323
  13.55–56: 191
  14.2: 190, 237
  15.7–8: 199
  15.24: 321
  16.14: 190
  16.18: 161, 263
  19.17: 248
  21.1–3: 291
  21.1–9: 283
  21.1–13: 298
  21.3: 293
  21.5: 88, 291, 292
  21.6–7: 291
  21.7: 293
  21.8: 291, 300
  21.9: 291
  21.10: 283, 290, 291
  21.10–13: 281
  21.11–13: 291
  21.12: 293
  21.13: 294, 297, 303
  21.23–25: 211
  21.42,44: 64
  21.43: 288
  22.10–11: 71
  22.31–32: 173
  22.32: 76, 100, 224, 303
  23.8: 36

INDEX

Matthew (*continued*)
23.13: 203
24.12: 251
25.21: 198
25.40: 48
26.2: 280
26.13: 48
26.38: 72
26.61: 310
26.62–63: 311
27.34,48: 304
28.20: 265–266

Mark
1.1: 37, 50
1.2: 133, 204, 206
1.1–3: 50, 205
1.3: 147, 206, 207
1.4: 228
1.5: 206, 211
1.7: 217, 219
1.7–8: 214
1.9: 239
1.10: 236, 294
1.13–15: 255
1.13–21: 257
1.14: 254, 257
1.16–17: 263
1.16–20: 255
1.17,20: 222
1.21: 255
1.21–22: 267
1.23–27: 267
1.30–31: 267
1.32,34: 267
2.16: 248
3.29: 114
4.9: 172
5.1–13: 225
6.8: 70, 199
6.14: 237
6.16: 190
10.18: 85, 119, 235
11.1–12: 283
11.2: 298, 301
11.4: 298
11.5: 298
11.8: 300
11.15: 283, 299
11.15–17: 282

11.17: 294
12.26–27: 125, 173
12.27: 125
14.34: 139
14.58: 310
14.60–61: 311

Luke
1.5: 180
1.11: 185
1.11,13: 189
1.13: 185
1.15: 143
1.17: 143, 148, 155, 186, 187, 200, 214
1.18: 195
1.19: 215
1.20: 196
1.20,64: 147
1.35: 187, 189
1.35–36: 143
1.39–41: 237, 238
1.41–42: 237
1.41,44: 81
1.42: 238
1.44: 145, 155
1.63: 148
1.63–64: 196
1.64: 148, 215
1.65: 188, 190
1.67: 193
1.76: 193
2.9–11: 49
2.14: 49
2.29–30: 323
3.2–4: 207
3.4–5: 195
3.5: 208, 237
3.5–6: 207
3.6: 208
3.7: 208, 211
3.7–9: 208
3.8: 209
3.9: 209, 210
3.15–16: 214
3.16: 214
3.21–22: 239
3.22: 74, 116, 294
4.13–16: 255
4.13–31: 257

4.14: 254
4.16,31: 254
4.18–21: 47
4.28–30: 256
4.31: 256
4.31–35: 268
4.38: 268
4.40–41: 268
6.45: 198
6.48: 168
7.28: 200, 201, 217
7.33: 211, 212
7.35: 96
7.37: 47
7.38: 248
8.14: 48
8.24: 170
8.26–33: 225
9.3: 70
9.19: 186
9.62: 286
10.6: 96
10.22: 52
10.41–42: 225
11.10: 154
11.15: 212
11.52: 217, 285
12.3: 141
12.50: 229, 247
14.28–30: 169
16.9: 216, 286
16.29: 177
18.8: 251
18.10–11: 203
18.14: 203
18.19: 119
19.29–41: 284
19.30: 298
19.33: 298
19.34: 299
19.40: 293
19.41,45: 299
19.41–46: 282
19.46: 294
20.6: 212
20.36: 132
20.37–38: 173
20.18: 64
22.27: 80

INDEX   341

22.28: 74
23.21: 48
23.36: 304
23.43: 309
24.14: 40
24.18–20: 40
24.27: 164
24.32: 44, 278

John
  1.1: 16, 37, 42, 52,
    55, 56–58, 64, 78,
    89, 90, 93–97,
    103, 104, 111,
    122–125, 128,
    195, 261
  1.1–2: 111
  1.1,4: 129
  1.1–5: 21
  1.2: 43, 94, 103,
    111, 112, 179, 263
  1.3: 22, 24, 25, 94,
    113, 114, 118,
    120, 122, 123,
    177, 221
  1.3–4: 57, 129, 139
  1.3–5: 66
  1.4: 22, 45, 65, 78,
    117, 124, 128,
    131, 132, 134, 135
  1.5: 22, 58, 134,
    139, 140, 156, 222
  1.6: 18, 23, 144
  1.6–7: 155, 196
  1.7: 8, 142, 143,
    155, 157, 222
  1.9: 45, 65, 66, 76,
    134
  1.10: 223
  1.14: 56, 90, 156,
    228, 263, 276, 314
  1.15: 171, 177, 178,
    197
  1.15–18: 152, 238
  1.16: 172, 177, 178,
    189
  1.16–17: 171
  1.17: 178, 180, 241
  1.18: 171, 172

  1.19: 180, 182, 185,
    210, 238
  1.19–22: 182
  1.19–23: 152
  1.19,20,23: 184
  1.20: 180
  1.21: 181, 184, 185,
    189, 190, 193,
    201, 204
  1.22: 184
  1.23: 147, 152, 181,
    183, 195, 197,
    199, 201, 205,
    215, 230
  1.24: 182, 206, 210,
    238
  1.24–26: 214
  1.25: 182, 202, 204,
    210, 212
  1.26: 212, 213, 218,
    221–223, 238
  1.26–27: 153, 181
  1.27: 213, 219, 223
  1.28: 228, 230
  1.29: 7, 36, 37, 62,
    80, 81, 237, 242,
    245, 247, 249–
    252, 276, 279
  1.29–31: 153
  1.29,36: 147
  1.30–31: 62, 81
  1.32: 143, 294
  1.32–34: 153
  1.33: 81, 116, 143,
    228
  1.36: 153, 239, 325
  1.38: 153
  1.39: 154, 263
  1.40–42: 263
  1.40–45: 325
  1.41: 40, 154, 325
  1.42: 155
  1.43: 239, 325
  1.45: 40, 325
  2.1: 256
  2.1–11: 286
  2.1–12: 290
  2.6: 11
  2.11: 270

  2.12: 254, 257, 265,
    266, 286
  2.12–15: 256
  2.12–25: 8, 19, 253
  2.13: 15, 257, 279,
    285, 325
  2.13–14: 280, 284
  2.14: 302
  2.14–16: 286, 293
  2.15: 302, 326
  2.15–16: 287
  2.16: 287, 294, 303,
    304
  2.17: 290, 304, 308
  2.18: 305
  2.19: 305, 308–310,
    322
  2.20: 312
  2.21: 310, 319, 321
  2.22: 322, 323
  2.23: 325
  2.23–25: 326
  2.25: 327
  3.1–2: 256
  3.18: 324
  3.22: 256, 257, 263
  3.23–24: 257
  3.25–26: 257
  4.1: 263
  4.2: 204, 216
  4.10: 229
  4.24: 41, 270
  4.25: 40
  4.25–26: 60
  4.38: 233
  5.17: 173
  5.19: 310
  5.27: 85
  5.39: 164, 199, 251
  5.46: 199
  6.35: 61
  6.48: 75, 277
  6.49,51: 232, 233
  6.50–51: 277
  6.51,33: 61
  6.53: 229
  6.53–56: 15, 276
  7.36: 196
  7.37: 195, 222

INDEX

John (*continued*)
8.12: 37, 45, 60, 65, 68, 70, 134
8.39: 173
8.56: 150
8.58,56: 172
9.1: 36
9.4–5: 66
9.5: 70, 88
9.39: 123
10.2: 59
10.7: 229
10.7,9: 127
10.8: 90
10.9: 37, 44, 45, 60, 151
10.11: 37, 60
10.11–12: 88
10.11,14: 127
10.18: 243
10.30: 52
10.36: 60
11.1,18: 225
11.3: 225
11.25: 37, 44, 45, 60, 70, 88, 89, 125, 173
11.39: 36
11.43–44: 310
12.1–2: 284
12.3: 47
12.12–15: 285
12.13: 300
12.14: 300
12.15: 88, 300
12.26: 68
12.27: 72, 139
12.36: 96
12.48: 123
13.2,27: 327
13.13: 60, 74, 88
13.25: 37
13.33: 7
14.2: 325
14.6: 37, 44, 45, 57, 60, 70, 127, 178, 180, 198, 229
14.9: 173
14.27: 168
15.1: 60, 74, 247

15.1,5: 65
15.5: 60
15.15: 74
15.22: 89, 90, 122
16.14: 128
16.33: 246
17.1: 60
17.3: 98
17.21: 68
18.33: 60
18.36: 60
19.23: 215
19.26: 38
19.28–29: 304
19.32–36: 276
19.34: 10
19.36: 307
20.17: 246, 247, 309
20.25: 8
20.29: 323
21.25: 46, 162

Acts
1.8: 152
1.20: 288
2.3: 247
2.27: 77
3.2: 303
3.22–23: 181, 193
4.11: 64
5.20: 303
5.29: 303
5.30: 303
5.36: 185
5.37: 185
7.49: 224
8.10,20: 82
8.16–17: 216
8.18–20: 216
8.35,32: 51
9.4–5: 48
13.10: 197
16.3: 43, 262
17.23: 262
17.28: 262
17.31: 85
19.2–5: 216
20.7–10: 163

21.14: 43
21.24,26: 262
22.22: 48

Romans
1.1–5: 112
1.3: 260
1.4: 260
1.5: 113
1.14: 159
1.16: 45
1.20: 73
2.16: 38, 50, 165
2.28–29: 42
2.29: 31, 86
3.13: 203
3.24: 59
3.25: 58, 82, 85, 88
3.25–26: 62
4.11: 173
4.17: 119
5.3–5: 69
5.6: 248
5.12,18: 261
5.13: 122
6.4: 70, 309
6.4–5: 306
6.5: 148
6.10: 46, 79
7.6: 41
7.8: 122
7.9: 122
7.14: 14, 230, 261
7.15: 261
7.24: 156
8.3: 138
8.15: 74
8.20: 54, 69
8.21: 58, 68, 115
8.21,19: 68
8.22: 54
8.31: 140
8.32: 248
9.11–14: 146
9.14: 85
10.6–8: 89, 124
10.15: 44
10.20: 223
11.7: 100
11.33: 71, 96

INDEX

12.6: 201, 219
14.9: 218
15.19: 161
16.25–26: 175

1 Corinthians
  1.2: 250
  1.5: 169
  1.24: 56, 62, 82, 84, 94
  1.24,30: 128
  1.25: 83
  1.26–27: 159
  1.30: 46, 59, 62, 84, 179
  2.2: 43, 46, 56, 102, 103
  2.4: 44, 158, 159
  2.5: 159
  2.6: 241
  2.7: 273, 319
  2.7–8: 314
  2.8: 241
  2.10: 96
  2.14–15: 131
  2.15: 261
  2.16: 319
  2.16,12: 38, 294
  3.1: 43
  3.19: 108
  4.9: 68
  4.13: 245
  4.16: 325
  4.19–20: 44
  5.7: 15, 273, 274, 275, 278
  5.8: 274
  6.7: 295
  7.6: 262
  7.12: 35
  7.17: 35
  8.2: 52
  8.5: 76
  8.5–6: 100
  9.20: 43
  9.20–22: 262
  9.22: 76
  10.1–4: 230
  10.2: 233
  10.4: 234

10.11: 41
10.18: 32
10.31: 89
11.1: 325
11.3: 84
12.4: 216
12.4–6: 114
12.7: 219
12.8: 136
12.12: 307
12.15–24: 307
12.25: 308
12.26: 308
12.27: 305
12.28: 36
12.31: 136
13.1–2: 199
13.10: 324
13.12: 52, 156, 324
13.13: 324
14.8: 199
14.24–25: 327
14.32: 187
15.15: 309
15.22–24: 309
15.24: 81, 266
15.25–26: 52, 315
15.26: 81, 248
15.28: 78, 81, 85, 248
15.45: 56, 78
15.49: 106
15.54: 306

2 Corinthians
  3.6: 47, 159, 161, 166, 167, 287
  3.15: 41, 297
  4.7: 38, 159
  4.10: 70, 79
  4.18: 73
  5.4: 69
  5.16: 102
  5.19: 37, 248
  5.21: 138
  6.18: 35
  7.9–10: 277
  10.2: 322
  10.3: 230
  11.6: 158
  11.29: 262

12.2: 33
12.2,4: 262
12.4: 176
12.5: 262
12.6: 213
13.3: 180, 266, 278

Galatians
  1.1: 300
  2.20: 38, 266, 306
  3.8: 173
  3.19–20: 151
  3.24: 273
  3.25: 41
  4.2: 41, 42, 232
  4.2,4: 273
  4.4: 41
  4.19: 52
  4.26: 296
  5.9: 41
  5.17: 79
  6.14: 306

Ephesians
  1.21: 51, 76, 133
  2.12: 176, 298
  2.14: 73
  2.20: 78, 88, 228, 305, 315
  2.21: 305
  3.5: 52
  3.5–6: 175, 176
  4.8: 247
  4.11: 36
  4.13: 307
  4.27: 327
  5.8: 130, 131
  5.30: 313
  6.12: 139, 296
  6.16: 170, 301

Philippians
  1.23: 54
  1.24: 54
  2.6–7: 248
  2.7: 80, 252, 260, 266, 326
  2.8: 261
  2.8,6: 80
  2.10–11: 231

Philippians (continued)
3.20: 106
3.21: 237
4.3: 244
4.7: 96, 168
4.13: 82, 325

Colossians
1.10: 43
1.15: 39, 55, 71, 73, 92, 99, 121, 145, 173, 178, 260, 314, 318
1.16: 73, 76, 315
1.16–17: 121, 221
1.17: 37
1.18: 58, 59
1.19: 46
2.3: 141, 159
2.9: 46
2.14–15: 246
2.16–17: 273
3.3: 156
3.4: 156, 180
3.11: 77

1 Thessalonians
5.5: 96

2 Thessalonians
2.3: 144
2.8: 108
2.11–12: 144

1 Timothy
3.15: 286
3.16: 151
4.10: 245, 252
6.11: 33
6.16: 127, 139
6.20: 166

2 Timothy
1.10: 139, 175
2.3: 177
3.16: 35
4.3–4: 277

Titus
3.5: 216

Hebrews
1.2: 113
1.5: 74
1.7: 49
1.14: 297
2.9: 86, 115, 127
2.11: 84
3.5: 41
4.12: 79, 203, 249
4.14: 34, 62, 86
4.15,14: 85
4.15: 84
5.6: 34
5.12: 55, 230
5.14: 241
7.11: 33
7.17: 34
7.26–28: 151
8.1: 243
8.5: 41, 240, 274, 322
9.5: 321
9.7: 302
9.23: 240
9.28: 85
10.1: 42
10.13: 248, 266
11.16: 125, 173
12.22–23: 273
13.2: 133

James
1.18: 58
2.18: 42

1 Peter
2.5: 88, 305, 314, 315, 317, 319
3.4: 31, 138
3.18–20: 218

1 John
1.5: 134, 138, 139
1.6: 137
2.1: 62, 82, 151
2.1–2: 82, 85, 88, 245, 252
2.2: 62, 82
2.9: 137
2.11: 137
2.23: 150
5.8: 229

Jude
3: 319

Revelation
1.17–18: 61
1.18: 78
3.7: 106, 164, 165, 217
3.12: 321
3.20: 39
5.1–5: 164
5.2: 217
5.6: 242
5.9: 242
6.9: 243
6.17: 66
7.2–5: 31
7.3–4: 32
10.4: 162
10.6: 303
10.10: 165
14.1–5: 32
14.4–5: 33
14.6: 14, 42
14.6–7: 50
16.5,7: 85
16.14: 66
19.11: 91, 106, 107, 109
19.11–16: 16, 21, 105
19.12: 109
19.14: 110
21.1: 306
21.6: 61
22.13: 38, 58, 61, 75, 77, 78

www.ingramcontent.com/pod-product-compliance
Lightning Source LLC
Chambersburg PA
CBHW032025290426
44110CB00012B/680